The Neoconservative Revolution

Jewish Intellectuals and the Shaping of Public Policy

This book, which will come as a surprise to many educated observers and historians, suggests that Jews and Jewish intellectuals have played a considerable role in the development and shaping of modern American conservatism. The focus is on the rise of a group of Jewish intellectuals and activists known as neoconservatives, who began to impact on American public policy during the Cold War with the Soviet Union and, most recently, were influential in the lead-up to the invasion of Iraq. It presents a portrait of the life and work of the original small group of neocons, including Irving Kristol, Norman Podhoretz, and Sidney Hook. This group has grown into a new generation who operate as columnists; in conservative think tanks such as the Heritage Foundation and the American Enterprise Institute; at colleges and universities; and in government in the second Bush administration, including such lightning-rod figures as Paul D. Wolfowitz, Richard Perle, Douglas Feith, and Elliott Abrams. The book proposes that the neocons have been so significant in reshaping modern American conservatism and public policy that they constitute a neoconservative revolution, as the book's title suggests.

Historian, social activist, and a prolific writer, **Murray Friedman** was appointed as vice chair of the U.S. Civil Rights Commission in Washington, D.C., by President Ronald Reagan and as acting chair following the death of the chairman. He was honored in 2005 by Temple University, which announced the creation of the Murray Friedman Chair in American Jewish History. In 2003, he served in a State Department delegation representing the United States in Vienna at a conference on racism, xenophobia, and discrimination. Dr. Friedman has written and edited numerous books, including *What Went Wrong? The Creation and Collapse of the Black Jewish Alliance* (1995), several volumes on Philadelphia Jewish history, and *The Utopian Dilemma: American Jews and Public Policy*. In addition, he has written articles in *Commentary, Atlantic Monthly, The Weekly Standard*, and *The New Republic* as well as in professional journals such as *American Jewish History*.

The Neoconservative Revolution

Jewish Intellectuals and the Shaping of Public Policy

MURRAY FRIEDMAN
Temple University

CAMBRIDGE UNIVERSITY PRESS
Cambridge, New York, Melbourne, Madrid, Cape Town, Singapore, São Paulo

Cambridge University Press
40 West 20th Street, New York, NY 10011-4211, USA

www.cambridge.org
Information on this title: www.cambridge.org/9780521836562

First published 2005

Printed in the United States of America

A catalog record for this publication is available from the British Library.

Library of Congress Cataloging in Publication Data

Friedman, Murray, 1926–
The neoconservative revolution : Jewish intellectuals and the shaping of public
policy / Murray Friedman.
p. cm.
ISBN 0-521-83656-5 (hardback)
1. Jews – United States – Politics and government. 2. United States – Politics and
government – 1945–1989. 3. Conservatism – United States – History – 20th century.
4. Jews – Intellectual life – 20th century. I. Title.
E184.36.P64F75 2005
320.52′089′924073 – dc22 2004019000

ISBN-13 978-0-521-83656-2 hardback
ISBN-10 0-521-83656-5 hardback

Contents

Introduction

American Jews in an Age of Conservatism

Why would I choose to write about American Jewish conservatism? Is there really much to say? As far back as most of us can remember, the vast majority of American Jews have been associated with liberalism, not conservatism. They have consistently supported public assistance for the poor and civil rights for the rejected. Second only to African-Americans, they have been the strongest supporters of the Democratic Party at all levels of government. From the 1930s until the start of the Cold War, a small but influential number joined the American Communist Party or were sympathetic to what they took to be its goals. For many, the far left was simply the farthest end of the liberal political spectrum.

But that was then. It is not Jewish liberals who have been making the news in recent years. It is Jewish conservatives with important positions in the administration of President George W. Bush. The Pentagon's Paul Wolfowitz and Douglas Feith; the National Security Council's Elliott Abrams; and Richard Perle, formerly of the Defense Policy Board, can be distinguished from moderate WASP conservatives not only by their ethnicity, but also by their militancy. Rather than descending from many generations of conservatives, they are mostly relatively new to the movement – and they have transformed it. Unlike traditional conservatives, they have proudly come to be called neoconservatives (or neocons).

Cheering them on have been such prominent and like-minded journalists and writers as William Kristol, editor of the Washington-based *Weekly Standard*, columnists David Brooks and Charles Krauthammer; Robert Kagan, an international affairs specialist and political scientist; Joshua Muravchik, a frequent contributor to *Commentary*; and Norman Podhoretz, longtime editor of *Commentary*, the neocon bible. For example, in response to findings by United Nations weapons inspectors and others that Iraq possessed "the elements of a deadly germ warfare arsenal and perhaps poison gases as well as the rudiments of a missile system," Kristol and Kagan at *The Weekly Standard*, along with a number of former government officials, urged

President Clinton in January 1998 to oust Saddam Hussein by mounting a ground invasion. Clinton, in fact, also believing the situation to be perilous and untenable, initiated at the close of 1998 Operation Desert Fox, a four-day missile and bombing attack against known and *suspected* weapons facilities in Iraq.[1]

The American invasion of Iraq has, arguably, left the nation more divided politically than at any time since the Vietnam War. The essence of the debate has revolved around the Bush Doctrine, which, after September 11, 2001, established the rationale for preemptive (unilateral, if necessary) military action "to strengthen our intelligence capabilities to know the plans of terrorists before they act and to find them before they strike" and "to pursue nations that provide aid or safe haven to terrorism."[2] Critics accused the hawkish neocons of unduly influencing an inexperienced chief executive and encouraging him to undertake a reckless, imperialistic adventure. William Pfaff of the *Los Angeles Times* "argued that the Bush Doctrine undermines the principle of state sovereignty which has hitherto been the bedrock of international relations and the basis of international order" by substituting not a new universalist and allegedly liberating principle, but to achieve American security, to which it implicitly subordinates the security of every other nation."[3]

Others took to more personal attacks against Bush or his neocon advisors. Jack Shafer, in the online magazine *Slate*, noted (albeit critically): "In a letter/photograph spread captioned 'Separated at Birth' in the September (2003) issue, *Vanity Fair* letter-to-the-editor writer Art Dudley attempts to draw parallels between Perle and Nazi Minister of Propaganda Dr. Joseph Goebbels. . . . Dudley writes: 'Here it is: the same arrogance, the same malice toward the photographer, the same all-around creepiness.'" A smaller number of writers and intellectuals, including Middle East scholar Bernard Lewis and diplomatic historian John Lewis Gaddis, perhaps this country's most eminent scholar of the Cold War, backed the administration.[4] Although critical of some of the language used by the Bush administration, Gaddis has argued, in his book *Surprise, Security and the American Experience* (2004), that the move has increased discussion within the Arab world about political reform.

There is no mistaking the emphasis placed by some on Jews as responsible for the war and a whiff – more than the whiff – of anti-Semitism that permeates some of the criticism. Writing in the left-wing *Nation* magazine, Eric Alterman said the "war has put Israel in the showcase as never before. . . . The U.S. Congress and White House puppets to Israel military policy have been consistent." Independent presidential candidate Ralph Nader told right-winger Pat Buchanan in an interview in June 2004, "Both parties concede their independent judgment to the pro-Israel lobbies." And a musical opened several months later in Manhattan attacking Bush, featuring Paul Wolfowitz wearing a yarmulke.[5]

A national security document of the United States ultimately embodied the president's doctrine in a formal statement in September 2002.[6] He had already followed up his State of the Union speech with a speech in June 2002 at West Point, where he declared that deterrence and containment were too little and again promised to "take the battle to the enemy."[7]

For the Bush team and its neocon advisors, September 11 was what Eliot A. Cohen, another of the neocon intellectuals, gave "the less palatable but more accurate name [of] World War IV. The Cold War was viewed as World War III."[8] The enemy was militant Islam. Al-Qaeda-style terrorism was just part of the assault. Attacks had previously occurred and were continuing to occur in Saudi Arabia, Nigeria, Kuwait, Indonesia, and Israel, as well as in Western Europe. Accordingly, we could not afford to sit still and wait for the next one. With the proliferation of weapons of mass destruction, the danger of mass casualties was such that aggressive action was warranted against terrorism's state sponsors – thus, the initial moves in this country for regime change in Afghanistan and war and occupation in Iraq. As foreign policy experts Ivo H. Daalder and James M. Lindsay note in a recent book, Bush has finally laid to rest the hallowed policy of deterrence, which had emerged from America's struggle to contain expansion of the Soviet Union in the nuclear age.[9]

The final determiners of the critical new defense and international policy were, of course, such strong-willed figures as Defense Secretary Donald H. Rumsfeld, Vice President Dick Cheney, National Security Adviser Condoleeza Rice, and President Bush, rather than the neocons. We must leave to history the final reckoning on the Bush Doctrine and the invasion and occupation of Afghanistan and Iraq. What is not in doubt, however, is the important role played by neoconservative intellectuals, not just in the case of the War on Terror but also in the development of public policies, thought, and debate for more than fifty years. Indeed, it's hardly an exaggeration to suggest that the neocons have been critical players in bringing about an Age of Conservatism in which we live today.

How did these conservatives, neo or otherwise, come to play such a role? Where did they come from, and what does their influence portend for America's future? These are matters I will examine in the pages that follow. Among the shibboleths to be challenged at the outset is the one holding that liberalism has been bred into the bone of American Jewry, as would appear to be the case from Jewish voting patterns since the days of the New Deal. In fact, there has always been a strand of *conservative* Jewish thought that has been little noticed. A number of scholars and historians, including Jonathan D. Sarna, David Dalin, the late Charles Liebman, and Jerold S. Auerbach, have begun writing about it recently.

Jews, according to Liebman, have been "folk-oriented" rather than "universalistic," "ethnocentric rather than cosmopolitan."[10] Dalin, on the other hand, traces this characteristic back to biblical and postbiblical times. "Over the centuries," he writes, "the preference for charitable lending . . . over what might be termed the more liberal alms giving, which I take to be a conservative trait or tendency, became a fundamental principle of the Jewish philanthropic tradition." This principle found its "most famous and enduring formulation," Dalin adds, in the Mishnah Torah, the basic guide to the laws and teachings of Judaism for some two thousand years. The great medieval sage Moses Maimonides taught that the highest form of charity lay in offering loans or jobs to indigents so that they could become self-supporting.[11]

In 1603, at the Jewish Council of Padua, Italy followed Maimonides' precept in a communal regulation requiring recipients of charity to engage in some form of labor. Traditional Jewish thought and society provided no precedent for living continually on welfare without engaging in some form of labor. No work, no welfare. "No beneficiary could evade this requirement."[12]

Edward S. Shapiro has noted the striking "difference between the Christian and Jewish attitudes toward wealth." Whereas the New Testament emphasizes the virtues of the poor over those of the rich, "The *Mishnah*, by contrast, asks . . . 'Who is rich? He who enjoys his wealth.'" Asked by a disciple how he might achieve eternal life, Jesus says "sell your possessions, and give to the poor, and then you will have riches in heaven." At another point, he says "it is easier for a camel to pass through the eye of a needle than for a rich man to enter the kingdom of God."[13] Over the years, Jewish authorities have viewed the Padua edict as a legal precedent. That's the conservative, and sometimes liberal, position today, as evidenced by President Bill Clinton's signing of the Welfare Reform Act of 1996.

Benjamin Disraeli, the nineteenth-century British statesman who was born a Jew but joined the Church of England and later became prime minister, believed that "all the tendencies of Jews were conservative." In his book *Lord George Bentinck*, he described Jews as "the trustees of tradition, and conservators of the religious element [whose] bias is to religion, property and natural aristocracy," adding that "it should be the interest of statesmen that this bias of a great race should be encouraged and their energies and creative powers enlisted in the cause of existing society."[14]

In the United States, Jewish political conservatism was evident from the founding of the republic until well into the twentieth century. Charity or *tzedaka* (its Hebrew translation) was a function of the Jewish community itself, not of government. Under the ground rules that the first Jews in New Amsterdam (later New York) worked out with its anti-Semitic governor, Peter Stuyvesant, in the seventeenth century, a certain opprobrium was directed against outside help. "So long as we are able to educate our youth in the Hebrew, send Passover bread or coal to suffering brethren, [and] preserve our own organizations for dispensing charity to our own poor," the *Occident*, the country's major Jewish weekly, editorialized in 1858, "we should be proud to decline contributions from any fund that belongs to the public for public purposes."[15]

In the nineteenth century, many Jewish leaders were also conservative on the issue of slavery; relatively few joined the abolitionists, and many, in fact, opposed them. "The link between prophecy and social justice, a staple tenet of Reform Judaism," Auerbach writes, "was less self evident in the nineteenth century than it became later." Isaac Mayer Wise, the most prominent spokesman for Reform Judaism, the leading Jewish religious body at the time, was more critical of abolitionists, whom he termed "wicked preachers" and "fanatics," than of slaveholders. He claimed to find justification for the practice in biblical texts. While Reform Judaism's Pittsburgh statement of principles, adopted in 1885, condemned the "evils of the present organization of society," it was not until the rise of the Protestant Social Gospel movement that it began to apply prophetic morality to industrial capitalism.[16]

Separation of church and state was not always one of the cardinal principles of Jewish public policy, as it has been of contemporary Jewish liberalism. Sarna has pointed out that for a long time Jews were more concerned about freedom of religion than freedom from religion. "[M]ost early American Jews accepted religious freedom as a right rooted within a religious context," he writes. "They defined it in the words of Mordecai Noah, perhaps the leading Jewish figure of the day, as 'a mere abolition of all religious disabilities.' This trend continued for about two thirds of the 19th century until a movement to Christianize the country brought Jews into a more absolutist or separatist position which found its fullest expression in the post World War II years."[17]

Before the coming of FDR, Jewish voting patterns were mixed. Although many of the Eastern European Jews flooding into this country at the turn of the last century were drawn to socialism, most divided their vote among the major parties.[18] The politically orthodox voted more often for Republicans than for Democrats in presidential elections from 1900 to 1928 (with the possible exceptions of 1900 and 1916).[19] Jacob Sapherstein, a Bialystock-born, Orthodox Jew who emigrated to the United States in 1887 and began publishing the *Jewish Morgen Journal*, later the *Morgen Zhurnal*, in 1901, turned his newspaper into the Yiddish voice of Republicanism.[20] In 1920, eleven Jews were elected to the House of Representatives in Washington: one socialist from New York, two urban Democrats, and the rest Republicans.[21] Of course, Republicanism was not then what it is today and contained many liberal or progressive features; but the fact remains, Jews were not always wedded to the Democratic Party.

The nation's most prominent and influential German-Jewish leaders in the early years of the twentieth century also tended to be conservative. New York bankers Jacob Schiff and Felix Warburg; Philadelphia bibliophile and jurist Mayer Sulzberger; Chicago Sears, Roebuck head Julius Rosenwald; and New York attorney Louis Marshall, second president of the American

Jewish Committee, were staunch Republicans and equally staunch adherents of the laissez-faire business philosophy their party stood for. Seeking to dissuade Schiff from voting for Democrat Woodrow Wilson in 1912, Marshall wrote to him that the GOP "in my judgment represents the principle of constitutional government as we have received it from the 'Fathers of the Republic,' and as such still merited Jewish support. It stands four square against the forces of socialism and radicalism . . . as contrasted with an unregulated democracy." During the subsequent Red Scare, Marshall argued that Bolshevism was the "creation of non-Jews" and that "the Jew is not by disposition a radical. He is essentially conservative, wedded to the ideals of his forefathers."[22]

Woodrow Wilson first broke the Republican association with Jews by receiving 55 percent of the Jewish vote in 1916.[23] Even so, Republican Warren Harding gained some 43 percent of the Jewish vote four years later; the rest went to Socialist Eugene V. Debs. In heavily Jewish Boston precincts, Harding received 59 percent.[24] With the coming of Franklin D. Roosevelt and the New Deal in the midst of the Great Depression, Jewish voters moved overwhelmingly into the Democratic camp.

What the foregoing suggests is that despite the popular image of pervasive Jewish liberalism, there has always been a significant conservative Jewish tradition in this country. Indeed, if one looks at the course of Jewish history, it can be said that liberalism is the newcomer to the Jewish political stage and that the Jewish trend toward greater conservatism, especially at state and local levels, is growing, as I discuss in the Epilogue.

Before going further, the reader needs a definition (at least *my* definition) of conservatism. As used here, conservatism denotes a body of thought that emphasizes the right of individuals in society to pursue their own interests with as little government interference as possible. Socialism is seen as a failure, while capitalism, with all its faults, is credited with having provided for the material well-being and individual freedom of increasingly larger numbers of people, both in this country and abroad.

Conservatives blame the New Left and the counterculture that spread during the Vietnam War era for a breakdown of societal values, as reflected in increased crime, violence, drug use, and sexual immorality (if indeed we can use that term seriously any more). A binding force for conservatives has been strong opposition to communism and, more particularly, to the aggressive designs of the Soviet Union before its collapse. (Of course, many Democrats and liberals also shared these concerns – Harry Truman launched the Cold War, which John F. Kennedy continued – but conservatives over the years have led the anticommunist crusade.)

Many of the neoconservatives whom I profile in the following chapters (Irving Kristol; his wife, Gertrude Himmelfarb; Daniel Bell; Nathan Glazer; and Norman Podhoretz, along with such non-Jewish allies as James Q. Wilson, Michael Novak, and Daniel Patrick Moynihan) were bitterly attacked as apostates from liberalism. Nonetheless, as their ideas gained broader acceptance, they won greater respect. Although older-generation neocons still see themselves as embattled outsiders, younger Jewish conservatives regularly express their views to large audiences on television talk shows and in mainstream newspapers and magazines.

Gary Dorrien, a historian respectful of the movement coming from a liberal perspective, notes in the Preface to his book *The Neoconservative Mind: Politics, Culture, and the War of Ideology* (1993) that the political scientist "Michael Walzer has rightly observed that neoconservatism is the only intellectual movement in recent American politics to successfully unite theory and practice."[25] Even Norman Podhoretz and Midge Decter, who have been bitterly reviled for embracing conservative views, have received relatively benign reviews for their most recent autobiographical works, particularly Podhoretz's *Ex-Friends* (1999).[26]

The neocon ascendancy in this country has taken shape against the backdrop of a growth in conservatism both in the United States and abroad, hence the title of this Introduction. A Gallup poll indicates that twice as many Americans (41 percent) view themselves as "conservatives" than as "liberals" (19 percent). Since the end of the New Deal and Fair Deal, Republicans have occupied the White House for much of the time. The demise of the Soviet Union and its turn toward private enterprise, the rollback of socialist systems in Africa and Asia, including, most notably, Communist China and Western Europe (Germany in particular), have accentuated the worldwide move to the right. (Although the conservative Margaret Thatcher is no longer in office in Britain, a later successor, Prime Minister Tony Blair, has often appeared Ronald Reagan–like at times, to the mortification of his own Labour Party.). Sociologist Alan Wolfe has written, "Across all of Europe and North America, the social democratic century has come to an end."[27]

Popular culture has also taken a shift rightward most recently. With some twenty million listeners, conservative Rush Limbaugh still dominates talk radio, not to mention Fox News, "the loud, flashy, right-tilting network," writes Jason Zengerle, "that in January 2002, overtook CNN in the ratings to become the most-watched news network in the country"[28] It may be a measure of the times that the widely viewed and award-winning television program *The West Wing* replaced liberal President Josiah Bartlet briefly in the fall of 2003 with the conservative Republican President John Goodman. Its producers brought in two consultants, one a former chief of staff to Ronald Reagan and the other a neoconservative, John Podhoretz, the son of two of the key figures in neoconservatism.

In one of his most memorable pronouncements, Irving Kristol, a former Trotskyite who became one of the movement's leaders, and indeed is widely seen as the father of neoconservatism, declared that a conservative is a liberal who has been mugged by reality. Reality came on September 11, 2001. The Islamist terrorists' destruction of New York's World Trade Center encouraged a national yearning for security and a new swing toward conservatism. A new generation of Jewish neocons have lined up behind the Bush Doctrine. Moreover, as threats to Israel's safety and security have mounted, coupled with an increase in anti-Semitism in Western Europe, Jews have a nagging sense that they remain an endangered people. The deeper their anxieties, the more likely their move to greater conservatism.

If one argues, as I do, that Jewish conservatism has played a little-noticed role in American social and political life for much of the last hundred years, one may wonder why it has gone largely unrecognized for so long. The reason is that relatively few historians have examined the subject of *American* conservatism, let alone Jewish conservatism. Liberal historian Michael Kazin put it this way: "Historians, like most people are reluctant to sympathize with people whose political opinons they detest. Overwhelmingly cosmopolitan in their cultural tastes and liberal or radical in their politics, scholars of modern America have largely eschewed research projects about past movements that seem to them either bastions of a crumbling status quo or the domain of puritanical, pathological yahoos."[29] Alan Brinkley has made the same point succinctly: "American conservatism has been something of an orphan in historical scholarship."[30] And Leo P. Ribuffo, a George Washington University historian who describes himself as "an unreconstructed McGovernite," compares the profession's neglect of the right to its earlier indifference to African-Americans, women, and industrial workers.[31] This volume can be viewed as part of the effort to create a historiography of American conservatism.

But what about *Jewish* conservatism? Indeed, for some, the term "Jewish conservative" is a contradiction in terms. One of the aims of this book is to refute that notion. For many Jews of any political persuasion, "Jewishness" is not measured by synagogue attendance or the formal aspects of faith, even though a number of the younger Jewish conservatives today are turning back to traditional religion. Many of the older generation of neocons profiled here, while proud of their Jewish ancestry, rarely attended synagogue. In an essay describing his political shift from left to right, Joseph Epstein observed that even for the non-observant Jew, Jewishness exercises "a subtle influence upon one's political consciousness," adding that his own conservatism resulted from his being "made aware of anti-Semitism as a principal fact of life."[32]

The subtlety goes even deeper. For Jews who reached their maturity in the 1930s and 1940s, the tendency was to equate Jewishness with political engagement on the side of the various shades of the left. What I am suggesting is that for most neocons, their move to the right reflected the fact that the leftist formulas for social change not only had played themselves out but also, as it turned out with communism, had led to totalitarianism and massive human suffering. Thus, among the neocons, there has been what historian Stephen J. Whitfield has called "an unabashed proclivity for intellectualism."[33] That may be what is Jewish about Jewish conservatism.

In a sense, all history is biography. The values and interests of individual historians often determine what they explore and not infrequently what they write about. I too have personally traveled the route of many of the neoconservatives described here. I grew up in a left-wing, working-class, immigrant-oriented environment in New York City. I attended a tuition-free municipal college – in my case, Brooklyn rather than City College, to which many of the neocons were drawn by economic necessity. (We used to refer to Brooklyn College as "the little Red school house.")

With time out for military service, I participated in the radical politics of the immediate postwar years. It pains me to recall that as a college student, I made streetcorner speeches from a wooden platform for Henry Wallace, who ran vainly against Harry Truman for the presidency in 1948. I was not put off by the fact that the American Labor Party, a Communist Party front, supported Wallace's Progressive Party. Shortly thereafter, and at the height of the loyalty investigations, I went to work in the Pentagon helping to write the history of the U.S. army in World War II. I was given access to classified information and feared that if my "radical" past were uncovered I would be fired as a "security risk." (They never found out!)

My experience, however, which I will touch on from time to time in this book, may add a small personal dimension to this account. Two books were critical to my intellectual evolution. The first was Arthur Koestler's *Darkness at Noon* (1941), his fictionalized version of the Moscow show trials. For the first time I began to question whether the communist and left-wing sympathies that were so widespread in my circle actually led to the good society. The second book was Whittaker Chambers' moving 1952 memoir *Witness*, describing his years in the underground as a spy for the Soviet Union and the exposing of Alger Hiss as a member of his espionage ring. I found Chambers' version of events compelling. I remained, nevertheless, a liberal civic activist even as I began graduate studies.

As a staff member of the centrist American Jewish Committee in Philadelphia, I grew increasingly concerned that Jewish civic policies were losing touch with groups that made up the old liberal coalition. *Overcoming Middle Class Rage* (1971), a collection of essays that I edited (with a Foreword by Senator Hubert Humphrey), warned that liberalism was losing its way and needed to become relevant to the times. In 1984, I published an examination of Jewish public policy, *The Utopian Dilemma*, which urged Jewish liberals to move beyond their earlier important contributions to create a fresh agenda for the closing years of this century. It is a measure of the ground I had traveled that this time the Foreword was written by the conservative theologian Michael Novak, and the cover carried a blurb by Jeane J. Kirkpatrick, the conservative political scientist and former ambassador to the United Nations under Ronald Reagan.

Following publication of an article I had written in 1981 for *Commentary* called "A New Direction for American Jews," President Reagan named me vice chairman of the U.S. Civil Rights Commission in Washington. Alas, in that post, both the left and the right clobbered me. But that's another story.

My goal here is to provide an examination of American Jewish conservatism that is both comprehensive and objective. I can do no less, for my first loyalty is to history rather than to social or political activism. I have sought to apply here the maxim of the eminent social critic James Q. Wilson, who notes, "I know my political ideas affect what I write but I've tried hard to follow the facts wherever they lead."[34]

A word about sources: my debt to George Nash, whose book *The Conservative Intellectual Movement in America: Since 1945* was first published in 1976 and brought up to date in 1996, can be measured by the fact that I have dedicated this book to him. He has truly been a mentor to me, as he has been to just about everyone who attempts to tell the story of conservatism in our society. Two books on neoconservatism have been especially important: Gary Dorrien, *The Neoconservative Mind: Politics, Culture, and the War of Ideology* (1993), and Mark Gerson, *The Neoconservative Vision: From the Cold War to the Culture Wars* (1996). The first is critical of the movement, the latter sympathetic. Both books are excellent (I note the perspective of each, since the subject is so suffused in controversy), but both have been overtaken by events, particularly the emergence of a new group of younger neoconservatives as well as the events in Iraq and Afghanistan, which have given the discussion of neoconservatism new momentum.

Turning back to the Cold War period, I found Jay Winik's *On the Brink: The Dramatic, behind the Scenes Saga of the Reagan Era and the Men and Women Who Won the Cold War* (1996) useful primarily because of excellent interviews with neoconservatives describing their firsthand and candid personal experiences. Anticommunism has been at the center of neoconservatism from 1947 to the collapse of the Soviet Union in 1990. The important books here dealing with McCarthyism and what I have called the liberal civil war and the liberal meltdown include Richard Gid Powers' *Not without Honor: The History of American Anticommunism* (1995) and *Venona: Decoding Soviet Espionage in America* (2000) by John Earl Haynes and Harvey Klehr. The essential background for my description, one necessary to understand the role of the neocons in and out of the Reagan administration regarding the dangers posed by Soviet imperialism and the collapse of the Soviet Union, can be found in Peter Schweizer's *Reagan's War: The Epic Story of His Forty Year Struggle and Final Triumph over Communism* (2002), which draws from materials found in Soviet archives.

Finally, Norman Podhoretz has written several memoirs describing the evolution of his thought and experiences that I have consulted closely. They include *Making It* (1967), *Breaking Ranks: A Political Memoir* (1979), *Ex-Friends: Falling Out with Allen Ginsberg, Lionel and Diana Trilling, Lillian Hellman, Hannah Arendt and Norman Mailer* (1999), and *My Love Affair with America: The Cautionary Tale of a Cheerful Conservative* (2000). Irving Kristol, arguably the founding father of neoconservatism, has been somewhat more reticent. The closest thing that we have of his version of events and experiences, apart from his articles, essays, and op-ed pieces, can be found in his thirty-eight-page "Autobiographical Memoir" that introduces one of his collections, *Neoconservatism: The Autobiography of an Idea* (1995). Regrettably, Nathan Glazer, another seminal figure, has not written his memoirs, so we have his version only in bits and pieces.

Obviously, I have had the assistance of a great many people in developing this account, but I have decided to mention just a few names here. In the course of my long career at the American Jewish Committee and as director of the Feinstein Center for American Jewish History at Temple University, I have interacted frequently with neoconservatives and others. I have sometimes found it difficult to distinguish between formal interviews with them and conversations held in the ordinary course of events. The Notes should give the reader some indication of the scope of my efforts.

Richard Orodenker, an award-winning writer and editor and a Penn State professor of English and American Studies, was instrumental in helping to whip the manuscript into shape. Richard is no stranger to the neoconservative movement, with his own longstanding ties to the National Association of Scholars, arguably the nation's leading nonpartisan organization devoted to a return to reasoned scholarship and democratic ideals in higher education. His was a great task, and any lingering errors in this text are my responsibility, not his. The second person I must acknowledge is Lewis Bateman, who originally commissioned this book when he served as editor for another publishing house. On his departure, the book became an orphan. I asked permission to withdraw it, and Lew once more came to my rescue. He encouraged me to complete it and saw me through the various processes by which the manuscript became a book. There is more to writing a book than getting your thoughts down on paper. Finally, I must express my appreciation to the Lynde and Harry Bradley Foundation for a grant that helped to defray certain expenses incurred in writing this volume, as well as other research on American Jewish conservatism, at the Feinstein Center for American Jewish history at Temple University.

1

Jews and the Making of the Cosmopolitan Culture

In the years following World War II, a "golden age" seemed to open up for Jews. "Suddenly," Irving Kristol remembered, "things were possible that seem[ed] utterly impossible."[1] Hitler's Holocaust had demonstrated the depths of human depravity at the cost of six million Jewish lives, but the battle against Nazism had been won. The United Nations was established to keep the peace, and a Jewish homeland was created. Anti-Semitism, while still a force to be reckoned with, seemed to be in retreat. The position of the Jew had been normalized, social critic Will Herberg proclaimed in his influential *Protestant, Catholic and Jew* (1955).

In the transformation of American society after the war, no ethnic group took greater advantage of the new emphasis on egalitarianism than the Jews. Their numbers were tiny even back then – there are still fewer than 6 million Jews in a national population of well over 220 million. Yet their influence in field after field – from law, medicine, entrepreneurship, and philanthropy to virtually all forms of high and popular culture – was extraordinary. "People talk about what Episcopalians have accomplished and their power," wrote the University of Pennsylvania sociologist E. Digby Baltzell, an Episcopalian, "but what Jews have done in the United States ... is now the great, untold story."[2]

It was not that American Jews merely began to win acceptance in the overwhelmingly Christian society, but rather that many became bright stars in a new cultural firmament. For example, seismic changes in literature in the postwar years saw the eclipse of an older generation of novelists and poets such as Ernest Hemingway, F. Scott Fitzgerald, William Faulkner, and T. S. Eliot and the emergence of such young Jewish writers, artists, composers, and critics as Saul Bellow, Aaron Copland, Leonard Bernstein, Philip Roth, J. D. Salinger, Norman Mailer, Arthur Miller, Herman Wouk, Bernard Malamud, and Alan Ginsberg. So stunning was the shift that critic Leslie Fiedler proclaimed "the great takeover by Jewish American writers."[3]

Miller became the preeminent American playwright and Bernstein the preeminent conductor-composer. Among social critics, Lionel Trilling was the dominant figure, one, according to David Hollinger, who "saw America afresh with details to which natives had grown blind or numb." Intellectuals such as David Riesman and Daniel Bell replaced religious leaders as "the most authoritative public moralists" for the nation.[4] In his first great book, *The Adventures of Augie March*, Saul Bellow, "a Jewish kid living in the Jewish neighborhood of Humboldt Park in Chicago" and later a Nobel Prize winner, told Americans that what was so heroic about this country was "not pioneers settling the West but city kids rising from poverty."[5]

The impact of Jews extended far beyond high culture. They taught Americans how to dance (Arthur Murray), how to behave (Dear Abby and Ann Landers), how to dress (Ralph Lauren), what to read (Irving Howe, Alfred Kazin, and Trilling), and what to sing (Irving Berlin, Barry Manilow, Barbara Streisand).[6] Jonas Salk discovered a way to defeat a crippling disease. The Sulzbergers demonstrated how to publish a great newspaper, the *New York Times*. Walter Annenberg showed how to make a huge fortune with a simple magazine listing television programs (*TV Guide*). Norman Lear's impact on TV (*All in the Family, Sanford and Son, The Jeffersons*, etc.) is still being felt. It is no exaggeration to suggest that during the "golden age," Jews, for better or worse, came to play a critical role in defining America to other Americans.

A more significant and perhaps more enduring measure of their advance was the increased presence of Jews on the faculties of universities that had previously excluded them. In 1946, there was not a single Jewish tenured professor at Yale. By 1960, 28 of the University's 260 full professors were Jewish.[7] Elsewhere, the advance was even more spectacular, especially in disciplines likely to impact on the broader culture. At the most prestigious institutions, professors from Jewish backgrounds accounted for 36 percent of law faculties, 34 percent in sociology, 28 percent in economics, and 26 percent in physics. They also constituted 22 percent of the historians and 20 percent of philosophers – disciplines that had systemmatically barred them just a few years before.[8] Furthermore, after the turn of a new century, the three schools that stood atop the elitist Ivy League – Yale, Harvard, and Princeton (as well as the University of Pennsylvania) – would all have had Jewish presidents.

In the pre-war years, the ranks of American intellectual life were augmented by a stream of Central European scientists, artists, musicians, philosophers, writers, political theorists, and political dissenters fleeing from Hitler, two-thirds of whom were Jewish.[9] Coming into their own now, they included figures from the famous "Frankfurt School" such as Theodor Adorno (half-Jewish), Max Horkheimer, and Leo Levinthal as well as Hannah Arendt, Albert Einstein, Eric Fromm, Ludwig von Mises, Leo Strauss, and Hans Morgenthau. Describing this remarkable group in *The*

Sea Change: The Migration of Social Thought 1930–1945, H. Stuart Hughes called them "the most abrasively critical, skeptical, and cosmopolitan within German-speaking Europe," suggesting that "their arrival was the most important cultural event of the second quarter of the Twentieth Century."[10]

The "Frankfurt School" was obsessed with the dangers of "thinking with the blood." They sought to wipe out fascism and anti-Semitism that had forced them to flee their countries. Most brought with them a Freudian/Marxist ideology and were suspicious of liberal capitalism. These ideas were embodied in Adorno and Horkheimer's *Dialectic of Enlightenment* (1944), a chapter of which on "Elements of Anti-Semitism" dealt with the potential dangers of fascism in the United States. They found this thesis (despite its improbability in this country) rooted not in mass discontent but in the injustices of the free market. Since the United States was the prototypical capitalistic society, American Jews, they felt, had much to fear in the basic economic arrangements of the society.[11]

While Adorno and Horkheimer never entirely abandoned their radicalism for liberalism, their association with the American Jewish Committee and their own growing doubts tended to temper this extremism and to bring them closer to the liberal ideology and psychological orientation that would define the Committee.

These years saw also the emergence of a new profession of public intellectuals, many from immigrant, Jewish backgrounds – men and women molded by the Great Depression and often radical in their politics, some of whose eventual movement to neoconservatism this book explores. "Assisted by a dose of barely digested Marxism, they simply transmuted the problem of their own future into a critique of the society," historian Henry Feingold writes.[12] A number found their way into the universities, in part because of the crush of returning ex-GIs, but largely as a result of the newfound status of the intellectuals. Such figures as Howe, Kazin, William Phillips (without a Ph.D.) and even Philip Rahv (who did not even have a B.A.) became professors. Columbia University conferred the Ph.D. on Glazer and Daniel Bell *after* they began to teach, in recognition of the work they had published.[13]

Many of these public intellectuals were associated with "little magazines" like the *Partisan Review*, *Commentary*, and *The New Leader* that reached only a small audience but proved to be breeding grounds for an amazing group of ambitious and thoughtful strivers. Writing for the *Partisan Review* (edited by Philip Rahv [born Ivan Greenberg] and Philips), which became the virtual house organ of the New York intellectuals in the 1930s and 1940s, signaled a sense of accomplishment. Despite its Marxist-Freudian origins and communist sponsorship when it was founded in 1934, the little magazine soon demonstrated a courageous anticommunism and opposition to the Soviet Union. It championed works of modern writers and encouraged postwar movements such as existentialism. "Critical debates once confined to these magazines were soon heard in academic departments, moving out from there to a wider, educated, public," Joseph Berger observed in his obituary of Phillips.[14]

By this time, New York had replaced Paris as the world's cultural capital and had begun to attract aspiring intellectuals, artists, and writers from all over the country. Midge Decter, who grew up in St. Paul and would later become a prominent neoconservative, was drawn to this "Jewish Camelot" by a new sense of possibility.[15] She was escaping what she feared would be a restricted and overprescribed life in Minnesota. Coming to Manhattan from Brooklyn "was liberation" for Irving Kristol. Brooklyn, where he grew up, was dull.[16]

The New York intellectuals (as Howe called them) focused on any number of subjects and jumped from one discipline to another.[17] For many, science and the psychological insights of Sigmund Freud replaced religion as the guiding principles of society. "Their outlook was cosmopolitan rather than provincial and their style was often abrasive," Henry L. Feingold writes. Any "cudgel was used to beat down the opponent in intellectual discourse."[18]

The New York intellectuals began their adult lives as outsiders in a WASP-dominated milieu. World War II, however, took them from their neighborhoods and broadened their experiences. The army was "like a graduate school for me," Howe said. Stationed in Alaska, he read books and began contributing "a book review here a book review there."[19]

The newly enthroned cosmopolitan or modernist perspective emphasized tolerance, relativism, rationalism and pluralism. It carried with it contempt for what was viewed as the backward, "provincial mind" as encouraging prejudice and conformity, as Terry A. Cooney has remarked about these intellectuals.[20] Religion (as Freud had taught them) was relegated to the periphery of modernist thought or, at best, would often end up governed by secular and rational philosophy. Charles Liebman has suggested the new Jewish elite were "'Judaizing'" the society, but less from the stance of historic and intrinsic Jewish values they sought to universalize than "in an effort to impose their own condition – loss of religious faith and a sense of estrangement – upon the society."[21]

At the outer edge of thought and behavior during the "golden age" stood the Beats, led by Allen Ginsberg, raised in an immigrant, Jewish household in Paterson, New Jersey, along with his friends, novelists William S. Burroughs and Jack Kerouac. Ginsberg's reading of his first major work, *Howl* (1956), in San Francisco put the Beat Generation on the covers of *Time* and *Life*.[22] Turning their backs on traditional and what they felt were "puritanical" standards and values, the Beats, Ann Douglas notes, made "hitchhiking, jazz, gender bending, left wing attitudes and high-style, low life de rigueur for anyone aspiring to 'hipster' status."[23] "No one knew it at the time," literary critic Morris Dickstein writes, "but what Ginsberg stood for was where a large part of American culture would soon be headed."[24]

Ginsberg was joined by Norman Mailer, whose postwar novel *The Naked and the Dead* (1948) exploded on the literary scene to wide acclaim. In a famous and bizarre essay, "The White Negro: Superficial Reflections on the Hipster," originally published in Irving Howe's magazine *Dissent* in September 1957 (to Howe's later chagrin), Mailer celebrated the "hipster" as a model character, conceding that he was a "philosophical psychopathic," who nonetheless ought to be admired because of his individualistic inclinations.[25]

The Jewish intelligentsia, notes Andrew R. Heinze, "created much of the American lexicon of self in the twentieth century, articulating the human desire for self expression and acceptance with such concepts as ego-id-superego, rationalization, projection, defense mechanism, identity, identity crisis, life cycle, inferiority complex, compensation, life style, peak experience, self actualization and I-thou relationship."[26] To be sure, the new Jewish cultural elite were hardly alone in encouraging new ways of thought and behavior. They tended to reinforce tendencies already present among the most de-Christianzed, liberal Protestants, "lapsed Congregationalists like the philosopher John Dewey."[27] Many Jewish writers took as their model the Anglo-Saxon critic Edmund Wilson and his broad-gauged surveys of modernism. Lionel Trilling, perhaps coincidentally, rented a Greenwich Village apartment across from Wilson where he could observe the great critic at work at his desk.[28] Simultaneously, broader segments of the American intelligentsia were moving in this direction. Alfred Kinsey, a WASP who grew up in Hoboken and South Orange, New Jersey, and did his major work at Indiana University, was determined to use science to free American society from what he saw as the crippling legacy of Victorian repression. Self-liberation was to be the model both in his personal life and for others. Kinsey's underlying message was that people should listen to their more open ideas of sex rather than to their conscience, their God, or their superego.[29]

But even as they were gaining prominence and influence, the Jewish intellectuals were not entirely at home in America. They neither belonged to their parent's immigrant culture nor felt fully part of American culture. They were often ambivalent or professed to be indifferent about their Jewishness.[30] Novelists Malamud, Bellow, and Roth objected to being pigeonholed as Jewish-American writers. Born Irving Horenstein in the heavily Jewish East Bronx, Howe Anglicized his name as a college student in 1940. During its first years of publication, the *Partisan Review* rarely made references to Jews or Judaism, Glazer notes in an interview. In its early years, Glazer adds, *Commentary* devoted little space to the state of Israel.[31]

With only slight exaggeration, Isaac Rosenfeld referred to the postwar Jewish cultural leaders as specialists in alienation.[32] Arthur Miller modeled Willy Loman, the protagonist of *Death of a Salesman* (1949), after his uncle Manny but never identified him as Jewish until, in a new Preface for the fiftieth anniversary of the play, he explicitly identified the Lomans as Jews who have lost their Jewishness; his 1948 novel, *Focus*, on the other hand, dealt specifically with anti-Semitism.[33] Similarly, Joseph Heller presented Yossarian, the most memorable character in his fictional classic *Catch-22* (1962), as an Assyrian, although Heller has more recently acknowledged Yossarian's Jewishness.

As a graduate student in the 1920s, Trilling – who came from a traditional family of Orthodox Jews from Bialystok, Poland – wrote for the *Menorah Journal*. As his career took off, he came to feel that "realizing one's Jewishness" was both "provincial and parochial." In an often-quoted statement, he denied finding anything in his professional or intellectual life that could be traced to his Jewish background. "I should resent it if a critic of my work were to discover in it either faults or virtues which he called Jewish," Trilling said.[34]

Cynthia Ozick, for one, has pointed out that when *The Diary of Anne Frank* was first brought to the stage in the 1950s, its message was one of universal human suffering. Only with a new version of the play in 1995 was Frank's Jewishness made explicit.[35] Ozick recalls that as a graduate student in Trilling's class at Columbia in the 1930s, she caused a stir by noting that Marx, Freud, and Einstein were all Jewish. "I was made to feel SHAME over having introduced the idea of Jewishness as a contributing force," she told the historian Susanne Klingenstein.[36] The Jews who moved into the academy were eager to throw over their immigrant origins and appear as scholars in the WASP mode.

Still, there was no mistaking the Jewish ambience of these Jewish intellectuals and the publications from which many of their ideas poured forth. Eric Bentley hailed the *Partisan Review* in 1947 as "the voice of the New York ghetto."[37] In listing the traits that linked his life with *Partisan Review*, Fiedler declared himself "an urban American Jew"; Howe made much the same point in an essay describing *Partisan Review* as full of "Jewish references, motifs, inside jokes, and even inside themes."[38]

Lack of religious faith and alienation from the broader society, together with memories of the pre-war Great Depression, drove many Jewish intellectuals left of center politically and often to the extreme left. Marxism and its various secular offshoots offered a sense of belonging. Jews found themselves welcomed in these movements and perceived the Soviet Union, whose official pronouncements proscribed anti-Semitism and discrimination, as the fulfillment of all these advantages. When the crimes of Stalin began to be exposed in magazines like *The New Leader*, *Partisan Review*, and *Commentary* and the Soviet system was revealed as chimerical at best, many of these same intellectuals refused to believe it, while others found themselves isolated philosophically.

Thus the paradox of the "golden age" for Jews: even as they were becoming more at home in America, they continued to feel uneasy. Although polls showed anti-Semitism declining, they feared the rise of demagogues who might capture the public imagination. "In the immediate aftermath of the Holocaust," writes historian Stuart Svonkin, "who was to judge whether the professional anti-Semite was a relatively harmless crackpot or a potential Hitler?"[39]

In response, Jews and Jewish groups, along with allies in the labor movement and aristocratic WASP circles, began an all-out assault on prejudice and discrimination and other forms of injustice directed against Jews and other excluded groups. The role of the American Jewish Committee (the Committee), the Anti-Defamation League (ADL), and the American Jewish Congress (the Congress) took on a newfound importance. This effort involved "a particular kind of social vision built around internationalism, liberalism and modernism" and stepped-up racial improvement efforts and "progressive" politics more generally, which exerted extraordinary influence in shaping American political, economic, and cultural life.[40]

No longer seeing themselves simply as Jewish "defense" agencies, Jewish civic bodies, which now referred to themselves as "community relations" bodies, broadened their agendas to support social welfare programs of all kinds as part of the effort to strengthen democracy. Increasingly, they employed social science research to combat bigotry against all outsiders in the society. Often working in collaboration with universities, they embarked upon scholar-activist programs to bring about social change. They came to play a central role in shaping the newly developing field of intergroup relations as an integral part of the liberal agenda.[41]

Patrician German-Jewish leaders created the Committee in 1906, initially to battle on behalf of the rights of Jews abroad. Seven years later, the ADL came into existence, focusing on discrimination within this country. The most militant and left-wing of these bodies, the Congress, founded in 1918, which was closer to the masses and the descendents of the immigrant generation, sought to fuse a fuller Jewish identification with the broader battle for human rights. In the postwar years, these groups developed a network of field offices in all the major cities of the country. Five years after World War II, the Committee's annual budget had quadrupled, from five hundred thousand to more than two million dollars. The ADL was not far behind. The Congress, the third of the "big three," grew even faster. In 1944, the National Community Relations Advisory Council (NCRAC – later the National Jewish Community Relations Council [NJCRC] and now the Jewish Council for Public Affairs) came into existence to coordinate the activities of all these groups along with other Jewish civic and religious bodies.[42]

Gone from top posts in these organizations were more conservative turn-of-the-century German-Jewish leaders such as Jacob Schiff, Louis Marshall, and Julius Rosenwald. In their place stood John Slawson (originally Slavson) of the Committee; Leo Pfeffer, Will Maslow, and Alexander Pekalis of the American Jewish Congress; and Isaiah Minkoff the NCRAC. The new leaders were professionally trained social workers and lawyers (what we call public interest officials today). Many came from socialist-labor backgrounds. Unlike their "benevolent patrician" predecessors, they devoted themselves full-time to civic activism.

Having grown up poor in Eastern Europe or in families of recent immigrants, they identified strongly with victims of poverty and other forms of social displacement. They were drawn to left-wing formulas, especially stressing the role that government could play in bringing about greater justice. They believed strongly that the battle against anti Semitism had not ended with the demise of Hitler but rather persisted in discrimination against Jews at management levels in industry and finance, in housing, in education, and at leisure resorts. Central to their belief was the idea that Jews could never feel safe unless prejudice and discrimination against *all* minorities were wiped out.[43]

The most influential of these bodies was the Committee, which in its early years had worked quietly behind the scenes with influential Americans to protect the rights of Jews. The group had a strong social-scientific orientation, sponsoring some of the original work on race relations of the distinguished Columbia social anthropologist Franz Boas. During World War II, Slawson, a social psychologist, who was appointed as executive head of the agency in 1943, gathered together a number of the European émigrés in the Frankfurt group for help in understanding the nature and origins of prejudice. Following the meeting, Slawson created a Department of Scientific Research, headed by Horkheimer. The chief product of this department was the five-volume series Studies in Prejudice. The lead volume was *The Authoritarian Personality* (1950).

In one of his most important moves, Slawson hired a young African-American psychologist named Kenneth B. Clark to prepare a study on the impact of discrimination on the personalities of young children, which the Committee planned to use for a 1950 White House Conference on Children. Clark completed his six-month study, which famously involved the use of "white" and "colored" dolls, in that year. His paper, based in part on the data developed in the Studies in Prejudice series, argued that legally enforced school segregation damaged black children psychologically and concluded that the average black American had been scarred by self-hatred.[44]

Speaking for a unanimous court in *Brown v. Board of Education, Topeka, Kansas*, in 1954, Chief Justice Earl Warren declared segregated schools unconstitutional in no small part based upon the psychological data of Gunnar Myrdal, Clark, and other social scientists in studies introduced by the Committee, the Congress, and various individuals and groups. Citing these studies in a famous footnote to the case, the first one on Warren's list was Clark's analysis.[45]

Operating from the premise that prejudice was partly a product of ignorance, the Committee and the ADL also stepped up their educational efforts.

During World War II, they had labored to make the point that it was Hitler versus the American people, not Hitler versus the Jews. The ADL now began a campaign utilizing radio and by 1950 was using television spots, clever jingles, blotters, filmstrips, and other media devices to teach Americans about tolerance. As Samuel H. Flowerman and Marie Jahoda of the Committee's Scientific Research Department noted in 1946, "It is, after all, not surprising in our industrial-commercial culture that ... the methods used to boost the sales volume of famous-brand toothpastes or soaps should be taken out of their commercial context and used in the battle against prejudice."[46]

The Jewish groups were careful to avoid the image of being narrow or parochial in their interests. The caption of one ADL blotter depicted a black youngster wiping away tears because he wasn't allowed to play baseball with white children. The caption read, "What difference does it make what his race or religion is? He can pitch, can't he?" The ADL enlisted Hollywood starlets in its effort; Bess Myerson, the first Jewish Miss America, joined the roster of speakers appearing in schools and auditoriums around the country, declaring, "You can't be beautiful and hate."[47]

Hollywood now joined enthusiastically in the cause of "attitude modification." Frank Sinatra appeared in *The House I Live In* (1945), based on the popular Academy Award–winning song. The next year, Laura K. Hobson's novel *Gentleman's Agreement* was the subject of a Twentieth Century-Fox film on anti-Semitism from the perspective of a white Protestant. The extraordinary thing about these films, John Mason Brown wrote in the *Saturday Review of Literature*, was that they opened up a subject not then publicly discussed.[48]

Maslow and Pekalis of the Congress, however, were convinced that institutional discrimination was the real target, rather than prejudice per se. Impatient with efforts at generalized appeals for tolerance, they were eager to prove that legal and legislative campaigns were the most effective means of public instruction. Toward the end of the war, the Congress created a new department under Pekalis, the Commission on Law and Social Action, which initiated efforts seeking through legal maneuvers to ban discrimination in education, housing, and employment on city and state levels during the 1940s and 1950s. They were soon joined by the other Jewish community relations agencies.[49]

In an essay, "Full Equality in a Free Society," published in 1945, Pekalis, the leading theoretician of the broadened Jewish thrust, wrote the credo of Jews and their organizational representatives, basing it on a secularized version of the Jewish mission. Pekalis called for an "active alliance with all progressive and minority groups engaged in the building of a better America." American Jews will find more reasons for taking an affirmative attitude toward being Jews, he declared, "if they are part and parcel of a great American and human force working for a better world whether or not the individual issues involved touch directly upon so-called Jewish interests." The tradition and fate of Jews, he argued, "are indissolubly bound to those of the forces of liberalism."[50]

In subsequent years, the Congress and the other Jewish bodies, along with non-Jewish partners such as the ACLU and the National Council of Churches, switched to a more aggressive liberalism. Discriminatory practices were challenged in state after state. The centrality of the Jewish groups to these efforts grew out of their sense of mission and their experienced professional staffs and equipment – mimeograph machines, for instance – that were used to organize these efforts. By the early 1960s, twenty states and forty cities had enacted fair employment practices legislation – laws covering some 60 percent of the national population and about 40 percent of minorities.[51]

Simultaneously, all of the major religious denominations of American Judaism formed social action committees immediately following the war. In 1949, the Reform movement laid the foundation for what would become its Social Action Center in Washington, DC.[52] During the 1950s, rabbinic groups adopted resolutions backing union workers (even as Jewish workers were fast disappearing). Reform bodies now also rallied automatically behind federally funded housing and medical care for the indigent as well as strengthening the United Nations. Conservative rabbis applauded (as did the Jewish defense agencies) when the Supreme Court handed down its historic decision banning school segregation in 1954. Even the Rabbinical Council of America, then a self-consciously "modern" Orthodox body, was intent on distinguishing itself from what it considered old-fashioned Orthodoxy and adopted a left-of-center politics. At its 1951 convention, it passed resolutions backing price and rent controls.[53]

In the late 1940s and 1950s, prior to the rise of Martin Luther King and the black protest movement, Jews and Jewish bodies pioneered much of what would soon become the civil rights revolution. These years marked the Jewish phase of the civil rights movement. Far-sighted as these moves were, they suffered nevertheless from a limitation that would become apparent only later. Legislation and educational efforts did not and could not overcome fundamental economic inequality in American life that resulted from years of disadvantage and discrimination, which limited opportunities for minorities. (Before long, such efforts by the Jewish agencies, coupled with King's and others' attempts to obtain greater integration into the society and the right of blacks to vote in the South and elsewhere, appeared too limited. A new generation of black militants would arise and transform the civil rights movement into a race revolution marked by the growth of black nationalism, efforts at empowerment, and sometimes old-fashioned anti-Semitism.)

The most visible expressions of the Christian character of the society at the time, however, were found in the public schools. Here compulsory prayers and Bible readings were recited daily. A number of public schools engaged in released-time religious instruction programs, in which children were permitted to leave their classes to study the Bible and religion. Some minority Christian and civil liberties groups had regularly challenged these practices, but Jewish bodies had held back, fearing that this would stir up anti-Semitism.

Fearing that mass action by the small Jewish community would have little weight, the Jewish community relations bodies also turned to the courts in one of their most important and far-reaching efforts – to redefine the meaning of separation of church and state. Jews felt uncomfortable and often intimidated about such practices as Bible reading and prayer, particularly because of its usually Christian character. Such practices were felt to be a private matter to be undertaken at home and in churches and synagogues. Earlier, bent on assimilation, they had been unwilling to see themselves set off from their neighbors.[54] But the postwar "golden age" had produced a new assertive spirit among Jews and their civic groups. "There was to be no going back to the marginalization of Jews by other Americans that existed before World War II," the historian Eli Lederhendler notes.[55]

In taking up this issue, Jewish groups were entering an area even more sensitive than race relations. By the end of the nineteenth and throughout much of the twentieth century, most Americans had come to accept a "generic, trans-denominational Protestantism."[56] That idea, however, was already being undermined at the close of the century by the arrival of large numbers of Roman Catholics and others outside the Protestant hegemony. The growth of the liberal, cosmopolitan culture with which Jews were so closely identified now reinforced itself and moved beyond these "de-Christianizing" perspectives, a movement already well along in more liberal Anglo-Protestant circles. Older stock WASP intellectuals such as Josiah Royce, Oliver Wendell Holmes, William James, and John Dewey had long ago broken with tradition.

While Jewish bodies framed the issue in terms of religious liberty, "their conceptual framework was not free exercise but anti-discrimination," the religion scholar Alan Mittelman has commented. The argument they developed was that the rights of their children were violated when they heard a government-required prayer in public school. School prayer "made them aware that they were not like everyone else."[57]

At heart here was a clash of cultures – the secular and ascendant cosmopolitan culture, in which Jews were now so heavily invested, and the older Christian and Tocquevillian tradition that religion is essential for a healthy civil society. In pressing now for a wall of separation between church and state, the Jewish groups also went beyond the position of a previous generation of Jews. For most of their history, Jews had sought not to separate religion from American life but to gain "equal footing" within it, according to Naomi Cohen, Jonathan D. Sarna, and David G. Dalin.[58] This meant removing Christian test oaths to run for public office and religious qualifications for voting. They did not seek the removal of religion from the "public square" until the latter part of the nineteenth century, when, concerned about missionary efforts and moves to declare the United States a Christian nation, some Jews began to seek a more strict separation, even as most of them went along with the practices of their Gentile neighbors.[59]

In the first years of the twentieth century, the politically conservative Jewish leader Louis Marshall sought accommodation between and among religious groups in the society rather than the rigid separation of religion from public life. Marshall had prepared the Committee's brief in *Pierce v. Society of the Sisters of the Holy Names of Jesus and Mary* in the 1920s, which had argued successfully that Oregon's Klan-sponsored law requiring all children to attend public schools was unconstitutional. Marshall also believed that released time for religious study during the school day was both constitutional and "highly commendable." He urged fellow Jews to support it, since "unless something of this sort is done, we shall have a Godless community."[60]

Marshall also favored compromise on Bible reading in the schools. In a letter in 1922 to his cousin, he wrote,

> Some method should be found by which all interested persons can agree upon a programme which will obviate the sound objections to the reading of certain portions of the Bible and at the same time confer upon the youth of this country the advantage of familiarizing itself with the noblest ethical teachings the world has yet known, couched in the purest of English.[61]

In 1957 (revised in 1971), a Joint Advisory Committee of the Synagogue Council of America and the NCRAC summed up the new body of thought among Jewish groups in a statement entitled "Safeguarding Religious Liberty: Jewish Groups." It announced "the shared conviction of all the organizations that . . . the wall of separation between state and church created by the Constitution must be scrupulously maintained."[62]

Church-state separation became the fixed view for many Americans and, more importantly, for most Jews. Leading the battle to establish this view was Leo Pfeffer of the Congress. During his forty years of association (1945–1985) with the Congress's Commission on Law and Social Action as staff attorney, director, and special counsel, Pfeffer advised, planned, and argued more church-state cases before the U.S. Supreme Court than anyone else in American history.[63] He was widely consulted by other groups and often ghosted their briefs, while writing widely on the subject.

The son of an immigrant Orthodox rabbi, Pfeffer explained in an autobiographical reflection in 1985 how his own thought had been shaped by two experiences. The first was his experience at Public School 15, just two short streets from his home. He was deeply troubled by the daily Bible reading by Miss Knox, "probably a Protestant lady." The second occurred in the middle of the 4A term, when school authorities began to consider introducing a released-time program. His parents promptly took him out of the school and enrolled him in a yeshiva.[64] The uncompromising Pfeffer conceded in his memoir, "My briefs, writings, and lectures manifest my commitment to absolutism in respect to all First and Fourteenth Amendment rights." Compromise, he felt, was too often the "starting point for further compromises."[65]

Pfeffer's remarkable insight was to join these battles through a series of "friend of the court" briefs. In 1947, he filed briefs in two historic cases before the U.S. Supreme Court: *Everson v. Board of Education*, challenging a New Jersey law that allowed state funds to be used for busing school children to religious schools; and *McCollum v. Board of Education*, which concerned an Illinois released-time program permitting school facilities to be utilized for religious instruction during regular school time.[66]

Separatism was not generally endorsed at the time. Indeed, it would be hard to exaggerate how foreign to the mind of most Americans this idea was. (So strongly did the Baptists object to it, they never released to the public Jefferson's letter [see note 63] containing the famous "wall of separation" statement.) The promotion of religion and morality along with education was seen by the founding fathers as a primary purpose of government.[67]

Nonetheless, filing briefs in *Everson* were not only the Synagogue Council of America and the NCRAC, the ACLU, and the Seventh-Day Adventists, among other ardently separationist bodies, but also the Joint Conference Committee, a collection of groups evolving at the time into the anti-Catholic Protestants and Other Americans United for the Separation of Church and State (now Americans United for Separation of Church and State). This old nativist order, in fact, initiated the case, according to University of Chicago law professor Philip Hamburger.[68]

The *McCollum* decision of 1948 (written by Justice Hugo Black), backed by the NCRAC, speaking for the community relations organizations, and by the Synagogue Council of America, representing all branches of Jewish religion, presented another irony. The McCullums were athiests. The Jewish groups felt they had a compelling interest in the case, given the abuses that sometimes resulted from released-time programs. They believed themselves vindicated when the High Court ruled that "both religion and government can best work to achieve their lofty aims if each is left free from the other within its respective sphere."[69]

Everson and *McCollum*, in which the Committee, the ADL, and Pfeffer's Congress were joined together, were crucial victories. They marked the first steps, writes religious historian Gregg Ivers, "to redefine the constitutional relationship between organized religion and the state." The decision also vindicated Pfeffer's belief that litigation could be a primary tool to achieve the Jewish agencies' objectives.[70] The political scientist Samuel Krislov has suggested that Pfeffer was "*sui generis* in the annals of modern constitutional litigation." No other lawyer "exercised such complete intellectual dominance over a chosen area of law for so extensive a period – as an author, scholar, public citizen, and, above all, legal advocate."[71]

In subsequent years, a parade of decisions increasingly backed by the major Jewish community relations agencies, which by this time had adopted Pfeffer's more aggressive legal tactics, effectively erected Jefferson's "wall" of separation between church and state. In the *Engel v. Vitale Regents* prayer case in 1962 – a case that Pfeffer opposed joining because the issues involved were too minimal, he thought – the Supreme Court ruled that even a nonsectarian, New York state–sponsored prayer (one that Marshall might have favored) was unconstitutional. The ruling upheld the contention of the Jewish agencies and other civil liberties bodies that such a prayer violated the "establishment" clause of the First Amendment.

And in *Abington Township School District v. Schempp*, a case brought by a Unitarian couple but spearheaded by the Philadelphia Jewish Community Relations Council, the High Court brought Pfeffer's long campaign to a final and successful conclusion. In his concurring opinion, Justice William Brennan declared, "Today the Nation is far more heterogeneous religiously, including as it does substantial minorities not only of Catholics and Jews but as well of those who worship according to no version of the Bible and those who worship no God at all."[72]

In its report to its members, the Congress declared it had achieved a "social revolution" for religious equality. This was hardly an exaggeration. "Jewish civil rights organizations have had a historic role in the postwar development of American church-state law and policy," Ivers agrees.[73] Joined now with the ascendant Jewish intellectual and cultural elite and with liberal Protestant and civil liberties bodies, Jewish groups had come to play a critical role in the "de-Christianization" of American culture.

There was a mild backlash from Catholics and conservative Protestants. A number of governors called for a constitutional amendment to permit school prayer, and the Catholic journal *America* warned of a rising tide of anti-Semitism. The magazine worried openly that Pfeffer and other Jewish agencies sought to "exploit all the resources of group awareness, purposefulness and expertise" of the Jewish community to frustrate legislative efforts that might provide grants or loans to church-related institutions.[74]

For the moment, however, such criticism, carrying with it a whiff of anti-Semitism, remained isolated. Carried on a wave of economic, political, and judicial success, Jews came to view the United States as a nation that was only nominally Christian. And in such a place, of course, Jews could and did flourish.

If Jews came to play an increasingly important role during the postwar years in shaping the liberal, cosmopolitan agenda, these years were not without setbacks. The most significant was Senator Joseph R. McCarthy's charges, beginning in 1951, of massive communist infiltration of the State Department and other agencies. As the Senate prepared to investigate them, communist North Korea invaded South Korea, drawing America into a bloody land war in Asia. In an unrelated matter, just weeks after the start of hostilities in Korea, the American Julius Rosenberg and his wife Ethel were arrested for passing atom bomb secrets to the Soviet Union. While McCarthy was not known to be an anti-Semite – several of his chief aids were Jewish – his efforts often seemed to target Jews who were drawn to liberal or left-wing causes.[75]

For four years, the country reeled as McCarthy and his right-wing sympathizers searched for traitors. He and other investigative committees cast a wide net, and they were none too meticulous in defining who they were looking for. Liberals, communists, and many in between found themselves targeted. The frenzy was sparked by the case of Alger Hiss, a former top official in the State Department, who had earlier been convicted of perjury in concealing his ties to Whittaker Chambers, an underground spy for the Soviet Union who had broken with communism in 1939. Not surprisingly, a number of Jews associated with left-wing causes were dragged before Congress and other investigative bodies. Some were fired from their jobs, and others were blacklisted. Jews and Jewish groups suddenly found themselves thrown on the defensive. In *The Authoritarian Personality* (which, coincidentally, was published at the height of the McCarthy era), Theodor Adorno and his colleagues viewed such right-wing behavior, along with anti-Semitism, as the product of authoritarian tendencies among some Americans.[76]

This view was elaborated upon by a group of liberal intellectuals following a Columbia faculty seminar on McCarthyism in 1954. The historian Richard Hofstadter, borrowing from Adorno, argued that McCarthyism was an outgrowth of the status anxieties of "pseudo-conservatives." His essay under that title appeared in *The New American Right* (1955), an influential volume edited by Daniel Bell, which was derived from the seminar (and was written mainly by Jews and widely publicized by Jewish community relations agencies). Hofstadter observed, "Pseudo conservatism is among other things a disorder in relation to authority, characterized by an inability to find other modes for human relationships than those of more or less complete domination or submission."[77]

In retrospect, it can be seen that the threat posed by McCarthyism, while deeply troubling to Jews and other liberals, was only a temporary setback. When McCarthy finally charged communist penetration of the U.S. army, even conservative Republicans concluded that he had gone too far. The Senate censured him in 1954, ending the reckless career of the Wisconsin senator, who died in 1957. Although the menace of McCarthyism faded away, there remained a conviction among his targets, many of them Jews, that any criticism of communism or of the Soviet Union was irresponsible "Red baiting."

McCarthyism created a deep fissure among individuals and groups on the left. Starting in the 1930s and gathering force in the 1940s, the failures of the Soviet dream and the crimes of Stalin became all too apparent to a number of Jewish intellectuals and others. Though hostile to McCarthyism because of his reckless tactics, many of these same liberals (a number of them ex-communists or leftists) felt that communists, fellow travelers, and other naïves posed a genuine threat to this country; that important sectors of government as well as other areas of society had, in fact, fallen under communist influence (see Chapter 5); and that the aggressive designs of the Soviet Union posed an immediate threat to the United States and the rest of the world. By this time, many of them had also come to believe that the Soviet Union was more of a threat than McCarthyism (which they viewed as a temporary problem, owing to the senator's self-destructive behavior) had ever been.

Although it was not apparent at the time, the rise of these Jewish anti-communists would before long transform the nation's political dynamic and become a catalyst in the growth of a conservative movement that would capture the White House and remain a force down to the present time.

2

The Premature Jewish Neoconservatives

For poor, young Jewish intellectuals in New York in the 1930s, City College was where the action was. In dingy, horseshoe-shaped alcoves lining the college lunchroom, the students spent hour after hour in ideological debate that was often more spirited and stimulating than the classroom lectures.

There were separate alcoves for Catholics, Zionists, and Orthodox Jews, but the pro-Stalinist and anti-Stalinist radicals made the most noise and commanded the most attention. The Stalinists in Alcove Two outnumbered the other factions and controlled the student newspaper, which defended the Moscow trials in editorials. They had close to fifty allies among City College's left-leaning faculty, and, Irving Howe remembered, one in their group, Julius Rosenberg, would later be executed along with his wife, Ethel, for conspiring to steal America's atomic secrets.[1]

The group in Alcove One was a mixed bag. Although they were all pretty radical in their college days, many would later make their names as prominent neoconservatives. They were united in their opposition to the Soviet dictator and often sought to provoke his backers (who were not permitted to speak to them) in Alcove Two. On other political issues, however, they disagreed with one another as often as not. For example, while Howe and Irving Kristol backed the revolutionist Leon Trotsky, who broke away from Stalin and was later murdered in Mexico, Nathan Glazer and Daniel Bell were anti-Trotskyites.[2] Alcove One's contingent also included Seymour Martin Lipset and Melvin Lasky.

Howe later recalled that you could walk into Alcove One at almost any hour of the day or night – many students had day jobs – and join in heated conversations about the Popular Front in France, Roosevelt's New Deal, the civil war in Spain, Stalin's Five-Year Plan, and "what Marx really meant." "I can remember getting into an argument at ten in the morning, going off to classes, and then returning at two in the afternoon to find the argument still going on but with an entirely fresh cast of characters," he wrote. Howe said his alcove took pride in at least dipping into James Joyce, Marcel Proust, and

Thomas Mann, whereas those in Alcove Two read "palookas like Howard Fast."[3] The battles between the communists and anticommunists became legendary. Kristol said they were fought over the "faceless bodies of the mass of students, whom we tried desperately to manipulate into the 'right' position."[4] But learning went on in these alcoves. In fact, Kristol believes that he left City College with a better education than students at more prestigious colleges received, "because my involvement in radical politics put me in touch with people and ideas that prompted me to read and think and argue with furious energy."[5]

Howe also recollected that many of these young Jewish intellectuals bore the "mark of Cohen" – that is, of philosophy professor Morris Cohen, who "like a fencing master facing multiple foes... challenged students to his left and to his right, slashing their premises, destroying their defenses.... You went to a Cohen class in order to be ripped open and cut down." It was from Cohen, Howe said, that he and other students gained their sharp, often abrasive intellectual style – intellectual life as "a form of combat."[6]

In the 1930s, before the crimes of Stalin became widely known, many Americans viewed communism as the outer end of the political spectrum. But not Cohen. While he spelled out all that was wrong with this country, he always reminded his students of the promise of American life. He helped them to see that an ostentatious alienation from society was not the only stance possible for an intellectual.[7]

While New York's free municipal colleges served as "yeshivas" for these secularized Jews, the University of Chicago was playing a similar role, but with a more conservative character. Its students included Saul Bellow, Isaac Rosenfeld, Delmore Schwartz, and Leslie Fiedler.[8] After graduating from City College in 1940, Kristol spent a year in Chicago, where his wife Gertrude Himmelfarb had a graduate fellowship. Bell taught there between 1945 and 1948. With many Trotsky sympathizers already in Chicago, Bell joined the Young People's Socialist League, the youth wing of the official Trotskyite organization.[9] But Chicago was also home for Milton Friedman, the conservative economist associated with the free market "Austrian school" of Ludwig von Mises and Friedrich Hayek, and it was the home of Leo Strauss, the conservative philosopher.

Kristol, Howe, Glazer, Bell, Sidney Hook, and other New York intelllectuals who would later enjoy such prominence in shaping the postwar American mind came out of the poor, working-class neighborhoods of Brooklyn and the Bronx. They were twice alienated – initially from an older stock Protestant elite, who dominated important areas of society, and secondly from the limiting experiences and religion of their parents. J. David Hoeveler, Jr., has suggested that the Great Depression drew them to socialism. It was seen as resolving "all their inner dilemmas about their place in society." It opened them "to the contemporary world and to a future world in which Jewish identity would not make any difference."[10] They were not only extrordinarily bright but also fiercely ambitious to place their mark on society as writers, thinkers, and public intellectuals. Norman Podhoretz, who grew up poor in the Brownsville section of Brooklyn, would later describe this drive to succeed in his 1967 memoir, *Making It*.

If City College and to a lesser extent the University of Chicago, along with various shades of left-wing thought, were starting points in the intellectual journey to neoconservatism of these young Jewish Americans, World War II was another. It took them out of their parochial neighborhoods and sent them to distant parts of the world. They met and interacted with Americans from other backgrounds and other parts of the country – an eye-opening experience for these essentially naïve young men. In an autobiographical fragment written years later, Irving Kristol told of training with soldiers from Cicero, Illinois, a famously corrupt blue-collar town that the boy from Brooklyn had never heard of. "I said to myself, 'I can't build socialism with these people. They'll probably take it over and make a racket out of it.'"[11] Nevertheless, Kristol admired their "can do" qualities. "They convinced me that they knew more about people than I did."[12] Bell put it somewhat differently: "I discovered that there were more things in heaven and earth than were dreamt of in the philosophy of Brownsville."[13]

Once sent overseas, exposed to the horrors of war, and stationed in Germany after the war, however, Kristol found that his fellow GIs were too easily inclined to rape, loot, and shoot prisoners. He concluded that only army discipline kept them in check.[14] Bell reacted similarly. He later told an interviewer of his fear of mass action, of "passions let loose." His fears reflected his Jewishness. "When man doesn't have *halacha* (Jewish law), he becomes a '*chia*,' an animal."[15] These intellectuals remained nevertheless firmly rooted in the left. Lewis Feuer, a graduate of City College in 1931, who was born in a tenement on the Lower East Side and made the transition in his career as a sociologist from Marxist orthodoxy to neoconservatism, was demoted from sergeant to private for trying to organize local workers in New Caledonia, a French possession east of Australia. Feuer argued that the Free French who held power there had forced the workers into slavery as they built airstrips for the Allied military. By the time of his death, however, a family member quotes him as saying, in his mantra about his abandonment of Marx, "For Hegel, I would not give a bagel."[16]

The novelist Herman Wouk, an Orthodox Jew who wrote about the war, viewed the conflict from a different perspective. He was a naval officer, while the others were Army grunts. Having taken part in eight Pacific invasions, winning four campaign stars and a unit citation, Wouk appreciated the Navy's tolerance of his special dietary practices. And his conflation of American and Jewish destiny is the final message Wouk leaves with readers in the closing pages of *The Caine Mutiny* (1951).[17]

The postwar years saw the gradual reconciliation of many of the young New York intellectuals with the society from which they had been alienated.

One historian has argued that neoconservatism began as a counterprotest against a generation of ungrateful children in the 1960s, although its roots predated that era.[18] The movement away from alienation and toward neoconservatism can be traced instead to a period in the 1950s, when barriers against Jewish admissions to colleges and graduate schools began to fall.

Later critics would accuse the neocons of becoming "apologists" for American culture. What they displayed, however, was gratitude and simple patriotism, a spirit that many intellectuals would have derided earlier. Podhoretz, who was a student at Cambridge during the McCarthy era, grew restless with the anti-Americanism he encountered in England and did not hesitate to say so. He wrote that the onslaught "did more than strengthen my deepening recognition that America was my true home; it also resurrected the patriotic zeal that I had grown up with as a child.... In its new incarnation, my patriotism took the form not of a vaguely exalted sentiment but of a clearly defined political position." He wrote later that the "unexpected patriotism" of the "family" – he meant his group of New York intellectuals – had developed in the 1950s.[19]

No doubt the growing success of the Jewish intellectuals and writers hastened their reconciliation with American life. The *Partisan Review* acknowledged this trend in a celebrated symposium, "Our Country and Our Culture," whose proceedings occupied three issues of the magazine in 1952. The purpose of the symposium, the editors declared, was to demonstrate that while they were still opposed to the bourgeois society's "philistine materialism," they were now looking at the country in a new way. "The tradition of critical nonconformism," as the editors put it, would survive, but in a different form.[20] Lionel Trilling stated it bluntly, writing that "an avowed aloofness from national feeling" could no longer be considered the "first ceremonial step into the life of thought." However, Norman Mailer, gaining a reputation as a leading young novelist, put himself on record as being in "almost total disagreement with the assumption of this symposium," a position he would repeat often in the coming years.[21]

Meanwhile, on a totally different level, the thought of Felix Frankfurter was also undergoing transition. An Austrian Jewish immigrant, Frankfurter had begun his career as a liberal Harvard law professor who had defended the anarchists Sacco and Vanzetti in the 1920s. He became an adviser to President Franklin D. Roosevelt's New Deal reforms, and when Roosevelt appointed him to the U.S. Supreme Court in 1939, his critics attacked him as a "radical" and a "judicial activist." But Frankfurter proved them wrong. On the bench, he became known for his independent thinking, his attachment to the Constitution, and his growing conservatism. He actually served as a brake on the court led by the liberal Chief Justice Earl Warren, who helped to overturn a record forty-five prior court decisions.[22]

In perhaps his most memorable dissent, Frankfurter held that the court majority was wrong in striking down a statute requiring children in public schools to salute the American flag. Jehovah's Witnesses had protested that this requirement profaned their religious beliefs. But Frankfurter argued that the government had the right to require the flag salute as a means of inculcating loyalty and national pride.

"One who belongs to the most vilified and persecuted minority in history," he wrote, "is not likely to be insensible to the freedom guaranteed by the Constitution." On a purely personal level, he would have preferred to join the court majority. "But as judges," he continued,

> we are neither Jew nor gentile, neither Catholic nor agnostic. We owe equal attachment to the Constitution and are equally bound by our judicial obligations whether we derive our citizenship from the earliest or the latest immigrants to these shores. As a member of this Court, I am not justified in writing my private notions of policy into the Constitution, no matter how deeply I may cherish them or how mischievous I may deem their disregard. . . .[23]

Frankfurter's attachment to government under law, guided by tradition and orderly change, was dramatically reflected in the implementation of the court's landmark 1954 decision against school segregation. He persuaded his colleagues, including Warren, to add a remarkable phrase to its finding. At his bidding, the unanimous court ruled that its decision ending separate schools for black and white children should be carried out "with all deliberate speed" (the key word being "deliberate"). It seemed like a contradiction in terms, but Frankfurter intended to give white Southerners especially time to adjust to a finding that would transform their social order. He felt (as conservatives tend to do) that while change was long overdue, it was also desirable to avoid major dislocation and to undergird order in the society.[24]

In their early years, the New York intellectuals had been drawn to a body of universalistic or cosmopolitan beliefs that allowed no room for religious faith. But Alexander Bloom's suggestion that there was "more style than substance" in this thinking was borne out when some in the group began to reassess the Jewishness from which most had distanced themselves.[25] Kristol wrote in 1948 in *Commentary* that he and others were seeking "to establish rapport with the Jewish tradition, heart in, head out."[26] One year later, he attacked psychoanalysis and its champion Sigmund Freud, who stood at the center of the newly enthroned cosmopolitan culture and for whom religion was a "mass obsessional neurosis."[27]

Kristol dismissed the widespread belief in the postwar cosmopolitan culture, and especially the Jewish response to it, that psychoanalysis offered solutions to individual problems and provided peace of mind. "Where once a Judaism liberated from the ghetto fled into the arms of a universal Pure Reason (which did, after all, proclaim honorable intentions), now a Judaism liberated from just about everything religious embraces psychoanalysis without a first thought as to the propriety of the liaison." Kristol also ridiculed the notion of a Hebrew Union College dean that religious teaching actually strengthened rather than weakened people's mental and emotional health. He took this to mean that "God is a fiction anyhow and He may as well make himself useful." He went on to argue that Moses "did not promise the Jews 'happiness,' nor did he say they should walk in the path of the Law because he thought it a virtuous law. The Law was true because it was divine – it was God's Law, a revelation of man's place in the fundamental constitution of existence."[28] In this and a number of his subsequent essays, including "Einstein: The Passion of Pure Reason," written in 1950, Kristol provided a respectful treatment of religion and the Jewish religious tradition and showed his mounting contempt for radical rationalism, especially among Jews.[29]

Kristol remained a secular Jew, but his mind was opening to the idea that religion embodied great truths of contemporary meaning to society. Other erstwhile radicals who would later become neoconservatives were undergoing a similar experience. In the 1940s, Bell and Glazer joined with Kristol's brother-in-law, Milton Himmelfarb, who was then the American Jewish Committee's director of information and research, in studying the work of Maimonides, *Mishnah Torah*. According to Bell, they met every Sunday for dinner and then sat around the table discussing the Spanish-born philosopher, physician, and rabbi of Cairo of the twelfth and thirteenth centuries. And since Maimonides codified the Talmud, the collection of writings that form the basis of religious authority for traditional Judaism, they learned about the faith of their fathers.

They came to understand also that the organized Jewish bodies did not embrace the whole of Judaism – that there was a need to include, as Harold Rosenberg (another member of the "family") put it, "the Jew whom the Jewish past has ceased to stir." Such a Jew, Rosenberg noted presciently, "may tomorrow find himself at the center of the movement toward the future."[30] Out of the study group's discussions, the idea to start a new magazine that would appeal both to intellectuals and to a broader educated Jewish public emerged. Thus, the American Jewish Committee founded the magazine *Commentary* in 1945.[31] The leading figure in bringing the magazine into existence was its executive head, John Slawson, who worried about the assimilation of Jews and saw the new magazine as a vehicle for Jewish survival in this country.[32]

As renegades from the Marxist notion that class determines every aspect of the life of society, a number of New York intellectuals found themselves increasingly drawn to the ways in which group identity and culture actually shape people's lives and behavior. As Bell put it, in an article in *Commentary*, "no one makes himself; nor is there such a thing as a completely cosmopolitan culture. The need to find parochial ties, to share experiences with those who are like themselves, is part of the search for identity."[33] In 1957, Glazer published his important sociological portrait *American Judaism*. And just one year after being named editor of *Commentary* in 1960, Podhoretz, in a symposium, Jewishness and the Younger Intellectuals, posed a series of questions for Jews. He wondered whether they felt any responsibility to continue the Jewish tradition. He asked what they would think if their children converted to another religion and what importance they gave to supporting Israel. There was significance in his merely raising such questions.[34]

Since the turn of the century, Americans and especially Jews had welcomed Israel Zangwill's cri de coeur that this country was "God's Crucible, the great Melting Pot, where all races of Europe are merging and reforming... Germans and Frenchmen, Irishmen and Englishmen, Jews and Russians – into the Crucible with you all! God is making the Americans." But in their seminal work, *Beyond the Melting Pot: The Negroes, Puerto Ricans, Jews, Italians and Irish of New York City* (1963), portions of which had appeared in *Commentary* earlier, Glazer and Daniel Patrick Moynihan demolished Zangwill's crucible. They argued that rather than uniting together in peace and harmony, people of different races, creeds, and ethnic backgrounds tend to gravitate naturally to their own kind. And the resulting tribal ties that the liberal, cosmopolitan culture believed stood in the way of a progressive society were, in fact, not only inevitable but also evidence of healthy human relations.[35]

Throughout the 1950s, the New York intellectuals remained firmly in the liberal camp. As Kristol once phrased it, "I believe the Negro's struggle for civic equality to be absolutely just, and the use of militant methods in this struggle to be perfectly legitimate." It was during this period, nevertheless, that the burgeoning conservatism of elements of the New York intellectuals first began to take root. While always supporting civil rights and government spending to curb poverty, the premature neocons were coming to see racial issues as nearly unsolvable. Glazer began now to explore the "unintended consequences" of government social programs. In a 1958 *Commentary* piece on Puerto Ricans, which later became part of *Beyond the Melting Pot*, Glazer charged that such well-meaning programs sometimes reinforced destructive behavior and that discrimination alone did not cause minorities to live in poverty. Indeed, Glazer believed that welfare dependency largely resulted from poor people's adapting to all of the services of the modern welfare state. He did not urge, however, that these programs be ended or changed radicially. "*Commentary*'s essays in the 1960s maintained that storybook integration and the eradication of black poverty would not follow the passage of any legislation or spending bills," Mark Gerson, a historian of neoconservatism, writes.[36]

Meanwhile, Podhoretz was also developing the ideas that would make him a key figure in the neoconservative movement. Podhoretz was the son of a milkman, and Yiddish was the primary language spoken in his home. During his early school years he spoke with an accent, telling a teacher he was "going op de stez" when he was going up the stairs. A teacher insisted that he take a remedial language class to improve his English and soon encouraged his aspirations to rise above his origins.[37]

His brilliance as a student gained him admission to Columbia at sixteen, when that university still maintained a quota system. Among his professors was Lionel Trilling, who took the young man from the "provinces" (Brooklyn, in Trilling's felicitous phrase) under his wing. At Morningside Heights, Podhoretz's "meritocratic convictions" were formed, along with the firm belief that education required the absorption of the best that Western civilization had taught.[38]

Simultaneously, Podhoretz studied at the Jewish Theological Seminary and later won scholarships at Cambridge University in England. Returning home, he was adopted by the New York intellectuals as their most precocious younger member. Trilling brought him to the attention of Elliot Cohen, the first editor of *Commentary*, and the young Podhoretz began to contribute articles there. He launched his career more fully as a literary critic on *Commentary*'s staff. As early as 1957, he had observed that liberalism lacked "a sufficiently complicated view of reality" and characterized it as "a conglomeration of attitudes suitable only to the naive, the callow, the rash."[39]

Podhoretz, according to Thomas L. Jeffers, was also beginning to take a stand on the side of more commonplace, bourgeois values.[40] The 1950s were beginning to show signs of what would later be called "new age" thought, including an emphasis on individualist behavior that was often self-indulgent and hedonistic. In the 1960s, this idea would burst forth in full force. In a piece he wrote for the spring 1958 issue of *Partisan Review*, Podhoretz expressed disdain for what he termed the "Know Nothing Bohemians," men like poet Allen Ginsberg (a classmate of his at Columbia) and novelist Jack Kerouac. Podhoretz argued, Ann Charters claims, that "their tremendous emphasis on emotional intensity, this notion that to be hopped up is the most desirable of all human conditions, lies at the heart of the Beat Generation and distinguishes it radically from the Bohemianism of the past."[41]

These two advocates of new age thought, Podhoretz felt, suffered from arrested development. Later, describing his "forty year war" with Allen Ginsberg, Podhoretz notes that at twenty-six, when the beatnik poet and his friends were celebrating individualistic expression and Ginsberg had published *Howl and Other Poems*, "I had married a woman with two very small children, thereby assuming responsibility for an entire family at one stroke. By the time 'The Know Nothing Bohemians' appeared a third child had come along with a fourth to follow in due course."[42]

Trilling did not have much use for Ginsberg, also his student, either. Upon the latter's return home in triumph to his alma mater from California for a poetry reading at McMillin Theater in 1959, Diana Trilling recalled the events of that evening, skewering Ginsberg in the pages of *Partisan Review*. She recalled how he had been expelled and later readmitted to Columbia after allegedly writing an anti-Semitic obscenity on a window. The thrust of the essay was of two forces – the academic and the bohemian – colliding.[43]

Although these Jewish intellectuals considered themselves "radicals," there was no mistaking their puritanical ways. In some cases, the standards inculcated by their immigrant parents remained in place even as they sought to reach beyond them. Trilling's wife, Diana, said that entering into a premarital sexual relationship with him was "the most courageous act of my life." Kristol later wrote that it never even entered his mind to begin an affair with Gertrude Himmelfarb before their marriage. And a lack of empathy for homosexuals, which Podhoretz carried into later years, may have been the rule rather than the exception among his peers.[44]

In some of the work of the premature neocons can be seen an emphasis on what later would be called "family values." Following up on his spectacular success with *The Caine Mutiny*, Wouk published *Marjorie Morningstar* in 1955, a celebration of Jewish suburban, middle-class values. Wouk would win no plaudits as a writer among the cognoscenti, but his heroine, critic Leslie Fiedler writes, was the first "fictional celebration of the mid-twentieth century detente between the Jews and middle class America."[45]

Kristol, who was almost always a step ahead of a number of the Jewish intellectuals in the evolution toward conservatism, later said that the U.S. army's rigidity and inefficiency convinced him of the stupidity of socialism. In *Encounter*, he wrote that it was reasonable "that something as important as Big Business should be managed by hard-faced professionals" rather than by, "say the editors of *The New Left Review*."[46] In *Commentary* in 1957, he affirmed "it was time now to say a good word for Horatio Alger's novels."[47] And at a time when most liberals (and most Jews) viewed the United Nations as the last, best hope for peace, Kristol harbored doubts about the organization. He foresaw that poor Third World countries with their socialist outlook would never find accommodation with the wealthy, capitalist West. Inevitably, the two outlooks would clash. It hardly came as a shock to him and other Jewish conservatives when, in the 1970s, the UN encouraged neutralism in the Cold War struggles and exhibited a growing antipathy toward the state of Israel.[48]

Along with Kristol, three other figures – Elliot Cohen, Lionel Trilling, and Leo Strauss – formed the nucleus of the emerging Jewish conservatism. Unlike his New York colleagues, Cohen, the son of an immigrant rabbi, was born in Iowa and raised in Alabama. He entered Yale at fifteen and graduated at eighteen, majoring in English literature and philosophy. At Yale he became president of the Menorah Society and later editor of the *Menorah Journal*, which sought to create a Jewish cultural vanguard to promote a Jewish cultural renaissance within the framework of a pluralistic society. It would stand for "a combination of anti-assimilationism and cosmopolitanism."[49]

In 1945, Cohen, a brilliant but erratic figure, was named the first editor of *Commentary*. Under his leadership, *Commentary* became an "ideological hothouse" of ideas, much like the role that City College's alcoves had played in the previous decade. Cohen recruited such stalwarts of the alcoves as

Kristol, Glazer, and Howe as editors or writers, along with art critic Clement Greenberg, social critics Robert Warshow and Robert Clurman, and novelist Saul Bellow. Soon Podhoretz joined the stable, and in 1960, after a brief interim (the troubled Cohen had taken his own life), Podhoretz became editor. Cohen's "grand design" for *Commentary* (described in its statement of purpose) had been to reconnect Jewish intellectuals to the Jewish community and bring their ideas to upwardly mobile Jews.[50]

Steven J. Zipperstein notes that in its "grand design," *Commentary* envisioned the prospect of Jews' feeling comfortable in America (although most of its writers still did not) while also being comfortably engaged in "a thick, porous, intense intellectual Jewishness." It sought to implode notions that Jews must choose with regard to their Jewishness between an unambiguous partisanship and its abandonment. It did so with intelligence unmatched by any other Jewish magazine in the country.[51]

Cohen hoped to arrange a marriage between Jewish intellectuals – the "family" – and the broader American culture, while promoting reconciliation between them and the Jewish community. "*Commentary* could be trusted," the critic Alexander Bloom writes, "to tell its readers what was right with American society rather than what was wrong."[52] It served as a forum for examining issues ranging from the Holocaust, Jewish identity in the Diaspora, and the moral and political bankruptcy of communism to the role of the intellectual in society. *Commentary* came to "fill the void for communal focus for many intellectuals which had been created after they had abandoned Marxism."[53]

Typical of *Commentary*'s commonsense approach was a 1953 piece by Clement Greenberg. At that time, intellectuals routinely denounced the invented word "middlebrow" as a term of opprobrium. Dwight Macdonald led the attack. He defined "middlebrow" as a capitalist "instrument... by which the bourgeoisie was anesthetized and thus made passive." But Greenberg, then perhaps the most influential art critic in America, liked the term. He said it expressed the "desire and effort of newly ascended social classes to rise culturally as well."[54]

"And while the middlebrow's respect for culture may be too pious and undifferential," Greenberg continued,

> it has worked to save the traditional facilities of culture – the printed word, concert, lecture, museum etc. – from the complete debauching which the movies, radio and television have suffered under low-brow and advertising culture. And it would be hard to deny that some sort of enlightenment does seem to be spread on the broader levels of the industrial city by middlebrow culture and certain avenues of taste opened.[55]

Cohen's views were very much like those of the Committee, the magazine's parent: "By the very nature of their ideals," historian Oscar Handlin wrote, "the founders of the Committee [which viewed itself as a non-Zionist but not anti-Zionist organization] had opposed any ideology that considered the United States as exile."[56] This gave rise to the unusual editorial freedom the magazine has enjoyed from the very outset and has maintained since, even when in later years it parted company with the Committee on many political issues.[57]

Commentary often published articles similar to those that appeared in the *Partisan Review*, which had "rejected Jewishness as a central defining feature."[58] When the youthful Podhoretz asked Cohen about this, the editor offered a ready explanation. The principal difference between the two magazines, he said, was that "we admit to being a Jewish magazine and they don't."[59]

But *Commentary* was not universally admired. Despite Cohen's attempts at reconciliation with the Jewish community, religious and Zionist critics charged the magazine, not without some truth, with ducking a number of Jewish issues. The magazine's critics further contended that *Commentary* was suspicious, even contemptuous, of certain aspects of Jewish life, which earlier had ensured Jewish vitality by relying heavily on Western or Westernized figures such as Kafka, Babel, and Freud. *Commentary*'s relentless defense of American values against the (more left-wing) faultfinders angered both Howe, who stopped writing for the magazine (even as he acknowledged the diversity of views there), and the sociologist Louis Coser. Howe and Coser believed that *Commentary* had lost its critical perspective, particularly, in their opinion, in having underestimated the threat to civil liberties represented by McCarthyism. To fill the void, they started *Dissent*, a rival magazine with socialist orientation, in 1954.

Lionel Trilling, whose early work had appeared in Cohen's *Menorah Journal*, would come to dominate the cultural life of the 1950s and beyond with his brilliance and prestige. Trilling's métier was literature (he was an authority on Matthew Arnold), but his essays on that subject had a political kick. A number of them appeared in *Partisan Review* and were later collected in his most important books, *The Liberal Imagination* (1949) and *Beyond Culture* (1965). Kristol later recalled that Trilling's essays "hit me with the force of revelation."[60] Trilling became Podhoretz's mentor, and Podhoretz later acknowledged in *Making It* the part Trilling had played in his life.

Trilling's brand of liberalism made him suspect among the "progressive" community, which dominated cultural and political thought at the time. Since there was no generally accepted and respectable conservative body of thought as yet, he remained, in Kristol's terms, a "skeptical, out of step, liberal" whom his students, and then only in later years, called a conservative.[61] In his novel *The Middle of the Journey* (1947) (a thinly disguised novelistic portrait of Whittaker Chambers, whom he had known at Columbia), Trilling decried the liberal surrender of a stable frame of reference for recognizing or responding to evil. In a long essay in *Partisan Review*, while praising the motives behind the Kinsey Report, Trilling was also critical of its "liberating" views. He found fault with Kinsey for allowing the notion of the natural to develop into the idea of the normal. Too sophisticated and cosmopolitan to accept the dull and materialistic culture around him, he worried nevertheless that the current liberal mode of thought and behavior was becoming distant from the true sources of life.[62]

In some respects, Trilling anticipated Allan Bloom's *The Closing of the American Mind* (1987), which would appear almost half a century later. Trilling suggested there were perils inherent in liberalism itself. Focused as it was on a general enlargement of freedom and the "rational direction of human life," liberalism, he wrote, tended to "constrict" its views of the mind and the world, simplifying them, ignoring complexity and evil and frequently becoming sentimental. It was his task, he believed, to remind liberalism that it must understand variousness and possibility, which "implies the awareness of complexity."[63]

In the Preface of *Beyond Culture*, Trilling recognized a classlike "populous group whose members take for granted the idea of the adversary culture." This New Class, as these intellectuals would soon come to be called by later neoconservatives (still echoing the older Marxist rhetoric), was contemptuous of Matthew Arnold's ideals of order, convenience, decorum, and rationality, the very essence of what Trilling believed to underlie successful societies. Worse, this small and encapsulated group was becoming "massified" as its work was more widely read by thought and idea disseminators. The disenchantment of the New Class with bourgeois ideals, he warned, was spreading to the nation's growing middle classes.[64] Trilling was coming from an opposite perspective. As he argued in the symposium Our Country and Our Culture: "The American situation has changed. There is an unmistakable improvement in the present American cultural situation over that of, say, thirty years ago."[65]

Even as Trilling attacked the adversary culture, he was nevertheless a part of it himself. He identified with a "cult of failure," which he described as "an old feeling... the feeling of my youth that if you made a success you were a fraud."[66] So the intellectual, Trilling seemed to suggest, had to be poor and suffering. By the early 1950s, this view contradicted that of his young disciple Podhoretz, who in *Making It* would describe (rather outrageously at the time) a career in the arts and literature as though it were one in the business world. Podhoretz appeared to be saying that rising out of the ghetto necessitated a change in class. Those who had done so could find acceptance, but the rule seemed to be that you had to look down contemptuously on the culture of your parents. Podhoretz stood here against "the cult of failure." By speaking out so brazenly, and in a manner that could be criticized as "cocky" and "self-inflating," he was exposing the hypocrisy of many members of the group of which he was a part.

Trilling, along with others, urged him not to publish the book. When it came out, Podhoretz faced scathing attacks. Diana Trilling, who was sympathetic, said it was as though he had written *Mein Kampf*. Norman Mailer, no stranger to outrage, also weighed in against Podhoretz. The New York literary intellectuals were "scandalized, shocked, livid, revolted, appalled, disheartened, and enraged."[67] Yet what Podhoretz had done was merely to heed what Trilling had taught him earlier, that it was the "intellectual's obligation to remain responsive to reality" – that and the duty to understand the nature of power and its uses. Later, as a full-throated neoconservative at a time when the Vietnam disaster had led many of his countrymen to hesitate to meet the challenge of the Soviet Union and the threats of hostile neighbors to Israel, he and his contributors would pound away in the pages of *Commentary* about the importance of a strong military and the need to use power in the nation's interest and on behalf of our allies.[68]

In terms of influencing budding Jewish conservatism and the broader conservative movement at this time, the most important figure was Leo Strauss. Born in a rural district of Germany in 1899 and raised in an Orthodox household, Strauss received his doctorate from Hamburg University in 1921 and came to the United States in 1938 to escape the Nazis. After teaching at the New School for Social Research in New York, he joined the faculty of the University of Chicago in 1949 as a professor of philosophy. He later was named Robert Maynard Hutchins Distinguished Service Professor at Chicago, where he taught until his retirement in 1968. A prolific scholar, he wrote more than a dozen books and over eighty articles.[69]

Allan Bloom, his friend and associate at the University of Chicago, traced the wellsprings of his conservatism to life in Germany, where Jews cherished the greatest secular hopes and suffered the most terrible persecution. He was a Zionist at a time when Zionism was not fashionable among the cosmopolitan elite. Indeed, most of his contemporaries scorned the teachings of Judaism. They saw themselves as children of the Enlightenment, who believed in rationalism rather than divine authority in human affairs.[70]

Although Strauss's philosophical views were complex, his central argument was relatively easy to understand: he held that the West, transfixed by modernism, utopian ideologies, and its new god, science, had lost its moral moorings. It stood in deep crisis due to a loss of purpose and required a return to an earlier classical tradition that focused on the "formation of character" as the central issue in life. This way of thought would be free from extremism because it understood that evil could not be eliminated and that man could achieve only so much through his own exertions. Hence, in the classical tradition, political expectations were limited. The classical tradition focused on the moral character of the individual rather than the liberal notion of "uninhibited cultivation of individuality." Such individualism, he felt, was undefined and ever changing, always subject to the shifting whims of fashion.[71]

Strauss linked the classical tradition to the Judeo-Christian tradition. Western thought, he believed, rested on this tradition, whose central figure was Maimonides, the thinker whom Glazer, Bell, Milton Himmelfarb, and other young Jewish intellectuals had studied at their Sunday dinners in the 1940s.[72] According to Maimonides, human reason alone could not solve human problems. Consequently, he affirmed the indispensability of revealed religion. Maimonides' views contrasted sharply with those of another Jewish philosopher, Baruch Spinoza. Strauss believed that Spinoza sought to free men from biblical restraints, because the state of nature knows no law and knows no sin. Spinoza, Strauss argued, sought to put his trust in each individual's power to understand and make decisions. The "explicit thesis of Spinoza's *Theologico-Political Treatise*," Strauss wrote, "may be said to express an extreme version of the liberal view." Spinoza thus found his home in the liberal, secular state, while the emerging conservative movement welcomed Strauss.[73]

Strauss also labeled as destructive such philosophers as Machiavelli, Hobbes, Rousseau, and especially Nietzsche. Rousseau's attack on the classical, biblical tradition changed the moral climate of the West and unleashed the romantic, radical spirit of modern Jacobinism. In Rousseau's concept of the General Will, Strauss found nothing less than "collectivized human passion" and "the modern idol of collective man." Nietzsche, however, was the ultimate villain in Strauss's cosmology. In declaring God's death and defining Christianity as a "slave morality," Nietzsche offered nothing in its place other than power itself, according to Strauss. He saw in this the beginnings of modern totalitarianisms and concluded that liberal political theory's emphasis on individual liberty, subjective morality, and the rejection of "natural rights" led to nihilism – indeed, was synonymous with nihilism. By turning away from eternal truth and timeless values and making man absolutely at home in this world, liberal political theory could only succeed in making man homeless.[74] Or so Strauss thought.

In his own lifetime, Strauss, who died in 1973, made no effort to gain broader appeal for his ideas. He detested moral indignation, finding in it a form of self-indulgence. To his students and admirers, however, he was from "a different planet." Encountering his work, Kristol writes in his autobiography, produced "an intellectual shock that is a once in a life-time experience."[75] Social critics such as Allan Bloom fell under his spell and entered public life "with a radically altered perspective."[76]

If Strauss was a seminal figure for conservatives in the 1950s, Will Herberg was their "rabbi," a term applied to him affectionately by Sidney Hook, himself a convinced atheist. (Hook's remark was prompted in response to Herberg's espousal of traditional Judaism as well as his strong support of religion in the public arena.) His evolution from left to right was typical of many of his Jewish contemporaries described here. He was born in Russia and came to this country as a child. His parents were "passionate atheists," committed to mankind's salvation through socialism. Herberg entered the communist movement while still a teenager, and later attended City College and Columbia University. For him, communism was a religious faith. The Soviet purges during the Spanish civil war and Stalin's alliance with Hitler in 1939 enabled Herberg to seek a replacement for the "god that failed."[77]

In 1947, he served as managing editor of *Plain Talk*, moving on to become publicity director and "philosopher in residence" for the International Ladies Garment Workers Union. Later he taught at Drew University.

Early in his development, Herberg discovered the prominent Protestant theologian Reinhold Niebuhr, whose *Moral Man and Immoral Society* (1932) would profoundly change his life. In it, he found a compelling liberal position – a combination of practicality and progressive thought. More than any American thinker, Niebuhr, who befriended Herberg, related theology to politics through a realistic assessment of human nature. At one point, Herberg contemplated converting to Christianity, but Niebuhr talked him out of it. Herberg turned to traditional Judaism, which, along with providing spiritual support, encouraged social activism without falling into the trap of utopianism. During this time, he met with rabbis and briefly attended the Jewish Theological Seminary. He became an Orthodox Jew and by the 1950s was publishing widely in *The New Republic, The New Leader, Commentary*, and *Christian Century*.[78]

Herberg's main contribution to emerging conservative thought (and here he can be seen as perhaps the most modern of the premature neoconservatives) was to call attention to the role of religion in society. Like Niebuhr, he felt the country needed a new spiritual foundation.[79] His book *Judaism and Modern Man: An Interpretation of Jewish Religion* (1951) was "a confession of faith" and declaration of total commitment on the part of one "whose trust in the idols of modernity has broken down and who is now ready to listen to the message of faith." Again like Niebuhr, Herberg sought a theology based upon a less optimistic image of man, one that recognized human sinfulness and limitations. His conservatism was rooted in the concept of natural law developed by Edmund Burke, the nineteenth-century British statesman and philosopher. Burke viewed religious tradition as the very basis of the political culture, the essential component for maintenance of social order.[80]

In siding with Burke and Niebuhr, Herberg was at odds with other members of the "family," many of whom remained cultural modernists. Most of the contributors to *Partisan Review* saw his evolution as a "failure of nerve" and an escape from the real world. Hook and Bell assailed Herberg for his belief that liberal democracy rested on religious truths about man's fallibility and that such truths were a bulwark against totalitarianism. Such opposition would ultimately drive Herberg into an alliance with more traditional conservatives like William Buckley and Whittaker Chambers, who considered the Cold War in part a religious war between believers and nonbelievers.

Herberg was among the premature neoconservatives to challenge a central principle of the regnant liberal and secular Jewish culture: that the Constitution required the absolute separation of church and state. As we have seen, this view of the requirements of the First Amendment had been vigorously pressed forward in the postwar years by the Jewish civic agencies, especially the American Jewish Congress, along with other civil liberties groups. They had successfully challenged Bible reading in the public schools and any form of state aid to parochial schools. So dominant had the "separatist" view become that even a nonsectarian prayer prepared by the New York Regents Board in 1962 was ruled by the Supreme Court in *Engel v. Vitale* to be a violation of the establishment clause of the First Amendment.[81]

For his part, during the 1950s, Herberg supported government aid to parochial schools as well as religion in the public schools. Writing in *Commentary* in 1952, Herberg called upon Americans of all faiths to rethink their views of separation. He was especially critical of Jewish supporters of this idea. "Judging by their public expressions," he declared, "they seem to share the basic secularist presuppositions that religion is a 'private matter' – in the minimizing sense of 'merely private' – and therefore peripheral to the vital areas of social life and culture." He called upon Jews to abandon "the[ir] narrow and crippling minority-group defensiveness," urged interreligious harmony, and declared that Jews had little to fear from proposals to extend limited federal aid to parochial schools.[82]

Anticipating recent discussions of government support for efforts to use churches to deal with urban problems, such as "charitable choice," Herberg believed that neither in the minds of the Founding Fathers nor in the thinking of Americans throughout the eighteenth and nineteenth centuries did the First Amendment imply an ironclad ban on government cooperation with religion or its support of related activities. In his writings at the time, Herberg spoke mainly to intellectuals, but he began a discussion that would grow louder in subsequent years. Six years after his 1952 *Commentary* piece, Rabbi Arthur Gilbert, interreligious affairs director for the ADL, expressed much the same concerns in a speech before the Central Conference of American [Reform] Rabbis (as did Professors Jakob J. Petuchowski at Hebrew Union College; Seymour Siegel at the Jewish Theological Seminary; and Milton Himmelfarb, research director at the American Jewish Committee). Central to their discussion was a sense that a bland deism, as Himmelfarb put it, was likely to erode the Jewish community itself.[83] More recently, such diverse figures as University of Chicago law professor Philip Hamburger, Yale law professor Stephen L. Carter, and historian Jonathan Sarna would, like Will Herberg, adopt a more expansive view of government involvement in what some have called the naked public square.

Throughout this period, the premature Jewish neoconservatives were still isolated voices in the national dialogue. They wrote for little magazines that mainstream America paid scant attention to, but they were testing fresh ideas that today are commonplace. More importantly, they were developing a body of thought that would help to undergird the growth of a new and more broadly accepted conservatism in the years ahead.

3

Forgotten Jewish Godfathers

In *The Fifties* (1993), David Halberstam describes briefly what he perceived to be a significant political shift in that decade. He writes that although the "traditional left" had been devastated by the "grimness of Communism" and the "success of American capitalism," there had arisen "a new kind of left" that was alienated from the mainstream in a different way. Instead of attacking capitalism for its failures, Halberstam says, the new left was "essentially criticizing America for its successes, or at least for the downside of its successes." He names sociologist C. Wright Mills as the key link between "the old left, Communist and Socialist, which had flourished during the Depression, and the New Left which sprang up . . . to protest the blandness of American life."[1]

Nowhere in his vast popular study, however, does Halberstam make reference to a growing conservative counterweight to the regnant cosmopolitan culture. His lack of knowledge or indifference reflects the failure of that culture to recognize an important new force that would soon affect the social and political landscape so dramatically. The fifties, in fact, witnessed an extraordinary burst of conservative intellectual energy that foreshadowed the conservative ascendancy of more recent times.[2]

The postwar conservative revival was kicked off in Britain with the publication of *The Road to Serfdom* (1944), Friedrich von Hayek's broad-gauged attack on collectivism, which became a major event in American intellectual life when it was published in this country. Hayek was heavily influenced by his mentor, the economist Ludwig von Mises, a student of market mechanisms, who was of Jewish origin and produced one of the most incisive critiques of socialism. A non-Jew, Hayek was part of a Jewish circle in Vienna that he admired for its talent, although others dismissed it as being alien.[3]

Next came Richard Weaver's *Ideas Have Consequences* (1948) and *The Ethics of Rhetoric* (1953) and ex-communist Whittaker Chambers's *Witness* (1952), his best-selling account of Alger Hiss's communist ties and Soviet espionage in the United States. The following years brought books by other conservatives such as Russell Kirk, Robert Nisbet, James Burnham, Garet Garrett, Clinton Rossiter, and Leo Strauss. Two nineteenth-century classics, Alexis de Tocqueville's *Democracy in America* (1835, 1840) and Edmund Burke's *Reflections on the Revolution in France* (1790), commanded renewed attention with their emphasis on custom and order as indispensable safeguards for society.[4] With the appearance of Kirk's *The Conservative Mind: From Burke to Santayana* (1953), which Whittaker Chambers in *Time* magazine called the most important book of the twentieth century, the movement became more conscious and overt.

In this eloquent and impassioned work, Kirk invited his readers to reject the liberal objective of "progressive" social change in favor of a society that encouraged social order and stability. Deeply attached to rural and ancestral ways, he laid out in 450 pages his belief in divine intent, the primacy of leadership classes, the inseparability of property and freedom, and the distinctions between change and reform. While man is not perfectible, he argued, he is capable of bringing about a reasonable degree of order, freedom, and justice.[5]

Kirk was critical of both capitalism and libertarianism. A biographer notes, however, that his feuds with both belied his fundamental faith in the essential justice of the market economy, which could be made to work in more humane ways, thereby not undermining social stability or the moral order. Especially important to Kirk was the relationship between tradition and natural law. Challenged by both the left and some on the right for defending the claims of tradition, custom, and habit (while simultaneously supporting universal and transcendent norms), Kirk conceded that tradition and custom must give way to the requirements of natural law.[6]

In the 1950s, Chambers, along with social critics James Burnham and Frank Meyer, spearheaded the growth of a militant and evangelistic anti-communism. In their view, the West was engaged in a life-and-death struggle with an equally zealous Soviet Union, whose armies sat astride a weakened Europe following the war, while our troops withdrew from the continent. Also apparent by this time, too, were the failures of British socialism, as contrasted with the "miracle" of West German economic recovery based on free market ideas. The 1950s saw, finally, an increase in Christian orthodoxy and church membership. These were the years of Billy Graham's "crusades" and the addition of the phrase "under God" to the Pledge of Allegiance. On the new medium of television, the ratings of the Rev. Fulton J. Sheen, a charismatic Roman Catholic priest, surpassed those of comic Milton Berle.[7]

The period also saw the emergence of a number of conservative publishing houses, which provided a platform for conservative writers and authors. Henry Regnery created the house that carries his name in 1947. His aim was to publish "feisty books, infamous in mainstream book publishing because of their complete lack of orthodoxy," note Stephen Goode and Eli Lehrer in a 1998 article. According to Regnery's son, Alfred, "What my father was doing was running what would now be considered a think-tank publishing company challenging the status quo."[8] Regnery brought out Kirk's *The Conservative Mind* as well as Buckley's *God and Man at Yale* (1951). Devin-Adair of New York was another active conservative publishing house. In 1955, Buckley launched the *National Review*, which soon became a rallying point for the new conservatism.

Like many of the New York Jewish intellectuals whose political educations began in their ethnic neighborhoods and in the alcoves of City College, another group of conservatives from Jewish backgrounds came to play important roles in the conservative resurgence. These "forgotten godfathers" (to borrow George Nash's term) shared, for the most part, with many of the premature neoconservatives the common experience of breaking with communism and the left, but they differed from them in important respects. The latter still saw themselves as liberals and supporters of the welfare state, even as some were having doubts. The "forgotten godfathers" moved directly into the conservative movement without any soul searching. When Daniel Bell accepted an editorship on Henry Luce's *Fortune* magazine, a pillar of American capitalism, for example, a debate erupted within "the family." Midge Decter remembers questions being raised: "Should he have taken the job? Had he, in his climb toward success, sold out?"[9]

The "forgotten godfathers" had no such doubts. They were not content simply to leave the old faith; they dismissed it totally in their fervent assault on communism and their new espousal of conservative causes. What they took strongest objection to was the liberal reliance on government to achieve social objectives. They resented also what they viewed as the ambivalence of many on the left toward the mounting Soviet threat.[10]

One of first Jews to defect to the right was Eugene Lyons (1898–1985). An immigrant to New York at the age of nine, Lyons saw widespread poverty as he grew up and yearned to do something about it. "I thought myself a 'socialist' almost as soon as I thought at all," he later wrote, "dreaming of becoming a writer for my side of the class war." He cheered the Russian revolution of 1917, worked on behalf of the anarchists Sacco and Vanzetti (who were executed after a controversial murder trial in 1927), and later found employment with Tass, the Soviet news agency, for four years. But while serving as a journalist in Moscow from 1928 to 1934, Lyons saw Stalin's handiwork up close and fell out with communism.[11] He returned home and published *Assignment in Utopia* (1937), which described the totalitarian system that some on the left continued to believe in. Four years later came *The Red Decade: The Stalinist Penetration of America*, his sharp indictment of communist influence here and the foolishness of Popular Front liberalism, which had sought to make common cause with Stalin prior to and during the war. Lyons was one of 140 prominent intellectuals who signed a 1939 open letter (organized by NYU philosopher Sidney Hook, among others) linking

Russia with Germany, Italy, Japan, and Spain as states where "totalitarian ideas" were enshrined. The letter attacking the Soviet Union appeared just two weeks before Stalin's pact with Hitler, which led to World War II. It denounced the "fantastic falsehood" that conflated the Soviet system with the few remaining democratic nations, and it renounced the belief that the Soviet Union served as a bulwark against fascism. Throughout the war and after, Lyons, who served as an editor of the *American Mercury* and later as an editor of the *Reader's Digest*, continued to warn of communist takeovers of U.S. labor unions and other institutions.[12]

Ralph de Toledano, a Sephardic Jew, was another early critic of communism. The Moscow show trials (which Lyons described) and the Soviet subversion of the Spanish Republic (to whose side it had come during the Spanish civil war in the late 1930s) helped to lift him from the Red haze in which he had been living. The final straw was the Hitler–Stalin pact.[13] By 1940, he had joined the editorial staff of the bitterly anti-Stalinist and vaguely socialist *New Leader*. After the war, he joined New York's anticommunist Liberal Party and briefly became a member of Americans for Democratic Action. During the Eisenhower years, he blasted the administration for being too moderate in its anticommunism. His main concern was whether the nation had the will to bring the Soviet Union down.[14]

Morrie Ryskind seemed an unlikely convert to conservatism. Following stabs at journalism and public relations, he enjoyed considerable success writing scripts for Broadway musicals and Hollywood. Ryskind supported left-wing causes, as was evident in his screenplays for *Strike Up the Band* (1930) and *Of Thee I Sing* (1931). As late as 1936, he still viewed himself as a socialist. But after moving to Hollywood and rubbing shoulders with communists in the Screen Writers Guild, Ryskind, like Ronald Reagan later, grew determined to fight their influence. He questioned the communist commitment to civil liberties and found much to agree with in Lyons' *Assignment in Utopia*. Drawn now to conservatism, he opposed President Franklin D. Roosevelt's bid for a third term in 1940, charging that the "imperial presidency " was a "horrendous insult to our political heritage." Ryskind openly attacked Roosevelt's attempt to pack the Supreme Court, just as he had publicly criticized the Moscow purge trials several years earlier.[15]

In 1947, Ryskind told the House Committee on Un-American Activities what he knew about alleged communist infiltration of the film industry. For his outspoken testimony, he was denounced as a Wall Street lackey and Red baiter. Fearful of adverse publicity, industry representatives urged Ryskind to tone down his attacks. Ryskind, who could earn $75,000 per script, balked. He was blacklisted and never wrote another script. His experience demonstrates that writers suspected of communist leanings like the "Hollywood Ten" weren't the only film industry professionals to find themselves unemployable because of their political views.[16]

Frank Chodorov made no effort to find common cause with other conservatives, yet he played an important though rarely recognized role in the movement. The son of a poor immigrant Jewish peddler, he was born in 1887, grew up on New York's Lower East Side, and attended Columbia, aspiring to be an English professor. Instead, Chodorov taught school, sold knit goods, and managed a clothing factory. Then one day he happened to read the economist Henry George, whose work he found prophetic. In short order, he became director of the Henry George School of Social Science.[17] That position stirred his interest in social reform. George held that land was a free gift of nature and that it was unfair for a few people to acquire great wealth by owning large tracts that increased in value. He proposed a single tax on this "unearned increment."

The views of Henry George strengthened Chodorov's growing libertarian beliefs. These were also reinforced by his friendship with Albert Jay Nock, a cultured but eccentric conservative with a deep distrust of government. By the late 1930s, Chodorov had become editor of the revived magazine *The Freeman*, a small conservative journal operating out of a run-down old building in New York owned by Alfred Kohlberg, a backer of many right-wing causes. But Chodorov didn't last long as editor. He was fired for espousing isolationism as clouds of World War II settled over Europe.[18]

Undaunted, Chodorov set out to shape the conservative movement. In 1944, on a shoestring budget, he began publishing *analysis*, a four-page monthly newsletter that proselytized for his classical libertarianism. In a promotional letter, Chodorov laid out his credo: *analysis* was an "individualistic publication" in the tradition of Herbert Spencer, Adam Smith, Thoreau, Henry George, and Nock. Later, he described it as standing for "free trade, free land and the unrestricted employment of capital and labor." Chodorov believed the state was the enemy of these ideas. He found it to be the institutional embodiment of political collectivism; furthermore, it employed force to accomplish its purposes and took whatever it had from the productive parts of the society. Inevitably, there is a tug-of-war between the state and the individual. Whatever power one acquires must be to the detriment of the other. He declared, "*analysis* looks at the current scene through the eyeglass of historic liberalism, unashamedly accepting the doctrine of natural rights, proclaims the dignity of the individual and denounces the forms of Statism as human slavery."[19]

Regnery, who described Chodorov as a "born pamphleteer," published three of his most successful ones: "Taxation Is Robbery," "From Solomon's Yoke to the Income Tax," and "The Myth of the Post Office." Devin-Adair published all four of his books, but they never reached a large audience. In 1946, *analysis* had fewer than 3,000 subscribers, and in 1951 he merged it with another small conservative publication, *Human Events*.[20] Even so, Chodorov gained some important admirers, including Buckley and M. Stanton Evans, who became a leader in the young conservative movement during Barry Goldwater's presidential candidacy. The Chodorov imprint, Evans said, was visible in every phase of conservatism's growth.[21]

As independent in his personal behavior as he was in his ideas, Chodorov made no effort to find common cause with other conservatives. Hayek's *Road to Serfdom*, he declared, was disappointing and silly. His views, however, were more in line with another tradition that found support among some Jews, libertarianism, which many historians have overlooked. From the late nineteenth century until just after World War I, anarchism, a precursor to libertarianism, was an important feature of Jewish thought that would continue to thrive among a number of Jewish intellectuals, including von Mises, Gary Becker, Murray Weidenbaum, Israel Kirzner, and Milton Friedman.[22]

Perhaps the most remarkable personality in the conservative coterie of this period was the hugely successful and wildly individualistic Ayn Rand. While Chodorov and other libertarians toiled in obscurity, their work recognized only by a handful of opinion makers, Rand took center stage as a celebrity and cult figure with a following of millions.

Rand was born, as Alissa Rosenbaum, in St. Petersburg in Czarist Russia in 1905. Her father owned a pharmacy, a rare business for a Jew in Russia. As a youth, she lived comfortably, receiving a private school education, and graduated from the University of Leningrad with a degree in history in 1924. With the coming of the Bolshevik revolution, her deep detestation of communism grew even deeper following the nationalization of her father's business.

In 1926, she moved to the United States and made her way to Hollywood. A chance meeting with producer Cecil B. DeMille led to work as a movie extra and scriptwriter. Then she began writing on her own, with stunning results. Her novel *The Fountainhead* (1943) sold 18,000 copies in the first year; by 1948, it had topped a half-million; the following year, the book was made into a movie. Reviewers attacked her second novel, the huge, sprawling opus *Atlas Shrugged* (1957), as wordy, didactic, and repetitious. One critic called it a "masochist lollipop." Yet it outsold *The Fountainhead*. By 1989, its sales had exceeded two million copies, and Rand's novels have continued to prove popular, with total sales of 20 million in 1989.[23] These anticollectivist volumes featured highly individualistic men and women and capitalist entrepreneurs, whose force and drive resist crushing conformity, permitting them to lead successful economic and sexual lives.

Wearing a brooch with a dollar sign around her neck to symbolize her belief that all virtues arise out of individual creativity and the pursuit of self-interest, she was a Jew by birth but not by belief. Though she never denied her Jewishness, she considered herself an atheist. Meeting William Buckley for the first time, she told him, "You are too intelligent to believe in God."[24]

Rand and the group that gathered around her gave the name "objectivism" to her philosophical doctrine that all reality is objective and all knowledge based on observed objects and events. In *The Fountainhead*, Rand has her central character, the architect Howard Roark, say, "This country was not based on selfless service, sacrifice, renunciation or any precept of altruism. It was based on a man's right to the pursuit of happiness. His own happiness. Not anyone else's. A private, personal, selfish motive."[25] According to Rand, mass democracy, egalitarianism, and the ideals of twentieth-century Christianity conspired against the individual.[26] Her philosophy, which placed the gifted individual at its center, came perilously close to that of Nietzsche's superman, a philosophy in its essence totalitarian. Wrote Rand, "I am challenging the cultural tradition of two-and-a-half thousand years."[27]

Though her plots were awkward and her language stilted, the force of her work struck a chord around the nation and the world. She appealed to those people, mostly in the middle and upper classes, who believed that big government was displacing the individual as citizen, as employee, as consumer. Humans, she believed, were being robbed of individuality while mediocrity was triumphing over society. Despite having lectured at such Eastern liberal establishment strongholds as Yale, Princeton, and Columbia, in 1964 she supported the ill-fated presidential campaign of conservative Barry Goldwater, whom she saw as the last breath of hope for capitalism in the United States.

There would have been no "objectivist" movement, however, were it not for Nathaniel Branden (Blumenthal), Rand's principal student and, for a time, her lover. He and his wife, Barbara, persuaded Rand to move to New York, where she gathered a circle of disciples, known as the Collective. Most of them were Jewish-Canadian relatives of the Brandens. Included in the group was Alan Greenspan, who would later play a pivotal role in steering the nation's economy as chairman of the Federal Reserve Board during several presidential administrations. He even got to read *Atlas Shrugged* in manuscript.[28] In a 1966 essay, obviously still under the influence of Rand, he wrote:

> Every movement that seeks to enslave a country, every dictatorship or potential dictatorship, needs some minority group as a scapegoat which it can blame for the nation's troubles and use as a justification of its own demands for dictatorial powers. In Soviet Russia, the scapegoat was the bourgeoisie; in Nazi Germany, it was the Jewish people; in America, it is the businessman.[29]

With Rand's cooperation, the Brandens launched an institute bearing his name to promote Rand's extreme libertarian views of objectivism.[30]

Murray N. Rothbard, a "fellow traveler" of the group (who was encouraged to divorce his wife on the basis of the group's "objectivist" philosophy) was another of the conservatives from Jewish backgrounds whose ideas about individual autonomy bordered on the eccentric. At various times, he found himself associating with and then breaking from Rand and Buckley. Born into a New York Jewish immigrant family with leftist sympathies (an uncle was an engineer on the Moscow subway), Rothbard ran the gamut, from supporting Strom Thurmond, the Dixiecrat Democrat, in 1948 to backing Democrat Adlai Stevenson in 1952 and ultraconservative Pat Buchanan in 1992. He had concluded as early as 1950 that even limited government was an untenable compromise. An enemy of the state in every shape and form, he didn't even concede that police power, common defense, and the court system were legitimate functions of government. To believe so, he thought, was to accede to the statists, who always sought to expand state power. Unlike Buckley, who had reconciled himself to the expansion of state power to counter the Soviet threat, Rothbard, who had no affection for Soviet rulers, insisted that they were not inherently aggressive. Later, during the student rebellions of the 1960s, he helped establish *Left and Right: A Journal of Libertarian Thought* and sought to forge an alliance with antistatists in the antiwar movement.[31]

The ever-present Jewish distrust of authority and power (whether linked to collectivist political models or not) also gave rise, following World War II, to a group of free market economists, the aforementioned von Mises, Becker, Weidenbaum, Kirzen, and Friedman. If Rand was bizarre and reckless, both in her lifestyle and the harshness of her economic theories, Friedman provided a solid base of thought and authority for the emerging American conservatism. Milton Friedman grew up in Rahway, New Jersey, beyond the influence of urban-based New York Jewish intellectuals like Kristol, Bell, and other members of the "family." In his youth, Friedman was "fanatically religious," but his religious orthodoxy soon faded. After completing undergraduate work at Rutgers University, he studied at Columbia and the University of Chicago. In Chicago, he met the woman, also an economist, who would become his wife in 1932. (The Friedman's 1999 joint biography, *Two Lucky People*, was indicative of the integral, if often unrecognized, part Rose played in Milton Friedman's work.) With academic positions hard to obtain in the 1930s, Milton and Rose Friedman went to Washington during the presidency of Franklin D. Roosevelt, whom they admired. They worked as statisticians until the University of Chicago hired Milton Friedman.[32]

During his long tenure there, Chicago became the center of free market economics. With his colleagues George Stigler and Yale Brozen, Friedman developed a way of economic thinking that became known as the Chicago School, which, like the Austrian school, was devoted to the free market, although Friedman's group was more interested in how government programs actually malfunctioned. This emphasis fitted in well with what might be called the "pragmatization" of conservatism.[33]

Nonetheless, Friedman frequently sided with von Hayek, his friend and colleague in Chicago, in his losing struggle against the economic policies of John Maynard Keynes. Keynes held that nations, in order to pull themselves out of economic depressions, should go heavily into debt to alleviate suffering. For decades, Keynesian economics held sway in the United States and Europe, and it still has its advocates today.

High in the Swiss Alps in 1947, Friedman attended the founding of an unusual group at Mount Pélerin. Convened by Hayek and von Mises (an old-fashioned European liberal), the meeting brought together nearly forty prominent European and American conservative economists. At the time, they constituted a breed apart. In their joint autobiography, the Friedmans remembered feeling "beleaguered in their own country"[34] by scholars, a number of them internationally famous. To be sure, socialist planning was growing throughout Europe, and in the United States liberal Democrats dominated the scene. The Cold War was already under way, and the threat of totalitarian communism loomed large on the horizon.[35]

Though lacking governmental influence, the Mount Pélerin conservatives sought nothing less than to launch an intellectual crusade opposed to postwar collectivism and to threats to individual freedom. "It showed us that we were not alone," Friedman said later of the importance of the Mount Pérelin Society, which still exists today. Indeed, the society came to serve as a rallying point for conservative economic thought, not just in the United States but also in other parts of the world.[36]

By the 1950s, Friedman was giving a twist to the Keynesian tail in works like *A Theory of Consumption Function* (1957). His great achievement lay in pointing out how capitalism had created both an increase in opportunities and wider material well-being. He met the liberal charge that capitalism was responsible for the Great Depression head-on in his *Monetary History of the United States, 1867–1960*, coauthored with Anna J. Schwartz (1963), in which he argued that it was "government mismanagement" of the Depression, not the free enterprise system, that was at fault. This theory of the Great Depression remains alive in conservative circles today.[37]

In *Capitalism and Freedom* (1962), a collaboration with his wife, Rose, based on a series of lectures Milton Friedman had given, the Friedmans made a daring and iconoclastic assault on the conventional wisdom of twentieth-century liberalism and what they viewed as liberal failures, such as restraints on economic freedom and the spread of the welfare state. The book was not reviewed by any major American publication, but it sold, nevertheless, more than 500,000 copies. The book demonstrated perhaps Friedman's greatest impact on conservative thought: his incisive challenges to liberal dogma.

Why should the federal government be responsible for the post office? Why should it control the price of gold? Minimum levels of financial support were necessary for public education, but why must the state have total control of the schools? Private enterprise, the Friedmans argued, should provide more of these services for profit. In what would become a central issue in educational debate in the 1990s and in the early days of the new century, he suggested educational vouchers "redeemable for a specific maximum per child or spent on 'approved' educational services."[38]

"The educational service," Friedman argued,

> could be rendered by private enterprises operated for profit, or by non-profit institutions.... In terms of effects, denationalized schooling would widen the range of choices available to parents.... Parents could express their views about schools directly by withdrawing their children from one school and sending them to another.... The injection of competition would do much, the Friedmans felt, to promote a healthy variety of schools. It would do much, also, to introduce flexibility into school systems.[39]

To advance the idea of educational vouchers in public education, the husband-and-wife team later set up the Milton and Rose D. Foundation, one of the several financial supporters of the educational voucher movement today. In addition to educational vouchers (now in place in a number of U.S. cities and recently ruled constitutional by the Supreme Court), Friedman can also be credited with the idea that led to the adoption of the all-volunteer armed forces.[40]

As his ideas gained wide currency, Friedman's influence grew. In the early 1960s, he joined Barry Goldwater's brain trust. He was elected president of the American Economic Association, won the Nobel Prize in economics, hosted and contributed regularly to the PBS television series based on his work *Free to Choose* (1980), and wrote a column in *Newsweek* magazine. He also dabbled in politics. Returning from a Mount Pélerin conference, he met William Baroody, another Goldwater associate and an entrepreneur of conservative ideas, who had established the American Enterprise Institute, a conservative think tank that would become influential during the Reagan years. Friedman joined its advisory committee.[41]

Thanks to Friedman and others, conservative thought began to gain greater form and substance. But the conservative political movement remained far outside the mainstream. Such blatantly anti-Semitic figures as Gerald Winrod, Gerald L. K. Smith, and Merwin Hart, as well as Robert Welch, founder of the right-wing extremist John Birch Society, all claimed to be conservatives. They gave the movement a bigoted and reactionary image at a time when memories of Hitler's racism were still fresh.

Internal divisions further weakened broader acceptance of conservative ideas. On one side stood Kirk, Strauss, Voegelin, Peter Viereck, and other "traditionalists," who were troubled by the growth of a rootless mass society and the excesses of individualism. The traditionalists emphasized that side of Edmund Burke that focused on the organic aspects of society and the unwritten contract between the dead and the living and the unborn as being more central to democratic freedom than free trade beliefs. At the opposite side of the political spectrum, Chodorov, Rothbard, and Ronald Hamowy emphasized freedom over order and pressed forward the idea of rugged individualism, almost to the point of anarchism. (Hamowy's opposition to state power, for example, was reflected in his advocacy of privatizing lighthouses.) At the other end entirely was Rand with her enthusiastic band of "objectivist" zealots, some of whom, in the 1970s, would join the New Left in pushing for total individual freedom and permissiveness.

Finally, there were the economic conservatives, who looked to the marketplace for the solution of many societal problems. Conservatives knew what they were against. For the most part, though, they did not know what they were for. "A distaste for Communism and socialism is not a program," Chambers told Buckley.[42] With such disarray, it was hardly surprising that Clinton Rossiter referred to the movement in his sympathetic study, *Conservatism in America* (1955), as "the thankless persuasion."

However, a critical figure stepped forward in an attempt to tie together these divergent conservative strands. Barely known today, Frank S. Meyer was born in 1909 and grew up in Newark, New Jersey. The son of a lawyer, Meyer lived in a comfortable Reform Jewish home. He studied at Princeton and the University of Chicago, nominally a student of anthropology but really specializing in left-wing agitation. He received a B.A. in 1932 and an M.A. in 1934 and then went on to Balliol College, Oxford, and the London School of Economics, from which he was expelled for radical activities. Edward Shils, later a professor of social thought and sociology at Chicago and a prominent conservative, came to know Meyer when both of them were students there. Meyer, Shils reports, would interrupt the lectures of Louis Wirth in Chicago with Marxist corrections, supplements, and reinterpretations.

Meyer hungered to find an anchor, his biographer reports, in a "depression wracked world" (which, consequently, had destroyed his father's business). He sought it at Oxford by studying Catholic theology and history, but soon turned to Marx.[43] Meyers made a reputation for himself as a radical student leader in England and later in the United States. Secretly, he joined the Communist Party, which instructed him to work as a student activist.[44] He quickly rose to the rank of education director, and by 1938 he was put in charge of activities for the Illinois–Indiana district.[45] When he soon became alienated from the party's slavish following of the Moscow line, he supported Harry Truman, but grew disenchanted with Democrats who called themselves liberals. Too many of them, he thought, were relativists who denied the existence of right and wrong and encouraged ideas that supported the growth of communism, including utopianism and a kind of Machiavellianism. The generation of the New Deal, he conceded, had been horrified by the violence and tyranny of the Soviets, but it had rejected moving away from government intervention in the society, which, in his view, could lead only to totalitarianism.[46] He came to believe that the "containment" policy endorsed by Truman and Eisenhower, which counted on the Soviet Union's self-destruction from within and embraced "peace" as the only objective, was inadequate. The USSR had to be brought down.

Meyer's agonizing reappraisal coincided with his reading of *The Road to Serfdom* and *Ideas Have Consequences*. Following service in the army, he made his final break with communism in 1945. Drawing on his own experience, Meyer wrote *The Moulding of Communists: The Training of the Communist Cadre* (1963), a chilling account of how the party created revolutionaries. "Leaving the Party," he wrote,

> is not simply a question of friends, associates, habits [but entails] the loss of a way of thinking, which makes it comparatively easy to find answers to everything: the simple moral problems of everyday life; how to vote in a trade-union meeting; what to think about the latest newspaper headline. Life for the Communist contains no mystery, and the fight back to the acceptance of the glorious human fate of living with mystery is difficult indeed.

Leaving the underground party entailed dangers, and, like Chambers, he took to sleeping with a loaded weapon next to his bed.

No longer willing to let anyone regiment him, Meyer moved now to the opposite shore, emerging as a prominent and deadly serious libertarian. This caused him to be hostile to liberals, some of whom still claimed that Marxists were "idealists," determined to do good.[47]

At the *National Review*, where he served as a senior editor, publishing a regular column, "Principles and Heresies," until his death in 1972, he gained recognition as a libertarian who slashed away at both the political left and the right. While denouncing the New Deal's liberalism and the activist Supreme Court under Chief Justice Earl Warren, he also assailed the new conservatism of traditionalists like Kirk. "Neither the welfare statist with his materialist ends nor the New Conservative with his spiritual ends is willing to accept freedom," he wrote in his best-known book, *In Defense of Freedom: A Conservative Credo*, originally published by Regnery in 1962.[48]

The fullest statement of his philosophy can be found in *In Defense of Freedom*, themes of which appeared as early as 1955 in his short essay "Collectivism. Re-baptized." One of the landmark books of the conservative movement, it argued that American conservatism was a composite of two broad streams of thought – individual freedom and tradition – that were historically in opposition to each another in Europe but that had been brought together and harmonized in the United States. The two principles, he felt, had been synthesized in the founding documents of the nation. In current thought, there were the traditionalists, who emphasized values, virtue and order, and the "libertarians" (with whom he was most closely associated), who stressed freedom and the importance of the individual. In this country, "the devotion to individual freedom merged with institutional arrangements of ordered liberty" made freedom possible. Indeed, liberty, he felt, was essential to the pursuit of virtue. The good life *is* the achievement of freedom.[49]

In an article, "Freedom, Tradition, Conservatism," originally published in *Modern Age* in 1960, Meyer sought to merge the two major contending elements of conservatism.[50] The article was later issued by Chodorov's Intercollegiate Society of Individualists as a pamphlet and then published by Holt, Rinehart and Winston two years after. "In Defense of Freedom" appeared under the original title, "What Is Conservatism?" The book contained essays by almost all the leading conservative lights, including Kirk, M. Stanton Evans, and Hayek (the latter arguing "Why I Am Not a Conservative"), with two pieces by Meyer.[51]

In asking "What Is Conservatism?" Meyer started off with a definition that built on its two main components as opposing the ideology behind "collectivist liberalism." He believed that "these two streams of thought, although they are sometimes presented as mutually incompatible, can in reality be united in a single broad conservative political theory, since they have their roots in a common tradition and are arrayed against a common enemy."[52] Shrewdly, he argued that there was consensus among the contending elements despite seeming contradictions. At the heart of their politics, all conservatives accepted "an immutable moral order" in addition to individual freedom. All distrusted the power of the state and social planning. Most of all, they shared "a devotion to Western civilization and awareness of the necessity of defending it against the messianic world-conquering intentions of Communism." Meyer, along with Buckley, believed that if the two poles of conservatism could be brought together in a crusade against communism and the Soviet Union, it could be taken out of the intellectual salon and gain political power.[53]

Together with Buckley, Meyer laid out a philosophical stance known as fusionism that brought the warring factions of conservatism together philosophically. The historian George Nash credits Meyer with winning the great debate then under way between the traditionalists and the libertarians. Under the banner of "fusionism," Nash concludes, Meyer effected a "strategic integration" of the conservative forces.[54] Meyer's recent biographer, Kevin J. Smant, goes further: Meyer was instrumental in the creation of the energetic and influential conservative political network (or "counter establishment," as some have called it) that came to full flower with the election of Ronald Reagan in 1980 and in the Republican takeover of the House of Representatives in 1994.[55]

The religious and Jewish identity views of these Jewish conservatives widely differed. There was, first, the strong gravitation of Jews, particularly their intellectual classes, to "causes," usually on the left. As many Jews began to move away from their religious tradition, they substituted a series of secular commitments aimed at making the world more just and humane. I have called this tendency "the Utopian dilemma" (in a book of that title [1985]), suggesting that Jews have often put broader public needs above their own immediate or direct interests. Of course, Jews have hardly been alone in searching for meaning and even transcendence in political arrangements and movements. What will surprise many is that this penchant for causes, usually of a secular character, could move a number of Jews to the right as well as to the left.

George Nash has suggested that in many other respects the "forgotten godfathers" were typically Jewish. With the possible exception of Frank Meyer, "all were first or second generation Americans." Lyons, William S. Schlamm, and de Toledano were immigrants to this country. On the other hand, Chodorov, Marvin Liebman, and Ryskind were born in New York of immigrant parents from Eastern Europe. Except for Schlamm, who was born in the Austro-Hungarian Empire and received his education in Vienna, the remainder grew up in the New York area. "Whether it was the Lower East Side, the Lower West Side, Brooklyn, or nearby Newark, New Jersey," Nash writes, "the sidewalks of New York were for most of them a formative cultural milieu."[56]

There was a second characteristic that politically conservative Jews shared with most of the Jewish intellectuals on the left. They, too, had been radicals. The temperamental maverick Chodorov disapproved of socialist "pundits," whom he viewed popping off in coffeehouses on Grand Street. Socialists had "an intuitive urgency for power, power over other people," he argued. While attending Columbia (class of 1907) he had "fought it out with the socialists." "Man's management of man is presumptuous and fraught with danger," Chodorov said.[57]

Finally, the new Jewish conservatives experienced the same anti-Semitism as other Jews. For Chodorov, at one point, it was anti-Semitic taunts while playing football at Columbia. He blamed religion, which he found "at the bottom of social discords." Thereupon, he embarked upon an "anti-God crusade," as he called it.[58]

On the other hand, some of the new Jewish conservatives – Ryskind, Will Herberg, and Strauss especially – felt a strong personal sense of Jewish identity that pervaded their thought and work. Religious orthodoxy and the preservation of a great tradition lay at the heart of Herberg's conservatism. Strauss respected Judaism's ways, loved its wisdom, and firmly identified with the Jewish people and with the Jewish state following the war. He described the force that drove his scholarly life as "the Jewish question."[59] He once wrote, "[I] was a young Jew born and raised in Germany, who found himself in the grip of the theological-political predicament."[60]

Strauss, however, traced this concern to liberalism. While he was aware of the defects and weaknesses of the Weimar Republic, he viewed liberalism as "devoid of any authoritative truth," a world in which all opinions, all preferences, and the individualistic style of thought and behavior had equal value. The result was a moral vacuum at the heart of liberal society, one that the most fanatical elements and totalitarian forces rushed to fill. Having experienced in Germany the same conditions of moral decay he saw emerging in liberal democracy in this country – which was, after all, the brainchild of modernity and the Enlightenment – he set out to combat rootlessness and the brutalities of the times.[61]

Strauss was hardly simplistic in his thinking. He knew that the same forces liberated by modernity had freed Jews from the burdens and limitations of the past. He sought to preserve the "virtues of modernity" while saving it from its vices. He found in Jewish texts – Maimonides, in particular – as well as in the classical tradition the "true promise of modernity." Never a practicing Jew, he nonetheless believed that religion and the "gods of shuddering awe" were necessary to civilize society and turn natural savages into husbands, fathers, and citizens.

But many other Jewish conservatives grew up outside the Jewish tradition or were in open rebellion against it. They were what Isaac Deutscher called "non-Jewish Jews," more comfortable in a world free of all forms of group identity. Rand made religious antagonism a fetish of her intense individualism (although her "objectivist" movement was made up almost entirely of Jews). Taking a position similar to Rand was de Toledano, a Sephardic Jewish immigrant whose conservatism was reflected in his bitter opposition to Stalinism. He even criticized the administration of moderate Republican President Dwight D. Eisenhower for not being tough enough on the communists. Yet so strongly did he resent identification with religion that he refused to accept the designation "H" (for Hebrew) on his army dog tags.[62]

Not all the Jewish conservatives supported Israel. William Schlamm, a close associate of Buckley's and a cofounder of *National Review*, opposed the Jewish state. Chodorov was also outspokenly anti-Israel. Ryskind, albeit identifying as a Jew, was a friend of Rabbi Elmer Berger, executive head of the bitterly anti-Zionist American Council for Judaism. Although Meyer was at first skeptical, he later supported the Jewish state, which he saw mainly as a Cold War ally.[63]

Still, the break with communism ("the God that failed") led some to a preoccupation with questions that were at heart religious. In his autobiography, *Lament for a Generation*, de Toledano wrote that the "desire for faith, taunting and appealing," had become "the central fact of our time." When man seeks to "become his own providence," he "exceeds his powers."[64] Chodorov, who described himself as an atheist after graduation from Columbia, later turned to "transcendence," as he acknowledged in an essay, "How a Jew Came to God."[65]

The problem these conservatives faced in dealing with their Jewish background was that the secular, liberal character of the Jews they were most familiar with left them with little to lean upon. Certainly, religious orthodoxy was out of the question, because it was part of a past from which they had sought to escape. Since religion walled off its adherents from the world, they saw it as out of touch with the times. As a result, men like de Toledano and Chodorov were drawn to the orderliness and traditionalism of

Roman Catholicism. Undoubtedly, their admiration and respect for Buckley, an ardent Catholic, had much to do with this as well. (Liebman entered the church under Buckley's sponsorship, but at his death in 1997 he had left the faith, according to friends.) For a while in the 1950s, de Toledano considered converting to Roman Catholicism. He sent a copy of one of his books to a Catholic bishop with the inscription, "From a Catholic fellow traveler."[66]

Herberg admired traditional Catholicism so strongly that he criticized the modernizing efforts of the church under Pope John XXIII. He argued that those who welcomed them were like Esau, "selling their spiritual birthright for a pot of lentils." Chodorov died in a Catholic nursing home, while Schlamm requested that a priest officiate at his funeral.[67]

In his deathbed conversion to Roman Catholicism, Meyer demonstrated the poignant appeal of the Roman Catholic faith to some Jewish conservatives. He had always been interested in religious issues, but he had shied away from institutional forms of religion. In a footnote in *In Defense of Freedom*, he wrote,

> That no civilization can come into being or develop without being informed by one kind or another of relationship between the men who make it up and God, I am certain; that Christianity, which informs Western civilization, is the highest and deepest relationship to the Divine that men can attain, I am also certain; but I am not able to say that any single institutional church is the bearer of God's spirit on earth.[68]

When Meyer was diagnosed with terminal cancer early in 1972, he spoke with a number of people, especially Monsignor Eugene Clark of New York City, an unofficial advisor to the New York State Conservative Party. Buckley also visited him near the end, remembering that Meyer had told him he would have converted years earlier were it not for the "collectivism" of the church since Vatican II and the fact that "I'm a Jew." It was especially difficult for him to have done so in the face of Jewish persecution, he indicated. Unlike the dominant secular Jewish ethos, the moral absolutism of the church appealed to him. Meyer died on April 1, 1972. The next day was Easter Sunday.[69]

Even as they moved to the other political shore, some of these early Jewish conservatives were not always comfortable with their comrades on the right. In a confidential memorandum written in January 1962, Liebman wrote that the John Birch Society did not speak for him. He noted that its recklessness hurt the conservative movement and that neither Young Americans for Freedom, which he had helped to create, nor *National Review* could control these extremists.[70]

De Toledano acknowledged that inveighing against centralism and devolving many federal government activities to the state level, where they could be closer to the people, had appeal. But it had "induced the unwary" into supporting "slavery in the past, racial stratification in the present."

Furthermore, it left them isolated from "the forum of intellectual exchange" and affected public opinion negatively.[71]

"In my early days of association with conservatives," Toledano wrote in his autobiography, "I had not yet differentiated between those whose position was based on evaluation of the issues and concepts which I could accept and those who lived in a haze of fanaticisms, an uproar of slogans, and an intellectual confusion of liberal proportions." In the ugly war against those who sought to obscure "the systematic infiltration of the government and other institutions by Communists," he felt no need "to scrutinize the standards and ideals of allies when adversaries surrounded me."[72]

Not the least of the problems some of these early Jewish conservatives faced was anti-Semitism among some elements on the right. Isaac Don Levine withdrew from the anticommunist *Plain Talk* he had founded in 1946 because he found the anti-Semitism of the magazine's readers troubling.[73] Sniping by anti-Semitic Russian nationalists forced Eugene Lyons to abandon the American Committee for the Liberation of the Peoples, which he had founded.[74] When "anti-Semitic blight" appeared at the *American Mercury* in 1955, de Toledano, Nash reports, "would have no part of a publication which even flirts with the anti-Semites." Visibly shaken, Ryskind urged *National Review* to take a stand against the magazine.[75]

Even *National Review* came under attack from a Jewish perspective. Strauss wrote in a letter to the editor on January 5, 1957, that an article in the November 17 issue had accused Israel of being "a racist state." "It is incomprehensible to me," he went on, "that the authors who touch on that subject are so unqualifiedly opposed to the state of Israel." A conservative, he declared, was a man who believes that "everything good is heritage," and he knew of no other country "in which this belief is stronger" than in Israel.[76]

A debate over the relative importance of freedom and virtue between Meyer and L. Brent Bozell, Buckley's brother-in-law, that was played out in the pages of *National Review* also troubled some Jewish conservatives. In order to "establish temporal conditions conducive to virtue," Bozell said, "it was necessary to "build a Christian civilization." Meyer vehemently disagreed. He warned that Bozell's prescription could lead to a theocracy, and such a development, he added, was certain to exacerbate historic Jewish fears of being overwhelmed by Christian society. In Meyer's view, unrestricted liberty, not religious dogma, was the central tenet of conservatism. Yet he soothingly contended that the traditionalist emphasis on virtue could be joined with the libertarian's emphasis on freedom in the process of "fusionism."[77]

In the 1950s and early 1960s, the embattled Jewish conservatives found few friends on the right or on the left. Nor was the Jewish establishment in their corner. The latter, they felt, used such legitimate fears as that of anti-Semitism to whip the Jewish community into a generally liberal posture. Lyons accused the Anti-Defamation League in 1951 of "a vicious attack" on the executive director of the American Jewish League against Communism. In 1964, Schlamm was also critical of "New York Jews" for "casting suspicion on every man of the American Right for rabid anti-Semitism – a "neurotic readiness" that was dangerous and unfounded. The following year, de Toledano alleged that the ADL was more interested in attacking the "radical right" than in tackling growing anti-Semitism among blacks.[78]

Neurotic or not, the "New York Jews" may have had a point. Early in 1961, the National Renaissance Party, an overtly anti-Semitic and right-wing organization, charged that Jewish intellectuals had been "ordered" to "infiltrate" and capture positions of leadership within the "conservative hierarchy." Among the Jews singled out were U.S. Senator Barry Goldwater (whose father was of Jewish descent); Roy Cohn, an aide to Senator Joseph McCarthy; Dr. Fred Schwarz (an Australian whose parents were born Jewish), head of the Christian Anti-Communist Crusade; columnist George Sokolsky; and Liebman.[79]

Liebman drew heavy fire for his association with Young Americans for Freedom (YAF) and his close ties with Buckley. In 1964, a YAF associate close to Birch Society founder Robert Welch attempted to take control of YAF away from the "*National Review* crowd." The attempt featured an undisguised anti-Semitic attack on Liebman as well as on Sokolsky and Goldwater, who was shortly to receive the Republican presidential nomination. A story appeared in *Spotlight*, the publication of the anti-Semitic Liberty Lobby, under the title "Kosher Konservatives." Another right-wing group described Liebman as "a fanatical Zionist," pointing out that just about all of YAF's office staff, except for "front men" like Richard Viguerie, was either Jewish or Negro.[80]

Liebman appealed to Rusher and Buckley for support. After a series of torturous maneuvers, the *National Review* side won out. The experience taught Liebman a lesson. Ever since then, he wrote in his autobiography, "I have been alert to and aware of the anti-Semitism that continues to lurk in the American right wing and that can be used as a cudgel at any time and against any one."[81]

4

The Liberal Civil War

In 1948, Alger Hiss, president of the Carnegie Endowment for International Peace, appeared headed for even greater responsibility. Tall and handsome and with an impeccable WASP pedigree, he had clerked for Supreme Court Justice Oliver Wendell Holmes, advanced in the State Department during World War II, and served as an adviser to President Franklin D. Roosevelt at the Yalta conference. There was talk of Hiss's becoming secretary of state. But then, on a sultry day that summer, his life fell apart.

Whittaker Chambers, a senior editor at *Time* magazine, identified Hiss before the House Un-American Activities Committee as a former member of the same secret communist cell that Chambers himself had belonged to before breaking with the movement. The episode caused an immediate sensation. Chambers was rumpled, squat, and little-known. His charges against a pillar of the liberal establishment stunned Hiss's friends.

In denying the charges, Hiss filed a slander suit against Chambers. But Chambers, who had originally tried to protect Hiss (whom he viewed as a friend) had to go one step further. He produced, from a scooped-out pumpkin on his Maryland farm, microfilm that he said Hiss had given him. The microfilm contained classified information that Chambers said Hiss had photographed from State Department files, to be turned over to the Soviets. The case dragged on through two trials. Finally, in 1950, Hiss was convicted of perjury, the statute of limitations having run out on espionage. He was sentenced to forty months in a federal pentitentiary. The Hiss case, however, continues to remain a subject of much dispute, and denial, in intellectual circles. An Alger Hiss Professorship exists today at Bard College.

The astonishing downfall of Alger Hiss marked a fateful turning point in American liberalism just as the Cold War was getting under way. In a rare public speech in 1946, Joseph Stalin had announced a five-year build-up, preparatory to the inevitable conflict with the West. The following year, at a meeting at Sklarska Poreba in Poland, his associate Andrei Zhdanov laid out the Soviet party line: the West and Soviet Union had to be seen as two irreconcilable camps. With its armies astride Western Europe, America having withdrawn its forces following the war, and Eastern Europe firmly in its orbit, the Soviet Union embarked confidently upon what it saw as an effort to export its system to the West and other parts of the world, based on Marxist laws of history.[1]

The first Hiss trial ended in a hung jury on July 6; the Soviet Union exploded its first atomic bomb on August 29; the People's Republic of China was formed on October 1. Three weeks into the second trial, the German-born physicist Klaus Fuchs confessed to British intelligence his role as an atomic spy. And while the invasion of South Korea by communist North Korea that began in 1950 and lasted to 1953 was undertaken at the initiative of its leader, Kim Il Sung, it had the approval of the Kremlin, which, along with China, supplied North Korea weapons and other equipment. This news of Stalin's build-up, Sam Tanenhaus reports, was received by liberals and others as a "declaration of World War III."[2]

Stalin was a revolutionary, diplomatic historian John Lewis Gaddis has written recently, based on research in Soviet archives and other intelligence information released in the past several years. Gaddis believes that a Cold War was "unavoidable." Stalin "never gave up on the idea of a world revolution." He "expected this to result . . . from an expansion of influence emanating from the Soviet Union itself."[3] To the day of his death, Gaddis added in a lecture after the publication of his book, Stalin thought that "the capitalist states would never join together to contain Soviet expansionism" because "Lenin had taught that capitalists were too greedy ever to cooperate with one another."[4]

Needing to close ranks within the Soviet Union and its satellite empire to conduct his adventures, the paranoic Stalin simultaneously launched an internal war against the Jews, who he felt were unreliable. During World War II, he set up the Jewish Anti-Fascist Committee as a propaganda tool to ensure international support. As his plans progressed, however, Zionist sentiment among Jews in the Soviet Union grew, especially with the appointment of Golda Meir as Israel's first ambassador to the Soviet Union.[5] The affinity between Soviet and American Jews and Israel, he felt, posed a serious threat to him.[6] In 1952, a year before Stalin's death, Rudolph Slansky, the former secretary general of the Communist Party of Czechoslovakia, was put on trial, along with thirteen codefendants, on charges of espionage and treason. Eleven of the defendants, including Slansky, were Jewish, and most of them, including Slansky, were sentenced to death and hanged.[7]

Although often seen as a reformer, Nikita Khrushchev, the first undisputed Soviet leader after Stalin, "adapted the revolutionary-imperial paradigm to the age of missiles," according to Vladislav Zukok and Constantine Pleshakov, leading to a major crisis when he placed missiles in Cuba.[8]

In the 1930s and during World War II, we now know, as a result of the recent opening of certain Soviet and American intelligence files and a number of publications of Yale Univerity Press based on them, that Moscow maintained a highly disciplined underground in Washington made up of Americans, like Hiss; Assistant Secretary of the Treasury Harry Dexter White; and Laurence Duggan, the head of the State Department's Latin American Division, among others, who regularly fed intelligence information to Soviet contacts in high, sensitive places.[9] Nearly every agency that dealt with classified information – the War Department, the State Department, the OSS, the Office of Postal and Telegraph Censorship, the ONI, and even the FBI – had been penetrated.[10] John Earl Haynes and Harvey Klehr, in their study of the Venona files released by the United States in 1995, conclude "that the Cold War had begun not after World War II but many years earlier."[11]

Stalin's nonaggression pact with Hitler in 1939 and the Soviet Union's invasion of Finland later that year caused outrage in the West that lasted only until Germany attacked Russia in June 1941. Then the gallant struggle of the Red armies against the Nazi legions won America's fervent admiration, which only grew stronger after the United States entered the war in December 1941.

This support of Russia crossed political and ideological lines. *Time* magazine named Stalin its Man of the Year in 1942, while *Time* and other Henry Luce publications likened the NKVD, Stalin's notorious secret police force, to the FBI, whose job was "tracking down traitors."[12] General Douglas MacArthur, no friend of communism, paid tribute to "that great [Red] army that fought so valiantly with us." Business executive Joseph E. Davies, who served as American ambassador to the Soviet Union during the war, was cleverly manipulated by the Soviet Union's murderous tyrant. In his memoir, *Mission to Moscow*, Davies defended the Moscow purge trials and pictured Stalin as a "cross beween an inspirational football coach and a benevolent scoutmaster." His book was later made into a successful motion picture.[13]

In the postwar years, Soviet and Marxist influence was especially strong in the labor movement in Western Europe and in intellectual and cultural circles in the United States and abroad. Arriving in London after the war, the South African novelist Dorris Lessing found in the communists the "most sensitive, compassionate, socially concerned people."[14] Such highly visible literary cultural figures as Random House's Bennett Cerf, author/critic Van Wyck Brooks, architectural critic Louis Mumford, and Archibald MacLeish, who served as wartime head of the Office of War Information, remained stalwart defenders of the Soviet Union's policies, believing them to be peacefully motivated.[15]

In 1948, Henry A. Wallace, former vice president under President Roosevelt and commerce secretary in the Truman adminstration, embarked upon a quixotic presidential bid under the newly formed Progressive Citizens of America banner, allowing key communists and party sympathizers to gain control of his campaign. Only later, when his career was in tatters, did he acknowledge mistakes and errors in judgment. The liberal historian

Arthur Schlesinger, Jr., later referred to such naifs as Wallace as "doughface progressives."[16]

Meanwhile, through Stalin "peace prizes" and carefully staged peace offensives in foreign capitals, the Soviets encouraged European and American artists and intellectuals to support its presumed benign intentions. In March 1949, a Soviet backed Cultural and Scientific Conference for World Peace was held at New York's Waldorf Astoria Hotel. The Waldorf Conference attracted 800 delegates, including such notables as Leonard Bernstein, Lillian Hellman, Norman Mailer, Langston Hughes, Paul Robeson, Arthur Miller, Dashiell Hammett, and their Russian counterparts like Dimitri Shostakovich, who denounced "hatemongering" and the thrust for world power of the new American "fascists." To critics, however, the Waldorf conference was a sounding board for pro-Soviet propaganda under the pretense of bringing peaceloving people together to stand against war.[17]

Through their well-oiled propaganda machine, communist leaders presented themselves (unlike their Nazi totalitarian counterparts) as caring, loving humanitarians worthy of trust. Their promises of rescuing the poor from the capitalist yoke, backed by the written Soviet constitution guaranteeing civil liberties and religious freedom, offered hope to the disheartened and help to those scarred by the Great Depression.[18]

Stalin was still regarded benignly by much of the media, even at the time of his death on March 6, 1953. The *New York Times* banner headline said nothing of the purges and gulags. His passing merely "brought to an end the career of one of the great figures of modern times – a man whose name stands second to none as the organizer and builder of the great state structure the world knows as the Soviet Union." The Soviets counted also on widespread American fear that nuclear conflagration would bring about acceptance of division of the world into Soviet and American "spheres of influence." The peace movement in this country, through groups like the Fellowship of Reconciliation, the War Resisters League, and the American Friends Service Committee, gradually revived themselves beginning in the mid-1950s.[19]

Jews especially were impressed with Soviet rhetoric prior to and during the war. Although most Jews were not communists, they were disproportionately represented in American radicalism and in the U.S. Communist Party. Jewish fears were stoked, finally, by Sen. Joseph McCarthy. To the degree that many Jews identified with the various shades of the left, they felt particularly threatened by what would come to be known as McCarthyism.

The Hiss trial and the execution of Ethel and Julius Rosenberg two years later sent shock waves through the Jewish community. Chambers's references to "Godless Communism" seemed to many secular Jews another heresy. Hook and de Toledano both knew that Chambers was telling the truth about Hiss; but why, Hook, a militant atheist, wanted to know, did he have to bring God into the discussion?

Agencies like the American Jewish Committee and the ADL had been battling the stereotype of Jews as communists since World War I. They saw in McCarthy's onslaught a hidden attack on Jews, even though McCarthy never assailed Jews directly and, in fact, employed Jews on his staff. They worried that Jews generally would be seen by their countrymen as communists, barred from government and other responsible places (as some indeed were) and subjected to a wave of anti-Semitism.

The Soviet threat, of course, did not go unchallenged. In Moscow, U.S. diplomat George Kennan composed his famous "long telegram" of February 22, 1946, warning the State Department not to expect an era of peaceful coexistence with the Soviet Union.[20] In an effort to expand its empire of communist satellites, the Soviets began exerting pressure on the government of Iran, threatening Turkey, and supporting civil war against the government of Greece. When the liberal government of Great Britain began to back away from Soviet aggression, Winston Churchill warned at tiny Westminster College in Fulton, Missouri, that an "iron curtain" had descended over the continent. President Truman delivered a message to Congress on March 12, 1947, calling for appropriations to Greece and Turkey to prevent a Soviet takeover. He further declared that America should become the defender of democracy in the free world.

As part of his Cold War strategy, Truman issued Executive Order 9835, which created a loyalty program to root out of government known communists, or those sympathetic to the movement, as security risks.[21] Truman's move involved some two million federal employees who were subject to background investigations. The attorney general also listed more than seventy front groups deemed subversive. These efforts aroused serious opposition in this country and abroad. Influential journals like *The Nation* and *The New Republic* mounted attacks on Truman's policies, as did several liberal groups. The leftist weeklies often followed the Soviet line. *The New Republic*, in fact, was owned and run at the time by Michael Straight, who later admitted to having been recruited by the British Soviet spy Anthony Blunt to serve the Comintern as an underground agent.[22]

Worried by what they saw as the rise of a reactionary tide (in 1945, Republicans had won control of both houses of Congress in November for the first time since 1930), a group of liberals, including Eleanor Roosevelt; historian Arthur Schlesinger, Jr., whose book *The Vital Center* (1949) had become the Bible of liberals; NYU philosopher Sidney Hook; theologian Reinhold Niebuhr; labor leader David Dubinsky, and others created Americans for Democratic Action (ADA) and set out to renew the liberal message against what they saw as the influence of communists and fellow travelers in this country.

A thought-provoking and serious anticommunism was voiced in the postwar years by, in addition to *Commentary* (see Chapter 2), such small but influential publications as *The New Leader* and *Partisan Review*. These magazines sought to describe and promote (perhaps with the exception of *The New Leader*) modernistic trends in art and literature, and produced a steady stream of anti-Stalinist criticism. *The New Leader* served also as a "way station" for newcomers and anticommunist writers, whose markets were limited by the political correctness of the times. Hook described the old Menshevik and Russian immigrant Sol Levitas at *The New Leader* as the "real center" of political anti-Stalinist thought and activity. Every major campaign against communism began at either Levitas's home or office, Hook said. Later, Levitas published the works of such legendary dissidents as Alexander Solzhenitsyn and Joseph Brodsky.

Financed largely by Dubinsky's ILGWU, *The New Leader* was among the first little magazines to call attention to Soviet harassment of Jews, including Stalin's murder of two Polish Bund leaders, Henryk Erlich and Victor Alter, who had retreated to the Soviet Union during World War II. In 1959, it devoted an entire magazine to the plight of Soviet Jews, although that issue had not yet reached the agenda of American Jewry. Two early Jewish foes of communism, Ralph de Toledano and Daniel Bell, worked for *The New Leader*.

In his staunch anticommunism, Levitas had much in common with conservatives at the time. Even as its commanding passion was anticommunism, *The New Leader* hewed to liberal orthodoxy and remained firmly on the left, playing a central role in the nation's passage of the first modern civil rights legislation in 1957. Levitas's conservative friend John Chamberlain parted company with the magazine, objecting to labor leader Walter Reuther's piece, which called on the government to create 60 million new jobs. Chamberlain labeled *The New Leader* "a study in equivocation."[23]

Closely allied to *The New Leader* was *Partisan Review*, edited by two New Yorkers of Jewish backgrounds, Philip Rahv and William Phillips. Its stable of heterogeneous and often squabbling writers included Edmund Wilson and his future wife Mary McCarthy, Dwight Macdonald, Delmore Schwartz, and Clement Greenberg. Although *Partisan Review* had been founded in 1934 as part of a communist cell, the John Reed Club in Greenwich Village, and initially financed by wealthy communists, its pro-Soviet sympathies did not last. By 1936, it had abandoned communism in favor of socialist politics and economics. *Partisan Review* writers and editors saw themselves as literary figures first and communists or party sympathizers second. Its pages also came to "perform a job of intellectual demolition on the Popular Front," moving in the 1940s toward a hard-line anticommunist posture.[24] Nonetheless, although *Partisan Review*, like *The New Leader*, was opposed to Stalin, *Partisan Review* backed Trotsky, who had broken with Stalin while remaining a communist; *The New Leader* was led by Mensheviks, who opposed both Trotsky's and Stalin's versions of Leninism.[25]

At the center of the *Partisan Review*'s approach, however, was its distaste for liberalism. As the nation approached World War II, the magazine opposed liberalism's nationistic ideal; afterwards, it rejected liberalism because the magazine's editors were convinced that too many liberals were pro-Stalinist. Dwight Macdonald would later describe this position as a form of conservatism "expressed in a radical language" because the magazine really "had no conservative vocabulary."[26]

An independent central figure worth noting here was the critic Hannah Arendt. Although her work was aimed at a general audience from a universalist rather than Jewish perspective, her Jewish experience is vital to understanding her thought. ("I am a German Jew driven from my Homeland by the Nazis," she wrote a decade after World War II.) With her book *The Origins of Totalitarianism* (1951) in mind, historian Stephen J. Whitfield writes, "No book was more resonant or impressive in tracing the steps toward the distinctive twentieth century tyrannies of Hitler and Stalin, or in measuring how grievously wounded Western civilization and the human status had become."[27]

The Origins of Totalitarianism provided an essential and largely missing rationale for anticommunism. It involved a detailed explanation of the roots and attributes of totalitarianism found in both communism and fascism. Prior to the war, totalitarianism was a term used only in describing fascism or Nazism. As a Jewish refugee scholar who had confronted some of the worst horrors of European tyranny, Arendt was able early to recognize the commonality of both systems.

Notable among the critics of communists, fellow travelers, and naïfs was the philosopher-activist Sidney Hook. Although he thought of himself as a socialist, no one, arguably, played a greater role in the shifting political thought of Jewish intellectuals, from radicalism in the 1930s to liberalism in the 1940s to a growing conservatism in the 1950s and beyond.

From his roots in Brooklyn's Williamsburg section, one of the poorest areas of Jewish immigrant settlement, Hook rose to teach philosophy at New York University. Contemptuous of Norman Thomas's brand of socialism, Hook had been a communist sympathizer as a youth. Communism seemed to him a workable antidote to the capitalist system, which, he believed, had broken down during the Great Depression. Increasingly, however, he was put off by the crudeness of what the Marxists called the "science" of dialectical materialism, a way of understanding reality, whether ideas, emotions, or the physical universe.

Hook hoped to reinvigorate communism, to forge a marriage of Marxism with the pragmatism of his mentor, John Dewey. In his brilliant, if somewhat didactic, study *Toward the Understanding of Karl Marx* (1933), he had argued that Marxism and pragmatism shared the same methodological empiricism. Both were realistic and materialistic and were based on human experience instead of abstract reasoning.[28]

Hook was unusual among the New York intellectuals on several counts. He was the only avowed Marxist on the faculty of a major university. He also knew more about the subject than anyone else. In addition, unlike many of his confreres, he was willing to play a public role in moving his ideas into a broader public setting. It was customary among the New York intellectuals to engage in "intramural, highly factional debate" about political issues, without going public for the most part. Only later, in the 1960s, did the *New York Review of Books* and *The New Yorker* provide the means for intellectuals to reach out to a broader readership to promote their ideas. Hook, however, reveled in his public role – "to distinguish historical truth from political falsehood." This included revealing the pernicious role played in the world by communists and the Soviet Union.[29]

In 1933, Hook, who was a fellow traveler but not a party member, met the nation's most influential communist, Earl Browder, for the first time. To Hook's amazement, Browder proposed that he create a national network of fellow travelers to spy on new military and industrial experiments and report back to the party.[30] Shaken by his exposure to a group that was apparently working to overthrow the U.S. government, Hook decided to start his own communist organization, the American Workers. However, he left intellectual control of the new party to his close friend and New York University colleague James Burnham, whom he had earlier attracted to Marxism.

In succeeding years, Hook was among the first within left-wing circles to break directly with Stalinism and the front groups supporting it. Earlier than most, he saw through the phony Soviet propaganda and its insidious pitch to the poor. He attacked the Moscow show trials of 1936 and 1937 and organized a Commission on Inquiry to expose the falseness of the kangaroo courts. He began writing a column for *The New Leader* in 1938 and, with remarkable foresight, predicted a Stalinist shift to anti-Semitism.[31]

The following spring, with the assistance of Frank Trager of the American Jewish Committee and the writer Ferdinand Lundberg, Hook organized the short-lived Committee for Cultural Freedom (CCF), with Dewey as its first chairman. Its statement of principles, drafted chiefly by Eugene Lyons and signed by 142 intellectuals, warned that a "tide of totalitarianism threatened the world." This was perceived as equating the Soviet Union with Nazi Germany and Stalin with Hitler, and it sent shock waves through the American intellectual community. The statement was sharply attacked by *The New Republic* and *The Nation*, which were busily engaged in furthering the Kremlin's Popular Front strategy. This brought forth a counterstatement from a group of 400 communists and fellow travelers, including Corliss Lamont, I. F. Stone, Dashiell Hammett, and Lillian Hellman, who called equating the Soviet Union with Nazi Germany a "fantastic falsehood." They also attacked Hook, Dewey, and other CCF members as "Fascists and allies of Fascists."[32]

At the time of the Waldorf Conference, Hook convened a meeting of some thirty local members of the CCF and others at the home of Dwight Macdonald, where Hook described the need to "expose the dishonesty of the upcoming Waldorf proceedings" and his proposal "to launch an educational counter campaign to expose the true auspices and purposes of the conference."[33]

Following the meeting, Hook submitted a lecture proposal to the Waldorf conference organizers, which was rejected. He then invited some two hundred sponsors to join him in protest. With the financial support of David Dubinsky's ILGWU, Hook rented a room at the Waldorf and organized a counter rally at Freedom House. An overflow crowd heard Hook, Schlesinger, and Eastman condemn Soviet repression of Soviet intellectuals. Following this meeting, a new organization, the American Committee for Cultural Freedom (ACCF), was established to broaden the fight for intellectual freedom.

The ACCF came under attack from left-wing critics like Christopher Lasch, among others. The latter called the intellectuals associated with the ACCF "servants of the secret police." Novelist Norman Mailer described them as "cockroaches in a slum sink." These attacks on its liberal bona fides took place despite the ACCF's protest against the execution of seven African-Americans in Martinsville, Virginia, in 1951 and its opposition one year later to Franco's Spain's gaining admission to UNESCO. It had also commissioned the book *McCarthy and the Communists* (1954), which deplored the senator's activities.[34]

By the time the ACCF was formed, the Cold War had intensified. North Korea, with Soviet backing, had invaded South Korea, and Soviet pressures were mounting in Berlin and elsewhere. Since the end of the war, liberal-left opinion had been divided in its opposition to Soviet expansionism and totalitarianism. Some justified the Soviet Union's relentless suppression of democratic possibilities in Central and Eastern Europe as necessary for its security needs or as a barrier to the triumph of reaction. Hook's ACCF, however, was limited in its ability to challenge this. It had no worldwide base. Recognizing the problem, a group of American intellectuals led by Hook and Burnham traveled in June 1950 to West Berlin, now the apex of the Cold War as a result of a Soviet blockade, to launch yet another Committee for Cultural Freedom. They sought to create, beginning with the conference they sponsored, an international organization, ultimately with headquarters in Paris, to gain the support of the world's intellectuals on behalf of the liberal democratic cause.

According to Hook, the new organization developed out of a discussion between Melvin J. Lasky, a strong anticommunist, and him in the late spring of 1949. Both men had been taken aback by the emergence of neutralism and anti-Americanism at the International Day of Resistance against War and Fascism in Europe. The West Berlin conference, which opened just as news broke of the communist invasion of South Korea, was organized mainly by Lasky and Michael Josselson, "two Russian Jews," as Edward Shils later described them, "[who] decided to save Western civilization." Lasky, one of Kristol's sparring partners in Alcove One at City College, had grown up in a Yiddish-speaking home in the Bronx prior to the war. He had remained in Germany afterwards, where he served as the poorly paid correspondent for *The New Leader* and *Partisan Review*. A short, stocky figure with oriental eyes and a Lenin-like beard, Lasky went on to edit *Der Monat*, a U.S. sponsored German intellectual magazine. Josselson, its executive director, was the son of a timber merchant, who had come to the United States in 1936.[35]

The conference took place on June 27 and 28, 1950, the day after North Korea invaded South Korea. It drew some 200 noncommunist writers and political activists, including François Bondy, Arthur Koestler, Lasky, Malcolm Muggeridge, Carlo Schmidt, Ignazio Silone, Stephen Spender, and Manes Sperber. It featured addresses and papers and an American contingent that included, among others, Burnham, Elliot Cohen, James T. Farrell, and the African-American journalist George Schuyler, in addition to Hook. The high point of the conference occurred on its last day, when Koestler strode to the platform of the Funkturn in the British sector of West Berlin to address an audience of 15,000.

Born in Budapest and educated in Austria and Germany, Koestler became a foreign correspondent for German newspapers prior to joining the German Communist Party in 1931. During the Spanish civil war, he fought on the side of the Loyalists and was imprisoned for a while by Franco's forces. Soon after leaving Spain, however, he left the Communist Party because of the Stalinist purges of 1936–38, noting in his letter of resignation the epidemic of charges of a Trotskyite–Nazi conspiracy, which he compared to the notoriously anti-Semitic *Protocols of the Elders of Zion*.[36]

Koestler's hatred of communism was initially expressed in *Darkness at Noon* (1940), one of the great political novels of the twentieth century, and in an essay in *The God That Failed* (1949). *Darkness* tells the story of an old Bolshevik, Rubashov, who, after being arrested by the Soviet secret police, is executed for crimes that he did not commit based on his forced confession. In his speech, Koestler declared that the traditional left-right, capitalist-socialist dichotomies were out of date. The old left, which had led the fight against injustice, had failed to lead the fight against the Soviet Union. He summoned his listeners to move against injustice there and wherever the Soviets were in control. The time had come to unite all elements of the left in this battle. He hailed the delegates' decision to create an international anticommunist body, with affiliates in various countries. Its goal was to unite prudent conservatives and sensible radicals. "Friends," Koestler exulted, "freedom has seized the offensive."

Returning home in 1951, Hook and Burnham formally organized the ACCF as an affiliate member of the international Congress of Cultural Freedom. Its office was at *The New Leader* offices in the Rand School in Manhattan, which served as the unofficial headquarters and clearing-house for ideas and meetings.[37] With its heavily Jewish leadership, the CCF now emerged internationally as the major vehicle of the liberal intellectual offensive against totalitarianism in all its forms. It opposed McCarthyism and supported Hook's call for McCarthy's retirement from American life. It kept conservatism at arm's length, although Burnham, who had moved to the right since his earlier association with Hook, became involved with that movement as it got off the ground. During its most fruitful years, from 1950 through 1958, the CCF operated offices in 35 countries and employed 280 staff members. It established a network of magazines in these countries, including *Survey*, *Preuves*, *Tempo Presente*, *Cuadernos* and, most importantly, *Encounter*, which was coedited by Irving Kristol and the poet Stephen Spender in London. Daniel Bell directed its seminar program from 1956 to 1957. Peter Coleman, historian of the Congress, credits it with helping to shatter the illusions of Stalinist fellow travelers, paving the way for Khrushchev's secret "crimes of Stalin" speech in 1956, and making Aleksandr Solzhenitsyn a cause célèbre.[38]

Before long, however, arguments developed that foreshadowed later divisions between liberals and neoconservatives. Hook came to favor an unfettered assault on communists and their underground apparatus. Included in that was his support of President Truman's unprecedented loyalty program to root out suspected subversives. Hook believed the government had valid reasons to root out infiltration in its ranks; those who hid the fact, after all, were operating secretly in the interests of a foreign power. With regard to the campuses, however, he accepted the right to teach and publish, regardless of heresy. Even the right of communists and fascists, he felt, must be safeguarded. He made a distinction, however, between the right to avow heresy and to engage in conspiracy, which he defined as playing outside the rules of the game. Propagandizing in class, for example, was outside the rules.[39]

In his history of the Truman administration, Arnold A. Offner observed that the loyalty program "jettisoned basic legal procedural safeguards, virtually included a presumption of guilt, and did not distinguish between sensitive federal jobs, such as atomic scientist, and clerk or janitor.[40] Also according to him, Truman's executive order opened the way for purges of government employees that helped set the stage for the anticommunst crusade of Senator Joseph McCarthy. David McCullough, in his biography, *Truman*, wrote of the loyalty program's "pernicious influence" and cited Truman's belated admission that it was "terrible.[41] Critics saw the loyalty program and the laws passed by Congress making it illegal to teach and advocate the violent overthrow of the government as first steps in the rise of American fascism.

To Hook, Kristol, Diana Trilling, and other liberals who had no use for McCarthy and who believed his anticommunism was dysfunctional, Lasky's conclusion made sense: "The historical uniqueness of Nazism," said Lasky, "should not blind us to the fact that morally and politially it is identical with Stalinism." He and the others never doubted that Stalinist aggression around the world constituted the primary danger to America and the West.[42]

Alleged left-wingers, however, were not the only targets in those difficult days. Some anticommunists who challenged the peaceful and benign intentions of the Soviet Union also suffered. Like Morrie Ryskind, who was blacklisted in Hollywood after testifying of communist influence there, certain anticommunist writers faced difficulty getting their books published. Publisher Victor Gollancz refused to look at George Orwell's *Homage to Catalonia* (1938), describing his experience with communist terror in the Spanish civil war, while another publisher turned down *Animal Farm* (1945) as an unhealthy anti-Soviet text. Arthur Koestler initially found it expedient to withdraw his name, and later his pseudonym, from the translation of *Darkness at Noon*.[43]

Hannah Arendt's *Origins of Totalitarianism*, which made clear that Soviet repression was every bit as evil and dangerous as Hitler's, could not find a French publisher.[44] At the height of the Hiss affair, Viking declined to publish an updated edition of *The Middle of the Journey*, Lionel Trilling's fictionalized account of Whittaker Chambers' life as a communist agent. Trilling was puzzled, but Chambers' biographer, Sam Tanenhaus, notes that there was good reason for Viking's reticence: its publisher, unbeknown to Trilling, was a communist who had volunteered his services to the Hiss defense team.[45]

A small number of hard-line Jewish anticommunists and others muddied the waters further. They admired McCarthy and fiercely defended him against numerous critics. This group included Roy Cohn, who was McCarthy's chief advisor; newspaper columnist and radio broadcaster Walter Winchell, who had a huge national following; and "China lobby" zealot Alfred Kohlberg. But their extreme views found little appeal in the Jewish community or among Americans generally.[46]

Some on the left by this time sought coexistence with the Soviet regime on almost any terms. By the close of the 1950s, the distinguished philosopher Bertrand Russell argued that if the Soviet Union could not be persuaded to accept reasonable proposals for nuclear disarmament, he would support unilateral disarmament and communist domination "with all its horrors." Writing in the fall 1960 issue of *Daedalus*, psychiatrist Eric Fromm pleaded "The Case for Unilateral Disarmament." The following spring, the Committee for a Sane Nuclear Policy (SANE) was formed, with Fromm as its head.[47]

Historian Henry Steele Commager declared "the new loyalty" to be mindless conformity: "the uncritical and unquestioning acceptance of America as it is." Irving Kristol disagreed. He said that investigations of suspected communist front organizatons were necessary and that those opposed were acting irresponsibly. Kristol singled out *Washington Post* editorial writer Alan Barth, who had written that FBI agents, by infiltrating the Communist Party, were invading the privacy of party members.

Diana Trilling, a former literary editor of *The Nation*, charged that Senator McCarthy's reckless depredations had so poisoned the atmosphere that all those who spoke out against communism were accused of engaging in McCarthyism. She recalled hearing the theologian Reinhold Niebuhr, relentless anticommunist though he was, denounce AFL-CIO head George Meany as a "Neanderthal man" because of his intransigence in dealing with communism in the unions. McCarthy had succeeded in "deforming" political thinking and polluting the political rhetoric, Trilling said.[48]

In her diary, Trilling poured out her irritation at Russell, who earlier had been among the first intellectuals to understand the nature of the Soviet threat, but who was now spreading the notion that the United States was nearing the condition of fascist Germany in the 1940s. "The idea that America is a terror-stricken country in the grip of hysteria is a Communist inspired idea," she wrote. Those who indulged in this type of talk, she thought, were adopting the tactics of McCarthy himself. She saw it as a "reasonable function of the legislative body" to investigate "the possibility of subversive influences on Government policy." Alger Hiss, she pointed out, was not an innocent liberal. Recognizing that McCarthy might have tarnished the reputations of some innocent liberals, she reminded her readers that "had it not been for the Un-American Activities Committee, Hiss's guilt might never have been uncovered."[49]

But she was not indifferent to the possible erosion of civil liberties resulting from overbearing government investigations. When J. Robert Oppenheimer, the scientist and wartime leader of the Los Alamos atomic bomb project, was investigated during 1952 and 1953 and finally denied clearance by the Atomic Energy Commission, a number of the premature neocons balked. According to the strict standards by which he was judged, "virtually anyone might fail," Diana Trilling observed. Having once "granted him clearance [when he was a fellow traveler], she argued that to take it away was only "tragic ineptitude."[50]

The liberal anticommunists represented by Hook, Kristol, and Diana Trilling, who distanced themselves from informants like Elizabeth Bentley and Whittaker Chambers in order to maintain their liberal credentials, nonetheless found themselves in an uncomfortable position. Diana Trilling acknowledged that the new "enforced alignment between reactionaries and anti-Communist liberals was distasteful and limiting." "The anti-Communist liberal," she wrote, must "insist on his right not to be labeled a reactionary just because reactionaries agree with him on this issue."[51] And she blamed McCarthy's campaign of character assassination for creating "an automatic association between any voiced opposition to communism and reaction." Before McCarthy, she said, anticommunism was still a liberal option. "All avowed socialists were anti-communists. "With few exceptions, all our anti-communist friends were liberals. Lionel Trilling and I would have been generally described as liberal anti-communists. The phrase had about it no hint of paradox."[52]

For these anticommunist liberals, McCarthy and McCarthyism were troubling, but not paramount. In fact, with McCarthy's censure in 1954 and his death three years later, the phenomenon was short-lived. The main issue for them continued to be the struggle with Stalinist expansionism and Stalin's sympathizers in this country and abroad. In an article in *Commentary* in 1953, Glazer expressed outrage that McCarthy remained in the Senate after his censure but declared that he posed no "imminent danger to personal liberty in the United States."[53] Elliot Cohen called him a blowhard propped up only by "the fascinated fears of the intelligentsia."[54] Anticommunist liberals were worried also by communist infiltration of government and other sectors of American life. With the opening of some Soviet files, materials needed for reaching a more complex understanding of the McCarthy era are now available. Historian Michael J. Ybarra notes that the Communist Party was "both a totalitarian organization in the thrall of a foreign enemy power and a political organization whose existence . . . was protected by the Constitution."[55] It was a gut-wrenching time, when real security needs clashed with the principled liberal belief in individual rights. No satisfactory resolution was ever found.

Moreover, the widespread penetration of the U.S. government – known to government authorities through the Venona files of the U.S. National Security Agency and other, then still unreleased, intelligence – spurred more respectable efforts to root out subversion. Despite many sincere and well-meaning communists involved in racial improvement and other legitimate social efforts, Haynes and Klehr, writing from the perspective of familiarity with the materials, conclude that "espionage was a regular activitity of the American Communist Party." Indeed, we now know that several hundred American communists, often at the highest levels of government, were spying for the Soviet Union and the CPUSA from beginning to end and were subordinate to Moscow. And while the information turned over to the Soviets by Julius Rosenberg was available from its agents elsewhere, Haynes and Klehr indicate that it advanced Soviet efforts to create nuclear weaponry two years sooner than expected and at a lower cost. As late as 1949, with the Cold War well under way, the KGB continued to utilize American communists as spies. In 1949, Judith Coplin, widely seen at the time as innocent, was arrested by the FBI in the act of turning over FBI counterespionage files to a KGB officer.[56]

The liberal civil war soon created a split at the ACCF. The agency had denounced McCarthy but failed to mount a full-scale campaign against him. Schlesinger and Trilling resigned in 1955, just as Whittaker Chambers was named to the agency's executive committee. Following Schlesinger's and Trilling's example were economist John Kenneth Galbraith, newspaper editor James Wechsler, and Harvard professor David Riesman. Schlesinger complained that the ACCF "was becoming more anti-communist than liberal."[57]

In turn, Hook believed that the international CCF in Paris had grown tolerant of totalitarianism and hostile to America's role in fighting communism. He wanted the organization to go beyond containment and seek the actual destruction of the Soviet empire, later a prime objective of the neoconservative movement. Liberal anticommunists had become bitterly divided. Hook felt a crucial point had been reached when, following the outbreak of the Hungarian revolution in 1956 (which was ruthlessly suppressed by the Kremlin), the organization quashed a reference to "the Soviet Empire" in a forthcoming resolution. Spender objected to it on the grounds that it was too "provocative."[58]

Some worried that confrontation with the Soviet Union might even threaten civilization, especially if the atomic bomb were ever used again. Shils, another of the disaffected liberals, credited this reluctance, however, to "the burden of 1917," the idea still resonant among some left-wing intellectuals that the Soviet Union, despite its imperfections, was "an advanced," arguably progressive, society because it had eliminated private property, capitalism, and the market.[59]

Throughout the early years of the ACCF, Kristol, Spender, and Hook had heard rumors about CCF ties with the CIA. They either discredited them or, as they later claimed, discounted them. As far as they were concerned, the battle against Soviet expansionism and communism was the transcending issue. So what if the government helped? Besides, as Daniel Bell argued, such funding would be a matter of concern only if the CIA had tried to influence ideas, which it certainly had not.

Kristol summed up this sentiment later in an article in the *New York Times Magazine* in 1968, following the public exposure of secret CIA financial assistance to the CCF and *Encounter* magazine. He argued that he had no objection to CIA funding for certain projects and under certain circumstances. He had no more reason to despise the CIA than he did the post office, he wrote. Both were exasperatingly inept. Schlesinger and Hook were even more accommodating when the matter of CIA backing was made public. They noted that the "progressives" received much of their money from sympathetic left-wing foundations; liberal anticommunists, on the other hand, were unacceptable to both right-wing and left-wing foundations and had no choice but to turn to the CIA.[60]

Peter Coleman points out that the CIA link was indeed important. The agency, for example, funded the 1950 Berlin conference at which Koestler laid down the gauntlet in the battle against communism. Joselson was, in fact, a CIA agent.[61] In April 1966, the *New York Times* began a series of articles describing the links between the CIA and the CCF and *Encounter*. The following year, in an article in the *Saturday Evening Post*, Tom Braden, a CIA operative in the 1950s, described the connection in some detail. Ironically, in much of Europe in the 1940s, socialists were the only people who cared about fighting communism, he declared.[62] The revelations about the CIA nevertheless produced a storm of disapproval, especially when they were confirmed at the height of the Vietnam War, a time when anticommunism appeared to some to have led the nation into a quagmire.

The breaking of the CIA story during a later phase of the Cold War, when this country's role in Vietnam was coming under sharp attack, however, should not take away from the critical, indeed crucial, role that the CCF played in its early phase. (CCF remained in existence until 1967, when it was closed down, although by this time its influence had dwindled considerably.) "Through its publications, conferences, and international protests," its historian Peter Coleman sums up,

> it kept the issues of Soviet totalitarianism and liberal anti-Communism to the fore in a frequently hostile environment. It cannot claim to have had the historic impact of Khrushchev's 'secret speech' in 1956 (or of Solzhenitsyn later), but it took and held the initiative in public education. By the end of the period, the propaganda of the Soviet Union and its fellow travelers was no longer credible.[63]

A crucial moment in the liberal civil war and the rise of neoconservatism took place even earlier. It was provoked by an article by Irving Kristol, "'Civil Liberties': 1952 – A Study in Confusion," in the March 1952 issue of *Commentary*. Kristol's career is a virtual road map of the path taken by some liberals on their way to becoming neoconservatives. Like a number of intellectuals prior to World War II, he and his wife, Gertrude Himmelfarb, had opposed what they saw as an imperialist war taking shape in Europe. Following Stalin's nonaggression pact with Hitler and the invasion of Poland in 1939, both came to see the world differently.

After the war, in which he served as an infantryman in Europe, Kristol, before leaving for England with his wife, sold a short story to *Commentary*, beginning an association with the magazine that would become a critical part of his life. On their return to this country in 1947, Kristol became a junior editor at *Commentary*. His passion was less for politics than for literature at first. Still not deeply involved ideologically, he found himself troubled by "the extraordinary profusion of opinions sympathetic to, even apologetic for, the Stalinist regime in Russia among many leading liberals." His first entry into politics was a review of a book by Carey McWilliams (a noted progressive), which he found to be a "discrete apologia for Stalinist fellow-traveling."[64]

Encouraged by the reception to the piece, he now tried his hand on the issue of McCarthyism. Kristol's "Civil Liberties" essay – the most controversial of his career – still arouses strong feelings today when it is recalled by old-timers. Dismissing McCarthy as a "vulgar demagogue," Kristol had rounded to the belief that it was the "fundamental assumptions" of liberalism that were the real problem. His article was a full-throated attack on those liberals who defended the rights of communists when the latter were bent on *destruction* of civil liberties and freedom more generally:

> Did not the major segment of liberalism, [he wrote] as a result of joining hands with the Communists in a popular front, go on record as denying the existence of Soviet concentration camps? Did it not give its blessing to the 'liquidation' of the kulaks? Did it not apologize for the mass purges of 1936–38, and did it not solemnly approve the grotesque trials of the old Bolsheviks? Did it not applaud the massacre of the non-Communist Left, by the GPU [the Soviet intelligence arm] during the Spanish Civil War?[65]

He was especially hard on Alan Barth (an editorial writer for the *Washington Post*), "who knows that, though a man repeat the Big Lie, so long as he is of liberal intention he is saved," and on Professor Commager, who "if he spent nearly as much time reading the records of the Congressional hearings as he does denouncing them, we should all be better off." Kristol's thesis was that "civil libertarians" like Barth and Commager, among others, had moved from the defense of the civil rights of communists to a defense of communists and communist activities. Liberals, he wrote, had contributed to McCarthy's rise. As for communists' losing their jobs for refusing to answer questions before Red-baiting members of Congress, Kristol had little sympathy. Communism was not just another idea; it was "a conspiracy to subvert every social and political order it does not dominate." Kristol ended his essay with a peroration: "For there is one thing that the American people know about Senator McCarthy; he, like them, is unequivocally anti-Communist. About the spokesmen for American liberalism, they feel they know no such thing. And with some justification."[66]

Kristol had come to believe that the right posed less of a threat to liberalism than did the left. Communist propaganda had gained such enormous success, Kristol would write in the piece "On Negative Liberalism" published in *Encounter* two years later, that it had induced the West and especially Western intellectuals to have a guilty conscience in their fight with communism.[67]

Kristol had caught more than a piece of truth in his 1952 essay, despite his overheated rhetoric. Bell had tried to get him, unsuccessfully, to soften the article and make it more ironic and balanced.[68] His characterization of procommunist intellectuals was right on the mark, and he noted correctly that following the emergence of McCarthy, some liberals, in effect, gave up the fight against Soviet aggression abroad in their zeal to confront the Wisconsin senator at home.

Kristol tended also to minimize much of the continuing liberal assault on communism. He failed to recognize that people like Norman Thomas, who complimented *Commentary* for publishing several critical articles on what he called "sentimental professional liberals," were honestly worried about the resurgent antiliberalism of the right.[69]

Missing from the torrent of criticism that descended on Kristol at this time, however, has been an attempt to understand where he was coming from. The sense that Kristol (and other premature neocons) felt they were shouting into the wind at a moment of great danger to this country and the West may account for some of his crankiness and exaggeration. "We knew about the Gulag before Solzhenitsyn and wrote about the new class before [Milovan] Djilas [the Yugoslavian dissident]," Hook wrote.[70] In part, of course, it was also the New York intellectuals' adversarial style. "It's been a good day. I've had three fights," Hook once remarked.[71]

Schlesinger reminded Kristol that while the New Deal had gone about the task of developing certain important reforms, it was the New York intellectuals, with whom Kristol was closely connected, who had supported proletarian revolution, whether led by Stalin or by Trotsky. It was the liberal Americans for Democratic Action, as well as such figures as Eleanor Roosevelt, Schlesinger himself, Niebuhr, and Chester Bowles, the leader in the battle against Henry Wallace's fellow traveling Progressive Citizens of America (PCA), who had contributed significantly to Wallace's defeat.[72]

By this time, Kristol, a close student and admirer of Leo Strauss, was moving away from his older liberal beliefs (although, as his friend Robert Nisbet has suggested, he did not know it at the time). He still considered himself a liberal – what else could he be, considering how liberalism had benefited Jews? As Trilling pointed out, liberalism was the only respectable intellectual tradition around. Spender, who knew him as his coeditor at *Encounter*, would soon complain that he no longer shared the liberal's sympathy with the plight of the economically and socially excluded.[73]

During a stint in Europe, Kristol and Himmelfarb had also come under more conservative influences. They were befriended by Malcolm Muggeridge, an editor of *Punch* and enfant terrible of British journalism, and Michael Oakeshott, one of the most distinguished conservative thinkers of the century, who had succeeded Harold Laski in his chair at the London School of Economics. "I found my conservative friends," Kristol would say in an unpublished interview, "far more interesting than the others." Kristol had not known any conservatives (as distinct from ex-radicals) who were breaking with *their* past beliefs. He was fascinated that his new friends "felt perfectly at ease with themselves as conservatives, neither apologetic nor unduly contentious."[74]

Kristol was hardly alone in his move to the right. Operating off the lessons of the Hiss case, Toledano found "[n]ew vistas opening up for him... and old ones shut off." He had learned, he writes, that while anticommunism "might be the battle cry," it was "a pointer on the road" as he set out to "reconsider the context of liberalism, the problems of conservatism, and the structure of my beliefs."[75]

As the debate over the goals and activities of the Soviet Union and communism escalated and the methods to be employed in countering that threat sharpened, many intellectuals on the left now found themselves being drawn in more conservative directions.

5

The Modernization of American Conservatism

"In the United States at this time liberalism is not only the dominant but even the sole intellectual tradition," Lionel Trilling wrote in the Preface to *The Liberal Imagination* in 1953. "The conservative impulse and the reactionary impulse do not... express themselves in ideas but only in irritable mental gestures which seek to resemble ideas." Trilling was saddened by liberals' inability to recognize the "powerful conservative mind" as a corrective needed to bring modern American liberalism back to its "primal imagination."[1]

Although a serious body of conservative thought was beginning to emerge, marked by the more cosmopolitan and humane impulses of F. A. Hayek, Leo Strauss, Eric Voegelin, and Michael Oakeshott, the chief characteristics of the Old Right prior to World War II included a fanatical opposition to Franklin D. Roosevelt's New Deal, resistance to international alliances (along with a bias in favor of protectionist trade policies), and complacent tolerance (occasionally even active support) of racial and religious discrimination against blacks, Jews, and other minorities.

In the early 1960s, there were "conspiracy addicts" who saw themselves as conservatives. Robert Welch of the John Birch Society, for example, believed that communists dominated most of America; outright bigots such as the fundamentalist minister Gerald L. K. Smith; Conde McGinley, publisher of *Common Sense*; Westbrook Pegler, the famous journalist; and Willis Carto, a founder of the the so-called Liberty Lobby, were convinced that the decline of this country was due to Jews and blacks. Fundamentalist ministers deplored the growth of humanism, liberalism, and secularism and saw authority in American life coming to an end.[2]

Conservatives had never been able to live down Mill's description of them as "the stupid party," and Jews had no trouble choosing the more liberal Democratic Party over a Republican Party, whose extreme right wing was unabashedly anti-Semitic. Their liberalism was reinforced after World War II by their oppositon to the "Radical Right," which Peter Vierick, himself a conservative, characterized as the "same old isolationist... revolt of radical Populist lunatic-fringers... only this time it is a Populism gone sour."[3]

The threat from the New Right came to preoccupy Jewish leaders. The co-heads of the ADL, Benjamin Epstein and Arnold Forster, made this point the central theme of their *Danger on the Right* (1964). Richard Hofstadter called the Goldwater campaign of that year an example of "the paranoid style" in American politics.[4] As a staff member of the American Jewish Committee, I recall being summoned with my colleagues to the agency's New York headquarters one day in 1964 by David Danzig, its brilliant program director. "The smell of fascism hangs in the air," Danzig declared ominously. Danzig was not alone. Liberal politics was the only politics Jews felt they could trust.

Such respectable conservative organizations as the Foundation for Economic Education, the Mount Pélerin Society, and the Intercollegiate Society of Individualists (ISI), the last run by Frank Chodorov, were small and little known, as were the handful of right-of-center publications that were up and running. *Human Events* had been established in 1944 as an organ of libertarian journalism, and the bitterly anticommunist *Plain Talk* was founded two years later. *Plain Talk*'s circulation never exceeded 12,000, but – funded by Alfred Kohlberg, the so-called "China lobbyist" because of his support for Chiang Kai-shek, president of the Republic of China – it kept going. It featured exposés of communist infiltration of government, such as its first-issue story of what would later be called the "Amerasia" case.[5] Edited by Isaac Don Levine (with Ralph de Toledano as an associate), *Plain Talk* soon moved beyond anticommunist research to become an enlarged publication that could deal with politics, the arts, literature, theater, book reviews, and current events from a conservative viewpoint. Following a meeting convened by former President Herbert Hoover at the Waldorf Hotel in New York, the publication was merged into *The Freeman*, the first issue of which appeared on October 2, 1950, with the declaration that one of its "foremost aims [will be] to clarify the concept of individual freedom and apply it to the problems of our times."[6]

Conservative Jewish activists, including Frank Meyer, Frank Chodorov, Morrie Ryskind, and Willi Schlamm, along with Yale graduates William Buckley and L. Brent Bozell, showed up to help. Between 1950 and 1954, the *Freeman* emerged as a voice in the young conservative movement. None of these publications, however, including the *American Mercury*, begun by H. L. Mencken in the 1920s as a literary and cultural journal, compared in influence or circulation to left-wing journals like *The New Republic* and *The Nation*. Conservatism, historian John P. Diggins writes, was "a mood in search of a master."[7]

And although Jewish activists stood in the wings, a devout Roman Catholic stepped forward to supply the necessary leadership. Generally eschewing the hard right's bigotry, William F. Buckley, Jr., pulled together often conflicting strands of conservatism and launched it down a new path. In intellectual thought, sophistication, and personality, he proved to be indispensable in modernizing the movement. By creating the conservative weekly *National Review* in 1955 (and the television program *Firing Line*, which first aired in April 1966), he catapulted the emerging conservative movement into the mainstream of American politics.[8]

Born in 1925, Buckley grew up in a strict Roman Catholic family, which informed his strong anticommunism. His biographer, John B. Judis, describes his father, a wealthy oil man who made his fortune in Mexico, as a racist, albeit otherwise a bright and intelligent man. The elder Buckley regarded Indians (the family was from Texas) and African-Americans as inferior, and he frequently attacked Jews. William F. Buckley, the youngest son, recounted later with little pleasure his unhappiness when his brothers went out to burn a cross on a lawn, leaving him behind because he was too young.[9] After studying briefly at the University of Mexico, he enrolled at Yale. During his undergraduate years there, he spent much of his time crusading against collectivism and secularism.

Buckley graduated in 1950 and published *God and Man at Yale* the following year. By Christmas, it had sold some twelve thousand copies, and by the spring, thirty-five thousand, reaching the *New York Times* best-seller list. In the book, he attacked the teaching of religion at Yale as devoid of any serious appreciation for its moral canon and the teaching of economics for its emphasis on the collectivist principles embodied in FDR's New Deal. He favored instead free market principles. He took after faculty members by name, accusing them of fostering atheism and socialism.[10]

One might have expected a great university steeped in the Protestant ethic to ignore the rantings of a single recent graduate – and a papist at that. But Yale took Buckley seriously. McGeorge Bundy, a member of the Yale faculty, guided by the new president, A. Whitney Griswold, wrote in the *Atlantic Monthly* that it was odd indeed "for any Roman Catholic to undertake to speak for the Yale religious tradition."[11] The book turned Buckley into an instant celebrity. For young conservatives beginning to stir, Gregory L. Schneider writes, it was a "manifesto akin to what C. Wright Mills' *The Power Elite* or Paul Goodman's *Growing Up Absurd* were for left-wing students."[12]

Buckley's friends wanted him to study under Hayek at Chicago, but he was also being sought after by the *The Freeman* and *The American Mercury*, where he had worked briefly. Neither, however, was a vital political publication, and *The American Mercury* had become overtly anti-Semitic since changing ownership in 1952. Like the Kennedys, the Buckley family knew and liked Joseph McCarthy. Buckley and his brother-in-law, L. Brent Bozell, penned *McCarthy and His Enemies* (1953), published at the time of the Army–McCarthy hearings, which led to the senator's downfall. Hardly blind to McCarthy's failures (the book contained sixty-three critical references to him), the book was, nevertheless, an apologia. The two young men opined, "We cannot avoid the fact that the United States is at war with international Communism." McCarthyism, as distingushed from McCarthy, they declared, was "using social sanctions to safeguard the American traditions." With liberalism dominating public policy discussion, and *The Freeman* reduced to a monthly, Buckley decided to start a new magazine to counter the saliency of *The Nation* and *The New Republic*. He wanted to integrate "the new anti-Communist conservativism" of James Burnham with the older tradition of Edmund Burke, thus answering "the fear of the present with the faiths of the past."[13]

Playing an important role in Buckley's planning for a new conservative magazine was William (Willi) S. Schlamm, another of the forgotten Jewish godfathers. Schlamm was a refugee from Austria. As a teenager, he had been a communist. By the 1930s, at the age of twenty-five, he broke with the party, becoming a well-known anti-Nazi and anti-Stalinist. In 1938, he published *Diktatur de Luge* (*The Dictatorship of the Lie*), a sharp criticism of Stalinism and the Trotsky trial; the following year, convinced that democracy had no future in Europe, he came to the United States. Schlamm worked briefly as a columnist for *The New Leader* and soon joined the editorial staff of *Time*, becoming a key foreign policy adviser and assistant to editor Henry Luce, who was himself moving increasingly to the right.[14]

During the war, Luce had encouraged favorable coverage of the Soviet Union, but under the influence of Chambers and Schlamm he came around to their way of thinking.[15] Schlamm pressed Luce to create a first-class anti-Stalinist intellectual journal that would feature such writers as W. H. Auden, T. S. Elliot, Arthur Koestler, George Orwell, and Lionel Trilling. He nominated himself as editor. Luce, however, worried by a dip in the economy, sold the title to Henry Regnery, who had a different idea for the magazine.[16] Frank Meyer's biographer suggests that the scheme fell through because Luce was "never a deep or original thinker."[17]

Schlamm, however, never relented. In 1951, he left *Time* and for the next three years helped to edit *The Freeman*, hoping all the while to establish a new conservative publication. At about this time, Schlamm edited and wrote the introduction to Buckley and Bozell's *McCarthy and His Enemies*. Buckley impressed Schlamm and shared his view that liberalism's dominance of the culture – liberals controlled some eight journals – had to be challenged.[18]

Aware that Buckley had access to funding, Schlamm broached the idea for an opinion magazine, originally to be called *National Weekly*. The weakness of *The Freeman*, Schlamm explained to Buckley, was the diffusion of leadership. He suggested that Buckley serve as editor-in-chief, fully expecting to strongly influence a twenty-eight-year-old feeling his way into the anticommunist movement.

With a $100,000 pledge from Buckley's father, Buckley and Schlamm wrote a prospectus intended to gain financial contributors and writers. The "political climate of an era," they declared, was a product of serious political journals. It was possible to overcome the jaded liberal status quo with the "vigor of true convictions."[19] Ryskind raised some $38,000 of the total of $450,000, not including the deficits Buckley anticipated in the first two years. Meanwhile, Schlamm worked closely with him in assembling the staff. When Buckley hesitated to go forward, Schlamm persevered. "Willi's point," Buckley recalled, "was that if you get twenty-five thousand readers, your subscribers won't let you die, and that proved almost exactly accurate."[20]

In November 1955, a few days before Buckley's thirtieth birthday, the first issue of *National Review* appeared. Buckley promised that it would offer a "responsible dissent from liberal orthodoxy." Schlamm, who wrote a column for the new publication, quickly became popular with its readers and with his coworkers. According to Alfred Kazin, who worked with him at *Time*, Schlamm possessed "all the patronizing charm of the Viennese cafe intellectual along with the cultural solemnity of the Jew brought up under German culture."[21] Buckley himself has described Schlamm along with Burnham as "his two closest partners" in this venture. William Rusher, publisher of *National Review*, called Buckley and Schlamm "one flesh." Schlamm was a genius, John Chamberlain, Schlamm's closest friend, later wrote, and "set Bill Buckley on a path that proved to be indispensable to conservatism."[22]

Before long, however, the two drifted apart. The independent, radical Schlamm advocated nuclear war against the Soviet Union. Buckley, who did not favor war over Eastern Europe, gradually eased Schlamm out until he resigned in 1957. Nonetheless, Buckley was always generous in crediting Schlamm's role in the enterprise.[23] Schlamm returned to Europe, where he wrote books on East–West relations and eventually came to be the owner and editor of a magazine, *Die Zeitbuhne*, that predicted the difficulties the West would face in countering the Soviet Union around the world. Following his departure from *National Review*, he began to write for John Birch Society publications.[24]

Unlike *The Freeman*, which had been secular in tone, *National Review* (with three Catholics among its editors and Will Herberg, an orthodox Jew, joining it shortly as associate and later religious editor) would be deeply concerned about religious and philosophical tradition. Whereas *The Freeman* had brought together the anticommunist approach of Levine's *Plain Talk* with the free market emphasis of Leonard Read's Founation for Economic Education, *National Review* added the traditionalist interests of Russell Kirk, the leading figure of Burkean conservatism in the United States.[25]

National Review was attractive and crisply edited, enhancing the message of the new conservatism. Buckley sought to distinguish the publication from the "irresponsible right." With his later celebrity status as a television star (through *Firing Line*), the suave and sophisticated Buckley put conservatism on the map. In the absence of *National Review* or some similar publication, there would probably have been no serious and popular intellectual force on the right in the 1960s and 1970s.

From 1955 to 1960, the editors of *National Review* poured forth a steady attack on the dominant liberal ethos, focusing on intellectual currents and party platforms. Most of their positions had been shaped by their personal experiences and the now-repudiated ideological convictions of the 1930s. Buckley argued in his 1959 book *Up from Liberalism* (modeled on Booker T. Washington's *Up from Slavery*) that this country – and this included Eisenhower Republicanism – had sacrificed its principles in the name of compromise. Liberals had emphazised the use of state power to foster equality and eliminate social and individual differences and had cast conservatism into an almost pathological mode of thought and behavior.[26]

National Review assembled on the masthead as editors or contributors many of the renegades from the various shades of the left as well as more established proponents of American conservatism, regardless of their special perspectives. Traditionalists like Kirk, Richard Weaver, and Donald Davidson, the libertarians John Chamberlain and Frank Chodorov, and ex-radical critics of statism like Max Eastman and Frank Meyer all vied with one another, not always comfortably, in this ecumenical brew. Typically, Kirk bristled at Meyers for criticizing him in *The Freeman* and attacked Chodorov's staunch individualism. (Later, Kirk would withdraw his name from the masthead.) Buckley remained the controlling figure, especially after Meyer had come forward as "the great conciliator" and "house metaphyician."[27]

Although *National Review* has often been characterized as militantly Catholic and Irish-Catholic, five Jews served on the original editorial board, including Meyer and Schlamm. Ryskind and Eugene Lyons were frequent contributors. Ralph de Toledano became the magazine's music critic, as well as its first pseudonymous Washington correspondent. The editorial board, however, did not always share a common view. During the 1956 election, the senior editors debated whether or not to endorse the reelection of Eisenhower. Burnham and Chamberlain argued against the president, while Schlamm and Meyer supported him. When the Soviet Union brutally put down the Hungarian revolt in 1956, Burnham feared aggressive U.S. opposition might trigger atomic warfare and was uncharacteristically hesitant. Schlamm and Meyer believed that Burnham's strategy meant capitulation. They won the editorial battle.[28]

Buckley, an ardent Roman Catholic, was particularly drawn to Herberg, whom he thought of as the "theological conscience" of the magazine. He saw him as countering the atheism of Max Eastman and others within the group. Herberg, as we have seen, was a sharp critic of the Jewish civic agencies during the postwar "golden age" of the 1940s and 1950s. He challenged the effort to remove religious practices from the public schools. In one essay, according to Buckley, Herberg argued that the prohibiton against paying attention to God in the classroom resulted in removing from students' intellectual consciousness the entire supernatural dimension, which could not be counterbalanced at home. Even when parents took children to church on Sundays, the impression was left that religion was at best a pleasant, useful, tribal convention, like golf or canasta.[29]

Herberg also used the pages of *National Review* to criticize the popular religious pieties of the 1960s and social justice papal encyclicals such as *Mater et Magistra* and *Pacem in Terris*. Of course, religion has been closely tied to politics at all times and almost everywhere in the world. But Herberg resented its growing leftward tilt. A "do-it-yourself" religion had emerged in which everyone was given license to become his own theologian. Herberg, now an orthodox Jew, was opposed to robbing religion of its transcendence. Like Strauss, he was a firm believer in natural law, which claimed that man-made law sprang from a power outside of man. Throughout the 1960s, Herberg fought the trend that replaced the hard-nosed but compassionate religion of Reinhold Niebuhr with that of the "human relations" and "rapping" theology of the Berrigan brothers and Harvey Cox.[30]

Another strong influence on Buckley's thinking was Whittaker Chambers. At one point, he considered naming him editor-in-chief of *National Review*. Sam Tanenhaus notes that as an undergradutate at Columbia in 1924, Chambers had developed close associations with Jews, who helped to shape his development. A product of a shabby WASP gentility, he grew up in a bizarre, anxiety-ridden household but eventually found his place among the precocious, urban Jews who dominated undergraduate intellectual life at Columbia. He established important relationships with Meyer Schapiro (later the nation's leading art historian), Clifton Fadiman, and Lionel Trilling. Jewish students introduced him to Marx and Lenin and gave him his cultural and political education. For the first time, he found himself in the presence of serious people, albeit from totally different backgrounds, with minds like his own. Trilling saw him as "hungry for a sustaining faith" and found his "commitment to radical politics to be definitive of his whole moral being."[31]

Chambers had sought to alert government officials early on about Soviet espionage in this country. Shortly after German troops invaded Poland and Hitler signed the nonaggression pact with Stalin, Chambers, along with Isaac Don Levine, met with Assistant Secretary of State Adolph B. Berle, Jr., to warn him of the underground Washington communist spy ring with which Chambers had been associated (citing Hiss and other figures). His warning, for reasons not entirely clear, was disregarded.[32]

Arthur Schlesinger, Jr., called Chambers "an ideologue with no mercy for the pragmaticisms of democracy," with "special contempt for liberalism." Although widely recognized as a spokesman for anticommunism and, by extension, conservatism, Chambers was no right-wing extremist. In fact, he drew a clear distinction between conservative politics and reactionary politics and held no brief for either the rich or businessmen as such. For him, the true meaning of capitalism and its partner, economic freedom, was to act as a countervailing force against totalitarianism.[33]

Chambers favored a "Beaconsfield position" (after Benjamin Disraeli) in which "objectives were weighed against historical possibilities." Conservatism, he felt, must accommodate to the hopes and needs of the masses. Although *National Review* championed the free market economics of von Mises, Hayek, and Milton Friedman, Chambers felt otherwise. "There will be no peace for the islands of relative plenty," he wrote in *National Review*, "until the continents of proliferating poverty have been lifted to something like the general material level of the islanders."[34]

When the Republicans lost ground in the House and Senate in the 1958 election (their worst defeat since the Great Depression), Chambers wrote Buckley, "It was the Old Guard the voters wiped out.... If the Republican Party cannot get some grip of the actual world we live in and from it generate and actively promote a program that means something to most people, why somebody else will."[35]

Despite his dread of communism and the Soviet Union, Chambers was not an admirer of McCarthy, although he never spoke out publicly against him. When *McCarthy and His Enemies* was published in 1954, Chambers began a correspondence with Buckley that ended only with Chambers's death in 1961. While Buckley's book was a defense of McCarthy, Chambers feared that the Wisconsin senator's blunders would discredit the anticommunist movement. He saw McCarthy as a "slugger" and "rabble rouser." When McCarthy died in 1957, Chambers summed up his career in this way: he had no understanding of communism; he knew only how to attack.[36]

National Review's governing principle was its opposition to liberalism. Buckley, joined by publisher William Rusher, along with Chambers, believed that all shades of the left shared the same materialist principles. It was the liberals, Buckley wrote in the first issue, who ran the country. Frank Meyer, in summing up the magazine's viewpoint, virtually dismissed liberals as weaklings incapable of effectively waging the Cold War against the Soviet Union. Charging that American liberals agreed with Russian communists on the "necessity and desirability of socialism," Meyer said that there were no "irreconcilable differences" between the two ideologies, only differences as to methods and means. As a result, Meyer alleged, liberals were unfit for the leadership of a free society and intrinsically incapable of offering serious opposition to the communist offensive.[37]

Although Buckley himself rarely used such intemperate language, which virtually accused liberals of disloyalty, *National Review* battled relentlessly against them. Buckley's most important contribution to the conservative movement, however, may have been his purge of its most extreme and bigoted elements. "Conservatism," he wrote, "must be wiped of the parasitic cant that defaces it." Responding to pleas from Ryskind and Kohlberg, Buckley decreed in 1959 that anyone of this character could not be on the masthead. None of its editors could write for *The American Mercury*, which had fallen into the hands of a bigoted businessman named Russell Maguire, who reprinted the anti-Semitic *Protocols of the Elders of Zion*. Buckley's decision to ban the bigots did not sit easily with Rusher and others; it would cost the magazine subscribers. Chambers, however, applauded: "Now what is good and strong outside us can draw to us. The dregs will be drawn to the dregs, and sink where they belong."[38]

Regarding the extremist John Birch Society, Buckley at first equivocated but later spoke out forcefully against it, even though its founder, Robert Welch, was a financial contributor to *National Review* and many of the magazine's subscribers were John Birchers. Welch, a pink-cheeked, white-haired, grandfatherly-looking candy manufacturer, had launched the society in 1958. Picking up the torch laid down by Joe McCarthy, the John Birch Society held that the American government was under the "operational control" of the Communist Party, with communists dominating "60 to 80 percent" of the country. In its wildest, most irresponsible allegation, Welch charged that President Eisenhower, a moderate Republican, was in fact a "conscious agent of the Communist Conspiracy."

Despite its recklessness, the John Birch Society, to which a number of veteran anti-Semites had attached themselves, found its niche. By the early 1960s, it had set up chapters in at least thirty-five states and collected more than $1.3 million in membership dues. On October 19, 1965, however, *National Review* finally weighed in with a special issue, "The John Birch Society and the Conservative Movement," denouncing Welch's group and dealing it a fatal blow. Included in the broadside were several columns by Buckley and others; statements by leading conservatives, including Barry Goldwater; and a two-page Principles and Heresies column by Meyer, declaring that the John Birch Society's "psychosis of conspiracy" threatened American interests.[39]

Meyer's piece was especially compelling. The heresies of the Birchers comprised no awareness of the essence of liberalism. "There is no room here for misplaced idealism, intellectual error, the lures of power, the weakness and vanities of men," he wrote. Liberals were wrong and misguided. Their ideas needed to be countered. But they were not part of a communist plot.[40] Although angry letters and subscription cancellations flooded *National Review*'s offices, its attack proved to be a critical moment in the development of a more responsible conservative movement.

One year later, Buckley was named host of *Firing Line*, a new program examining often controversial issues on national public television. With his cultured phrasing and his penchant for big words and obscure terminology, Buckley seemed like an actor on stage, yet he expressed his opinions often brilliantly and always evidenced his intellectualism. His years on public television would vastly widen the audience for his views. Meanwhile, the John Birch Society faded into obscurity.

When Alabama's segregationist Governor George C. Wallace formed his American Independent Party, persuaded General Curtis LeMay to be his running mate, and began his third-party campaign for the presidency in 1968, *National Review* came out against him. Once again, Meyer's role was critical, according to his biographer. Meyer argued in a column in May 1967 that Wallace was "the radical opposite of conservatism" and would "poison the moral source of its strength." Wallace's brand of populism "would substitute the tyranny of the majority over the individual," said Meyer, adding that Wallace stood squarely against the traditional conservative position of limited, constitutionalist, republican government. Buckley described Wallace privately as "Mr. Evil." He invited him on *Firing Line*, where he denounced him as a racist who had protected blacks inadequately in Selma.[41]

During this period, too, Meyer and Chambers assailed the libertarians Murray Rothbard and Ayn Rand as extremists who made a fetish of selfishness defined as individualism. Meyer accused Rand of calculated cruelties and of depicting an "arid subhuman image of man." Chambers, in a *National Review* piece, "Big Sister Is Watching You," likened "Randian man" to "Marxian man," in that each was made the center of a godless world. Chambers was also critical of her for seeming to suggest that we should be governed by a technological elite of gifted individuals; he thought this smacked too much of totalitarianism. *Atlas Shrugged*, he wrote, "consistently mistakens raw force for strength." Summing up his argument, Chambers declared, "From almost any page of *Atlas Shrugged*, a voice can be heard... commanding: 'To a gas chamber – go!'" Rand fired back, denouncing *National Review* as the "worst and most dangerous magazine in America."[42] It was not until 2003 that a Rand accolyte, Alan Greenspan, took Buckley to task for his treatment of the writer: "Someone has finally defined the rational morality underlying capitalism," the economic savant wrote, "and you treat it in such a vulgar manner."[43]

Buckley himself, as we have seen, remained a staunch supporter of McCarthy. After his death, the *National Review* eulogized him in two consecutive issues, referring at one point to his "vivid moral sense," and Buckley published a sympathetic novel, *The Red Hunter* (1999), which declared, "It was one of McCarthy's ironic legacies that it became almost impossible in future years to say that anyone was a Communist, because you'd be hauled up for committing McCarthyism."[44] Several of the Jewish members of his team shared Buckley's view. When McCarthy died, Schlamm wrote a *National Review* eulogy declaring, "I shall be perfectly satisfied to be called for the rest of my life a McCarthyite."[45] In *Faith and Freedom: The Journal of Spiritual Mobilization*, Frank Chodorov praised the Buckley–Bozell book. Twenty-eight right wing partisans (among them Chodorov, Toledano, and Lyons) wrote a letter to seven hundred newspapers in 1953 arguing that while McCarthy was being treated unfairly by the media, fellow traveler Owen Lattimore was finding his book, *Ordeal by Slander*, mindlessly praised. Meyer did not get involved deeply in the debates about McCarthy, but he felt the Wisconsin senator was a positive force in the battle against communism, mainly because he was *not* subtle.[46]

The views about McCarthyism of others in Buckley's circle of Jews were somewhat more ambivalent. Taking issue with Hook and Bell, who wondered why people who had broken with communism in the 1930s were willing to tolerate McCarthy's methods, Herberg refused to indulge in what he called the "liberal hysteria" about "hysteria." Writing, curiously, in the social democratic and liberal journals *The New Leader* and *The New Republic*, Herberg admitted that McCarthy was a "classical rabble rouser," but he explained him away by suggesting that he was symptomatic of American mass politics as practiced by Roosevelt and even Eisenhower. Herberg was also outraged by comparisons between the Wisconsin demagogue and Hitler.[47] "The danger today," Lyons added to the controversy in 1953, "is not hysteria but complacency."[48]

Toledano later wrote in his autobiography that he had become "hostage to the McCarthy forces" by the "malevolence of the opposition." It was not that he and others did not know McCarthy's limitations and his nihilism, but rather that "we were surrendering to an urgency engendered by the stubborn inability of some of our leaders to acknowledge the danger within" – President Truman's "red herring" remarks, for example, in the Hiss case. McCarthy, he claimed, was "a tough fighter who had seized the Communist issue and succeeded in making the public take heed where our intellectual onslaughts had failed."[49]

The fact remains that Buckley and his Jewish contingent flunked on the threat that the Wisconsin zealot posed. They did not understand that in battling against communism they had to be especially zealous in distinguishing between communists and simply liberals and naïfs, even when some liberals themselves hesitated to oppose the dangers that McCarthy created for a democratic society. For that matter, Buckley and his Jewish circle were also slow to recognize the implications of the civil rights revolution. For the most part, they did not recognize the terrible toll racism took on black Americans, and they played hardly any part in the struggle against it. As late as the 1960s, much of the Deep South resembled apartheid South Africa. Following the 1954 *Brown* decision banning segregated schools, many conservatives defended the South's control of its schools. Buckley also argued that the "claims of civilization (and of culture and community) superseded those of universal suffrage." What force and circumstance had created could not be immediately solved by the central government. The problem had to be solved locally and in the hearts of men. In effect, he conceded to Southern resistance and argued that black self-help ought to be the major instrument of needed change. Along with Herberg, Buckley was opposed to Dr. Martin Luther King's nonviolent marches as destructive of social order.[50]

Meyer was opposed to the Supreme Court's school desegregation decision on constitutional grounds. He felt the court was making social policy rather than simply interpreting the Constitution. Buckley and Meyer did put local conventions and states' rights ahead of cries for justice – a common failing of many conservatives. They also opposed President Eisenhower's enforcement of integration in Little Rock in 1957, and subsequently the marches, freedom rides, and civil rights legislation of the 1960s. On the other hand, when massive resistance in the South resulted in violence at the University of Mississippi and in Selma, Alabama, *National Review* lashed out against it: "The cause of principle is never served by jeering mobs," it declared. It also opposed the disenfranchisement of African-Americans.[51]

For the most part, Buckley, Meyer, and *National Review* avoided the argument that blacks were inferior to whites. In *Up from Liberalism*, nonetheless, Buckley declared that allowing blacks to vote threatened the superior "cultural advancement" of whites. Accepting black demands for independence and "one man, one vote" in South Africa, he also believed, was inviting a return to barbarism. This put him in conflict with the growing neoconservatism of Irving Kristol, who, in reviewing the book, found Buckley's opinions too extreme. He felt also that Buckley undermined his own credibility by criticizing Social Security laws. By 1965, however, the magazine "had slowly grown in sympathy for the civil rights movement," according to Meyer's biographer. The fact remains, though, that the marriage between Buckley's conservatism and Jewish neoconservatism, which had always favored civil rights, was still some years off.[52]

Although the *National Review*'s circulation rose to a respectable 100,000 subscribers by 1964, establishment journalists and intellectuals continued to write it off. John Fischer, the editor of *Harper's*, dismissed *National Review* as "an organ, not of conservatism, but of radicalism." This view was further developed by Richard Hofstadter, Daniel Bell, and other writers in *The New Right*. Writing for *The New Republic* in 1962, historian Irving Brant said the American right was essentially made up of "the John Birch Society at the lowest level of intelligence and *National Review* in the higher altitude of right-wing sophistication." But, he said, the two extremes were as "alike as two yolks in one egg."[53]

To Meyer and many of Buckley's people, winning the Cold War trumped almost everything. Meyer joined Burnham and others in pressing forward for the liberation of Eastern Europe from Soviet control, while complaining that Eisenhower had failed to reverse the disastrous foreign and domestic policies of Roosevelt and Truman. The time had come to take the Republican Party back. He was outraged also by the policies of the Kennedy administration, which would take the first steps in what would later be known as détente. For Meyer, this course of action meant only appeasement and retreat.[54]

At the close of the 1950s, though little noted by liberals and the establishment media, conservatism was becoming transformed. Historian George

Nash traces this growth to an intellectual community that was formulating alternatives to liberal orthodoxies and the development of a number of instruments serving to unite that community with grassroots rebels. One important vehicle, alongside *National Review*, was the Intercollegiate Society of Individualists (ISI), created in 1953 by Frank Chodorov as a counterbalance to what he felt was the corrosive influence of the left, especially on college campuses. (Following Chodorov's death in 1966, the name was changed to Intercollegiate Studies Institute.)

Although Chodorov persuaded Buckley to serve as ISI's first president, he did not enjoy sharing the spotlight with the young tyro and soon took the job himself. In a jocular tone, he wrote Buckley: "Am removing you as president. Making myself pres. Easier to raise money if a Jew is president. You can be V. P. Love Frank."[55]

Chodorov declared that the most important development of the twentieth century had been the transformation of the American character from individualist to collectivist through such instruments as the Intercollegiate Socialist Society (later the Student League for Democracy). He traced the long, slow process by which this transformation had taken place through the capture of the country's most vigorous young minds. Socialists had taken fifty years to transform the American character; consequently, another fifty years would be necessary for those who believed in individual freedom and a free market economy. The task for conservatism, he said, was to engage in such a process, no matter how long it would take.[56]

Chodorov's strategy for change was taken from Richard Weaver's *Ideas Have Consequences*. Since a more thoughtful kind of conservatism felt itself under siege and easily misrepresented because of anti-Semitic and fringe elements within the movement, ISI never sought wide publicity. This probably accounts for its being so little known today, despite the critical role it played in the coming American conservatve ascendency, according to E. Victor Milione, Chodorov's successor.[57]

ISI commissioned and distributed on campuses essays and monographs such as Weaver's "Education and the Individual," Herberg's "What Is the Moral Crisis of Our Time?," Kirk's "Standardization without Standards," Albert Hobbs's "The Integrity of the Person," and William H. Peterson's "Private Sector and Public Sector: Which Is Which and Why." A series of publications aimed at the young was also created, including *The Individualist*, which reprinted the best articles from student newspapers, and *Under 30*, which became the *Intercollegiate Review*, the ISI flagship publication. By the early 1960s, ISI was mailing conservative literature to 40,000 students. A number of ISI chapters at college campuses had been formed. Seminars and summer programs, along with fellowships, provided students with firsthand exposure to these ideas.[58]

Buckley, Meyer, and Kirk were often invited by ISI leaders to speak before college audiences. However, Buckley objected to being hailed as a "celebrity."

He wrote Chodorov in 1953: "If they would only get it into their heads that we don't care about crowds of 1000; a crowd of 30 (provided the 30 are intelligent and conscientious) would serve our purposes better."[59]

Among those who would emerge as prominent conservatives in the coming years were Edwin J. Feulner, Jr., later president of the Heritage Foundation, a prominent conservative think tank in Washington; and William Kristol, an ISI activist and later Vice President Dan Quayle's chief of staff and now a leading conservative writer and TV pundit.

One of the most brilliant of the new conservative student leaders (althought not a Jew) was M. Stanton Evans. In his book *Revolt on the Campus* (1961), Evans described presciently three "bursts of rebellion" against liberalism. One moved directly into the GOP, another into a premature effort at a new organization, and the third into the "exotic recesses of Bohemia," each reflecting frustration "with the conformity of liberalism." While none was successful in "turning back the liberal orthodoxy," he wrote, they reflected young people's unhappiness "with the conformity of liberalism."[60]

By the late 1950s, ISI, Nash observes, was "doing for conservative youths what other groups were doing for adults. It was giving them an intellectual home and a focus for disparate energies." By this time, ISI had also developed a series of campus chapters, which became an important vehicle for the recruitment and training of students into the conservative and, shortly, the Goldwater movement.[61] "Through ISI, I received books by Frédéric Bastiat, Frank Chodorov, and F. A. Harper as well as the newsletter *Human Events*, and I became aware of the existence of conservative publishers – Henry Regnery and Devin Adair," wrote Evans, then a Yale freshman. "It was a discovery beyond price, for it meant I was no longer alone."[62]

Some of the students trained by ISI went on to form Young Americans for Freedom, which soon became better known than ISI. YAF actually grew out of the executive committee of Youth for Goldwater, which had been organized to support the Arizona senator's abortive bid for the GOP presidential nomination in 1960. A day after the Republican convention, Goldwater met with the group at its invitation and urged them to "turn your group into a permanent organization of young conservatives."[63]

One of those most active individuals in launching YAF was not a young college student but an experienced public relations man, one who had helped Buckley raise funds for *National Review*. Marvin Liebman belonged to that generation of Jews searching for new meaning in their lives following their break with communism. At first he found that sense of purpose in Zionism. During the late 1940s, he became associated with the militant American League for a Free Palestine, whose hero was Peter Bergson and the underground Irgun Zvai Leumi organization in Palestine. Bergson, along with Ben Hecht and other Broadway celebrities, fought British imperialism as Jews outside of organized Jewish life. Late in 1946, Liebman embarked on the *Ben Hecht*, a vessel named after the playwright that was secretly engaged in running refugee Jews to Palestine. When the ship was picked up by a British destroyer before it could land, he spent fifteen days in a detention camp in Cyprus. During this time, he came to believe that Jews all over the world were one big family. As late as 1951, he marched in a May Day parade; but when South Korea invaded North Korea, he was finished with the far left and undertook to fight it in any way he knew how.[64]

As an account executive for a public relations firm (he had set up his own firm), Liebman set about organizing the Committee of One Million, which sought to combat Chinese communism. Utilizing techniques he had learned in his Communist Party days, he was among the first to discover the importance of mailing lists, now a prime organizational and financial tool of the conservative movement.

Liebman urged Buckley to encourage the nascent conservative youth movement. At the 1960 Republican convention, which Buckley covered for *National Review*, Buckley and Liebman were impressed with two Youth for Goldwater leaders, Douglas Caddy and David Franke. They were "ambitious, sophisticated, smart," Liebman noted "and, I was soon to learn, ruthless in pursuing their political agenda."[65]

Following the convention, Liebman persuaded Buckley to invite a number of young conservatives from ISI chapters and elsewhere to a conference at his family estate in Sharon, Connecticut, in mid-September to form what would become YAF. Close to 100 activists from 44 colleges and universities in 24 states showed up. Joining them were *National Review* editors and other conservative figures, including Meyer and Evans. There were several Jews present at Sharon, including a Harvard student who later would become a pillar of the religious right, Howard Phillips, and Richard Schuchman, a graduate of the prestigious Bronx High School of Science and at the time a student at Yale Law School. Schuchman would become national chairman of YAF in its early years. He was named to this post probably to avoid the public perception that the conservative movement was mostly Catholic and anti-Semitic.[66]

Evans was the principal author of what became known as the Sharon Statement, the statement of principles for the new organization that was adopted there. Echoing Meyer and Buckley, as well as the conservative intellectual legacy of the 1950s, the Sharon Statement fused together traditionalism, libertarianism, and anticommunism. It emphasized that freedom was "indivisible" and could not "long exist without economic freedom." The statement declared that government had only three functions: "preservation of internal order, the provision of national defense, and the administration of justice." To go beyond these functions, it said, would diminish order and liberty. Noting that the group met at a "time of moral and political crisis," it warned that "the forces of international Communism" were the single greatest threat to liberty. And in phrases that would be echoed by Ronald Reagan twenty years later, it concluded that only by seeking a victory over communism could Americans defend their way of life. Coexistence with the Soviet Union, the statement made clear, was not the answer.[67]

Following the Sharon meeting, Franche was installed as an intern at *National Review* and Caddy went to work at Liebman's firm. Although "Buckley's inspired philosophical example" and Rusher's political connections had brought the future YAFers and other young conservative leaders to Sharon, Liebman was the key figure in the creation of what one historian has called "the most important organizational initiative undertaken by conservatives in the last thirty years." "My midwifery of that was purely ceremonial," Buckley later said.[68] Caddy, elected president of YAF, used Liebman's office as his base of operations. By January 1961, YAF was counterpicketing in Washington against those protesting HUAC. A few months later, when the organization packed the Manhattan Center in New York for a Goldwater rally, its period of political activism had begun.

The Sharon conference has been described by the new conservative historiography as "one of the most significant student meetings of the 1960s." It helped to launch the movement that would win the White House for conservatives in 1980. Yet it gained little recognition at the time. The media missed what one historian has called the "real story" of the 1960s. While the media covered extensively the activities of the New Left and Students for a Democratic Society as they protested the war in Vietnam and embraced radical new lifestyles, they paid little heed to conservative students, even though they far outnumbered the radicals. SDS, formed in 1962, had perhaps 2,000 members at its peak; YAF, created two years earlier, had more than twice as many members (other estimates had the figure as high as 25,000 members at 115 colleges and universities).[69]

It is not surprising, perhaps, that YAF was largely ignored. It drew its support not from the affluent Ivy League, which produces so many of the nation's leaders in politics, business, and culture, but from smaller, poorer colleges with vocational orientations and strong religious allegiances. Catholic institutions including St. John's, Fordham, and Villanova, along with such campuses as the University of Dallas, were major centers of this new movement. Their students did not make headlines by burning draft cards. For the most part, they favored the fighting in Vietnam. In any event, the widespread image of the nation's youth taking to the streets to protest the war was misleading. The fact was that most Americans supported President Johnson's escalation of U.S. involvement in Vietnam. Robert S. McNamara, Johnson's secretary of defense, has written that polls in May 1967 showed "public sentiment" favoring a "widening of the war." He reported "slightly stronger support for increased military pressure than for withdrawal."[70]

The sixties were not a radical decade but a polaraized one. Both the conservative Sharon Statement and the leftist Port Huron Statement, written by Tom Hayden and adopted by SDS, argued that the time was ripe for an ideological crusade. Both attacked the dominant liberal paradigm but from opposite ends of the political spectrum. With his customary insight, Daniel Bell foretold this in *The End of Ideology*, in which he argued that the United States was vulnerable "to the politics of disaffection."[71]

Only recently, with the development of a historiography of American conservatism, has its side of the story begun to be reviewed.[72] The writing of the history of the 1960s has largely been in the hands of student activists of the period, such as Todd Gitlin, Maurice Isserman, and James Miller, who graduated into professional academics. In all fairness to these historians, a number have revised their earlier views. Nine years after writing his book on the rise of the SDS, Miller expressed regret at ignoring the importance of conservative activists. "In terms of the political history of this country," Miller declared, "the New Left just isn't an important story." The historian Thomas Sugrue has made a similar point. "The Promethean adventures of the New Left and the counterculture aren't all that relevant to understanding the Sixties"[73]

One of the few commentators who recognized the meaning of the conservative uprising was Murray Kempton, the iconoclastic columnist who delighted in "smiting both sides." "We must assume that the conservative revival is the youth movement of the sixties," Kempton wrote after a big YAF rally in Madison Square Garden in 1962. But he tempered his observation by noting that the conservative youth movement "may even be as important to its epoch as the Young Communist League was to the thirties, which was not very."[74]

In 1964, young conservatives discovered Senator Barry Goldwater, a right-wing senator from Arizona, and helped him to win the Republican presidential nomination. Goldwater's background was unusual. His grandfather, Michael "Big Mike" Goldwater, was a Jewish immigrant from Poland who, with his brother Joseph, had built a successful dry goods business in the wide open Arizona territory of the late nineteenth century. Baron Goldwater, who was Big Mike's son and Barry's father, established one of the most successful department stores in Phoenix.

Baron married a woman who traced her ancestry back to Roger Williams in Rhode Island. She was an Episcopalian, and Barry would be brought up outside Phoenix's Jewish community. "Only about five hundred Jews lived in Arizona in 1907," Goldwater writes in his autobiography. "By 1920, when I was eleven years old, there were fewer than 1, 200 Jews here." He went on to say that neither his father nor any member of his family took part in the Jewish community. "I'm proud of my ancestors and heritage. I've simply never practiced the Jewish faith.... In the jargon of today's sociologists, we've been assimilated. We're Americans." His collaborator on his autobiography reports, however, that one of the central forces shaping Goldwater, alongside the "can do" culture of the Southwest, was the "legacy of his Jewish immigrant grandfather."[75]

Unlike Joseph Lieberman, the Democratic candidate for vice president in 2000, Goldwater did not run as a Jew and did not seek the support of other Jews. He did not go out of his way to support Israel, either. On the other hand, he never disavowed his Jewish antecedents. He liked to quip that since he was half-Jewish, he could only play nine holes at restricted country clubs. At his funeral in 1998, the rabbi emeritus of Phoenix's Temple Beth Israel delivered the traditional Jewish prayer for the dead, "El Maaleh Rachamim."

Whether Goldwater should be seen as Jewish is an open question. The historian Jacob Marcus has declared that "any individual with one Jewish parent is a Jew, even if 'born' and raised as a Christian." Based on this, another American Jewish historian, Moses Rischin, writes that Goldwater was "the first major party Jewish candidate for the presidency."[76] Goldwater was aware, however, that his Jewish background was a detriment to running for high national office at that time. Approached to run for president, prior to 1960, he admitted having several drawbacks, including his Jewish name.[77]

Goldwater had been drawn to the writings of such conservative thinkers as Hayek and Kirk and to *National Review*, which, he said, "burst on us like a spring shower, proclaiming that the liberals were all wet."[78] When he was elected to the Senate in 1952, Goldwater initially seemed to be in over his head. His performance was lackluster, and he later confessed to the *Saturday Evening Post* in 1963 that he did not have "a first class brain."[79] Following his reelection in 1958, however, he became the ranking Republican member of the Senate Labor Committee. Its Republican counsel, Mike Bernstein, who often quoted such intellectuals as Hannah Arendt and Joseph Schumpeter, took Goldwater under his wing. A few months after the 1960 election in which John F. Kennedy defeated Richard M. Nixon, Bernstein prepared a position paper suggesting how Goldwater, who had also vied for the nomination in 1960, could try again as neither a stereotypical conservative nor a "me too" moderate but rather as someone who represented forgotten voters in the great middle class.

The "forgotten Americans" became a key element in Goldwater's conservative manifesto, *The Conscience of a Conservative* (1960). The book quickly became a best-seller, having sold 3.5 million copies by the time of Goldwater's nomination in 1964. Its theme offered the central strategy for conservatives seeking public office.[80] Conservative youth groups discovered in his "principles of conservatism" a rejection of the Eisenhower legacy of coexistence and compromise with liberalism – the first statement of conservative political belief around which they could rally. Conservatives found themselves heavily divided over Richard Nixon in 1960. Despite his strong anticommunism, Nixon left many of the new conservative activists underwhelmed by his association with New York Governor Nelson Rockefeller and his selection of Henry Cabot Lodge, the very epitome of Eastern liberal Republicanism, as his vice presidential candidate in his race against Kennedy.[81]

Earlier, in December 1959, Buckley's *National Review* sponsored a debate on the question "Nixon or Not?" Toledano took the affirmative position, arguing that turning Nixon aside would only give comfort to liberals. Nixon was, at least, a strong anticommunist.[82] Meyer, however, urged the young student activists not to waste their energies on Nixon and traditional politics but to build a significant conservative challenge.[83] In our era, Meyer declared, in a manner Jewish neoconservatives would adopt later, "a revolutionary force" had shattered "the unity and balance of civilization." Conservatism should not be limited to an uncomplicated reverence for the past, which is the essence of natural conservatism. The conscious conservative, he proclaimed, was required to become, in a nonpejorative sense, an ideologue, with a clear understanding of how principles and institutions and men affect each other to form a culture and a society.[84]

When, early in 1963, Buckley told Meyer that Goldwater was "perhaps not... our man, Meyer shot back, "[T]he only firm reponse I can make is: he's the only man we've got. I think it is vital to find a center around which to consolidate political conservatism." He also thought Goldwater had a chance to win and was convinced that a quiet conservative majority existed in the land, particularly from a voting perspective, in certain key regions. Meyer was right. He was just twenty years too early.[85]

Liebman took charge of the New York operation to draft Goldwater for the Republican nomination. He launched a statewide fund-raising effort utilizing Eddie Rickenbacker, a World War I hero and former chairman of Eastern Airlines. On May 12, 1964, a rally choreographed by Liebman before a sellout crowd at Madison Square Garden "gave final credibility" to the draft campaign.[86] Although few Jews were involved in Goldwater's run for the presidency in 1964, his Jewish "brain trust" included Liebman, Milton Friedman, Frank Meyer, Charles Lichtenstein, and Harry V. Jaffa, a Straussian scholar at Claremont Men's College in California. Ayn Rand was also an ardent and public supporter. Jaffa helped to write the most famous speech of the 1964 campaign, Goldwater's "take no prisoners" exhortation in accepting the GOP nomination at the Cow Palace in San Francisco, after turning back the GOP's liberal wing headed by Rockefeller and Governor William Scranton of Pennsylvania. "I would remind you," Goldwater said in its most familiar passage, "that extremism in the defense of liberty is no vice. And let me remind you also that moderation in the pursuit of justice is no virtue."[87]

Although Goldwater was soundly defeated by President Lyndon B. Johnson, conservatives found reason for hope in the rubble of the Democratic landslide. Goldwater had gained nearly 40 percent of the vote. His strength was centered in the South, where he won five states, and the Middle West, forging a new Republican base. He proved to be the catalyst for a movement that would take the country by storm less than two decades later.[88] In October alone, 2,500 new members joined YAF; after the 1964 campaign, five chapters were chartered in one day. Following the election, the American Conservative Union was founded as a "graduate YAF."[89] In New York, the Conservative Party, founded in 1961, grew even larger, and Meyer was intimately involved in its activities. Two years after Goldwater's defeat, the Conservative Party surpassed the Liberal Party to become the third largest party in New York state. A few years later, it supported Buckley's brother James, a Republican, in his successful race for the U.S. Senate.

The Goldwater campaign had another unforeseen consequence. It led directly to the creation of a new technique of direct mail solicitation, which revolutionized campaign finance for all parties, although at this time it gave greater influence to a small group of people on the right, led by the former YAF executive director (and Liebman protégé) Richard Viguerie and others who shared his beliefs.[90] In the early 1960s, Liebman had kept the names of contributors on three-by-five cards. In September 1965, he turned over to Viguerie all the direct mail responsibilities of the American Conservative Union, which Liebman had helped to establish. Viguerie began using card files and then computers to send letters to prospects, "who because of their previous contributions to conservative candidates or organizations, were likely contributors to the conservative cause." The mailing list accumulated during the Goldwater campaign became the foundation of all subsequent organized political activity on the part of American conservatives.[91]

In retrospect, one can see that Goldwater's race in 1964 helped to transform conservatism from a small, largely intellectual phenomenon into a significant grassroots movement. Near the end of that campaign, a retired movie actor delivered a televised speech for Goldwater that was more impressive than any given by the candidate himself. Two years later the former actor, Ronald Reagan, was elected governor of California.

6

The Liberal Meltdown

Few decades in American history have been as tense, tumultuous, and troubling as the 1960s. In this brief span, the nation's social fabric was torn apart by three assassinations of major national leaders, widespread racial disorder, numerous student rebellions, a disastrous ground war in Asia, and government duplicity on such a scale that Americans began to distrust their leaders. It appeared for a time that the center might not hold.

Although a civil insurrection was avoided, the 1960s left their mark on the country's psyche and took their toll on the dominant political party. Except for Eisenhower's two terms as president, liberal Democrats had ruled the land from the depths of the Great Depression in 1932 through 1968. In addition to enacting such progressive legislation as Social Security, Medicare, and Medicaid and successfully prosecuting World War II, liberals gained crucially important civil rights for Southern blacks, who had been denied them since Reconstruction. It was a stunning achievement.

Yet the shattering events of the 1960s began the meltdown from which liberalism and the Democratic Party have never fully recovered. The formulas for change embodied in the New Deal, the Fair Deal, and the Great Society had not reached down deeply enough into the smoldering ghettoes. Malcolm X, perhaps the most prominent of a new class of black militants, warned in January 1964 that the "streets are going to run with blood." Between 1964 and 1968, there were 329 riots in 257 cities, climaxed by death and destruction in the Watts section of Los Angeles in April 1968 following the murder of Martin Luther King.[1] King's assassination was followed by that of Democratic presidential candidate Robert F. Kennedy. In the summer of 1968, the Democratic National Convention in Chicago was disrupted by protests against U.S. fighting in Vietnam. Mayor Richard Daley's club-swinging, steel-helmeted police broke up the disturbances but were nationally criticized for overreacting. During the 1970 fall semester, bombings took place at a number of institutions; classes at Rutgers University in New Jersey, for example, had to be vacated dozens of times because of such threats.

In the 1950s, Lionel Trilling had warned of the rise of an adversary culture, a culture in revolt against the ordinary norms of the society; but by this time, the adversary culture had reached a point that even Trilling could hardly have foreseen.

Although urban rioting had subsided by 1969, the threat of disorder persisted. A new class of black activists arose. Such figures as Stokely Carmichael and H. Rap Brown did not identify with King's integration efforts. Denouncing the civil rights gains of the 1950s and 1960s as too little and too late, they called for black control of the schools, businesses, and other institutions in their neighborhoods. As journalist Brent Staples reported, television cameras trained on "scowling Black Panthers who spoiled for battles and called for 'offing the pigs.' ... The Panthers were supranormal men, walking versions of the cities on fire, tumescence on two feet. They shouted 'motherfucker' in mixed company."[2]

The new militants were, in fact, revolutionaries. African-American extremists joined white allies in an assault on the most basic institutions of the society. "The New Left of the late 60s," John B. Judis notes, "dreamed not of America's salvation but of its destruction." When the radical Weathermen took over SDS in 1969, it changed the name of SDS's newspaper, *New Left Notes*, to *Fire*. "The new revolutionaries steeled themselves for a life of sacrifice and eventually death in the service of world revolution. Huey Newton, the co-founder of the Panther Party, described its program as 'revolutionary suicide.'"[3]

The radicals identified themselves with the efforts of people of color around the world to overthrow colonial rule and seize power. In this superheated atmosphere, Israel came to be seen as an outpost of Western imperialism in the Middle East. American Jews were perceived as part of the oppressive white power structure – merchants and landlords exploiting poor inner-city blacks.

For Jews, this was both sad and ironic. Persecuted through the centuries themselves, they felt a special affinity for society's outcasts. Through much of the 1900s, Jewish leaders had worked to secure equal rights for African-Americans. Joel Spingarn, for instance, was instrumental in the founding and early work of the NAACP; Louis Marshall, the second national president of the American Jewish Committee, served as the NAACP's unpaid counsel before it assembled its own legal staff; Samuel Liebowitz, a New York lawyer, led the successful acquittal of nine black youths falsely accused of raping two white women in Scottsboro, Alabama, in 1931.

In the 1960s, liberals like Allard Lowenstein and Edward I. Koch were among the disproportionately represented Jews who marched with Martin Luther King. Two Jewish youths, Andrew Goodman and Michael Schwerner, who came to Philadelphia, Mississippi, to fight for black voter registration, were murdered, along with a young black activist, James Chaney, by Klansmen during the Mississippi Freedom Summer of 1964.

Moreover, Jews often found themselves victims of the racial disorder that swept through urban America in the 1960s. Much of the destruction centered on Jewish-owned businesses and rental units in the ghettoes. As a staff member of the American Jewish Committee in Philadelphia, Pennsylvania, in 1968, I opened a file on incidents involving Jewish merchants. In the following four years, I found that twenty-two Jewish businessmen had been killed in robberies and twenty-seven shot or severely beaten. At one point, I visited a Jewish grocer and his wife in the southwest section of the city. They told me of their fears, of their being subjected to continual harassment. A few days later, the newspapers reported that robbers had murdered the grocer.[4]

This tense period of American history contributed to a deepening sense of anxiety among Jews concerning their very Jewishness. Simultaneously, events in Israel led to a change in the attitudes of many American Jews of various political persuasions. The Six Day War in June 1967 and the Yom Kippur War in 1973 awakened fears of a new Holocaust, even though Israel decisively defeated its foes in both conflicts. In 1968, Meir Kahane, a Brooklyn rabbi, founded the Jewish Defense League (JDL), whose aim was to defend Jews with "all necessary means," including the use of violence. Although most Jews rejected the JDL's extremism, its slogan, "Never again," struck a responsive chord. Many Jews concluded that they could no longer remain passive when Jewish lives or rights were threatened. Milton Himmelfarb, the AJC's research director, observed in *Commentary* in October 1967 that Jews "were now reconsidering who were their friends and enemies. They were becoming as suspicious of the left as of the right; they had more faith in states and armies and less trust in talk and diplomacy. Jews were becoming if not quite conservative, at least 'Whiggish.'"[5]

The Vietnam War was the final blow to the liberal consensus. Since the end of World War II, liberals had for the most part stood firm against international communism and Soviet imperialism, and they had strongly supported Cold War initiatives. The electorate backed their candidates and their policies. But as the body bags came home from Southeast Asia and antiwar protests exploded on campuses and elsewhere, the nation's mood changed. Americans lost their taste for combat. Many grew angry, frustrated, and disillusioned by the tragic waste of lives and resources and by official lies concerning the outcome of the conflict. Under Democratic administrations and Republican ones, the government kept promising victory, when the inevitable outcome was defeat. The deceptions of Lyndon B. Johnson's administration followed by Richard M. Nixon's Watergate cover-up caused the American people to lose confidence in their leaders. Many came to believe that government, by its very nature, could no longer be trusted.[6]

Nonetheless, as conservative political scientist James Q. Wilson points out, there was much that was positive and right in the protests of the 1960s.

This was true especially for those young people who put their lives on the line to challenge segregation and voting rights restrictions against African-Americans in the South. The widespread materialism that so many enjoyed, even as they protested against it, was unnerving to youthful idealism. It is still not clear how some of the 1960s "peaceniks" came to ally themselves with terrorists (including the Weathermen), murderous gangs (like the Black Liberation Army) and hit squads (like the Huey Newton faction of the Black Panthers). Ex-radical Peter Collier would later call it "an Oedipal revolt on a grand scale; a no fault acting out ... whose mischief turned homicidal somewhere along the way."[7]

Of course, denouncing government was hardly new. What was most devastating in the 1960s, however, was the abject surrender of many in this country's leadership classes, including important elements of the intellectual and cultural elite, to the new revolutionaries. Aristotle and Tocqueville had taught "that when the fundamental principles guiding a society cease to be observed and defended by these classes, revolution takes place."[8] Fearing social disruption, many within the country's political and cultural elite – social activists and scholar/policy specialists especially – came to argue that disrupting the complacency and indifference to the excluded in society was necessary in order to bring about social progress. In a Foreword to a pamphlet that I commissioned for the AJC on racial disorders in Philadelphia (and on which I look back with some embarrassment), Dean Alex Rosen of the New York University School of Social Work wrote, "Behavior, even shocking, seemingly pathological behavior, has meaning." Scholars and social scientists, he declared, were beginning to view such inner city violence "as a form of inarticulate language in which one group communicates with other significant groups about its feelings, its problems, its life circumstances, its desperation."[9] In the same vein, scholar/activists Frances Fox Piven and Richard Cloward argued, "Rent strikes, growing crime, [and] civic disruptions" are "the politics of the poor."[10]

In its 1968 report on the nation's civil disorders, the commission headed by Governor Otto Kerner of Illinois focused on white racism as the underlying cause of the disorders. "What white Americans have never fully understood – but the Negro can never forget – is that white society is deeply implicated in the ghetto," said *New York Times* columnist Tom Wicker in his Introduction to the report. "White institutions created it, white institutions maintain it, and white society condones it." The report, in effect, absolved rioters for destroying their own poor neighborhoods and implied that blame should be placed elsewhere.[11]

The Kerner Commission report drew heavy fire from conservatives. Frank Meyer, writing in *National Review* on March 26, 1968, blasted it as "one of the most preposterous ebullitions of the liberal spirit ever seriously submitted to the public." It put the blame everywhere except "upon the rioters and upon liberals who, with their abstract ideology, prepared the way for the riots by their contempt for social order and their utopian egalitarian enticement and incitements."[12]

In Detroit, well-meaning business executives formed a committee in 1967 that actually funded street fighters, Tamar Jacoby reports in *Someone Else's House: America's Unfinished Struggle for Integration* (1998). One gang leader, who wrote newsletters calling for the murder of police officers, received $250,000. Very little of the $10 million that the committee spent helped common people; most of it went for barely disguised "riot insurance." When Coleman Young, a tough union radical, became mayor of the city in 1974, he made police reform the first order of business. Reform *was* necessary, and Young made some useful changes; but crime shot up, and whites fled the city. Weakened by economic changes and out-migration, Detroit literally fell apart.[13]

The New Deal and early Great Society programs viewed poverty as a temporary condition that could be corrected with government assistance, so long as the poor were honest and industrious. A new thought emerged in the 1960s that poured cold water on that premise. In *The Poorhouse State* (1966), Richard Elman mocked the traditional virtues of self-discipline, modesty, and hard work. He called instead for greater dependency: "We of the rising middle classes must somehow dispel our own myth that we are not dependent. We must try to create even more agencies of dependency, and we must make it possible for all to make use of them equally."[14]

In an article in *The Nation*, Piven and Cloward went a step further. They recommended that American cities be plunged into "a profound financial and political crisis" as a result of "a massive drive to recruit the poor onto the [welfare] rolls." They called for "bureaucratic disruption in welfare agencies" as well as "cadres of aggressive organizers" and "demonstrations to create a climate of militancy." If local officials did not respond adequately, they might face more rioting. And government, caught in such a bind, would provide a guaranteed income, thus putting an end to poverty in the United States.

The article, which created a sensation in left-wing circles, generated requests for 30,000 reprints and led to the formation of the National Welfare Rights Organization (NWRO).[15] George Wiley, the first head of the NWRO, remarked that the genius of the Piven and Cloward approach was that "generosity now would reduce dependency later." A new brand of antipoverty law, pressed forward by antipoverty advocates, lawyers, and social activists, soon took shape and was ultimately sanctioned by the courts. It sought to establish nothing less than a special, subsidized existence for the poor.[16]

Looking back twenty years later, *New York Times Magazine* writer Jason De Parle argues that "the bureaucracy's first response was to open up the tap. Under Mayor John V. Lindsay, New York reduced its [welfare] application to a single page of self-declared need. Its Welfare Commissioner became known to detractors as Mitchell (Come and Get It) Ginsberg."[17]

The nation's welfare population expanded astronomically. Between 1945 and 1960, it had grown by only 47,000 in New York City. Between 1960 and 1965, it increased by more than 200,000 to 538,000. After that, despite a record economic boom, New York's welfare population exploded. In 1971, the city counted an extraordinary 1,165,000 cases. Similar expansions were experienced in Illinois, California, Pennsylvania, and Ohio. By 1994, 5.1 million families were receiving welfare checks. That accounted for 15 percent of American families with children.[18]

What stood behind the welfare revolution, wrote Fred Siegel,

> was a new conception of liberalism that would play itself out in a variety of areas, from the idea of victimless crimes to the rights of the homeless, but that first appeared in connection with welfare. Dependent individualism yoked together the ACLU's conception of an absolute right to privacy and the life style of one's choosing (regardless of the social cost) with an equally fundamental right to be supported at state expense.[19]

Fresh from his role as assistant secretary of labor under Presidents Kennedy and Johnson, and now director of the Harvard–MIT Joint Center for Urban Studies, Daniel Patrick Moynihan wrote in *Commentary* that the "conceptual difficulties" of the War on Poverty was a result of "the work of intellectuals." He singled out those liberal, policy-oriented intellectuals who gathered in Washington and came to power in the early 1960s and who propounded a fairly radical critique of American society. "It was not, after all, just by chance that a large scale program to provide employment for adult men – a traditional anti-poverty measure – was left out of the poverty program, while the quite unprecedented community action programs were left in, and indeed came to be the center of the effort." The result "was to raise the level of perceived and validated discontent among poor persons with the social system ... without improving the condition of life of the poor." Was it conceivable "that this had *nothing* to do with the onset of urban violence?" Moynihan asked.[20]

The most striking example of the capitulation to the new radicalism occurred in New York under Republican Mayor John Lindsay, the liberal Republican chief executive. A former congressman from Manhattan's "silk-stocking" district and vice chair of the Kerner Commission, Lindsay took credit for keeping the lid on during the racially troubling summers in the 1960s. But as Vincent J. Cannato reports in *The Ungovernable City: John Lindsay and His Struggle to Save New York* (2000), there were smaller-scale disturbances, dismissed as minor, on his watch in various parts of the city. Murders increased by 137 percent in the Lindsay years, and his administration was accused of being soft on crime, the latter charge leveled with good reason at August Heckscher, his parks commissioner. Heckscher claimed to have found "an element of truth" in the argument that vandalism was simply one way of using the city's parks. Lindsay sought to effect an alliance with the new protest movement. "Our experience is that some good can come of confrontation politics," a spokesman for his administration said.[21]

Near the close of his first term as mayor, Lindsay teamed up with McGeorge Bundy, a former national security adviser, in a remarkable attempt to improve New York's woeful public schools through an unusual alliance with some of the new black activists. Slender, with sandy hair and pink cheeks, Bundy reflected, as did Lindsay, an upper-class expectation that he was destined to lead. In retrospect, however, one can see that both WASPs were in over their heads.[22]

Born into New England privilege and schooled at Groton and Yale, Bundy served as a Harvard professor and dean before becoming President Kennedy's national security advisor, where he fitted in neatly with the administration's "Camelot style." As president of the Ford Foundation, Bundy presided over major funding for programs involving social improvement. He was drawn to the idea of giving residents in some of New York's black neighborhoods greater say in the governance of their schools through what came to be called "community control."

The concept of community control or "power to the people," as it was termed in the 1960s, had originated with Preston Wilcox, an adjunct professor at the Columbia University School of Social Work, and the black community activist called Malcolm X. They believed that since blacks lived in a segregated world, they should take control of that world. Stokely Carmichael (later known as Kwame Toure) carried the concept further in his book *Black Power* (1967), written with the political scientist Charles Hamilton. Carmichael argued that control of ghetto schools "must be taken out of the hands of 'professionals,' most of whom . . . had long since demonstrated their insensitivity to the needs and problems of the black child." He and his followers saw "community control," not only of schools but also of police departments and hospitals, as a means of separating African-Americans from white society and giving them full control of their lives. That's not what Bundy and Lindsay had in mind. They viewed such efforts as interim steps toward full inclusion of blacks into, rather than their separation from, the broader society.[23]

Facing a tough reelection campaign, Lindsay mobilized black activists against the remnants of the old liberal and white ethnic machine. His welfare department head said it was a chance "to put black militants on the community action payroll and use them as a battering ram." Liberal foundations including the Ford, Taconic, and New World Foundations considered it an opportunity to create a political alliance of the top and the bottom against the middle, according to Cooper Union history professor Fred Siegel.

After narrowly winning a second term in a multicandidate race, Lindsay began the educational experiment in Brooklyn's Ocean Hill–Brownsville section. Initially, it appealed to the Jewish-dominated United Federation of Teachers and its longtime leader, Albert Shanker. But no one had foreseen the program's inherent radicalism. What the Ocean Hill–Brownsville leaders wanted was publicly financed black-nationalist schools on the order of those advocated by black nationalist Marcus Garvey in the twenties.[24]

In line with this ideology, the residents' planning council, in consultation with Ford officials, appointed an African-American, Rhody McCoy, as school superintendent. McCoy, a follower of Malcolm X, proceeded to fire nineteen teachers and supervisors, most of whom were Jewish. McCoy accused them of being uncooperative. He also encouraged "community activists" in the use of race-baiting tactics against both whites and blacks.

Shanker, a labor leader with one of the strongest records of civil rights activism in the country, blamed Bundy for the experiment that had gone awry. He believed the Boston Brahmin actually wanted to destroy public education.[25] Infuriated by the firings, Shanker proceeded to shut down New York City's entire public school system in a series of strikes in 1967 and 1968. The turmoil that followed was devastating. One black activist attacked Jews directly at the African-American Teachers Forum. He declared that Jewish schoolteachers had "educationally castrated" black pupils and taken part in "horrendous abuse of the [black] family, associates and culture."[26]

Lindsay had little knowledge or understanding of what was going on in the neighborhoods. Bundy was similarly uninformed, but he remained unfazed. "The idea is to do things society is going to want after it has them," he declared, shortly after taking over the reins at the Ford Foundation.[27]

The experiment a failure, the Ocean Hill–Brownsville school board was suspended. For some African-Americans, the episode may have represented an assertion of their right to control their own destiny, but for an important segment of the Jewish intelligentsia (the soon-to-be-called neoconservatives), along with many middle-class Jews and white ethnic Roman Catholics, it signaled the collapse of the liberal coalition in which they had been joined together since the early days of the New Deal. "Outer-borough Jews and white Catholics," an historian of the Ocean Hill–Brownsville confrontation writes, "began to forge a race-based alliance that would shift the electoral politics of the city rightward."[28]

In 2002, some thirty-three years later, the idea of school decentralization or community control was finally scrapped. The New York state legislature gave former businessman and Mayor Michael R. Bloomberg, a Republican, control of the school bureaucracy. He began a process of abolishing the local school boards in thirty-two New York City communities. This time, the black and Hispanic neighborhoods that had earlier pushed for decentralization were ready to forsake the idea, but by now, many middle-class whites had moved to religious and private schools or to the suburbs.[29]

As a result, the gulf between blacks and Jews widened. Any incident could unleash citywide charges and recrimination. A nasty episode at the Metropolitan Museum of Art made matters worse. "Harlem on My Mind," which opened in January 1969, was the largest exhibit ever mounted by the

Met. In describing frictions that had developed between blacks and Jews, the black woman who wrote the catalogue declared that "behind every hurdle that the Afro-American has to jump stands the Jew who has already cleared it." She said that their contempt for Jews made blacks feel more completely American in sharing a national prejudice. Although the catalogue drew widespread criticism, Thomas Hoving, the museum's patrician director, stood by it. "Her statements are true," he said. "So be it." He later acknowledged that he had been indiscreet, but the publication was not withdrawn.

The collapse of important sectors of the country's leadership class could also be seen in their response to the Cold War. Following victory in World War II, the foreign policy establishment stood at the height of its power and influence. President Truman's key advisers (dubbed "the wise men" by Walter Isaacson and Evan Thomas in their book of that name) included Clark Clifford, John McCloy, George Kennan, Robert McNamara, McGeorge Bundy and his brother, Bill, as well as Secretary of State Dean Acheson. Kennan had been a key figure in helping to launch the Cold War with his famous "long telegram" to the State Department in 1947, warning of Soviet intentions and the need to combat them.

The "wise men" believed they had learned the lessons of the pre-war period: appeasement of tyrants was a sure way of courting disaster. They addressed Soviet aggressive designs in the world by creating, as Acheson put it, "situations of strength."[30] They had a firm sense of direction and the character to follow through on their designs. Acheson helped to convince Truman to abandon Roosevelt's policy of cooperation with the Soviet Union and adopt one of containment, according to Richard Gid Powers.[31] Clifford, who believed that military power was the only language the Russians understood, wrote legislation in 1947 establishing the CIA. He was also one of the architects of the Truman Doctrine, which sought to protect Greece from a potential communist takeover.[32]

In the early stages of the Vietnam War, the "wise men" supported American involvement. They believed in standing firm against the spread of communism. McNamara, who was secretary of defense when the fighting escalated, did not object to its being labeled "McNamara's war" in 1964. It was an important conflict, he said, and he was happy to be identified with it. Liberal opinion makers also backed the fighting. At the start of America's defense of South Vietnam in 1961, the *New York Times* editorialized that every effort should be made to save the situation. Four years later, with this nation deeply committed, the *Times* declared that the motives of the war were "exemplary" and that every American "can be proud of them...." Later that year, it added, "and virtually all Americans understand that we must stay in South Vietnam for the near future."[33]

As the war dragged on and casualties piled up, the *Times* changed its tune. Earlier, it had deplored "precipitate withdrawal" as the advice of only "a few pacifists here and the North Vietnamese and Chinese Communists." By the early 1970s, it was calling for such a withdrawal.

Meanwhile, the erstwhile "wise men" turned against the combat they had once favored. They turned not only against the war they had helped to create and maintain but also against one another. In his memoirs, McNamara declared that he and his colleagues had been terribly wrong. At one point, McNamara even contemplated suicide. Clifford admitted that he "was part of a generation that I hold responsible for our country's getting into the war." He said he "should have reached the conclusion earlier that our participation in that war was a dead end." Clifford succeeded McNamara at the Pentagon in 1968 and employed his considerable powers of persuasion and knowledge of the levers of power in Washington to keep President Johnson from escalating the war further. Out of government, he worked to end the arms race.[34] Anticommunism, including the earlier role of the foreign policy elite in attempting to overcome the aggressive designs of the Soviets in the world, came to be seen as the catalyst of the entire Vietnam fiasco.

As long as Johnson was president, most of the "wise men" in his administration did not challenge him, or complained only mildly. But with Johnson's decision not to run and Richard Nixon's election as president in 1968, some of these same "wise men" became openly and sharply critical not only of the nation's involvement in Vietnam, but of anticommunism itself. Many of them, in fact, embarked upon an effort to convince their countrymen that this country's role in the Cold War had been a dreadful mistake from the very beginning.

Kennan was among the first to oppose the strategy he had done so much to formulate. He was turned off, he said, by what he declared was the militarization of containment. Testifying before Senator Fulbright's Foreign Relations Committee in 1966, he intimated that his original proposals had been misapplied and misunderstood. He denounced Radio Liberty and Radio Free Europe as "outworn relics of the Cold War."[35]

Privately, Kennan went a bit further. Reflecting his growing dislike for American politics and the vulgarization of American culture, he dismissed the idea that there were any moral differences between the Soviets and the United States. He said the Soviets perhaps performed better in handling their affairs.[36]

This was a far cry from his historic 1947 memorandum, in which he had written,

> The thoughtful observer of Russian-American relations will find no cause for complaint in the Kremlin's challenge to American society. He will rather experience a certain gratitude for a Providence which, by providing the American people with this implacable challenge, has made their entire security as a nation dependent on their pulling themselves together and accepting the responsibilities of moral and political leadership that history plainly intended them to bear.[37]

The Bundy brothers joined Kennan, Clifford, and other former Cold Warriors in speaking out against the nation's national defense and foreign policies. McGeorge Bundy helped to create the "Gang of Four," a group of distinguished former government officials (Bundy, McNamara, Kennan, and Herbert Scoville) who spoke out against American nuclear policies. Bundy wrote *Danger and Survival: Choices about the Bomb in the First Fifty Years* (1988), but his most important effort was an article in *Foreign Affairs* in 1983 calling for an end to the U.S. policy of first use of nuclear weapons to stop a Soviet invasion of Europe.

In the Senate, J. William Fulbright led the attack on what he termed American arrogance of power. As early as 1965, he had grown suspicious of anticommunism as a guide to foreign policy. In a speech in June 1965, the influential senator saw the terror of Stalin's time as having largely disappeared: "As it becomes clear to each side that it is safe and profitable to do so, ideological barriers can be expected to gradually erode away.... Communists have unalterable bonds of humanity with all other men and these bonds of humanity can be the instrument of change." In 1972, he declared that Radio Free Europe, which had been beaming radio signals into the Soviet bloc since the 1950s to challenge the information its peoples were receiving, "should take [its] rightful place in the graveyard of cold war relics."[38]

Fulbright rejected the very idea of "victory over Communism" and warned against "setting up a savage dichotomy between the Communist and Western world," one "true and good[,] the other unalterably evil."[39] In reality, the situation presented just such a dichotomy, and when Ronald Reagan called the Soviets an evil empire in the 1980s, he struck a chord with the neoconservatives. The latter were also opposed to the war in Vietnam, which they felt to be the wrong war in the wrong place at the wrong time, but as Robert Kagan points out, they refused to become "quasi-isolationists."[40]

The Cold War was fought with words as well as military power. In this battle, the country's cultural elite – scholars, historians, filmmakers, novelists, historians, and journalists – were as influential as government officials in shaping the nation's attitudes. In the late 1960s and 1970s, a revisionist view of the origins and nature of the Cold War took shape. David Halberstam's Pulitzer Prize–winning book *The Best and the Brightest* (1972) put forth a view that came to dominate liberal thinking. As Kagan summarizes Halberstam, the Cold War was "part mistake, part right-wing conspiracy, and part creation of the capitalist class." It did not involve "a conflict of principles – American democracy versus Soviet communism – and it had little to do with Soviet expansionism." Halberstam wrote, "Two great and uncertain powers were coming to terms with each other, a task made more difficult by their ideological differences (each believed its own myth about itself and it adversary)." He said they were "like two blind dinosaurs wrestling in a very small pit. Each thought its own policies basically defensive and the policies of its adversary basically aggressive."[41]

Halberstam's portrayal of the origins and nature of the Cold War was carried much further by revisionist historians William Appleman Williams and Gerald Kolko. They blamed the Cold War on Truman's belligerence and saw it as a manifestation of imperialist America's and capitalism's bid for global hegemony, utilizing its atomic monopoly.[42] On college campuses, an adversary culture ridiculed virtually every aspect of a bourgeois society. In English literature, the Western canon composed of "dead white European males" went out of fashion. Sociology departments came to be dominated by devotees of the New Left, while philosophy departments championed Michael Foucault's theory of relativistic deconstructionism. The intellectual underpinnings of the New Left emerged through the magazine *Studies on the Left*, which served as a spur in the founding of SDS, historian Ronald Radosh notes.[43]

Revisionists acquitted the Soviet Union of any responsibility for the Cold War. While denouncing the United States, some romanticized this country's enemies – the Vietcong, the Cubans, and fighters for Third World liberation across the globe. Student radical leader Abbie Hoffman proclaimed in a letter to his brother in 1970, "All America is a prison. The President is a warden and the people are all inmates."[44] Hoffman's erratic behavior made him an unreliable social critic, but Susan Sontag, who burst onto the literary scene in the mid-1960s, provided a degree of respectability to the new sensibility. Although claiming Lionel Trilling as a major influence, Sontag cast aside his realism and openly sided with communist North Vietnam. In her long essay "Trip to Hanoi" (1968), she wrote that North Vietnam "deserve[d] to be idealized," a conclusion she came to at about the same time she found the "white race" to be nothing less than "the cancer of human history."[45]

Along with other icons of the contemporary culture, including Hollywood actress Jane Fonda, who traveled to North Vietnam during Christmas 1972, and writer Mary McCarthy, Sontag hoped America would lose in Vietnam. She declared that the United States had become a "criminal sinister country," possessed by the "monstrous conceit that it was empowered to dispose of the destiny of the world." She also glorified the Cuban revolution. Cubans, she reported, possessed a "southern spontaneity" that "our own too white, death-ridden culture denies us." Following her visit to Vietnam in 1969, short story writer Grace Paley, a prominent member of the literary association PEN and a recipient of a number of literary prizes, spoke of how well American prisoners of war were being treated there.[46]

Poet Robert Lowell contributed prestige and sincerity to demonstrations against the war in Vietnam; Leonard Bernstein arranged his famous chic reception at his home for Black Panthers; and Norman Mailer, locating self-realization in fantasies of violence, provided literary coverage, Irving Howe noted, for the most extreme elements of the counterculture. Even Martin Luther King, Jr., in moving beyond his civil rights agenda to include opposition to the Vietnam War in his social program, found Americans to be "glutted by our own barbarity."[47]

Popular novels like Graham Greene's *The Quiet American* (1955), John Le Carré's *The Spy Who Came in from the Cold* (1965), Joseph Heller's brilliant comic World War II novel *Catch-22* (1961), along with Stanley Kubrick's witty movie *Dr. Strangelove* (1964) and the film *Seven Days in May* (1965), based on a best-seller, drove home a message of America's moral bankruptcy. Le Carré's spy story suggested that both sides in the Cold War were equally flawed. Heller's novel mocked patriotism, big business, and loyalty (one character signs hundred of loyalty tests a day just so he can prove to be more loyal than anyone else). World War II became a metaphor for Vietnam as well as a subtle attack on this country's role in the Cold War. In *Dr. Strangelove*, Kubrick depicts a psychotic general named Jack D. Ripper, who dispatches on his own initiative a nuclear strike on the Soviet Union.

It was not that these artists and writers were pro-communist or pro-Soviet (Kubrick, too, in portraying the Soviets as demented, demonstrated the sort of ideological parity these artists and writers seemed to be striving after), but their work, which was funny and at times brilliant, blurred any difference between the East and the West and seemed to question the necessity of bringing down the Soviet Union. This perspective is still evident in some of the historiography of the Cold War. In his *Culture of the Cold War* (1991), from which a number of the above illustrations are drawn, historian Stephen J. Whitfield argues that while the Soviet Union remained a dangerous and thoroughly undemocratic foe, "it became de-totalitarianized around 1956 with the repudiation of some of Stalin's excesses." Its leaders became "less demonic," he writes. "The culture of the Cold War decomposed when the moral distinction between East and West lost a bit of its sharpness, when American self-righteousness could be more readily punctured, when the activities of the two super powers assumed greater symmetry."[48] Of course, this view was lost on the citizens living behind the Iron Curtain, who rose in the late 1980s to throw off once and for all the yoke of this presumably more benign Soviet communism that had evolved.[49]

The most important journal that mirrored these radical currents was the *New York Review of Books*, founded in 1963 and modeled after the London *Times Literary Supplement*. Its stable of writers was drawn mainly from the New York intelligentsia, including Hannah Arendt, W. H. Auden, F. W. Dupee, Ralph Ellison, Mary McCarthy, Robert Penn Warren, and Edmund Wilson. In its early years it also published such premature neoconservatives as Bell, Decter, Gertrude Himmelfarb, and Podhoretz. As the Vietnam War intensified, however, the *New York Review* shifted to an explicitly radical critique of American society.

In its February 23, 1967, issue, Noam Chomsky, the linguist-turned-leftist social critic, unleashed a harsh attack on anticommunist intellectuals like Bell, Kristol, Walter Rostow, and Arthur Schlesinger for getting the nation into Vietnam. He called them death camp paymasters. Several months later, in the April 20 issue, Jason Epstein, in an essay called "The CIA and the Intellectuals," attacked liberal anticommunists associated with the Congress for Cultural Freedom for having accepted financial support from the CIA. Epstein suggested that their views about the Soviet Union had obviously been influenced by such payments.

The *New York Review*'s most daring issue, however, was published on August 24, 1967. With racial rioting sweeping American cities, it printed a diagram of a Molotov cocktail, with instructions on how to make one. The issue also carried an article by Andrew Kopkind, in which, he opined, "Morality, like politics, starts at the barrel of a gun." The uproar was such that the editors backed off, claiming that the Molotov cocktail article was "a joke."[50]

For many liberals, the goal was "a new humanity," built around ideas of social justice. But as the rebellion deepened, it sometimes trailed off into violence and decadence. "It must be a really wonderful feeling to kill a pig [murder a policemen] or blow up a building," Columbia student activist Mark Rudd exulted. Militant Jerry Rubin cited another aspect of the 1960s ethos: "Pot is central to the revolution. It weakens social conditions and helps create a whole new state of mind."[51]

Even those on the left who disapproved of the new radicalism (and perhaps most did) were nonetheless reluctant to speak out against it. Irving Howe, who continued to view himself as an outspoken socialist, criticized what he called the rush to celebrate "a radicalism of gesture." In his memoir, he later wrote,

> Some intellectuals were swept away by their outrage over the Vietnam War. A few were excited by the rekindling of old Marxist sentiments they had supposed would never again be put to use. While I felt little admiration for these people, I could at least understand what made them behave as they did. The intellectuals who infuriated me were those who kept their heads sufficiently to scorn the ideological vagaries of the late 1960s and yet, from a wish to stay on good terms with the spirit of the times, assumed an avuncular benevolence toward the New Left.[52]

He and Michael Walzer, his coeditor at *Dissent*, hoped vainly for a "progressive" third force to emerge from the Vietnam tragedy. Since it did not, this small pocket on the left offered only feeble resistance to the liberal meltdown.

Even as some students at elite colleges continued to trash their campuses, influential elders embraced the youth culture. "I believe in trusting the young," the Nobel Prize–winning chemist James D. Watson declared.[53] In the opening sentence of his report as chair of the commission investigating the Columbia student rioting of 1968, Harvard law professor Archibald Cox described contemporary students as "the best informed, the most intelligent," and "the most idealistic" generation "ever born in America." Lionel Trilling sharply disagreed with this assessment. "In his high estimate of the young," Trilling wrote, "Professor Cox accepted the simulacrum for the real thing." "The great store now placed on selfhood and the energies of the self" was triumphing "at the expense of the conceived and executed life," Trilling declared. Once young people had sought to emulate their elders in chosen ways of conduct; now they were following a new ideal of life as unfixed and improvisational.[54] But Trilling himself hesitated to challenge the temper of the times more openly. They could not afford to antagonize the young, he told Gertrude Himmelfarb.[55]

A number of post–World War II cultural Cold Warriors developed second thoughts about what they termed a "paranoid anti-Communism." Arthur Schlesinger, Jr., was among them. As a leader of "vital center liberalism" in the 1950s, he had described the anticommunist crusade as "a just cause" and "the brave and essential response of free men to Communist aggression." Later, however, he rejected identification as a "Cold War liberal." In a 1967 *Commentary* symposium, Liberal Anti-Communism Revisited, Schlesinger declared, "Obsessive anti-Communism blinds its victims to the realities of a changing world." He went on to explain that with the emergence of Red China we were now living in a poly-communist world. The nationalistic feelings of long-submerged peoples were becoming more important. But communism had proven to have little appeal among those people. In arguing this way, Schlesinger ignored the threat of force and totalitarian suppression that the Soviet regime exerted in world affairs, in its own country, and in its satellite empire.[56]

Years later, in reviewing Sidney Hook's memoir, Schlesinger dismissed Hook as one of those people who "are transfixed by the communist issue for all their lives." It was Hook's "obsessive" anticommunism, Schlesinger explained in his own Pulitzer Prize–winning memoirs, that resulted in Hook's move to the right. This led neoconservative critic Hilton Kramer to remark that Schlesinger was "more effective than any of the others in transforming himself from the very archetype of a Cold War liberal into the newer, more stylish, born again model."[57]

The same liberal meltdown that was developing in the United States was making itself felt within intellectual and cultural circles in Western Europe. Raymond Aron, a friend of the fellow traveling Jean Paul Sartre and a cofounder of the left-wing periodical *Les Temps Moderns*, stood up to the challenge created by the dominant left-wing thought surrounding him. Hardly an admirer of the United States, he nonetheless refused to see the world in Manichean terms (i.e., as a confrontation between good and evil), but he understood "that in many circumstances, particularly when democracies face tyrannies, sides had to be chosen and action taken."[58]

In the 1960s and the years that followed, America appeared to have lost its bearings. The Vietnam disaster and the tawdry Watergate affair contributed to the breakdown in the nation's morale. Jimmy Carter would soon speak of a national "malaise," one that lasted well into the Reagan years and beyond. In 1960, three out of every four Americans indicated that they trusted government. By the 1990s, only one in five agreed. "A self confident nation believes it can control its own destiny," conservative columnist David Brooks wrote, shortly after September 11. "It assumes that if it launches an initiative it will be able to complete it, so it is more prone to launch new initiatives. When it starts down a road, it does not allow itself to be paralyzed by the commentators who warn that the path leads to a quagmire."[59]

The neoconservative impulse that Brooks speaks about today with such confidence began to emerge only at this point (it was too inchoate to call it a movement), as a reaction to the liberal meltdown and the loss of confidence of many Americans. A group of primarily liberal Jewish intellectuals now came forward to challenge the despairing spirit of the times, the counterculture, and most especially what they believed to be aggressive Soviet designs in the world. Despite the tragedy of the Vietnam War, they refused to see America as morally bankrupt, and they viewed the Soviet Union as a serious threat that had to be confronted. They opposed the "new morality," with its emphasis on the "sovereign self." As a result, they found themselves questioning many of the beliefs and political attitudes that had previously guided them. In the process, and without setting out to do so, they would lay the foundation for a new model of Jewish conservatism.

7

The Rise of the Neoconservatives

Irving Howe has said that when intellectuals are moved to action, they create a magazine.[1] Irving Kristol is a case in point. He helped to advance the embryonic neoconservative movement in 1965 by founding *The Public Interest*.

At the time, Kristol's social and political views were undergoing change. Although he had known poverty firsthand and was sympathetic to the goals of Lyndon B. Johnson's Great Society, his skepticism of government planning had led him to believe that poverty could be overcome only by gradual economic growth that brought with it greater economic opportunity for outsiders. A disillusioned liberal, he feared that radical dissent had fallen prey to leftist totalitarianism. He shared with traditional conservatives their distaste for the eruptions of the counterculture. Yet he had no faith in the anti–New Deal, anti–Fair Deal conservatism advanced by Barry Goldwater's 1964 campaign. "We are children of the Depression," his wife, Gertrude Himmelfarb, told an interviewer, "and are committed to the New Deal kind of welfare state – by present terms, a very minimal welfare state. Social Security is something we regard as a very good thing."[2]

Kristol considered Bill Buckley's *National Review* "too strident," insufficiently "analytical" and "intellectual." He rejected also *National Review*'s "hostility to the New Deal and its enthusiasm for Jeffersonian individualism."[3] On the other hand, he distrusted what passed for social scientific thought embodied in the poverty programs, and was troubled by what he perceived as the vague, unfocused idealism of left-wing ideologues. Diana Trilling was similarly dismissive. As she put it, "The idealist finds virtue only where he is not – in the country which is not his country, in the class which is not his class."[4]

Kristol found himself increasingly attracted to certain virtues he found in daily American life, especially the pragmatic style and centrist characteristics of its political parties, its social pluralism, and its tolerance, if not encouragement, of experimentalism in the arts. He was no longer prepared to go shopping for new models of social perfection.

As the War on Poverty proceeded, he began to write occasional pieces for *The New Leader* expressing his doubts about government economic planning. He, along with his friends Nathan Glazer and Daniel Patrick Moynihan, thought of themselves as public intellectuals, in contrast with the campus professoriate, some of whom were deeply involved in shaping and carrying out Johnson's War on Poverty. Although intellectuals themselves, the incipient neocons were less ready to rely on social scientific "truth" entrenched in a left-wing ideological framework as a means to bringing about the good society.

Kristol linked the crisis of liberalism, especially among Jews, to Jewish history and the impact of the Enlightenment. The Jewish tradition (and the Christianity that grew out of it), he believed, took two forms that were closely related to the underlying tensions within that tradition. Religious orthodoxy sought the betterment of man through moderate improvements in daily life and within existing institutions. It tended to be stoic and taught that evil could ultimately yield to good, but it accepted as a given the inherent unfairness in life.

In contrast to this view stood the prophetic tradition, sometimes called Gnosticism, which shifted the emphasis away from the inner self and one's spiritual needs to the outer areas of public life, in which moral and social redemption presumably could be found. The prophetic or Gnostic model associated with the liberal/left sought to make man whole by changing the institutional arrangements of society and was best embodied in the French Revolution and some of the radical movements that flowed from it.

The second tradition – the Anglo-Scottish or British Enlightenment – sought incremental change. The first tendency yielded Robespierre and Saint-Simon; the other, James Madison and Adam Smith. For Kristol, the realistic and conservative character of the American Revolution accounted for its success. America's leaders "understood that republican self-government could not exist if humanity did not possess ... the traditional republican virtues of self-control, self reliance, and a disinterested concern for the public good."[5]

Hence, Kristol formed a vision of a magazine that would be objective in its outlook and free of the jargon of both the right and the left. He discussed the idea with Daniel Bell, his friend from City College's alcoves and now a leading sociologist. Bell was heavily analytical. He disliked ideological posturing and political extremism. Although both were strong anticommunists, their styles were different. Kristol's anticommunism was based on a fundamental distrust of what he saw as the left's romanticism; his work was sometimes polemical. Bell was more deliberative in the explication of his ideas.

The two men shared a desire to assist the underprivileged and to encourage those facing discrimination, but they were becoming doubtful of government-mandated solutions. They wanted better jobs, education, and housing for African-Americans, but they did not feel that this required racial disorder or black nationalist formulas for change. "Opposition to scattered-site housing and to pushing aside privileges, won at great effort through past struggles, should not be interpreted as the opposition by racists," Kristol wrote. Bell, too, was troubled by what he considered the faulty research and foolish conclusions of social scientists, whose findings were often cited in support of liberal programs. He once told an interviewer that he and Kristol both encountered difficulty finding publishers for their "relatively skeptical, anti-utopian writings."[6]

The two men discussed the idea for a nonideological magazine that would encourage solidly based research and that could be used by policy makers and like-minded intellectuals. The journal's financial backers, Warren and Anita Manshel, Martin Segal, and Harry Kahn, were Jewish, but later several conservative foundations would pick up the costs of the publication.

The first issue of *The Public Interest* came out in the fall of 1965, edited by Kristol with the aid of a secretary. (Kristol was shortly joined by Bell; although Glazer eventually replaced Bell, Kristol basically ran the magazine.) The quarterly took its title from an observation of columnist Walter Lippmann: "The public interest may be presumed to be what men would choose if they saw clearly, thought rationally, acted disinterestedly and benevolently."[7]

Among the "disillusioned liberals" whom Kristol persuaded to write for him was Daniel Patrick Moynihan. As assistant secretary of labor in the Johnson administration, Moynihan had written a paper early in 1965, "The Negro Family: The Case for National Action," in which he had warned that the disintegration of black families had reached a point of "social pathology." In support of his argument, Moynihan cited alarming rates of black unemployment, welfare, and illegitimacy. Although he emphasized that "white America broke the will of the Negro people" and urged the federal government to adopt policies, especially in education and government, "designed" directly or indirectly to enhance "the stability and resources of the Negro American family," he came under sharp attack. He was portrayed as a reactionary and even a bigot for "blaming the victims."[8]

Wounded, Moynihan left the administration just before *The Public Interest* began publication. He moved closer now to Kristol and the group who would soon come to be called neoconservatives. Kristol had published one of his first articles in *The Reporter* in 1959, which had put him in touch with another of his City College friends, Nathan Glazer, who was then deeply involved in his studies of ethnicity. With Glazer, Moynihan coauthored a seminal study of ethnicity in New York, *Beyond the Melting Pot* (1963), which challenged the widely held belief that America's immigrant tribes would blend into a "homogeneous end product."[9]

In a speech before ADA in 1967, Moynihan spoke out against the racial disorders in the cities. He did not think that liberal pieties would cure the problems of the black underclass. In a passage that came to the attention of Richard Nixon, he added, liberals must "see more clearly that their essential interest is in the stability of the social order" and "make alliances with conservatives who share that concern." When Nixon was elected president in 1968, Moynihan took his own advice. He joined the White House staff as assistant to the president for urban affairs. While never ceasing to think of himself as a liberal, his biographer, Godfrey Hodgson, reports, he shared the president's resentments about orthodox liberalism.[10]

Kristol and Moynihan, along with Seymour Martin Lipset, James Q. Wilson, and Bell, troubled by the harsh ideological debates of the mid-1960s, were among the early contributors to the journal. *The Public Interest* thus provided a home for a small but important group of contrarians, many of them Jewish, at a time of political crisis and liberal meltdown. Hodgson notes that Moynihan and his friends, who shared "his dark mood of resentment, misgiving and foreboding," no longer had to feel alone.[11]

Although the circulation of *The Public Interest* has always been small (at the start of the Reagan era in 1980, it had reached only 15,000 subscribers), its influence quickly grew. It soon became the rallying point for sociologists, economists, political scientists, and other intellectuals disillusioned with "social engineering" and government intervention in the economy. They scorned academics (especially those who had brainstormed Lyndon Johnson's War on Poverty), street demonstrations, and "community control" of public schools as "the old, sour, Socialist wine in the bottle of political expediency."[12]

If Kristol and Bell shared certain assumptions, however, they viewed social issues differently, although the spectrum of differences was narrow. As Bell recalled in his memoirs, Kristol was moving in a more conservative direction, even as he continued to publish articles with which he disagreed. His exposure "to intelligent, thoughtful, and lively conservatives" in Great Britain had influenced him in some measure. By contrast, Bell would later describe himself as "a socialist in economics, a liberal in politics, and a conservative in culture."[13] Other early contributors stood somewhere between Bell and Kristol.[14] Bell resigned in 1973 because he thought the journal was becoming too conservative.

When *The Public Interest* began publication, Johnson's War on Poverty was at its peak of influence. Michael Harrington's unflinching study of poverty in the land of opportunity, *The Other America* (1961), had made an enormous impact. President Kennedy had asked for a copy from Walter Heller, chairman of the Council of Economic Advisors, who recommended that such a "war" be declared. That fell to Johnson, after Kennedy's assassination in 1963. In 1965, Medicare, Medicaid, the Voting Rights Act, and federal aid to education became law.

Kristol initially took a nuanced position. In a special issue of *The Public Interest* in 1974, dealing with the lessons of the Great Society, the guest editors concluded that there had been "many partial, but genuine successes" in the War on Poverty. What troubled them was the way the war had been conducted. (Under Kristol's guidance, the magazine demanded hard numbers and incisive thinking to provide a rational basis for public policy.) Glazer did not wish to view complicated public policy issues simply as crude power struggles, in which old-fashioned reactionary forces opposed the "better" interests of society.[15]

The Public Interest sought to be neutral on such issues, but the evidence showed the expected gains of the Great Society to be largely ephemeral. What emerged at *The Public Interest*, then, was a body of thought that, while not liberal, was not strictly conservative. Its writers, admirers of Reinhold Niebhur's compassionate pragmatism, were troubled by the unintended consequences of well-meaning poverty programs and other social experimentation. Moynihan developed a compelling critique of the tendency to base radical and poorly-thought-out policy reforms (such as busing for racial balance in the schools) on questionable data. He and other writers rejected the New Left's utopianism, the idea that poverty could be cured by militant, even revolutionary, political action. "Someone," Kristol wrote, had "to continue talking modest sense, even if grandiose nonsense was temporarily so very popular."[16]

As a result, *The Public Interest* was soon filled with criticism of Great Society programs and warnings about the dangers of unintended consequences. Nathan Glazer, Edward C. Banfield, Roger Starr, and Aaron Wildavsky described the inadequacies of the Great Society's housing and welfare policies. James Q. Wilson underlined the problems of government bureaucracy and attacked liberal approaches to America's racial policies. Daniel P. Moynihan signaled in 1967 that the country's War on Poverty was in as much trouble as the hapless war in Vietnam. The next year, John H. Bunzel provided a negative picture of black studies on campuses, a generation before multiculturalism became a subject of controversy.[17]

Meanwhile, Kristol, echoing Frank Meyer, argued in *The Public Interest* that liberalism was creating a class of dependents while expanding the class of public sector functionaries.[18] More than a century earlier, Alexis de Tocqueville had advanced a similar argument in his *Memoir on Pauperism* (1835); in 1983, *The Public Interest* reprinted part of Tocqueville's essay, with an introduction by Gertrude Himmelfarb. Charles Murray took on the issue more directly in his book *Losing Ground: American Social Policy, 1950–1980* (1984). By 1995, criticisms that had first germinated in *The Public Interest* led finally to the enactment of welfare reform legislation that was signed into law the following year.

Kristol described the body of ideas that came to be known as neoconservatism as "a new synthesis." In economics and social policy, he wrote, "it feels no lingering hostility to the welfare state, nor does it accept it resignedly, as a necessary evil." What the neocons sought, he said, was to "reshape" the welfare state "along more modern lines. They wanted to attach to it the *conservative* [his italics] predispositions of the [American] people."[19] Gerson has cited yet another goal. The neocon analysis of the unintended consequences of government programs, especially during Lyndon Johnson years, made neoconservatives "rethink the emphasis they placed on the efficacy of expert knowledge and technical solutions."[20]

The neocons clearly differed from traditional conservatives like Friedrich von Hayek and Russell Kirk. The latter looked back nostalgically to a pastoral America of small towns and tight communities; the former, on the other hand, felt at home in the modern industrial world. The most fundamental ingredient marking neoconservatism has been its realistic and pragmatic approach to problems. The neocons found themselves at odds with that form of conservative libertarianism that seeks individual freedom, unrestrained by government. While increasingly doubtful of governmental solutions to problems, neocons were not hostile to government itself, particularly programs like Social Security. They saw no road to serfdom, as Hayek predicted, in the welfare state that they themselves had played no small role in creating.[21]

On foreign policy matters, in which neoconservatives would have enormous influence in the administrations of Ronald Reagan and George W. Bush, Kristol declared, "the goals of American foreign policy must go well beyond a narrow, too literal definition of national security."[22] Thus, the next generation of neocons – Paul Wolfowitz, Richard Perle, and Kristol's son, William (through his own magazine, *The Weekly Standard*) – helped to persuade President Bush to pursue the war on terrorism by invading Iraq in March 2003.

When neoconservatism's other "founding father," Norman Podhoretz, was appointed editor of *Commentary* at the age of thirty in 1960, he inherited a publication that under Elliot Cohen had become, arguably, the leading journal in American Jewish life. At a time when assimilation was the trajectory of most American Jews, Cohen expressed little interest in issues pertaining to Israel (at least initially); Podhoretz, however, came to back the Jewish state wholeheartedly (particularly in light of growing threats to Israel's safety and security). He also began to focus *Commentary* pieces more on the problems facing Jews around the world. Most intellectuals on the left had little sympathy for such thinking. As Cohen later wrote, intellectuals viewed this country as a "bourgeois, narrow-minded, puritanical society" run by businessmen for profit alone. Alienation was a badge of honor.[23]

Podhoretz inherited a publication that was in a position to become even more influential. Like *Commentary*'s parent organization, the American Jewish Committee, Cohen had been slow to recognize the importance of Israel. After 1948, however, Cohen became fully supportive of the Jewish state and began to broaden the magazine's scope. Podhoretz made it even more of a general magazine, albeit one loyal to Jewish concerns and intellectual interests.[24]

Podhoretz began his career at *Commentary*, however, somewhat alienated himself. Too young to have participated in the bitter ideological wars of the 1930s and 1940s, he grew up suspicious of the country's Cold War policies during his studies at Cambridge in England.[25] Although he had written for the anticommunist *Partisan Review*, he allied himself with the New Left by opening up *Commentary*'s pages to the "progressive," democratic socialist, and even anarchist thought that was blowing in the wind. Following his takeover as editor, *Commentary* would speak not about what man is, or what he was, but what he might become.

Under his direction, *Commentary* became perhaps the first magazine of any significance to pay serious attention to radical ideology. Contributors included Michael Harrington, Staughton Lynd, H. Stuart Hughes, and Edgar Friedenberg. Podhoretz welcomed Norman Mailer's ideas concerning instinctual freedom. He sought out and published a series by Paul Goodman that traced the malaise of the individual to the rise of the organization man. Under the title *Growing Up Absurd* (1960), Goodman's screed became a best-seller. Podhoretz also defended a black revolutionary in North Carolina and cooperated with the leftist Institute for Policy Studies, run by radicals Marcus Raskin and Arthur Waskow. In a brief history of the magazine published in 1995, *Commentary*'s editors acknowledged that in Podhoretz's earlier phase the journal had articulated and developed "the ideas that simultaneously encouraged the emergence of a new radicalism and helped to give it legitimacy."[26]

Podhoretz's greater "openness" at first won the approval of many on the left, including socialist Irving Howe. It gave the latter hope, coupled with the promises of the new Kennedy administration, of a burst of liberal thought and activism.[27] Podhoretz's move leftward was also precipitated by Khrushchev's de-Stalinization speech, which encouraged him to believe that if the Soviet Union could turn the corner, the Cold War need not be permanent.[28]

As the 1960s wore on, Podhoretz began to move away from this radical posture. He refused to accept the "apocalyptic notion" that American society was "hopelessly, incorrigibly corrupt." In 1962, Tom Hayden, a prime mover in the creation of SDS, offered Podhoretz the "Port Huron Statement" (soon to become the bible of the New Left) for publication. Podhoretz rejected it as intellectually shallow. Even though it eschewed violence, Podhoretz found the statement to be more conditional than principled, and he anticipated correctly that the type of humanism embodied in it carried the seeds of a later authoritarianism.[29]

Podhoretz's break with the liberal left was gradual. It had begun about 1967, but by 1970 his conversion to neoconservatism was complete. Kristol was his mentor, although the two men started out on shaky ground. Kristol privately did not think well of Podhoretz's *Commentary* and thought that Podhoretz's gradual movement rightward was the result of his "residual loyalty to the idea of the Left." In his own writings, unlike those that appeared in Kristol's *Public Interest*, Podhoretz could also display an in-your-face attitude.

Commentary's new brand of conservatism differed from *National Review*'s in style, if not substance. Buckley was urbane, witty, and made friends even with those with whom he disagreed. Podhoretz was more the street fighter, with a "take no prisoners" attitude. "The neoconservatives seemed less interested in promoting dialogue with opponents than in demolishing them," Dorrien observes, with Podhoretz clearly in mind.[30] Podhoretz often delighted in shocking sensibilities. In his famous essay "My Negro Problem and Ours," he described his experience as a Jew growing up in Brooklyn, coddled by his mother while physically being attacked by black toughs. In seeming to suggest that black Americans were more primitive than their white counterparts, he came close to crossing the line between observed behavior of kids and the kind of generalized racial stereotyping so widespread in the land.

Podhoretz admitted, with extraordinary candor and occasional self-mockery, that his rise (and that of most intellectuals) was fueled by the lure of fame and fortune: "I am a man who at the precocious age of thirty-five experienced an astonishing revelation: it is better to be a success than a failure."[31]

Such frankness, his talent for self-promotion, his delight in being outrageous, and his willingness to take risks brought down a torrent of vitriol from fellow intellectuals and friends, later to be described sadly in his various memoirs. There was no mistaking, however, his passion for the causes he espoused. His astonishing plea in "My Negro Problem and Ours" for racial intermarriage as a means of solving the racial problem may have been naïve, but it was a reflection of his serious concern about the intractability of racial injustice in this country. Even as he went through his "radical phase," he was never far from mainstream liberalism.

Podhoretz grew increasingly impatient with political radicals, who were disrupting campuses, shouting down speakers, staging sit-ins, and, in general, behaving irresponsibly. He was also appalled at the emergence of anti-Semitic elements among radical leftists and black militants. He had little use for those who would end the Cold War on Soviet terms. It was one thing to say the Soviets were not entirely responsible for the Cold War; it was another to seek unilateral disarmament. It was one thing to say that the programs of old-line civil rights organizations had not been responsive to the needs of the black masses; it was another to suggest that they were in collusion with racists to keep blacks down. One could be critical of American society, Podhoretz believed, but not nihilistically dismissive of our entire democratic system. Having grown up in a Brooklyn tenement, he felt that the country had been generous to him and many others from his generation and that it deserved some measure of gratitude.

The movement towards neoconservatism marked the development of a form of revisionist liberalism, which embraced the goals and tactics of the older socialism and its New Deal variation; but there was no mistaking the newer and more original conservative themes that were emerging. Both *The Public Interest* and *Commentary* now sought a more sympathetic understanding of capitalism as the basis for the freedoms and material well-being of increasing numbers of Americans and other Westerners. Furthermore, the fledgling neocons shunned containment of the Soviet Union. *Commentary* took the vanguard in encouraging the forces of disintegration within the Soviet Union and Eastern Europe – a far cry from the Nixon/Kissinger policy of détente. Indeed, Podhoretz had reached the conclusion that the leaders of the antiwar movement "were not against the [Vietnam] war at all but only against one of the sides fighting it." Even veteran socialist Norman Thomas noted that the chief organizers of antiwar demonstrations were more infatuated with the Vietcong than with peace.[32]

Podhoretz had grown up believing in "good liberal fashion" that African-Americans were disadvantaged and discriminated against – as, of course, they were. But as a child, he also realized that he belonged to another minority that suffered ill treatment at the hands of those he felt should have been on his side. "Neither rich, nor powerful," he wrote in "My Negro Problem and Ours," he disliked blacks for the way they brutalized him but also admired them, for "they were tough, beautiful, enviably tough, not giving a damn for anyone or anything." Thus, early on, he learned the law of the streets. "If one thing ties neoconservatives, Likudniks, and post-Cold War hawks together," Ian Buruma concludes, "it is the conviction that liberalism is strictly for sissies."[33]

Commentary trumpeted the outbreak of hostilities against the New Left with a series of articles. Irving Howe launched a blistering barrage against the intellectual fellow travelers of the New Left. He accused them of supporting illiberal reaction in order to remain in harmony with the temper of the times. Howe described the New Left as "ambitious, self-assured, at ease with prosperity while conspicuously alienated, unmarred by the traumas of the totalitarian age, bored with memories of defeat and attracted to the idea of Power."[34]

Diana Trilling followed up with "On the Steps of Low Library," an impassioned report on the student uprising at Columbia University. She termed it an assault on liberalism in its "lawlessness and refusal of reasonable process." In "The Case of the *New York Review*" (November 1970), the sociologist Dennis Wrong opened a direct attack on the publication. Its contributors, Wrong declared, were engaged in intellectual treason, aiding and abetting the most reactionary elements in the land. By this time, the *New York Review* had retreated somewhat. It no longer carried the writings of Stokely Carmichael,

Tom Hayden, or Andrew Kopkind. But Wrong was unforgiving. He said that its contributors had failed to learn the lessons of the anti-Stalinist intellectuals of the 1940s and 1950s.[35]

Commentary's shift toward conservatism was most evident in its response to the Vietnam War. In the early 1960s, Podhoretz's position on the war had been little different from that of his fellow radicals, and he was one of the war's earliest opponents (as were Glazer and Bell.) Podhoretz agreed initially with Hans J. Morgenthau, the noted theorist of the school of *Realpolitik*, and General Maxwell Taylor that it was the "wrong war in the wrong place at the wrong time." But his reasoning was very different from theirs, which held:

> American intervention in Vietnam was not a mistaken extension to Asia of the strategy of containment that had worked so well in holding the Soviet Union back in Europe; it was a criminal act of imperialism aimed at suppressing the legitimate national aspirations of a downtrodden dark-skinned people. It was the 'wrong war,' not because it was a wasteful and imprudent use of American power, but because it was morally evil; it was the 'wrong place' not because it was a foolishly chosen political and military field on which to hold the line against the spread of Communism, but because the fight being conducted by the Communists there was a fight for freedom that deserved our sympathy, not our opposition; and it was the 'wrong time' not because conditions in the United States were unfavorable to the building of support for such a war, but because *any* time was the wrong time for such a war.[36]

Podhoretz was "disgusted" by leftists who cheered for the North Vietnamese. "Never having believed that America had committed a crime in entering the war," he wrote, "nor in its conduct of it, I did not share Norman Mailer's wish to see this country humiliated." Only when the defeat of South Vietnam seemed inevitable and President Nixon ordered the return of heavy bombers to North Vietnam did he become reconciled to the fact that an American defeat was preferable to escalating the war further. But he took no joy in that fact and understood too fully the horrors that would follow.[37]

In addition, *Commentary*'s increasing attention to Jewish affairs, both at home and abroad, reflected Podhoretz's growing fear of the transformation of the civil rights revolution into a race revolution and the rise of black anti-Semitism. The Six-Day and Yom Kippur Wars had spurred an intensification of Jewish feeling on his part and among many Jews. In the August 1968 issue of *Commentary*, Podhoretz published Emil Fackenheim's famous essay "Jewish Faith and the Holocaust," which contained the much-quoted passage contending that after Auschwitz the most heinous sin for a Jew was to be an accomplice to the further destruction of the Jewish people and thus to grant Hitler a posthumous victory.[38]

In the 1970s, Podhoretz launched what became one of *Commentary*'s most enduring campaigns: an all-out assault against racial preferences. Supporters of such forms of affirmative action have long argued that taking race into account in the admissions policies of colleges and universities, for example, was necessary to redress discriminatory policies of the past (although recently they have contended that such practices are vital for the promotion of "diversity" on campus). Podhoretz likened such preferences to quotas, which he and other opponents said violated the U.S. Constitution.

Fellow neocon Nathan Glazer echoed much of the Podhoretz argument. In his influential *Affirmative Discrimination* (1975), Glazer opined that he would have been prepared to accept such preferences if the plight of the poorest blacks could be ameliorated. In practice, such affirmative action benefited only the black middle class; it did nothing to help those who most needed help – residents in the inner city. In the process, it encouraged a white backlash and devalued the accomplishments of those African-Americans who were admitted by virtue of their own achievements rather than because of their skin color. Affirmative action was a way for liberals to avoid the real problems of black America, Glazer said, some of which were cultural and therefore not "politically correct" enough to discuss.

The neocons believed that Jews, because of their small numbers, were especially vulnerable to discrimination. There was unmistakable irony here. Beginning in the 1920s and in subsequent years, upper-class Protestants had sought to limit the enrollment of Jews in elite colleges, universities, and medical schools by establishing quotas. In lowering the admission requirements for African-Americans and other heretofore excluded groups, the effect would be the same, even if the purposes were now more benign. Podhoretz saw these new quotas as a political strategy of the left and a fundamental break with the traditional liberal idea that all Americans should be treated on merit rather than as members of a group.

The New Left, the neocons believed, was not good for Jews, in part because its major targets often ended up being Jews – teachers (as in the aforementioned Ocean Hill–Brownsville brouhaha), small merchants, university professors (through racially oriented hiring), landlords, and other professionals. These comprised "all the roles Jews play" in American society, Glazer wrote.[39] Largely dormant until the Six Day War, the anti-Jewish bias of the New Left emerged sharply following the Jewish state's unexpected quick victory.

In "Revolution and the Jews" (February 1971), *Commentary* took aim directly at Jews in the New Left. Articles by Glazer, Walter Lacquer, and Robert Alter worried about a possible backlash against Jews, first for their role in the antiwar movement and second for their role in challenging broader American values and traditional lifestyles. As the ideas of the New Left spread, Podhoretz predicted, the statute of limitations on criticizing Jews (in place since the Holocaust) would become inoperative. Many white radicals, along with some black militants, had come to see Jews as privileged and oppressive.

Neocons worried also about the changes that "vital center" liberals were undergoing. "The new *Commentary*," Dorrien writes, "would have no place for social democrats like [Irving] Howe or [Michael] Harrington."[40] What had started out as an attack on the illusions of the liberal movement from within was now expanding into an effort that could outstrip the earlier anticommunism of Sidney Hook in the 1950s. A new-style Jewish liberalism-cum-conservatism was taking shape.

Michael Harrington has been credited with having coined the term "neoconservatives" in the late 1960s to describe a group of his old socialist allies who had turned away from the true faith.[41] A number of the early neocons demurred initially from such a characterization. From immigrant backgrounds themselves, neocons still associated conservatism with golf, country clubs, the Republican Party, big business – a sort of "*goyishe*" fraternity – and with the ideological posturing of right-wing fanatics. They viewed traditional conservatives as having little empathy for the underdog and the excluded in society. They thought of themselves as dissenting liberals, "children of the depression," as Midge Decter declared, who "retained a measure of loyalty to the spirit of the New Deal." Had "conservatism been dominant among my precursors," she added, they would have "ruled me out." She was not prepared to give up the term "liberal" in order to contend with people determined to "abscond with its good name."[42]

This impulse was developing simultaneously in Europe, led by Paul Johnson, former editor of the socialist weekly *The New Statesman*, in England, and by Jean-François Revel in France, who took issue with his intellectual counterparts on the French left, particularly Jean-Paul Sartre. The European neocons were responding to many of the same forces at work in the United States, but with local variations. Johnson was troubled by the growing power of the British trade unions, which were more socialistically inclined in Great Britain than in the United States. Revel worried that Sartre's ilk, while willing to overlook Soviet crimes, saw no irony in viewing the United States as the greater threat. Podhoretz began publishing these two voices regularly.[43]

Podhoretz now drew closer to Kristol. Subsequently, the two men became, in effect, indistinguishable. Concluding a half-hour broadcast of *Firing Line* with Podhoretz, Buckley, who was a friend of both men, thanked "Irving Podhoretz" for being with him.[44]

The neocons held stubbornly to their liberal credentials even as their views were undergoing change. In a 1966 article, "The Negro Today Is Like the Immigrant Yesterday," Kristol called for increased welfare benefits for those who needed them. The year before, he opined, "I believe the Negro's struggle for civic equality to be absolutely just" and "the use of militant methods in this struggle to be absolutely legitimate." Podhoretz shared Kristol's distress at the intractability of racism. Both men doubted, however, that civil rights legislation and government spending on antipoverty programs, which they supported, would solve the problems of African-Americans, primarily because of the tendency of people to stick to their own groups (as Glazer and Moynihan had previously argued). "*Commentary* essays in the 1960s," Mark Gerson claims, "maintained that storybook integration and eradication of black poverty would not follow the passage of any legislation or spending bills."[45]

Even as they embarked upon a new trajectory, the neocons retained close ties to elements of the labor movement, which was engaged in countering Soviet penetration of labor unions abroad. In February 1965, Podhoretz published Bayard Rustin's article "From Protest to Politics," in which Rustin, a prominent African-American leader, called for abandoning tactics of civil disobedience, nonviolent demonstrations, and other forms of "direct action," which may have been effective earlier, and turning to political action and "programs for full employment, abolition of slums, the reconstruction of our education system, [and] new definitions of work and leisure." What Podhoretz found attractive was Rustin's willingness to abandon revolutionary action and work through the system. After all, Podhoretz argued, wasn't the election of Lyndon Johnson a triumph over "the forces of racism and reaction united behind Barry Goldwater"?[46]

Ironically, the neocons shared one characteristic of the New Left: Jewish leadership. Leftists Abbie Hoffman, Jerry Rubin, and Sidney Blumenthal stood on one side; Kristol, Podhoretz, and Glazer on the other.[47] The leading publications on both sides of the divide were edited by Jews as well: *Commentary* (Norman Podhoretz), *The Public Interest* (Irving Kristol), and the *New York Review of Books* (Robert Silvers, Barbara Epstein, and Jason Epstein.) In some respects, the coming struggle between liberals and conservatives was a struggle within the Jewish community.

As the weaknesses of the Great Society and the liberal meltdown became apparent, the term "neoconservative" assumed an honorific standing among this little band of frustrated liberals. Gertrude Himmelfarb, the Victorian scholar, reminded her husband, Irving Kristol (who from the outset was not uncomfortable with the term), that the British labels "Tory" and "Whig" had also begun as insults and only later gained respectability. For his part, Moynihan, an Irish neocon, likened the Jewish neoconservatives to "good Catholics who were excommunicated." He quipped, "OK, we're Protestants."[48]

The neoconservative impulse was the spontaneous response of a group of liberal intellectuals, mainly Jewish, who sought to shape a perspective of their own while standing apart from more traditional forms of conservatism. Kristol called neoconservatism "a new synthesis." In economics and social policy, he wrote, "it feels no lingering hostility to the welfare state, nor does it accept it resignedly as a necessary evil." The older style liberalism became an issue for Kristol and the neocons, for example, when the American work ethic was eroded, or when the redistribution of income interfered with economic growth, or when egalitarianism came in conflict with liberty. Kristol wished "to reshape... [an older-style liberalism] – so as to attach to it the *conservative* [his italics] predispositions of the people, to rid it of its "paternalistic orientation."[49] The neocons were as one, however, with those on the right in recognizing the continuing threat of Soviet aggression and the need to convince their countrymen of this danger.

At first, more traditional conservatives at *National Review* did not know what to make of their unexpected allies. They saw little difference between liberal anticommunists and fellow-traveling members of the New Left. An ex-leftist, Frank Meyer, summed up this view:

> 1)... contemporary liberalism is in agreement with Communism on the most essential point – the necessity and desirability of socialism; 2) that it [liberalism] regards all inherited values – theological, philosophical, political – as without intrinsic virtue or authority; 3) that, therefore, no irreconcilable differences exist between it and Communism – only differences as to method and means; and 4) that in view of these characteristics of their ideology, the Liberals are unfit for the leadership of a free society, and intrinsically incapable of offering serious opposition to the Communist offensive.[50]

Still, these traditional and paleoconservatives (as some of them would soon come to be called) could not help but sit up and take notice. They knew that something important was happening. In 1970, *National Review* commented favorably on Podhoretz's new views, but wondered whether they would stand the test of time. "They [the neocons] are insufficiently rooted in serious political realities... or coherent intellectual tradition," the magazine said. Several months later, an editorial applauded *Commentary*'s article "Revolution and the Jews," noting that only a few years earlier, such an article would have been unthinkable in that journal.

The *Wall Street Journal*, the flagship of business conservatism, found Podhoretz to be an "improbable conservative" but approved of the work that he, Kristol, Glazer, and Decter were doing. "A "pro-American type of intellectual is starting to speak up," the newspaper exulted. And in its March 9, 1971, issue, *National Review* extended an invitation to *Commentary*: "C'mon in, the Water's Fine."[51]

If traditional conservatives hesitated to embrace the neocons, the suspicion was mutual. Kristol conceded that Buckley was charming and likeable but thought he and his magazine were prone to be "crackpotty."[52] He found *National Review*'s antiliberal polemics "sophomoric." "It seemed "simple-minded," he wrote, "in its 'anti-statism' in general and its contempt for all social reform in particular." He found its reaction to the New Deal "a species of political hysteria."

Kristol and other neocons also took sharp issue with *National Review*'s insistence that liberalism and communism were nothing more than two sides of the same coin. Slogans like "the road to serfdom" and states' rights hardly stirred neocons as they did Meyer and Chodorov. Later, however, Kristol acknowledged he was wrong in dismissing Buckley's journal so casually. He discovered that it was linked to a movement that trained several thousand young conservatives to take control ultimately of the Republican Party.[53]

Podhoretz recalled that early on he was "fiercely against" the view of Buckley and Chambers that the primary difference between the two superpowers was religious faith in the United States and state-ordered atheism in the Soviet Union. For Podhoretz, the struggle was clearly between democracy in the West and totalitarianism in the East.[54] Before long, Buckley and Podhoretz began to reach out to each other. In 1972, the two men entered into a cordial correspondence. The following year, Podhoretz invited Buckley to participate in a *Commentary* symposium. An alliance was subtly being forged.

Kristol, meanwhile, was coming to question certain aspects of capitalism. Businessmen, he believed, needed to be protected from themselves. They did not know how to think politically or defend themselves ideologically. "Large corporations today," he wrote in the spring 1973 issue of *The Public Interest*,

> happily publish books and magazines, or press or sell records, or make and distribute movies, or sponsor television shows which celebrate pornography, denounce the institution of the family, revile the 'ethics of acquisitiveness,' justify civil insurrection and generally argue in favor of the expropriation of private property and the liquidation of private industrialists.... Our capitalists promote the ethos of the New Left for only one reason: they cannot think of any reason why they should not.[55]

Kristol challenged businessmen to take the offensive and offered to help. Renegades from the left, like him, knew the enemy best.

Fate soon intervened. Robert Bartley, a young conservative journalist in the *Wall Street Journal*'s Washington bureau had been reading *The Public Interest* and was much impressed. Worried that the country was coming apart, he sensed something new and fresh in the land. Bartley knew that the traditional voices of conservatism, like *National Review* and the *Journal*, were important but could not generate the support and authority in influential circles that these former leftists could. Bartley phoned Kristol for an interview, and in May 1972 his article "Irving Kristol and Friends" appeared. The piece gave Kristol broader exposure than he had been receiving in his magazine and other little magazines. Soon after Bartley was appointed editor of the *Journal*'s editorial page, Kristol became a frequent contributor, later joining its board of contributors. In turn, the approach that the renegade liberals were formulating in *The Public Interest* became more "analytical, skeptical, and implicitly ideological" in the *Journal*'s editorials.[56]

Also about this time, Kristol joined New York University's faculty as a Luce Professor, a post arranged for him by his old mentor, Sidney Hook. He spent eighteen years at NYU, later holding a John M. Olin Professorship. With lots of free time and lengthy vacations, he was able to develop his ideas more thoughtfully.[57]

One of those intrigued by his thinking was William Baroody, Sr., head of the American Enterprise Institute (AEI), a small conservative "think tank" in Washington, D.C. Baroody, an intellectual entrepreneur, had refashioned a floundering think tank into the American Enterprise Institute for Public Policy Research in 1960 as a way of challenging the influence and liberal ideas of the Brookings Institute, another think tank operating in the nation's capital. In order to be effective, he knew he had to create an academically respectable organization. One of his first moves was to bring aboard the University of Chicago economist Milton Friedman, arguably the individual most responsible for reviving free market ideas in the post–New Deal era. Baroody had been reading *The Public Interest* and the *Wall Street Journal* closely. Baroody's vision, however, went beyond the free market to include religion, political philosophy, and the social sciences generally.[58]

When Baroody asked Kristol to join AEI, the move enraged Goldwater conservatives, who were major financial supporters of the organization, according to Kristol. Leftists of any stripe were not welcome.[59] Baroody, however, ignored them. He went on to recruit a cadre of resident scholars, many of them Democrats and neocons, which over time included Jeane Kirkpatrick, President Reagan's ambassador to the United Nations; theologian Michael Novak; and former Hubert Humphrey speech writer Ben Wattenberg. Later, such conservatives as Robert Bork, Antonin Scalia, and Laurence Silberman found a haven at AEI.

The invitation to Kristol came at the right time for him and his wife. New York was the center of the arts, the media, and finance; but the Kristols were policy wonks. Washington represented the real world of power. Kristol was only fifty and had visited Washington only once for a single day, to try to persuade Walter Lippmann to write an article for *Encounter* (unsuccessfully, as it turned out). On a more personal level, his children and grandchildren lived there. The Kristols were becoming increasingly isolated in New York, where their ideas went against the grain of liberal orthodoxies. Kristol took a sabbatical leave from NYU in 1976–77 and resigned his Luce Professorship two years later to join the AEI in the nation's capital. His wife developed a similar relationship with the Woodrow Wilson Center.[60]

AEI was among the first of the conservative think tanks and foundations to spread modern conservative doctrines through seminars, position papers, and grants to scholars. It would be joined shortly by the revived Harry and Lynde Bradley Foundation, the John M. Olin Foundation, the Manhattan Institute, the Ethics and Public Policy Center, and the Heritage Foundation, which was founded in 1973 by Paul Weyrich and Ed Feulner, products of Chodorov's ISI network.

These developments marked a new stage in the institutionalization of conservative ideas and conservative politics. Previously, conservatism had been a politics of frustration – in Daniel Bell's words, "the sour impotence of those who find themselves unable to understand, let alone command the complex society that is the polity today."[61] In conservatism's next stage, largely through the efforts of Buckley and Meyer at *National Review*, a broad unity of its contentious elements was achieved. Buckley increased the influence of his brand of conservatism by moderating its rough edges and banning anti-Semitic appeals. Even so, conservatism remained relatively powerless politically. In some respects, its influence had declined in the 1960s and 1970s. But the rise of the neocons in the 1980s strengthened the movement and enabled it to project modern, conservative ideas that were in tune with the feelings and needs of ordinary people.

Leaders of the movement found a patron also in William E. Simon, a wealthy businessman and philanthropist, who was equally influenced by them. Simon, who had served as secretary of the treasury under Presidents Nixon and Ford, was determined, as president of the John M. Olin Foundation in 1976, to establish what he called a "counter intelligentsia" in order to save the Republican Party. "American business," he believed,

> should funnel desperately needed funds to scholars, social scientists, writers, and journalists, who understand the relationship between political and economic liberty . . . [and whose work will] dissent from the dominant, socialist-statist-collectivist orthodoxy which dominates much of the media, in most of our universities, among many of our politicians, and tragically, among not a few of our top business executives.[62]

As far back as the 1930s, conservative foundations had supported the Liberty League and other right-wing groups with their free enterprise message. But they had showed little talent in dealing with "the things of the mind." Kristol hoped to become something of "a liaison between the intellectuals and the business community."

In 1978, Kristol, together with Simon now, forged an alliance that may be said to have launched the conservative foundation/think tank movement that has sparked the movement from left to right in recent years. They created the Institute for Educational Affairs (renamed the Madison Center for Educational Affairs in 1990) to penetrate college campuses with conservative ideas, just as Chodorov had done in the 1950s. The IEA made its first $50,000 grant either to the Federalist Society at Harvard or to the University of Chicago Law School (Kristol does not remember which). Kristol also convinced Simon of the need to fund a conservative press on college campuses to combat liberal dominance and to prepare students with conservative leanings for media and intellectual careers. At the University of Chicago, Norman Podhoretz's son, John, along with John Podhoretz's roommate, founded *Counterpoint*, a conservative literary journal. At Dartmouth, Dinesh D'Souza was among conservative students who aped the tactics of the New Left by making a student publication, *Dartmouth Review*, more strident and confrontational. By 1986, the conservative campus press had grown into a network of some sixty publications, according to Sidney Blumenthal. "If you are a conservative on campus, you should not feel lonely," Kristol told an interviewer.[63]

Graduates of these publications, D'Souza and John Podhoretz in particular, have become important sources of conservative thought in books and other publications. Kristol also arranged grants for the creation of *This World*, a scholarly publication examining the connection of religion and society. Its first editor was an alumnus of *The Public Interest*. It later became *First Things*, now the country's leading scholarly, conservative publication dealing with religion and society, edited by Richard Neuhaus. In 1985, Kristol arranged a grant of $600,000 from Olin to start up a new magazine in international affairs, *The National Interest*, to parallel the role of *The Public Interest* in domestic issues and to counter the more establishment and liberally oriented *Foreign Affairs*.

Much like Felix Frankfurter, who acted as a one-man employment agency for young liberals in New Deal agencies, Kristol recruited "Straussians" and other conservative talent for the accelerating conservative movement. He helped Leslie Lenkowsky win appointment to the Smith Richardson Foundation, a strong advocate of free market capitalism. Lenkowsky later headed President George W. Bush's Corporation for National and Community Service. Simon hired another Kristol protégé, Michael Joyce, initially as executive director of the Olin Foundation. When Joyce moved on to the Lynde and Harry Bradley Foundation in Milwaukee and became a prominent neocon in his own right, his successor at Olin was another Kristol favorite, James Piereson, a faculty member at the University of Pennsylvania. At Bradley, Joyce gave stipends to Strauss disciples Clifford Orwin and Thomas Pangle at the University of Toronto; Ralph Lerner and Allan Bloom at the University of Chicago; Walter Berne, a political scholar at Georgetown; and Berne's student James H. Nichols at Claremont.[64]

According to Jacob Weisberg, other beneficiaries of Kristol's networking and fund-raising skills included moralist William Bennett and conservative writer Charles Murray. Bennett is said to have been assisted by the Kristols in winning his first important national job as chairman of the National Endowment for the Humanities. Kristol also helped to obtain funding for such conservative magazines as *The American Spectator* and *The New Criterion*.[65]

As Kristol's influence grew, he and other neocons like Michael Novak and Allan Bloom came under sharp criticism from liberals and other critics on the left. Kristol, in particular, was accused of being a propagandist for big business, not above deriving financial benefit from conservative foundations. In *The Nation*, Jon Weiner reported that Kristol had received $376,000 as John M. Olin Distinguished Professor at the New York University Graduate School of Business Administration and John M. Olin Fellow at AEI. Michael Lind accused Kristol and other neoconservatives of having thrown aside their liberalism on economic and civil rights issues and converted, or pretended to convert, to the view of the older Republican right. The neocons' former liberalism, Lind charged, was never as deep as their ambition.[66]

In truth, Kristol had begun to write favorably about the spirit of capitalism in the 1950s and had expressed reservations about the welfare state long before his association with conservative think tanks and foundations. In working with more conservative foundations, he and his fellow neocons challenged more liberally oriented foundations such as the Ford and Carnegie Foundations, the Twentieth Century Fund, and the Brookings Institution, which dominated the public policy agenda at the time and continue to remain powerful forces. It was Carnegie, after all, that invited the Swedish sociologist Gunnar Myrdal, whose book *An American Dilemma* (1944) was to provide intellectual scaffolding for the civil rights revolution, to study "the American Negro Problem." Rockefeller Foundation money supported Dr. Alfred Kinsey's research into American sexual behavior in a bid to free Americans from "Victorian repression." The Ford Foundation under McGeorge Bundy was responsible for the Ocean Hill–Brownsville "community control" experiment in Brooklyn in 1968.[67]

Although critics have accused conservative think tanks and foundations of seeking to "buy" conservative thought and ideas, the assets of these groups do not begin to match those of the larger "progressive" bodies. The *New York Times* reported on May 20, 2001, that compared to the Ford Foundation's $14 billion in assets, Bradley had about $750 million, Olin $100 million, and Scaife $36 million.

The neocons also faced attacks from the reinvigorated paleoconservatives. The two groups were heirs to two different intellectual traditions. The paleos followed the thinking of Edmund Burke and Thomas Carlyle, who emphasized religion, social hierarchy, and status. The neocons were direct descendents of the Enlightenment; their ideas included free markets, democracy, individualism, equal rights, and, later, Marxist theories of class struggle and greater government intervention in society.[68]

For Kirk and other more traditional conservatives, neoconservatism represented a schism in the left (like the Trotsky faction of the Communist Party). Kirk did not consider it an authentic variety of conservatism. "The neo-conservatives," he declared, "were often clever but seldom wise." He viewed their movement as "a little sect," lacking "in the understanding of the human condition, and in the apprehension of the accumulated wisdom of our civilization."[69] He pointed out that for a long time the neocons had shared all the underlying principles of liberalism, including continued support of the welfare state. Kirk was right, of course. Glazer conceded as much when he noted that the differences between the neocons and liberals "do not have anything to do with deep, underlying, philosophical positions." Their differences, he said, were related to "fact and common sense." The neocons sought practical answers to contemporary social and economic problems, which traditionalists often examined from a religious or moralistic point of view.

Then there was the matter of the neocon attempt to take over the entire conservative movement. Kirk felt they were upstarts who acted as if they had invented conservatism.[70] Clyde Wilson, a University of South Carolina historian, agreed: "Our estate has been taken over by an imposter, just as we were about to inherit."[71] Stephen J. Tonsor put it more graphically: "It is splendid when the town whore gets religion and then joins the church. Now and then she makes a good choir director, but when she begins to tell the minister what he ought to say in his Sunday sermons, matters have been carried too far."[72]

Another source of friction between the two groups was their differing views on Israel. Many on the right believed that the backing the neocons gave to Israel reflected a fanciful, democratic globalism rather than genuine concern for American interests. Kirk complained that the neocons often mistook Tel Aviv for the "capital of the United States." Provoked, Decter charged that Kirk's sentiments echoed the old anti-Semitic canard of "dual loyalty."[73]

Over time, neocons and more traditional conservatives, if not the paleos later represented most prominently by Pat Buchanan, who sought the Republican presidential nomination in 1992, moved closer together. Neocons picked up a number of traditionalist themes. Decter frequently criticized the feminist and gay movements.[74] According to Edward Shapiro, Kristol "always sounded like a traditionalist, despite his claim that the essence of neoconservatism is the defense of bourgeois democracy."[75]

Moynihan, as a domestic policy adviser to Richard Nixon, had persuaded the president to give a speech advocating a downright radical idea, the Family Assistance Plan. Intended to stop fathers from leaving home so that their families could qualify for welfare, the plan sought to make available a guaranteed income to the unemployed and a supplemental income to the working poor. Nixon made the speech and sent the legislation over to Capitol Hill. Although Democrats, unwilling to allow Nixon to garner any credit for what they saw as an exclusively liberal idea, stalled the bill and forced Nixon to give up on the idea, Moynihan's ideas would evolve in the earned income tax credit as well as recent welfare reform legislation.[76]

Although Kristol flirted with joining the Nixon administration at Moynihan's behest, his brief association with the Republican president encouraged Kristol's later association with the GOP, especially following the defeat of Cold War Democrat Henry Jackson's bid for the presidential nomination in 1976. Before long, neocons joined the boards of the Heritage Foundation and the Ethics and Public Policy Center.[77]

Buckley and his coterie at *National Review* likewise were gaining respectability as influential voices on the national scene. When the *National Review* celebrated its tenth anniversary in 1965, House Minority Leader Gerald Ford attended. *New York Post* newspaperman Nick Thimmesch called it "the nation's best Tory magazine." *Washington Post* columnist David Broder observed that Americans could now get respected conservative opinion written "with style and wit." The "*National Review* crowd," he wrote, acted as "guardians and advisers to many of the groups that seek to influence the Republican Party, notably Young Americans for Freedom, the Young Republicans, the American Conservative Union, and the Intercollegiate Studies Institute." Moreover, *National Review* had been "scrupulously careful to disassociate itself from Bircher extremists." It did so ahead of many national Republican leaders.[78]

Traditional conservatives such as Meyer were coming to realize that under certain circumstances it might be desirable to work with liberal allies. The neocons, meanwhile, were distancing themselves even further from their leftist roots. Allied with business groups that they had formerly spurned and the broader conservative movement, they broke with mainstream liberal Jewish intellectuals. The question was, who had changed more, the neocons or traditional liberals?

Actually, as has been suggested earlier, the neocon break with the left had begun in the 1950s. "When Irving Kristol was executive secretary of Sidney Hook's American Committee for Cultural Freedom," Michael Harrington recalls, "one learned to expect silence on those issues that were agitating the whole intellectual and academic world."[79]

Harrington, still a socialist, set out now to create a marriage between the Old Left and the New Class. Earlier, Harrington, writer-critic Irving Howe, and other Jewish intellectuals had founded the journal *Dissent.* The magazine, while staunchly anticommunist, reflected older, socialist ideals. Amused at the infighting among New York Jewish intellectuals, Woody Allen suggested that *Commentary* and *Dissent* ought to combine under the title *Dysentery.*

In a *Partisan Review* article, "This Age of Conformity," which became the basis of *Dissent*'s founding theme, Howe attacked liberal anticommunists for becoming too complacent in American society. But liberals brushed aside the criticism. "Behind Mr. Howe's perspective," Kristol wrote, "there lies an unexamined premise: that there is something unnatural in an intellectual being anything but politically radical, a man of the left."[80] For Irving Kristol, neoconservatism was less a political posture than simply an expression of good common sense.

8

Neoconservatives and the Reagan Revolution

The 1972 election marked a turning point in the evolution into neoconservatives of some of the Democratic liberals. Until then, except for Kristol, who had voted for Nixon in 1968, and Moynihan, who had entered the Nixon administration, the neocons had remained loyal Democrats. Since the start of the Cold War, they had supported hard-line anticommunism and strong national defense, which had generally been endorsed by both political parties.[1]

In the view of most neocons, McGovern, a former Henry Wallace supporter, turned his back on this tradition in his 1972 campaign. His call for cooperation with the Soviet Union ignored, or at least minimized, what they perceived as the perils posed by that country's aggressive designs in the world. They were deeply suspicious of a candidate for president who charged that American foreign policy was based on "outdated stereotypes of military confrontation and power politics."[2] Indeed, these disgruntled liberals were convinced that the McGovernites had hijacked their party and jettisoned liberalism as they had known it.[3]

Although McGovern lost forty-nine of the fifty states and was finished politically, his dovish views resonated within important elements of America's intellectual and cultural elite. The Cold War had been waged as a siege in Europe and as a series of duels elsewhere, chiefly in Korea and Indochina. The Nixon administration's policy of détente had accommodated the status quo by relying heavily on a huge build-up of nuclear weapons by both the United States and the USSR to maintain the peace. Both superpowers knew that they faced obliteration if either pushed the nuclear button. Robert S. McNamara, secretary of defense in the Kennedy Adminisraton, had coined the acronym MAD (Mutual Assured Destruction). Its underlying premise, laid out in a speech in 1962 at the American Bar Association, held that once the superpowers had acquired a certain level of retaliatory power, neither would dare to attack the other. Both sides were vulnerable to destruction. In one of its more bizarre interpretations, one of the earliest

MAD advocates argued that if the United States was to feel secure, it had to assure itself that the Soviet Union had the ability to destroy it.[4]

The Vietnam debacle shifted the balance of power. It emboldened the Soviet Union and its satellites, who gained momentum in such Third World countries as Angola (to which Cuba sent troops and other military support) and Ethiopia, and in the Middle East, where the Soviets provided Arab countries with arms and political support in their confrontation with Israel and in Nicaragua. By contrast, in the United States (particularly following the Watergate scandal) pessimism permeated the corridors of influence. Henry Kissinger, Nixon's secretary of state, questioned the meaning of military superiority in an age of nuclear weapons. "He felt we are compelled to co-exist." Even after leaving public office, Kissinger continued to believe (as he declared in January 1977) that achieving nuclear superiority in strategic weapons was "extremely unlikely... and the obsession with it distracts me."[5]

According to Admiral Elmo R. Zumwalt, Jr., Kissinger saw the country moving toward a secondary role vis-à-vis the Soviets. Zumwalt, a former chief of naval operations, quotes a personal conversation with Kissinger, widely recognized as the most prominent advocate of *Realpolitik* in the Hans Morgenthau tradition, to this effect: "The U.S. has passed its historic high point, like so many other civilizations, and cannot be roused to the political challenge. We must persuade the Russians to give us the best deal we can get."[6]

The hallmark of détente in the 1970s was the Strategic Arms Limitations Talks (SALT), initiated by Nixon and later backed by President Carter. Its central thesis was that an arms race inevitably led to war. The country had to remain militarily strong, but at least the arms race itself could be managed by rational, intelligent individuals on both sides. Arms control came to be seen as an impediment to nuclear arms competition and a means of easing the tensions between the superpowers.[7]

The basic configuration of the Cold War – Soviet domination of Eastern Europe and its growing influence in other parts of the world, including the Middle East – was generally accepted by this country's foreign policy elite. Following the Truman years, President Eisenhower, his secretary of state, John Foster Dulles, and even Nixon, the 1950s Cold Warrior, who scorned Democratic diplomacy and once referred to Secretary of State Dean Acheson's "College of Cowardly Communist Containment," had rallied around the concept of détente as the vehicle for achieving world peace. Nixon and Kissinger had been rattled by the Vietnam War. They continued to view the world through the prism of the Cold War, but unlike Acheson and the "wise men" of an earlier generation, they could not see the possibility of victory. Indeed, historian Peter Schweizer has argued, perhaps with some exaggeration, that the only time there had been an extended period of peace between the superpowers was when a balance of power had been reached; thus, the United States had a stake in keeping the Soviet Union from falling.[8]

Liberal intellectuals also called attention to Soviet economic strength vis-à-vis America during this period. The Harvard economist John Kenneth Galbraith, according to Schweizer, declared that "the Russian system succeeds because, in contrast to the Western industrial economies, it makes full use of its manpower." Most fatuously, MIT economist Lester Thurow wrote in his textbook, "Today [the Soviet Union] is a country whose economic achievements bear comparison with the United States." Following a trip to Moscow in 1982, Arthur Schlesinger, Jr., reported, "I found more goods in the shops, more food in the markets, more cars in the street – more of almost everything, except for some reason caviar." He dismissed those in the United States who felt the Soviets were "on the verge of economic and social collapse.[9]

In reality, while the Soviet Union was receiving high marks from some misinformed scholars, its internal conditions were steadily worsening. Although it remained very strong militarily on the continent and elsewhere, its economy was dysfunctional, political corruption was ubiquitous, and its party leaders operated from an untouchable bastion of self-indulgnce. Moreover, in its satellite states, seething resentments threatened to bring down the system.

Daniel Patrick Moynihan, one of the public figures to recognize early on the Soviet Union's internal weaknesses, warned that it remained a menace. It might desperately attack oil-producing regions as a way to reverse the decline at home and preserve national unity. Employing the coercive power of a police state, it succeeded in concealing its economic difficulties and maintaining internal control. As a result, the Soviet Union spent heavily on armaments. Able to concentrate on the build-up of its military power, it extended its influence worldwide, while quietly disintegrating at home. Long before his presidency, Ronald Reagan understood this. He had declared as early as 1963 that the United States operated the world's most efficient and powerful economic machine, while Russia and China found themselves in the grip of feudalism.[10]

Even so, there was no denying the Soviet military build-up in the 1960s and 1970s and into the 1980s. Thomas Powers, a journalist specializing in intelligence matters, reported in a lengthy postmortem on the later Soviet demise that the percentage of its GNP devoted to the military, and especially to the massive build-up of strategic nuclear weapons, was at levels approaching those of World War II, far greater than the Pentagon's slice of the American GNP.[11]

Far from opting out of the arms race, as McNamara had predicted, the Soviets accelerated their build-up. Schweizer writes that "with the stroke of a pen" in 1969, General Secretary Leonid Brezhnev committed the Soviet Union to dedicating "almost one third of its gross national product to military needs." Between 1962 and 1972, the Soviets deployed five new intercontinental ballistic missiles (ICBMs), and were building between 200 and

250 new silo launchers and four new types of ballistic missile submarines each year. By 1971–72, they possessed 1,510 ICBMs, roughly 500 more than the United States.[12] After the signing of the SALT agreement in 1972, the build-up would become even more rapid.[13] By 1975, Henry Kissinger announced that Soviet adventurism had returned, aided by an unprecedented panoply of modern arms.

Less than two years into the Carter administraton, Secretary of Defense Harold Brown, one of the few hard-liners in the administration, told the Senate Foreign Relations Committee, "We have found that when we build weapons, they build. When we stop they nevertheless continue to build."[14] Meanwhile, Georgi Arbatov, the head of Moscow's Institute for the Study of the USA and Canada, claimed nuclear superiority for the Soviet Union: "...we [have] surpassed the Americans in the number of delivery systems, megatonnage, and throw-weight in strategic arms, and also in medium-range weapons."[15]

Soviet strategists from the 1960s onward argued that as a result of nuclear weapons and intercontinental weapons, warfare had been revolutionized. Soviet experts minimized MAD and arms limitations and concentrated on how to win wars.[16] Far from accepting a stalemate on the NcNamara model, the Soviet Union was strengthening its first-strike capabilities.[17] Even though the Soviet Union had signed the 1972 and 1975 Biological Weapons Conventions, banning the development, production, and stockpiling of biological agents for offensive military purposes, the Soviet government secretly initiated an effort to modernize its biological weapons and even to invent new ones.[18]

The Soviet Union took the American MAD policies as a sign of weakness. In 1972, Arbatov told a Soviet audience that Nixon had signed the SALT treaties because "new... conditions had forced him to do so."[19]

Despite his own domestic problems, Brezhnev insisted the Soviets were winning the Cold War. "The general crisis of capitalism continues to deepen," Brezhnev exulted in 1976. "Events of the past few years are convincing confirmation of this."[20] Soviet military publications (one of the few places Soviet intentions were visible) indicated that Moscow believed nuclear weapons might not just deter, but might actually overpower the West.

As late as Reagan's election in 1980, even with the knowledge of his hard-line approach, Moscow continued to be optimistic about its nuclear superiority. By this time, the Soviets had begun to deploy their greatly feared SS-20 missiles, aimed at Western Europe. In the Kremlin, Ambassador Oleg Grinevsky recalled that discussions revolved around America's loss of the arms race. He boasted that the Soviet Union was at the peak of its powers. General Adrianna Danilevich boasted that the SS-20 was a breakthrough. The United States had nothing like it. "We were immediately able to hold all of Europe hostage."[21]

To many of the disaffected Democrats, détente's sapping of the West's will during the Nixon–Ford years had permitted the Soviets to consolidate and then to extend their global power reach, while America's military forces and strategic position had deteriorated. The anti-anticommunist movement was letting the Soviets win the Cold War. It had captured the commanding heights of the culture and represented a serious threat to Americans, to Western freedom, and, not least important, to Jews and Israel.

Even before the reelection of Nixon in 1972, a number of Jewish liberals, including Midge Decter, Norman Podhoretz, and Ben Wattenberg, embarked upon an effort to recapture the Democratic Party and to restore it to its earlier strong anticommunist posture. The figure they gravitated toward for replacing "McGovernism" was the liberal, strongly anticommunist Senator Henry Jackson of Washington state. "Scoop" Jackson was a hard-liner; he had led the fight to attach an amendment to the Strategic Arms Limitations Treaty (SALT I) that would, in effect, have kept American armaments on a par with those of the USSR. Under the amendment's clumsy wording, the president was prohibited from allowing the United States to fall to "levels of intercontinental strategic forces inferior to the limits provided for the Soviet Union."

In another move with special appeal for American Jews, Jackson sponsored an amendment to the United States' 1972 trade agreement with the Russians that linked human rights and trade with the Soviet Union. The most-favored-nation trade arrangements with the Soviets would be dependent upon granting their citizens the right to emigrate. Although the amendment, which was enacted into law, did not say so explicitly, it was primarily aimed at ending the ban on the emigration of Soviet Jews to Israel.

Nixon and Kissinger opposed the Jackson–Vanik amendment. They believed it interfered with diplomatic efforts to come to some agreement with the Soviets. Jackson was seen as willing to sacrifice American economic interests – more trade and the ability to use economic ties as leverage on issues such as arms control and Vietnam. For them, Jackson's championing of Soviet Jewry was a cynical ploy, reflecting the senator's eagerness to become president.

Whatever his ambitions, Jackson had broader goals. He sought to convince Americans that beyond the photo opportunities of summitry and the ceremonies surrounding détente signings, the Soviet Union had not changed. The threat it posed, he believed, would remain in place until it became a democratic nation. You can tell what sort of "neighbor" a particular regime is likely to be, he told one observer, by looking at how it treats its own people.[22] In pursuing his goals, Jackson proved to be extraordinarily effective. Within a year after Nixon's resignation in 1974, he had forced the Ford administration to scuttle plans to grant economic concessions to Moscow in exchange for political cooperation.

Following the 1972 election, a number of disgruntled liberals, Max Kampelman, Jeane Kirkpatrick, Podhoretz, and Moynihan among them, formed the Coaliton for a Democratic Majority (CDM) in an effort to pull the party back to the center. Jackson became its honorary chairman. (Hubert Humphrey was scheduled to become his cochair, but an aid persuaded him that to do so would not sit well with the liberal wing of the party.) Mapping strategy in a draft prepared by Decter, they countered McGovern's theme, "Come home, America," with "Come home, Democrats."[23]

Among the disaffected Democrats was Eugene V. Rostow, a former Yale Law School dean and an undersecretary of state in the Johnson administration. Rostow, who had been named for Eugene V. Debs, the five-time Socialist candidate for president between 1900 and 1920, prided himself on being a tough-minded liberal in a nuclear age. As head of the CDM's defense task force in 1974, he wrote in an article titled "Defining Détente in Terms of the United Nations Charter," published in the *New York Times*, "We confront two implacable facts: the Soviet military build up is continuing at an ominous rate, and Soviet political policy is more and more obviously fixed in a mood of muscular imperialism."[24] By 1975, Rostow had concluded that the Democratic Party "didn't want to hear from us anymore" and needed a new chorus, a nonpartisan group of heavyweights."[25]

"By God, why don't we just do it?" Rostow asked in a letter to a group that included Paul Nitze, a Washington insider who had worked closely with Dean Acheson in shaping the Truman administration's response to the Soviet Union in the early days of the Cold War. Rostow later met with Nitze and former defense secretary James Schlesinger. The upshot was the formation of the Committee on the Present Danger (CPD) on March 12, 1976, with headquarters in Washington, D.C. Its purpose was to alert American policy makers and the public to what its founder perceived as the continuing, ominous Soviet threat.

Rostow was named chairman of the CPD. Also on board were former treasury secretaries Henry H. Fowler and Charles Walker, along with David Packard, cofounder of Hewlett-Packard, the computer manufacturer. Among Jewish members of the group were Sovietologist Richard Pipes, Podhoretz, Decter, Paul Wolfowitz, and novelist Saul Bellow, who said he was "appalled by the self-hypnosis of intellectuals" unable to comprehend the nature of the Cold War.[26] Exactly one year before his first inauguration, Ronald Reagan paid a visit to Washington, where he was named to the executive committee of the CPD.[27]

CPD leaders believed that the Soviet Union had achieved superiority in arms by concentrating its modest resources there and setting aside the broader needs of their people. They were opposed to arms limitations programs such as SALT II. Podhoretz worried particularly about this country's "spiritual Finlandization," a reference to that country's autonomous but submissive stance. Because Soviet leaders were seen as even more ambitious than

Hitler, the CPD pressed for an array of strategic weapons, including the B-l bomber (plans for which Carter would later cancel), to meet the challenge. It emphasized the danger of Soviet political blackmail as a result of its nuclear might; since the Kremlin "thinks it could fight and win a nuclear war." Pipes argued, the United States required weapons and strategies designed to preempt the Soviet Union before such a war started, or to win a war if one broke out. The next decade would be given over to the struggle against growing Soviet power, for the sake of national survival. Freedom was the ultimate prize, and a higher level of U.S. military spending was the driving need.[28]

Both the CDM and the CPD began laying the basis for a new counterestablishment – in effect, a government in waiting. Formerly liberal Democrats now found themselves increasingly in alliance with more conservative organizations such as Young Americans for Freedom, Paul Weyrich's Committee for the Survival of a Free Congress, and the Conservative Caucus. This last organization was linked to a group called the Emergency Coalition Against Unilateral Disarmament, which used mailing lists supplied by Richard Viguerie, the Liebman-trained operative. Shortly before the 1976 election, Rostow joined the National Strategic Information Center, a conservative lobbying group.[29]

There were, of course, obstacles to a coalition between traditional right-wing conservatives and the neocons. These revolved mostly around attitudes toward the welfare state and organized labor, with whom neocons maintained strong ties. They were moving closer, however, on issues such as affirmative action, busing to achieve school desegregation, and the perceived excesses of the feminist movement. Most important, together they tended to focus more and more on what they viewed as the Soviets' thrust for world domination. This, along with common stands against SALT, troop withdrawal from South Korea, the Russians in Cuba, the Cubans in Africa, the Russians and Cubans in Nicaragua, and restraint in Iran made them increasingly partners. Less was heard from them concerning underclass problems, the growing gap between rich and poor, the broken health care system, and failing schools – issues that had troubled the generation of young Jewish intellectuals in CCNY's alcoves during the Depression.

These increasingly alienated and more centrist liberal Democrats challenged the nation's intelligence community as understating the Soviet strategic threat. Early in 1975, the President's Foreign Intelligence Advisory Board approached Nixon with the suggestion that he appoint an outside and independent group to review CIA estimates. As head of the CIA under Gerald Ford, George Bush formed such a committee (known as Team B), headed by Richard Pipes, a Polish-Jewish immigrant and professor of history at Harvard. Other members included the American historian Oscar Handlin, the Sovietologist Adam Ulam, and several others, all reflecting a point of view different from that of other intellectuals, who were supportive of the Arms

Control and Disarmament Agency, SALT, and détente. Individuals associated with the CPD, along with high-level businessmen and former government officials, joined Pipes in the project. Once in place, Team B began to create a parallel draft of the annual assessment of Soviet offensive missile power formulated by the CIA (known as Team A).[30]

Throughout his career, Pipes had consistently characterized the Soviet Union as an aggressive, imperialistic power.[31] The Team B report declared that the "evidence indicated beyond reasonable doubt that the Soviet leadership did not subscribe to MAD but regarded nuclear weapons as tools of war whose power employment in offensive as well as defensive modes, promised victory."[32] The CIA, it concluded, had significantly underestimated most elements of Soviet power, including even such key measures as the accuracy of Soviet nuclear missiles. Wolfowitz, then an expert with the Arms Control and Disarmament Agency, wrote a section of the report on the importance to Soviet strategy of intermediate-range missiles. He would later tell an interviewer that he had never gone along with Team B's belief that the Soviets believed they could fight and win a war, but that he still thought the report was a useful guerrilla attack on conventional détente.[33]

The Team B report, in fact, provided intellectual fodder for the efforts of the CPD, which held its first press conference at the National Press Club in Washington, two days after the 1976 election, to announce its existence. Although the media ignored the CPD initially, by late December 1976, when the Team B report was leaked to the media, it would begin receiving attention.

The Team B report came under heavy fire from members of Congress, editorial writers, and columists from the *New York Times*, the *Washington Post*, and the Washington *Star*. The gist of the criticism, then and now, was that Pipes and the neocons had exaggerated the threat posed and that the Soviets were falling apart economically and socially. The result, critics said, had been to cause this country to waste funds on a military build-up that might be better used for social improvements at home. Some viewed the report as a crude political ploy to pressure incoming President Jimmy Carter, who had pledged to pursue SALT II negotiations and to cut back the defense budget by five billion dollars. At a farewell address at the National Press Club early in January 1977, Kissinger dismissed the plan as nothing more than an effort to "sabotage SALT II."[34]

When the revised text was finally approved by the Senate Foreign Relations Committee in 1978 (with the assistance of Moynihan, who by this time had become a New York senator), Team B's view of détente and Soviet designs remained unchanged. The influence of the report on government and public opinion was very powerful, as even its critics conceded. It was not so much that its revelations were new (they were not), but rather that they stimulated and justified doubts already in existence. Proponents of MAD were put on the defensive. A year later, Moynihan wrote that "Team B's notion that the Soviets intend to surpass the United States in strategic arms" and are in the process of doing so, "has gone from hearsay to respectability, if not orthodoxy" in "what might be called official Washington."[35]

By the time the CIA passed on its own penultimate draft assessment of Soviet strategy to the White House, CIA officials were thrown on the defensive, according to Derek Leebaert, a professor of government at Georgetown University: "The weight of scholarly opinion today is that while Team B went too far, it made the National Intelligence Estimates more rigorous.[36]

Following the election, Wolfowitz and Richard Perle spent one night writing a twenty-three-page, single-spaced memo on Salt II for the newly elected President Carter, to be used in negotiations with the Soviets. They called for deep cuts in the Soviet and U.S. missile forces and demanded reductions not only in Soviet intercontinental ballistic missiles but also in intermediate-range missiles. The United States, they argued, should have the option, forbidden under SALT I, of developing heavy ICBMs of its own; the cruise missile program should continue apace. As a result of Jackson's role as the Senate's leading expert and critic of SALT, the memo was widely circulated within the Carter administration, although the response was cool.[37]

CDM also provided Carter with a list of sixty neoconservative candidates for jobs in his administration. They included political scientist Kirkpatrick, Washington insider Max Kampelman, Glazer, and Perle. They were completely frozen out. They were offered only the minor post of special negotiator for Micronesia. Carter believed that the neocon leaders were too hawkish, too mired in the Cold War. Initially, he did not put much stock in warnings of Soviet expansionism. He had argued in his victorious campaign against Ford that economic and social problems would weigh heavier in the future than the "military-security problems, which have dominated international relations since World War II."[38]

As his secretary of state, Carter chose Cyrus R. Vance, who represented liberal, establishment thought. Vance had once declared that Leonid Brezhnev was a "a man who shares our [this country's] dreams and aspirations," and he would later resign in protest over Carter's decision to attempt a military rescue of American hostages in Iran in 1980. Against the advice of Jackson and Moynihan, he named Paul C. Warnke as his chief SALT negotiator. Early in 1975, Warnke had written that the "injection of American firepower into a local conflict is rarely compatible with our foreign policy interests."[39]

This dovish observation had drawn fierce criticism from hawkish neocons. But the incoming Carter team (save Brzezinski) was distinctly unfavorable to the Team B report. Carter went even further. In a speech at Notre Dame on May 22, 1977, he said the nation must overcome its "inordinate fear of Communism." He proposed that the Soviet Union join with the United States in joint activities in the Third World to improve conditions there.[40] Upon entering office, Carter abolished the Foreign Intelligence Advisory Board as part of his effort to stigmatize this inordinate fear of communism. His assertion came just a few months after Ethiopia's strongman, Mengistu Haile

Mariam, told the Cuban ambassador he planned to "follow Cuba's example" but needed the "necessary quantity of weapons" to maintain power. Moscow quickly agreed to send first Soviet advisiors, then 11,000 "internationalists," to be followed by tens of thousands of Cuban troops to this "choke point" on the Red Sea.[41]

The enraged neocons saw Carter's administration moving perilously close to "New Left" McGovernism. The CPD went on the warpath. Once Salt II was signed, the committee attempted to finds ways to block its ratification.[42]

Mounting its attack on what it saw as Carter's policies of appeasement and naïvite, CPD singled out Vance for withering criticism and reserved some of its heaviest guns for George Kennan. Although Kennan had been out of government for more than a quarter-century, he remained an authoritative figure because of the role he had played earlier in providing the rationale for the Cold War. His defection from these policies and testimony before the Fulbright Committee and elsewhere infuriated neoconservatives. In an essay in a German magazine in 1976, Kennan declared that the Soviet threat was not really a threat at all, since the the West had little to defend as a society. He said that Western civilization was "succumbing day by day to its own decadence, sliding into debility on the slime of its own self-indulgent permissiveness."Asked in an interview how Europe or the United States should defend themselves, he responded, "with passive resistance, which would prevent a foreign occupier from dominating a conquered country." Rostow dismissed Kennan as a man who is "exhausted, disillusioned and nearly without hope." His views typified, he said, "a fashionable post-Vietnam mood about foreign affairs."[43]

In fact, many neocons might have agreed with Kennan on America's slipping social standards. X-rated films, outrageous "rap"music, the foul language and sexual content condoned in various media, along with a growing divorce rate, fewer intact families, and violence in the schools, certainly gave evidence of American permissiveness. In suggesting that the West was in a death spiral, however, and that its day might be done, Kennan went too far for the children of the "tenement trail."

CPD publications, public opinion polls, and press conferences, along with cold facts and figures on the strategic balance, later marked a shift in administration policy and public opinion. When in the spring of 1977 CPD issued a policy statement, "What Is the Soviet Union Up To?," written by Richard Pipes, the response and tone of major news agencies to CPD became more positive. They carried interviews with Rostow and Nitze and described the committee as "a public interest group" and "an organization comprised of many leading Americans from all segments of the political sprectrum." When Reagan took office, the mood embodied in the Team B report was on the rise, and the work of the neocons and their allies was being put to good effect.[44]

In the early postwar years, anticommunism in America had been dominated by the Protestant leadership class and the Roman Catholic clergy. Most of the latter, like Father Edmund A. Walsh, Jesuit dean of Georgetown University's Foreign Service School; Father John F. Cronin, the Baltimore priest who battled communism in the labor movement; and Cardinal Francis Spellman, New York's influential prelate, were Irish. William Buckley at *National Review* was an Irish-Catholic, as was, even more prominently, Senator Joseph R. McCarthy. For them, communism was the anti-Christ. American Jews, while showing little sympathy for communism, rarely joined in the crusade aganst it.

In the 1960s, a curious role reversal took place. John F. Kennedy, the nation's first Roman Catholic president, downplayed his Catholicism, and Pope John Paul XXIII moderated the church's stand, encouraged dialogue with communism, and denounced nuclear power. It was at this point that the Jewish neocons came forward as a primary group in support of militant anticommunism.[45]

Podhoretz was now fully prepared to turn his back on the McGovernites and proponents of détente who had taken control of the Democratic Party in an effort to "help revive the American will to resist Soviet expansionism."[46] In an extravagant assertion, but one not without a measure of truth, historian Richard Gid Powers writes, "During those bleakest winter days of American anticommunism..., [o]ne man summoned the will, the strength and the imagination to commence the giant task of rebuilding the anticommunist coalition. This was Norman Podhoretz."[47]

Podhoretz galvanized those moving into the neoconservative ranks. "I can fix the exact moment when I – a reader of *Commentary* since my teens – was shocked to attention by an item in the magazine unlike anything I had ever read," Harvard Yiddish scholar Ruth R. Wisse recalls. She described a July 1970 article by Podhoretz."By setting Vietnam within the context of U.S. History and the history of human civilization, he was saying that revulsion against a mistaken or misfought war cannot become an excuse for ideological pacifism; that despite its ugliness and inefficiency, the reality of war remains the final safeguard of freedom.... Its truth struck me particularly as a Jew."[48]

Commentary became a force behind the Iron Curtain as well, providing encouragement to the restive peoples there. Neil Kozodoy and his colleagues at the magazine would hear from Poles and Hungarians and later Czechs that the magazine was being received and read, and that specific articles had been translated and distributed in *samizdat* versions.[49]

A central element in Podhoretz's evolving views, which would soon become his and many of the neocons' governing principle, was the question, "Is It Good for the Jews?," the title of a February 1972 *Commentary* piece. In "My Negro Problem – and Ours," his sense of Jewishness seemed almost attenuated. He wondered "whether [Jews'] survival as a distinct group was worth one hair on the head of a single infant." He recognized why Jews had struggled so hard to survive as a distinct group, but with the loss of that earlier theological memory, he wrote, "I am less certain as to why we still do."[50]

During the second half of the 1960s and the 1970s, his sense of his own Jewishness intensified, reflecting what Irving Howe called the immigrant "weight of fear of living on the edge of unforeseen catastrophe."[51] The idea that Jews were increasingly on the fringes became evident to him as the civil rights revolution was transformed into a race revolution, bringing with it greater black anti-Semitism and a racial spoils system benignly described by its advocates as affirmative action.

The new anti-Semitism reached its apotheosis when the United Nations, despite the United States' objection, adopted a resolution equating Zionism with racism. By this time, Podhoretz was convinced that the postwar "statute of limitations" on anti-Semitism was no longer in effect. Increasingly, neocons came to believe that the Jewish state's ability to survive – indeed, the Jewish community's will to survive – was dependent on American military strength and its challenge to the Soviet Union, the primary backer of Arab countries in the Middle East. The most ardent enemies of Jews and Israel were no longer on the right, Podhoretz professed, but on the left.

Podhoretz denies, however, that his move to the right resulted solely from the perceived growth of anti-Semitism and the threat to Israel. He traces it instead to the anti-Americanism on the left, which for him, a poor kid from Brooklyn who was able to rise in American life, was the crowning indignity. The rest came later.[52]

Commentary's strong, even militant, Jewish posture was something new. During the 1940s and 1950s, it had been "suspicious, even contemptuous of many aspects of bourgeois, Jewish life that had in the past appeared to guarantee the culture's viability," Stephen J. Zipperstein points out. It substituted "an uncertain, Jewishly ambiguous diet of Western or Westernized masters." The "first question we should ask" with regard to Jewish culture, Elliot Cohen wrote in May 1947, "is not whether it is Jewish but on a par with the best in the culture in general."[53]

In the magazine's early issues, Israel had received comparatively little attention. As late as the early 1960s, Podhoretz dealt with Jews through articles on Jewish culture and history that were, like Podhoretz, "not especially religious nor much Zionist" either.[54] *Commentary* articles now came to emphasize threats to Jews and the safety and security of the Jewish state. By the 1980s, nearly half of Podhoretz's writings on international affairs centered on Israel and these dangers.[55]

Among the most important essays Podhoretz published at this time was Moynihan's "The United States in Opposition." Following his stint in the Nixon administration, Moynihan returned to Harvard, where he received a chilly homecoming. Recognizing perhaps that his views on urban affairs would not receive a hearing, his interests turned now to foreign affairs. He argued that the UN had come largely under the influence of a collectivist, Third World ideology. It was time for the United States to "go into opposition" at the UN, indeed time "that the American spokesman [should come] to be feared in international forums for the truths he might tell." Secretary of State Henry Kissinger brought the piece to the attention of President Ford, and in May 1975, Moynihan was appointed U.S ambassdor to the UN.

Moynihan embarked upon a campaign at the UN against those socialist Third World countries. He met head-on the attempt to isolate Israel in world opinion. When Idi Amin, president of Uganda and the incumbent chair of the Organization of African Unity, arrived in October to speak at the General Assembly, Moynihan took the gloves off. Amin began his speech with boilerplate anticolonial rhetoric and then went on to attack Israel. "How can we expect freedom, peace and justice in the world," he asked, "when such a powerful nation as the United States of America is in the hands of the Zionists." He called for "the expulsion of Israel from the United Nations and the extinction of Israel as a state." Moynihan had nothing but contempt for pompous, murderous Amin. In a speech in San Francisco at the annual AFL-CIO convention a few days later, Moynihan declared,

> It is no accident that on Wednesday 'His Excellency Field Marshal Al Hadji Amin Dada, President of the Republic of Uganda' – to give him his UN title – called for the extermination of Israel as a State. And it is no accident, I fear, that this 'racist murderer' – as one of our leading newspapers called him this morning – is head of the Organization of African Unity.

Democracy was under attack, Moynihan said. "There was blood in the water, and the sharks grow frenzied." Under way was a "systematic effort to create an international society in which government is the one and only legitimate institution."

The response was explosive. Many felt Moynihan had gone too far. Amin soon introduced his infamous resolution at the UN declaring that Zionism was a form of racism. The resolution was introduced on the thirty-seventh anniversary of *Kristallnacht*, the night when the Nazis smashed the windows of Jewish-owned businesses and burned synagogues all over Germany. Moynihan waited until after the successful vote to deliver his most famous speech. He began, as he would end, with several lines penned by Norman Podhoretz. "The United States rises to declare before the General Assembly of the UN, and before the world, that it does not acknowledge, it will not abide by, it will never acquiesce in this infamous act." As a senator, Moynihan led the campaign for repeal of Resolution 3379, which was ultimately revoked on December 16, 1991. His real concern, however, was not so much Arabs or Jews – or Israel, for that matter – but Moscow, which stood behind these efforts.[56]

Carter, who succeeded Ford, was seen by the neocons as fundamentally hostile to Israel, a view brought home to them sharply in the "Andrew Young affair." Young's appointment as U.S. ambassador to the United Nation had been greeted intially with enthusiasm by Jews. As Martin Luther King's lieutenant, he had displayed strength and courage on civil rights battlegrounds. But in the summer of 1979, the *New York Times* and *Newsweek* reported that Young, in apparent violation of a U.S. policy against negotiating with terrorist groups, had met secretly in New York with the PLO's UN ambassador. At first, the meeting was dismissed as accidental. It soon became apparent, however, that it was a full-scale exchange.The subsequent uproar forced Young to resign.

The following March, Young's successor at the UN, Donald McHenry, supported a Security Council resolution declaring Jerusalem occupied territory and charging Israel with extraordinary human rights violations. Once again, Carter backed away, blaming the episode on a mix-up in instructions. To the neocons, Carter's foreign policies looked, in the words of Jeane Kirkpatrick, like "McGovernism without McGovern."[57]

Another disappointed Democrat was Morris Abram, former president of the American Jewish Committee and this country's former human rights representative to the UN. A Southern Jew, who had courageously fought the Klan, Abrams had worked with Attorney General Robert Kennedy to free King from a Southern jail and had pressed forward the litigation that led to the Supreme Court's "one man, one vote" ruling. As president of Brandeis, he was shocked when black students seized the administration building and proclaimed Brandeis "Malcolm X University." In the election that fall, Abrams voted for Ronald Reagan, the first time he had voted for a Republican presidential candidate.[58]

Awakening belatedly to the fall of the Shah in Iran and the Soviet invasion of Afghanistan, and facing an election against hard-liner Ronald Reagan, Carter reversed his ground. By the summer of 1977, in language that echoed the Team B report, his Presidential Review Memorandum 10 sought the "ability to prevail" in the event of war. In a speech before the Business Council on December 12, 1979, he committed the nation to an average real increase in defense spending of five percent for the next five years. He decided also, along with NATO, to deploy 572 intermediate-range nuclear force (INF), Pershing II, and ground-launched cruise missiles in five countries in Western Europe in 1983. The Soviet Union had 1,000 such missiles in place, aimed at the heart of Western Europe. The U.S. had none on the continent at the time. The Soviets did not budge. In turn, Soviet Premier Leonid Brezhnev called for a moratorium on all medium-range missiles as a "peace gesture," a move that would confirm the Soviet Union's military advantage. Despite his hardened line, Carter could not bring himself to mention communism in his 1980 State of the Union address when referring to this country's resistance to any outside force attempting to gain control of the Persian Gulf region.[59]

Hoping that the president had abandoned his reservations about the use of force and might seek their help in the upcoming election, the CPD met with him again in the White House on August 4, 1977. Things did not go well. He expressed some sympathy with their views but made it clear he felt public sentiment would not support a large defense budget and attendant preparations for intervention. He did not agree that he had erred earlier and refused to conduct any housecleaning that, in the words of Senator Moynihan, would replace members of his administration with "people whose past judgments comport to the administration's new policies."[60]

When Carter appeared lukewarm following Podhoretz's "impassioned plea" for a strong human rights offensive against the Soviet bloc, the neocons were convinced that Carter had not changed significantly. "Carter was telling us that he was going to pursue the 'Andy Young foreign policy' [finding accommodation with Israel's enemies]," Elliott Abrams, who was present at the meeting, later said. Jeane Kirkpatrick, who was also there, described the meeting as a failure. It threw "cold water on whatever hopes we had that Iran and Afghanistan would have a broad effect on the president's foreign policy orientation."[61]

The mood of the meeting left everyone discouraged. Testifying before the Senate Budget Committee in March of the following year, Rostow warned that unless the administration increased the defense budget by a substantial amount, "our security position will continue to erode, and our foreign policy to decline in influence."[62] At the dawn of the 1980s, the neocons felt the outcome of the Cold War was seriously in doubt.

Reagan's decision to run for president marked the final break of these liberal Democrats with their old party. Reagan would become the first presidential candidate since the days of Truman to take the offensive ideologically and politically against the Soviet Union. In his unsuccessful challenge to take the Republican nomination away from President Ford in 1976, he had made Kissinger and détente a campaign issue. During his 1976 and 1980 presidential campaigns, Reagan backed the CDP's view of the dangers of the SALT treaties and of SALT II in particular.[63] His extraordinary confidence – generally alien to the sour pessimism of the GOP – in the superiority of American society and his determination to succeed in overcoming Soviet communism was, in effect, a return to the earlier liberal worldview.[64]

Reagan was a genuine neocon. For most of his life he had been a liberal Democrat. He joined the Republican Party only in 1962. "I didn't leave the Democratic Party," he was fond of saying. "The Democratic Party left me." Reagan had watched the duel between Kennedy and Khrushchev in October 1962, when the Soviets placed missiles in Cuba. While the conventional wisdom has it that Kennedy behaved firmly and responsibly during that crisis, he felt that Kennedy had given up too much. He faulted him for maintaining existing policy, which agreed that the United States would not invade the island. "Are missile bases enough," he asked publicly, "or will we insist on freedom for all Cubans?" In the months that followed, he made a number of suggestions as to what this country should do next. When the Kennedy administration set out to develop an arms control agreement, he wrote an article urging that our goal should be not to coexist with communism but to defeat it.[65] When Reagan announced in 1979 that he was running for president, the KGB wrote a secret analysis of him. Unlike Kennedy, who, the Soviets conjectured, vacillated and changed his mind, Reagan was accorded greater respect. They viewed him as "a firm and unbending politician from whom words and deeds are one and the same."[66]

Although liberals dismissed him as a dim bulb, Reagan had an instinctive feel for traditional power politics. His relentless anticommunism dated from his years as president of the Screen Actors Guild in Hollywood, when radicals had plotted to take over the union.[67] In moving to the right, he had steered clear of McCarthy, who, he said, "went with a scatter gun and lumped together fellow travelers, innocent dupes, and hard-core Communists."[68] In his primary race for governor in 1966, he denounced the John Birch Society, declaring the great majority of its members to be "crackpots or hysterical about the threat of Communist subversion." He had been swept into office as governor of California in the aftermath of the Berkeley Free Speech Movement of 1964 and the Los Angeles racial disorders of 1965.

Reagan was keenly aware of the Soviet Union's internal weaknesses early on and made every effort to capitalize on them. As early as 1963, he declared that the United States enjoyed the most efficient and powerful economic machine in the world and that Russia and China, by contrast, were "in the grip of modern-day feudalism." He urged placing as much strain as possible on the feeble Soviet economy, assisting its enslaved satellites while denying any economic concessions to the Soviets themselves.[69]

With Jackson gone and Moynihan unavailable as a candidate for the presidency, the neocons turned to Reagan. A number of neocons and CPD members, along with Milton Friedman, served as advisors in his 1980 campaign. Of his seventy-six advisers during the campaign, twenty-two were members of the Mont Pélerin Society, and he cited Hayek and von Mises most frequently.[70] Podhoretz's *The Present Danger* (1980), which warned of the "Finlandization" of Western democracies, became the campaign bible. During the campaign, and echoing the CPD line, Reagan took the position that the United States needed to redefine the power balance after a decade of military and political decline. In turn, President Carter, despite his growing awareness of Soviet aggression, positioned himself to the left of Reagan, claiming that he was the "peace" candidate. He promised to resubmit SALT II to the Senate after the election.[71]

Reagan's triumph in the election provided the neocons with their version of John F. Kennedy's Camelot. *Commentary* became the White House's favorite political journal, and some sixty members of the CDP were recruited to work for the new president. Several of them would later become important players in the second Bush administration.

Paul Wolfowitz joined George Shultz at the State Department, where he stood as the point man when the administration withdrew its support from Ferdinand Marcos and helped bring to power the democratic opposition in that country. Following his service there, he served as ambassador to Indonesia, the fourth largest country in the world and the nation with the largest Muslim population, a post that provided him with background for his later crucial role in the second Bush administration.[72] Podhoretz's son-in-law, Elliott Abrams, was named assistant secretary of state for international organizations, and Perle, Senator Jackson's assistant, was appointed assistant secretary of defense. Max Kampelman headed the administration's arms control negotiations.Two neocons, first Rostow and later Kenneth Adelman, served as director of the Arms Control and Disarmament Agency. A neocon ally, William Bennett, headed the National Endowment for the Humanities and later took over as head of the Department of Education. Pipes directed the East European and Soviet Affairs division of the National Security Council. Chester Finn and William Kristol worked for the Department of Education. Morris Abram, a bitter oponent of racial quotas, was named vice chairman of the U.S. Civil Rights Commission. And when Congress formed the National Endowment for Democracy to spearhead the ideological war against the Soviet Union, Reagan selected Carl Gershman, an ex-leader of the Young Peoples Socialist League (YPSL), to direct it. Although it would shortly adopt a hard line in international and national defense matters, *The New Republic* complained that "Trotsky's orphans" were taking over the government.[73]

Podhoretz failed to get the post as head of the U.S. Information Agency, for which he was sometimes mentioned. He met, however, from time to time with Secretary of State Shultz, CIA director William Casey, and Reagan himself. Meanwhile, he kept publishing articles in *Commentary* that reminded his readers of the favorable military balance the Soviets still enjoyed in the world.

After reading her November 1979 article in *Commentary*, "Dictatorships and Double Standards," President Reagan named Jeane Kirkpatrick, a registered Democrat and CPD member, as U.S. ambassador to the United Nations – the first woman in history to hold that post. Earlier that same year, Kirkpatrick, a political scientist, had written an article titled "Why I Am Not a Republican." "The problem," she declared, "is that the Republican Party has not articulated any inclusive vision of the public good that reflects concern for the well-being of the whole community. It has been left to the Democratic Party to make clear that in a civilized society, people must look out for one another, and devise, however ineptly, the mechanisms for doing so."[74]

The double standards referred to in her *Commentary* essay were in response to what she felt to be the blunders in the Carter administration, which took a hard line on human rights violations committed by right-wing regimes but remained relatively indifferent to the systematic abuses of communist regimes. The essay, written several months before the overthrow of reactionary regimes in Iran and Nicaragua, made a distinction between totalitarian governments, whose coercive hold on their peoples prevented change, and authoritarian regimes, who were capable of being persuaded to grant human rights. She made it clear that she favored the encouragement of liberalizaton and democratization among friendly allies, but never at the expense of an existing government that was fighting for its life against violent forces.[75]

In demonstrating support for the latter, she provided the neocon rationale for silence, at least publicly, at the behavior of those right-wing regimes that Reaganites backed in Central America and other parts of the world as part of the effort to defeat Soviet expansionist designs. Kirkpatrick had formed her views on totalitarianism in her graduate school days at Columbia, where she encountered survivors of Hitler's death camps. Her views were crystalized when she heard Hannah Arendt speak at the New School for Social Research. Arendt, who taught that the left was just as capable of mounting terror as the right, was one of the shaping forces of neoconservatism.[76]

In the charged rhetoric characteristic of many of the neocons, Kirkpatrick, like Moynihan before her, led the fight at the UN for halting the spread of communism throughout the world and in providing support for Israel. Like Reagan, who had known and worked with Jews all his life, Kirkpatrick saw Israel as a young country of hard workers, pioneers taming a stubborn land. For those uncomfortable with her hard line, she came to be known as "the ambassador from *Commentary*."[77]

The neocons reinforced Reagan's hard-line beliefs on international communism and provided much of the administration's ideological energy, giving the Reagan revolution "its final sophistication." The effort to expand the scope of democracy and freedom supplied a moral dimension even in light of its support for certain regimes that sometimes deviated from this principle.[78]

Reagan set about implementing his ideas for rebuilding America's military forces through a measured modernization of obsolete systems. He also launched the Strategic Defense Initiative (SDI) and, most importantly, mobilized public opinion in this country and abroad behind his hard-line policies, particularly in Eastern Europe.

Reagan found himself confronted by Democrats in Congress, who by 1982 refused to fund the MX missile and hoped to undermine his efforts in other ways. He was buoyed, however, by a National Intelligence Estimate that his military build-up was causing consternation in the Kremlin. The report also showed that economic growth in the Soviet Union was stalling and that the advantages the Soviets had gained over the West militarily could not be sustained.

Less than a year into his presidency, Reagan went before the British Parliament. In a prophetic speech, he announced a campaign for democracy and an ideological war with the Soviet Union. Much like Churchill had done at

Fulton in his "iron curtain" address, Reagan declared that the Soviet Union, "the home of Marxist-Leninism," was gripped by "a great revolutionary crisis" and that a "global campaign for freedom" would ultimately triumph. With this speech, Reagan opened a new chapter in the Cold War, one that would leave "Marxism-Leninism on the ash heap of history."[79]

The *Times* scoffed. Missing from his plan, it declared, was any formula for utilizing Western economic strength "to promote political accommodation." *Time* magazine's Strobe Talbott declared the speech to be "dangerous bear-baiting," "extremist," and "militant."[80]

Out of the Westminster speech came another initiative, the National Endowment for Democracy (NED), a special favorite of the neocons, which would provide money to overseas organizations active in promoting democracy in their countries. Reagan seized on the idea, which had first been proposed by Georgetown University professor Allen C. Weinstein. To lead the effort, the NED turned to a former social democrat, Gershman, a former aide to Bayard Rustin during the struggle for civil rights who now worked with Ambassador Kirkpatrick at the UN. Soon the NED was engaged behind the Iron Curtain, coming to the aid of the Polish Solidarity labor union and Czechoslovakia's Charter 77 movement. One grant funded efforts to publish a Russian version of George Orwell's *Animal Farm*, as well as other anti-totalitarian tracts.[81]

Reagan's vision was implemented through a series of top secret national security directives, starting in 1982. These directives argued that the United States would attempt to "neutralize" Soviet control over Eastern Europe. He authorized the use of covert action and other methods to back up anti-Soviet groups in the region. Pipes, who had served as an advisor to Reagan during the campaign and on the transition team for the State Department, joined the administration following the election as part of the National Security staff in charge of the Eastern European and Soviet desk. Pipes was charged with laying out the philosophy and design of the Reagan thrust.

Working out of his crowded third floor office in the Old Executive Office Building, Pipes came up with a forty-three-page paper eventually known a NSD 75, confirming the arguments of the neocons and what Reagan intuitively felt himself. Starting from his basic position that détente had been a mistake, he argued that since the Soviets were inherently aggressive, it was vital to change the system. Thus, NSSD 75 determined that the U.S. had to pursue three objectives: weakening the Soviet economy further, weakening the power and privileged position of its leadership elite, and gradually democratizing the Soviets. By forcing them to compete with us in a military build-up, we would create further pressures on the regime and among its satellites and substantially lower its rate of growth and capital investment.

NSSD 75 declared also that the Soviets should be denied access to the West's technology. The United States should press forward covert efforts on behalf of democratic movements behind the Iron Curtain, especially in

Poland. Pipes was angered at the failure of the CIA to alert the administration to Soviet plans to use Polish troops against Solidarity. The document came to Reagan's desk in December 1982, and he promptly signed it.[82]

Unlike previous administrations, Reagan aggressively supported, with CIA funding and moral backing, dissenters in Eastern Europe and guerrilla insurgencies against Soviet client states. In the summer and early fall of 1981, for example, Soviet-backed Warsaw Pact troops moved to suppress the Solidarity labor movement. Troops were moved to the border, and Polish security forces invaded their own country, rounding up 5,000 Solidarity activists.

In the discussions that followed, the president was absolutely livid, Richard Pipes recalls. A strong protest in a letter to Brezhnev was drafted by Pipes, and was backed by Jeane Kirpatrick over the opposition of the State Department, which sought a calmer response. Reagan took to the airways in a speech, drafted mainly by Pipes, to announce an embargo against Poland and the Soviet Union. Poland would now lose its most-favored-nation trading status. Tariffs were raised on its exports to the United States, and no further financial credits would be extended to the Polish government. Even more signficant, Reagan issued a decree banning the sale of oil and gas technologies to the Soviets, in connection with a gas line they were looking to build, a decision that cost them billions. Reagan's determination to nurture freedom in Poland won him few plaudits among his critics. George Kennan described calls for freedom in Poland as inevitably self-defeating and detrimental to détente.[83]

Another forceful critic of détente in the Reagan administration, particularly on arms control, and a major figure in pressing forward the "Reagan doctrine," was Richard Perle. Perle was named to the important post of assistant secretary of defense for international security policy, a position known as the Pentagon's "little State Department" because it encompassed the full range of policy, from relations with the Soviet Union, NATO, and Europe to economic and strategic issues.

Perle grew up in the Hollywood Hills in California. Like so many of the neocons, he was not from a pedigreed, Ivy League background. While in high school, he dated the daughter of Albert Wohlstetter, a mathematician and leading theoretician of nuclear war, who worked at the Rand Corporation. Wohlstetter was the grand old man of the neoconservative hawks. Wohlstetter gave him his article on strategy, "The Delicate Balance of Terror," which had been published in *Foreign Affairs*. It questioned the ability of the United States to withstand a surprise Soviet atomic attack. In the spring of 1969, Wohlstetter offered him a job as senior researcher in Washington with the Committee to Maintain a Prudent Defense Policy, formed by him and Paul Nitze. One of Perle's tasks was to provide information in support of the antiballistic missile (ABM) defense system, which was designed to destroy incoming missiles while they were still in the air.

Perle arrived in Washington in November 1969 as an opponent of the Vietnam War and soon joined "Scoop" Jackson's staff. He thought of himself as a social democrat – a liberal on domestic issues and firmly anticommunist on foreign policy. He worked with Jackson in the battles over SALT I, the ABM treaty, and SALT II. He also helped to develop the Jackson-Vanik legislation in 1974 that sought as its major goal to pressure the Soviets into permitting Jews to leave the USSR. Disdaining what he termed Carter's "prudish moralism," Perle, like Morris Abram, voted Republican in a presidential election for the first time in 1980.

His influence in the Reagan administration grew out of the confidence Secretary of Defense Caspar Weinberger showed in him, as well as his formidable intellect and experience fighting rearguard battles against arms control while working under Jackson. During his years in Washington, he created a network of allies, friends, and informants throughout the intelligence community, the Capitol, and elsewhere in government, most of whom stayed in close touch with him, even as they worked at their regular assignments. Weinberger gave him a free hand in dealing with Soviet and arms control policy and consistently backed him at the White House. As a result of his unquestioned skills, and what some critics called his Machiavellian political tactics, he came to be known as "the Prince of Darkness."[84]

Perle, like other neocons, believed that under Carter and some of his predecessors in the White House, the United States had encouraged appeasement of the Soviet Union. In an article published in 1979, "Echoes of the 1930s," he argued that "anyone who has studied the interwar period and reads today's newspapers tends to experience an uneasy sense of deja vu." He recognized that the Soviet Union was an impoverished power. He recognized also that it was not guided by "a latter-day version of prewar German policies" and that Brezhnev was not "another Hitler"; but, as he testified before a congressional committee in 1985, the Soviets were like a "hotel burglar [who] goes down a corridor trying all doors until he finds an open door and in he goes." The Soviets, he believed, were determined to achieve nuclear superiority and a first-strike capability. They supported Marxist guerrilla movements of national liberation as part of the Brezhnev doctrine of permanent socialist revolution.[85]

Perle was convinced, following the Desert One disaster in Iran, where a number of American soldiers lost their lives in the failed attempt to rescue American hostages, and the Soviet invasion of Afghanistan, that the American people had elected Reagan because they wanted the United States to change its policies toward the Soviet Union. Less than three months after taking office, Reagan boldly began that change by moving to deploy Pershing II and cruise missiles in Western Europe.

What followed was a worldwide movement encouraged by Moscow to halt the deployment. In Britain, the out-of-power Labour Party called for unilateral disarmament (150,000 people rallied in Hyde Park in London).

On April 4, 1981, some 150,000 angry protestors, many with small children at their side, took to the streets of Bonn, demanding that the United States halt the spread of nuclear missiles. Six months later, 250,000 protesters packed the public squares in West Germany in opposition.[86] As Perle and Weinberger continued to hang tough, the State Department urged negotiations aimed at finding some kind of accommodation with the Soviet Union. A nuclear freeze resolution was passed by the House of Representatives, 278–149. In June 1982, an antinuclear rally in New York City attracted 700,000 people – the largest demonstration up to that point in American history.[87]

Meanwhile, former Vice President Walter Mondale, who would run against Reagan in 1984, claimed this country had "ceded the moral high ground" to Moscow. Senator Edward Kennedy explained that Reagan and his advisors "are talking peace in 1984" preparatory "to making war in 1985."[88]

Perle now seized on a Pentagon study to propose that both the United States and the Soviet Union remove all their missiles from Europe. This dramatic zero-level option would require the Soviets to dismantle their SS-20s aimed at Western Europe; in return, the United States would not deploy any of its 572 missiles. The plan was frankly aimed to be part of the propaganda wars under way, as well as to strengthen Western defenses. Perle assumed the Soviets would never accept it. But in light of severe opposition in Western Europe, including opposition among some European leaders, to the deployment of American missiles, it was meant to serve as a concession to those who felt Washington was being overly aggressive. Perle's plan was opposed by the State Department, which felt the Soviets would never accept it (they were willing to permit higher Soviet numbers to remain in place). Presented by Weinberger, Perle's plan was backed by Reagan. By the close of 1981, Perle's zero-level option strategy was unveiled as President Reagan's "first major foreign policy speech."[89]

Reagan's Strategic Defense Initiative (SDI), derided by critics as a costly "star wars" (from the science fiction film) fantasy, drew strong support from Perle. Reagan viewed SDI as a population shield that would employ modern technology to destroy incoming missiles. The concept came from Edward Teller, a distinguished, albeit eccentric, nuclear physicist refugee, who shared Reagan's hard-line views about dealing with the Soviet Union. Reagan pushed the initiative on his own. While Perle was aware of the president's rhetorical excesses and the extraordinary difficulties in bringing the idea to fruition, he seized upon it as consistent with the 1972 antiballistic missile treaty because of its defensive nature.[90] Perle joked, "It was a good movie in which the good guys won."[91]

SDI would never be a perfect shield, but even an imperfect shield was better than nothing, Perle believed. It would engage the Soviets in a high technology race that they could ill afford and force them back to the negotiating table. Much of the public believed Reagan's rhetoric, and the growing popularity of SDI helped to undercut the power of the nuclear freeze movement in this country, if not in Europe.[92] Of all the measures undertaken by the Reagan administration in the confrontation with the Soviets, this was perhaps the most important. It might or might not stop a nuclear strike, but it would worry Soviet military planners and make it easier to drive a favorable deal in arms control talks.[93] The issue for Perle and the neocons in the administration was not simply the opposition of the Soviets but pressures from the State Department, which sought a more accommodating role in what it deemed to be the interest of working out a peaceful accommodation with the Soviets.

In 1992, out of government, Perle published a novel, *Hard Line*. In the Introduction to the novel, the narrator, loosely based on the author himself, declares,

> What is particularly galling is the claim made by liberals of the period that the Soviet Union never really threatened the Free World, that the Pentagon overstated Soviet military power to justify huge military budgets, that liberal policies of restraint, no less led to the Western victory in the Cold War and the subsequent breakup, first of the Warsaw Pact and then the Soviet Union itself. In their view, the American president was at best a minor player and even a bystander witnessing events he neither understood nor influenced. The real hero was Gorbachev who deescalated the tensions and sought reform.[94]

Gorbachev knew the Soviet economic situation left them in no position to meet such a challenge. At the summit conference at Reykjavik in Iceland in 1986, Gorbachev offered a number of significant concessions but insisted that they be coupled with the agreement that SDI be confined to the laboratory and not field tested. According to Jay Winik and David Frum, some of Reagan's advisors were inclined to accept the offer. Perle dissented, and Reagan went along with him. Finally, in 1987, Gorbachev, recognizing that the United States would go forward on SDI no matter what he did, found himself compelled to sign the Intermediate Nuclear Force (INF) Treaty for Europe. The deployment of the missiles in Western Europe, along with the controversial SDI program, were critical in forcing the Soviet Union to retreat.[95]

Democrat Zbigniew Brzezinski, Jimmy Carter's national security advisor, believes that the Cold War was won at Reykjavik.[96] Similarly, political scientist Robert Kagan has maintained that Reagan's commitment to SDI panicked Soviet leaders into believing that a radical restructuring of their economic system was necessary for them to compete in a new arms race (both quantitatively and qualitatively) that they could not afford, thereby moving them to seek a respite from the Cold War.[97] Soviet Ambassador Anatoly Dobrynin has written in a memoir that Reagan's unwavering commitment to SDI and vastly higher Pentagon spending turned the tide. "No matter what diplomatic tack Moscow examined or actually took," he recalls, "the Reagan administration proved impervious to it. We came to realize that in contrast to most presidents who shift from their electoral rhetoric to more centrist, pragmatic positions by the middle of their presidential term, Reagan displayed an active immunity to the traditional forces, both internal and external that normally produce a classic adjustment."[98]

Gorbachev's selection as general secretary by a coalition of the foreign ministry, the military, and the KGB was, according to Georgy Shakhnazarov, a foreign policy adviser to Gorbachev, the result of "internal domestic pressures and Reagan's rigid position and that of his administration."[99]

Under President Clinton, research was scaled back significantly or canceled in the 1990s. Curiously, when the National Missile Defense Act of 1999, which called for deploying such a missile defense system, was enacted by Congress, Clinton signed it into law, thus making possible the Reagan vision.[100]

In the shaping of the policies of the Reagan administration, such figures as Kirkpatrick, Rostow, Podhoretz, Pipes, and Perle played a critical role. By the latter part of the 1980s, the very force of Perle's ideas, and the fierce energy he exerted in advancing them, made him perhaps the central figure here, save Reagan himself. While working at *Time* magazine, Strobe Talbott, who would later become the number two man in the Clinton State Department, sized up this influential neocon: "Perle ended up having more impact on policy in arms control than any other official in the U.S. government."[101]

9

Nicaragua: The Cold War Comes to This Hemisphere

One of the most difficult problems the Reagan administration and its neocon advisers faced in the heightened confrontation with the Soviets was the situation in Central America. Here the issues of human rights, articulated so eloquently by Moynihan and Kirkpatrick at the UN and in other forums, collided with the need to counter Soviet influence in the United States' backyard in Central and Latin America. The Soviets, in fact, had become interested in opening a new front in the Cold War by supporting leftist insurgencies in this part of the world.

There is some dispute among the authorities I have consulted as to when this new strategy took concrete form. According to Peter Schweizer, a fellow at the Hoover Institution of War and Peace at Stanford University, who has had acccess to KGB files, the Soviets began to provide financial support and weapons to a guerrilla army, the Sandinista Liberation Front (FSLN), which was waging a decade-old war against the bitterly hated Somoza regime in Nicaragua, as early as 1966. While some people in the West viewed the Sandinistas, a coalition of groups with different ideologies, as a democratic ally in overthrowing a widely acknowledged reactionary regime, the Soviets, Schweizer asserts, looked upon them as a vehicle for penetration into this hemisphere. The Soviet Union wanted not only to overthrow the Somoza regime but also to install in its place the Sandinistas, led by Marxist-Leninists, Daniel Ortega and his brother Humberto.[1] Michael Radu, a scholar at the Foreign Policy Research Institute, on the other hand, holds that following the Soviet misadventure in Cuba (precipitating the missile crisis and Bay of Pigs fiasco of 1961), the Soviets learned a lesson, following which they backed off. The Cubans under Fidel Castro remained, however, wedded to implementing Marxist-Leninist beliefs of world revolution in that region, with which Soviet leaders, it can be extrapolated, were sympathetic, although at times they could be publicly critical of Castro's calls for world revolution in the hemisphere.[2]

Under pressure from the Carter administration, which cut off aid to the Somoza regime, the regime fell in July 1979. A broad coalition of groups, including the Sandinistas, took over. The State Department viewed the Sandinistas as dedicated to democracy; their pro-Soviet bent, it was felt, was due to to the fact that Somoza had "radicalized the opposition." The administration decided to treat the new regime with good will, according to historian Theodore Draper.[3] Appearing before the Senate Foreign Relations Committee, Deputy Secretary of State Warren Christopher reported that the Sandinistas were prepared to build "a new Nicaragua through popular participation that is capable of meeting basic human needs." Christopher was instrumental in getting a $75 million aid package through Congress.[4]

The Sandinista takeover in Nicaragua, Cuba's menacing gestures, and the triumph of the communists on the small island of Grenada created an opening for the Soviets in Latin America. KGB General Nikolai Leonov, who had predicted a Sandinista victory, now began to think how to consolidate the power that had been placed in Soviet hands.[5]

The Ortega brothers, dedicated Marxist revolutionaries, proved to be as repressive as the autocrat they had driven from office. They shut down the Catholic Church's radio station and its Commission for Justice and Peace, which looked into infractions of religious and civic rights; hounded labor unions; persecuted indigenous peoples; and harassed *La Prensa*, the distinguished independent newspaper owned by the widely respected Chamorro family. Sandinista mobs roamed the streets terrorizing opponents. Even radical Marxist and other supporters, who had worked with the Sandinistas before the overthrow of the Somoza government (including Edén Pastora and the poet Gioconda Belli), soon found Humberto to be conniving and without principles and Daniel "a manipulating, dark character." At the beginning of 1984, Belli came to question the wisdom of the Sandinista leadership, even as she remained loyal to it and to her dream of a free Nicaragua:

> The Revolution slowly lost its steam, its spark, its positive energy, to be replaced by an unprincipled, manipulative and populist mentality.... We were feeling more and more like spectators to a process that continued to live off its heroic, idealistic image even though in practice, it was being gutted and turned into an amorphous, arbitrary mess.[6]

In 1980, Violetta Chamorro, who had run *La Prensa* following her husband's assassination in the closing days of the Somoza rule, resigned from Ortega's provisonal government. She later told a joint session of the U.S. Congress on April 26, 1991, that she had become disillusioned. Daniel Ortega, according to Draper, now emerged as the "Nicaraguan Castro." In March 1980, Ortega sent a delegation to Moscow and entered into economic, technical, and scientific agreements with the Soviet Union. Cuban advisors moved into Nicaragua. The Sandinista government now moved to support the leftist elements seeking to overthrow the government of El Salvador.[7]

Meanwhile, the Sandinistas developed close ties to Yasir Arafat's PLO. Their members trained in Palestinian camps and joined in PLO raids on Israel. In turn, the PLO delivered arms to Nicaragua. Arafat was cheered when he opened a PLO embassy in Managua in July 1980. "The triumph of the Nicaraguans," he declared," is the PLO's triumph."[8]

With military support from the Soviet Union and Cuba, the Sandinistas sought to destabilize U.S.-backed regimes in Honduras and Guatemala as well as in El Salvador.[9] As they became aware of the propaganda possibilities in South America and Central America, the Kremlin's investment politically and militarily in the latter grew substantially. A CIA report noted that the number of shipments to Cuba reached "the second highest annual total on record." By 1985, the Sandinistas had received some one billion dollars in Soviet aid and could boast of 350 tanks, advanced Soviet artillery, and a number of MIG-25s. Much like Cuba during the Kennedy administration, Nicaragua had become the primary outpost for the penetraton of the Soviet Union into the hemisphere.[10]

In the post–World War II years, both Democratic and Republican administrations had reacted strongly to any Soviet or communist moves to spread Soviet influence throughout the world. President Kennedy, it will be recalled, challenged the placement of missiles in Cuba and forced their removal. During the Carter years, however, it was felt that revolutionary change was sweeping the world and that the United States should place itself on the side of those seeking to replace reactionary regimes and support human rights. Not long after taking office, Carter spelled out his goals in a major address at the University of Notre Dame. Although this country was still suffering from the trauma of Vietnam, much good could come from this catharsis, Carter said. It might help return us to our real values. The danger came not from communism but from a failure to concentrate on human rights. In focusing on this, Carter presumably felt that we could overcome Soviet penetration in the area and simultaneously achieve humanitarian objectives.[11]

The Carterites (including chief advisers like Secretary of State Cyrus Vance) believed that the primary cause of human rights violations grew out of this country's role in the Cold War. Carter's United Nations ambassador, Andrew Young, argued that the Cold War mentality encouraged "an apparatus of repression" and "imperialism, neocolonialism, capitalism, or what have you." Carter and his advisors, however, seemed to be more interested in human rights violations by those nations in Central America who were resisting Sandinista efforts to destabilize them. When, late in 1979, Carter was visited by Polish Communist Party head Edward Giereck, the president refrained from criticizing his abysmal human rights record, according to a classified White House transcript.[12]

Before joining Carter's National Security Council, even Zbigniew Brzezinski, who later gained a reputation as a hard-liner in dealing with Soviet aggressive designs in the world, joined in the conventional view of the foreign policy elite that a new era had dawned. In Between Two Ages, a symposium originally sponsored by the Council on Foreign Relations (and published by Yale University Press in 1971 as *Between Two Ages*), Brezezinski spelled out the new "realities" as applied to Latin America. Despite the Cold War, he wrote, we needed to recognize the lessening of ideological competition, the importance of global interdependence, as well as growing Third World expectations. He called for abandoning the Monroe Doctrine, which for much of our history had sought to keep foreign influence out of the Western hemisphere. Sol Linowitz, who headed a national commission on U.S. relations in Latin America, took a similar position: "The changing realities of interrelationships required that power needed to be used to advance moral not economic or political goals."[13]

At one point, Christopher told hesitant members of the Senate Foreign Relations Committee that "the driving consensus among Nicaraguans" was "to build a new Nicaragua through popular participation that is capable of meeting basic human needs."[14] Confronted with what turned out to be a Marxist revolution in Nicaragua that was attempting to expand into nearby El Salvador and elsewhere in the area, Carter sought to use the power of persuasion and economic aid to get the Sandinistas to follow a more democratic and pro-Western approach, according to Robert Kagan. This view forswore the use of force and in its place pursued universal moral goals, while minimizing the commitment of Fidel Castro and the Sandinista leadership to Marxist-Leninist expansionist policies.[15]

Carter's policies bore some resemblance to the ideas of the New Left, although the neocons believed that such utopian globalism coincided with the liberal meltdown that had taken shape during and following the Vietnam War. The Carterites felt the country could move on from the despondency caused by the Vietnam failure to build a more humanistic society by lining up on the side of change.

On Christmas Day of 1979, a major Soviet military aircraft landed at the Kabul Airport in Afghanistan, followed soon by a number of transports containing hundreds of Soviet commandos, with accompanying equipment; the invasion of that country was under way. Carter was thunderstruck. A few days earlier, he had sat with his advisers and committed himself to détente and arms control with the Kremlin. He was prepared also to push hard for Senate approval for a SALT agreement. With the fall of the Shah in Iran, the taking of American hostages there, and Soviet successes in Nicaragua, Ethiopia, and Grenada, his policies quickly fell into disarray. Vance called for moderation, perhaps a verbal rebuke of the Soviets; but Brzezinski, now turned hawk, opposed this view sharply. Carter now sided with Brzezinski. Shortly before leaving office, he suspended U.S. aid to Nicaragua.[16]

Shortly before the Sandinistas came to power in Nicaragua, Ronald Reagan had warned that the Cuban-trained rebels were armed, dangerous, and devoted to building another communist country in Central America.[17] The incoming Reagan administration's hard-line approach for dealing with the situation hewed closely to the analysis of, and the plan laid out by, Kirkpatrick in her *Commentary* essay "U.S. Security and Latin America," a follow-up to her earlier essay "Dictatorships and Double Standards." Noting the strong military build-up in Cuba, including supersonic aircraft like MIG 21s and 23s that could be quickly armed with nuclear weapons, as well as the use of some 50,000 Cuban troops and military advisers in Africa and the Middle East, Kirkpatrick warned: "The deterioration of the U.S. position in the hemisphere has already created serious vulnerabilities where none previously existed, and threatens now to confront this country with the unprecedented need to defend itself against a ring of Soviet bases in and around our Southern and eastern borders."[18] This was the stance of CPD and a newly formed neocon vehicle, the Committee for the Free World, organized and run by Midge Decter. In a full-page ad that appeared in the *New York Times* on April 6, 1981, the group laid out the claim that the war in El Salvador "depends on weapons supplied by the Soviet Union through such client states as Cuba, Nicaragua, Vietnam and others." It went on to repeat the Kirkpatrick thesis that the result of a revolution in El Salvador would not bring "progressive" change but "totalitarian regimes."[19]

Once Reagan was inaugurated in January 1981, he moved sharply away from Carter's policies in Central America. The Republican platform had called for the overthrow of the Sandinista government. In February, the administration suspended the last $15 million dollars of the $75 million aid package to Nicaragua. The new president increased U.S. military aid to El Salvador, Honduras, and Guatemala and ordered the CIA in 1982 to support covertly an armed rebellion against Sandinista rule in order to overthrow the government.[20]

The situation, however, was complex. In one sense, Carter was right: problems in the area did, in fact, have a lot to do with existing social and economic inequities, not just with Soviet subversion. On the other hand, the Reaganites were also correct, as one report prepared for the State Department pointed out, in assuming there had been a "decision by Cuba with Soviet-bloc support, to organize and arm guerrilla forces under Marxist-Leninist control" after the Sandinistas' victory in Nicaragua and that "El Salvador became a target with the expectation that Communist-bloc training and supplies would bring a quick victory to Cuban-backed elements here." At their height, Soviet- and Cuban-supported guerrilla movements, according to the report, were operating in a dozen countries in the area.[21]

But the president and his advisers faced strong popular opposition to the direct use of military force in Central America and a Congress unwilling to support even sending military advisers to the area. This post-Vietnam view was backed by many elements of the cultural elite. In *The Tailor of Panama*, for example, John Le Carré continued to savage this country's Cold War policies, taking a satirical swipe at American military postures in Central America. The Reaganites were forced to select what one called "the low-ball option," which translated into covert support for military rebels (the Contras) in Nicaragua seeking to overthrow the Ortega regime.[22]

In linking its activities in Central America to Soviet efforts to spread communist influence to other parts of the globe, the Reagan administration and the Contras were faced with intense criticism and opposition, both at home and abroad. Stephen Schwartz observes that Nicaragua became "a virtual obsession of 'progressives' liberals and ultra leftists alike." The baby boom or Vietnam generation remained "radical about foreign policy in Central America."[23] Latin America specialist Mark Falcoff writes that "no anti-Communist insurgency in history – including the rebel movement in Afghanistan – ever received such negative treatment in the American press, particularly in television news." The Contras were accused of committing atrocities and of being mercenaries who were in the pay of fascist remnants of the bitterly hated Somoza regime, which many had fought against.[24]

Although the totalitarian direction of the Sandinista government was well known, the center of the discussion shifted away from Managua to Washington and to Reagan's policies. Central America, Schwartz suggests, was "a final attempt at revitalizing the 1960s" – a "politics of perpetual rage" similar to an obsession with "an almost forgotten past" to be found outside of the United States, lingering only in Scandinavia and West Germany.[25]

Nowhere were these attacks on Reagan and the neocons more evident than in Congress. Most Democrats felt that U.S. efforts were embroiling the nation in overseas adventures, and they worried that they were not receiving reports on covert activity. They also focused heavily on the human rights abuses of U.S. allies in the region.

Such opposition was embodied in the several Boland Amendments enacted in 1982 and 1984, which barred the CIA and the Department of Defense from supporting "military or paramilitary activities" in Nicaragua.[26] Democratic Representative Edward P. Boland headed the Select Committee on Intelligence. He was convinced, he said in taking over this committee in the early 1980s, that the CIA had spied on American citizens and attempted to assassinate foreign leaders. Insisting that he was in "complete sympathy" with the effort to curb communism and to destabilize nearby countries, he maintained that the Reagan administration's approach was duplicitous and dysfunctional.

The first Boland Amendment prohibited the CIA and the Defense Department from utilzing funds "for the purpose of overthrowing the Government of Nicaragua or provoking a military exchange between Nicaragua and Honduras."[27] Opposition to Reagan's plans solidified, partly because the Reaganites faced conflict and indecision within their own ranks and partly because they developed a poor public relations campaign to defend their actions. For all these reasons, the neocons felt, as an article in *Commentary* put it, that this country was "Losing Central America."[28]

It was not until Reagan delivered a prime time, nationally televised speech on May 9, 1984, that the administration finally made a more fully thought-out case for aid to the Contras. Lou Cannon, in his biography of Reagan, sees aid to the Contras as linked to a continuation of the policy of resistance to Soviet expansionism that the United States had followed since 1947 (when President Truman provided military aid to a conservative Greek government then involved in a civil war with communists and clients of Moscow). The difference between the Contras and the Greek situation, however, was that support for the Contras involved backing an insurrectionary force against a duly constituted government, which had overthrown a despotic regime.[29]

Although Reagan had laid the foundation of the "Reagan Doctrine" in his Westminster speech in London on June 8, 1982 (the phrase was the brainchild of Charles Krauthammer, another of the emerging Jewish neocons), the actual substance did not appear, as we have seen, until nearly a year later in NSD DD-75, the document largely developed by Richard Pipes. The Reagan administration, especially the State and Defense Departments, were often more conflicted about its meaning than the phrase implies; but the media picked up on the term, and it stuck as a reflection of Reagan's Cold War goals and policies.[30]

Under congressional pressure, Reagan authorized Secretary of State Shultz to enter into discussions with the Sandinistas. The talks dragged on, but by January 1985 Schultz had concluded that the Sandinistas were not serious and broke off discussions. In the meantime, the Sandinistas continued to rule by oppression and outright terrorism. Emboldened by congressional restraints, and further fueled by the CIA's ineptness in laying mines in Sandino harbor (in violation of international law), Ortega flew to Moscow to seek $200 million in aid. By this time, only the far left in this country wanted to abandon the Contras entirely. In the summer, the administration easily got through Congress legislation (which had been voted down earlier, on April 23, 1985) providing for humanitarian aid (food, clothing, and medical supplies) for the Contras.[31]

Shultz decided to pull together the various strands that made up U.S. policy in Central America. Seen as a moderate in the hawkish Reagan administration (liberal columnist Tom Wicker described him as the "steady man" on a ship of conservative loonies), he endorsed, at a February 1985 congressional hearing, Reagan's much-debated Central American policies. His full support rocked administration critics.[32]

With the administration policies in Central America bogged down, Shultz changed his team. Unwilling to rely on "the wise men," who earlier had guided Cold War policies and subsequently had turned against them, he turned to Elliott Abrams, whom he installed as assistant secretary of state for Latin American affairs (a job requiring oversight of more than thirty nations and a staff of two hundred) to monitor the Contra operation, even as Colonel Oliver North, representing the National Security Council, was conducting his own shop in the White House – at times illegally, critics later charged – in support of the Contras.[33]

The thirty-seven-year-old Abrams had grown up in the 1960s in a kosher home in the Hollis Hills section of Queens. "My parents were strict," he says. "Everybody went to a movie, and I always had to call home at nine-thirty." (He did not see himself any worse for it. "I went to my high school reunion and I saw wreckage.")[34] His immigrant parents had sent him to a small progressive school in Greenwich Village, where his classmates included a future black radical, Angela Davis, along with the orphaned children of Ethel and Julius Rosenberg. At the height of the student rebellions, he entered Harvard, where he defined himself as a liberal Democrat and opposed the Vietnam War. He served as national chair of Campus Americans for Democratic Action and was a strong supporter of Hubert Humphrey. As a result, he came under attack by the SDS. "I didn't change my view about liberalism," he later said. It "changed my feelings about liberalism."[35]

Following graduation and additional education at the London School of Economics, Abrams practiced law in a "white shoe" WASP New York firm. Bored, he turned to Richard Perle, whom he knew casually through his ADA connections, and joined the staff of Senator Henry Jackson. Perle excited Abrams's interest further when he told him of the senator's efforts on behalf of Israel and of his strong pro-defense and anti-Soviet posture. Perle arranged for Abrams to come to Washington, where he got a job on the Permanent Subcommittee on Investgations. In 1977, he worked for Senator Moynihan, who presided over a group of young, ardent neocons. Abrams moved up rapidly, becoming chief of staff. Before long, he was a regular in the neocon camp (he married Midge Decter's daughter, Rachel, in a ceremony officiated by Rabbi Seymour Siegel, one of the few publicly outspoken neoconservative rabbis. Moynihan and Jackson signed the *ketuba*, the Jewish wedding contract.)[36]

In 1980, Abrams campaigned for Reagan. At thirty-three, he was rewarded with the post of assistant secretary of state for international organizations. Within the year, he moved on to become assistant secretary of state for human rights, where he sought to rebuild the bureau and expound a conservative theory of human rights. He quickly made his mark by preparing a memo to Secretary of State Alexander Haig late in 1981, in which he argued that on the grounds of both morality and political necessity this country had to prove itself just as committed to fostering democracy in nations governed by allied dictatorships as it was in those ruled by communist enemies. It called also for neither coddling friends nor simply criticizing foes, but rather for making hard choices. "Human rights," the memo noted, breaking with

Carter's ineffective human rights crusading, "is not advanced by replacing a bad regime with a worse one, or a corrupt dictator with a Communist politburo." "I start from the premise," Abrams declared, "that the world is a dangerous place."[37]

Kagan credits Abrams's memo with establishing the origins of the Reagan Doctrine. Indeed, the Reagan administration, in its first year in office, did not use the word "democracy" in dealing with the Third World. In his speech at Westminister, Reagan, hewing to the line set out in Abrams' memo and the Pipes-shaped NSDD 75, went beyond this. He called for support for democratic change everywhere. He cited specifically Solidarity's struggle in Poland and the "decay of the Soviet experiment."[38]

As a major shaper of Reagan's policy in Central America, Abrams was hailed early on by Democrats and Republicans alike for compiling a good record on human rights and democratic reform in Chile, El Salvador, and other countries governed by anticommunist dictatorships. When, after five years in the human rights post, he was asked by Shultz to take over the job of assistant secretary of state for inter-American affairs (the bureau overseeing all of Latin America), his nomination did not sit well with elements of the right. Senator Jesse Helms held it up for a short time.[39] Abrams's new post required him to work with the Defense Department, the CIA, and with the White House and National Security Council. He was now in a position to help formulate and implement foreign policy in the region. Abrams successfully helped to unify the contending elements among the Contras so that their public face became not that of the bitterly hated "Somocistas" but of more democratic elements. In doing so, he fought a number of bureaucratic battles with the CIA, which saw human rights violations as an ugly but necessary part of war and failed to understand the ideological side of the battle.[40]

On January 7, 1984, the CIA, with the approval of President Reagan, placed magnetic mines in three Nicaraguan harbors; more were added a month later. It soon became known that the Contras were not responsible. Several ships were damaged, including a Soviet oil tanker. Congress was furious. The Senate Select Committee, chaired by Senators Goldwater and Moynihan, was by law supposed to be informed of such covert operations. Moynihan considered the move to be a challenge to American constitutional government.[41] The result was a second Boland Amendment, harsher than the first. It cut off any military or paramilitary aid to the Contras for about a year. Reagan signed it, as he had the first Boland Amendment. As Congressman Dick Cheney of Wyoming said without enthusiasm, it was a means to force the Contras "to lay down their arms."[42]

In the meantime, the Sandinistas overplayed their hand. In November 1985, a Nicaraguan helicopter brought down by Contra forces at the Honduran border was found to be filled with Cuban troops. Abrams went before a congressional committee the following month to report that intelligence sources had found "a massive Soviet and Cuban intervention" in Central

America. He warned that we might soon see Cubans moving into a "combat role in North America." A car accident later in the month in Honduras resulted in the discovery of weapons, money, and communications paraphernalia from Nicaragua, meant for Salvadoran guerrillas. Ortega implied in response that if the Contras were receiving anti-aircraft equipment from the U.S., he could send similar equipment to other countries in the region.[43]

Reagan and Abrams pressed Congress to go beyond providing only humanitarian aid to the Contras. The failure to offer military aid had been a disaster for the Contras. By the early part of 1986, the nearly two-thirds of their fighters in camps just over the border from Nicaragua were in desperate shape. The movement stood in danger of collapse. The elevation of Abrams to assistant secretary of state for Latin American affairs marked the final step in moving from a policy of limited objectives and halfway measures to all-out war on the part of the Reaganites. The president opposed any further negotiations with the Sandinistas.

When most House Democrats (and a handful of Republicans), who advocated further negotiations with the Sandinistas, voted against a military aid package for the Contras of over $100 million, the Sandinistas sent 1,500 men to attack a Contra base in Honduras. The move placed the administration in a new and better posture on Capitol Hill. Speaking before the Coalition for a Democratic Majority, Senator Sam Nunn of Georgia, the most influential Democrat on arms control in Congress, warned that "the end of all aid for the Contras would be a victory for the Sandinistas." With the assistance of other Democratic moderates such as Rep. Les Aspin, Jr., the chairman of the House Armed Services Committee, the administration was able to get through, narrowly, an aid package that would include military assistance for the Contras,[44] but this was somewhat down the road and could be stymied. Meanwhile, the Contras were in trouble.

As Abrams planned to make the Contras more inclusive of broader groupings of Nicaraguans, he asked skeptics to be patient with his reform efforts. "We just got rid of 'Baby Doc,'" he said in 1986, in reference to the recent ouster of the Haitian dictator. "We're about to get rid of Marcos [in the Philippines], and in two years we'll be rid of Pinochet [in Chile]. Certainly, we can have Contra reform."[45]

In the meantime, some $27 million in humanitarian aid for the Contras was running out. Shultz asked Abrams to handle the matter. Abrams asked the sultanate of Brunei for the loan, although he had no idea how to set up a secret account. Abrams asked Colonel North for the use of North's secret Swiss bank account, unaware of the broader purposes for which North was using this account. Abrams exhibited some naïveté, as he had no way of knowing if the Brunei money would ever have been used for the purposes he sought. He later conceded that "the line between feeding and clothing a resistance force and helping it to fight is a difficult one to administer."[46]

Simultaneously, and without Shultz's knowledge, the administration was raising money privately for the Contras through Taiwan and Saudi Arabia (countries friendly to the United States) as a way to get around the Boland Amendments. It was not illegal to do so, but it clearly violated the spirit of the amendments. When Shultz found out, he did not tell Abrams. From the White House, Colonel North was running a resupply operation for the Contras, which included sending them military arms. Abrams was not let in on this either. As North put it early in 1986, Abrams was Shultz's boy. He could not be trusted.[47]

Doggedly, Abrams plowed ahead with public disavowals of any official administration military aid to the Contras in Nicaragua. When he was asked at a Senate Foreign Relations Committee session if the United States was involved in helping out the private support network aiding the Contras while the Boland Amendments were in effect, he replied that it was not, repeating the assertions later. When a CK-123 Caribou plane containing a thousand pounds of ammunition, jungle boots, and AK-47s was brought down by a Sandinista surface-to-air missile over Nicaragua in 1986, Eugene Hasenfus, a CIA operative who was aboard the plane, admitted that the agency was coordinating the effort.

"I know nothing, still don't know anything, about the mechanisms by which money was tranferred from private groups that have been raising it to the Contras," Abrams told the Senate Select Committee on Intelligence late in 1986, on the very day President Reagan and Attorney General Edwin Meese were holding a press conference admitting the diversion, following the plane incident.[48]

Administration leaders and insiders he had worked with at the CIA watched silently as Abrams hanged himself in his public defense of the administration on the Hill. Following the plane incident, Abrams received permission from Shultz to go back to the Senate committee to amend his testimony; but throughout his various appearances, he failed to volunteer information about his negotiations with Brunei because of the secrecy that had been promised.

In their zeal to obtain support for the Contras, a number of Reagan officials, including National Security Adviser John M. Poindexter and his "action officer," Col. North, in effect went into business for themselves, concealing what they were doing from Congress. The matter became especially egregious in light of what came to be known as the Iran-Contra affair, in which some 2,000 TOW missiles and 240 Hawk spare parts were sold to Iran, with the cooperation of Israel, in the hope of obtaining freedom for the American hostages being held there and providing aid to the Contras indirectly through the surplus from the sale. Reagan's role in Iran-Contra remains ambiguous. He claimed he knew nothing of Iran-Contra, while accepting responsibility for its having occurred on his watch (a rationale that satisfied no one). There is no indication, however, that Abrams was involved in the affair, despite his knowledge of the plane incident, about which he said nothing in his testimony.[49]

Following the Hasenfus incident, Poindexter resigned. He was later convicted of conspiracy, lying to Congress, defrauding the government, and destroying evidence about the scandal. On October 7, 1991, Abrams pleaded guilty in the U.S. District Court for the District of Columbia to two counts of withholding information from Congress. He was placed on two years' probation, with one hundred hours of community service. The probation officer called his offense a "momentary lapse in judgment." In 1992, on Christmas Eve, President Bush pardoned five members of the Reagan administration, including Abrams, in one of the last stages of the Iran-Contra affair.[50] Later, both Abrams and Poindexter received high-level appointments in the second Bush administraton.

Like a number of neocons in government, Abrams's instincts tended to be those of the policy advocate rather than the bureaucratic insider.[51] "Theory was everything to them," J. David Hoeveler, Jr., writes. "[T]hey were strikingly indifferent to the vulgar real world."[52] Abrams admitted in an interview that "neocons were a strange combination of naiveté and sophistication." They did not fit in well with hard-line Republican politicos. They were primarily idea men and women, not organizers or administrators, and least of all politicians. As intellectuals, they were more interested in symbols and exhortation than in the accommodation and political compromise at the heart of the political process.[53]

In their efforts to counter Soviet penetration into Latin America during the Cold War, the Reaganites and neocons in and out of government sometimes closed their eyes to human rights violations and other corruption by this country's allies, from drug trafficking to failure to halt torture of suspected dissenters from government policies. In a case that made legal history, a jury ruled in 2003 that two El Salvadoran generals living in this country could be held accountable even if they did not execute an order or have personal knowledge of such torture.[54]

The issues that the Reaganites and their neoconservative advisers faced were excruciatingly difficult. The United States was engaged in a Cold War in which victory was far from assured. With the fall of the Soviet Union, it is easy to overlook the depth of the crisis faced by the country in the 1970s and 1980s, both internally and overseas. At one point, El Salvador's rebels, brandishing Soviet-made AK-47 assault rifles, invaded its capital and seized entire neighborhoods. The country, which was receiving U.S. support, was about to experience its own Tet offensive. In 1979, communists seized power in Grenada.

These successes sparked a mood of optimism within the Soviet bloc. "For thirty years we have been isolated, on our own," Fidel Castro exulted to East German leader Erich Honecker, with whom he was meeting secretly, "[and] now there are three of us in the region: Grenada, Nicaragua, and Cuba. Grenada has important implications in the Caribbean, where there is instability, after the success of the revolution in Nicaragua."[55] The Reaganites and their neocon advisers could not accept this situation. In 1983, Reagan ordered a strike against Grenada, which was quickly overrun.

Even with the passage of time and the possibility of a more balanced perspective, it is not clear what alternatives the administration had. The idea that "social change" required the United States to work with "historical forces" was a simplistic, Marxist notion that was especially galling to neoconservatives. In her articles in *Commentary*, Kirkpatrick disputed the early Brzezinski thesis in *Between Two Ages* "that the world is changing under the influence of forces no government can control." She chided Cyrus Vance for arguing that "we can no longer stop change than Canute could still the waters."[56]

In the meantime, and in spite of the inconsistencies and contradictions and ambiguities in Central America, the impact of the neoconservatives and their efforts in the area of human rights widened. In its discussions with the Soviets, the administration and its neocon brain trust emphasized such issues – the Achilles' heel of the Soviet empire. Max Kampelman, another neocon from a Jewish background, played a key role. Kampelman had been active in the CPD, serving as its counsel. Unlike Perle, Kampelman, a practicing lawyer, was a Washington insider, drawn to public service. He saw the Soviet Union as oppressive, cruel, and, most importantly, dangerous. Like the other neocons, he believed the Cold War was not to be managed; it was to be won.

Kampelman came to the ranks of the neocons as a Hubert Humphrey Democrat. He was less comfortable with Carter than with Walter Mondale, who persuaded him to serve as cochair of the U.S. delegation to the "Helsinki Review." In 1975, in the spirit of détente, some thirty-one nations, including the Soviet Union, concluded a two-year series of conferences on security and human rights issues. They then gathered in Helsinki to sign what became known as the "Helsinki Final Act," which laid out guidelines for appropriate international behavior.

In an opening address to the thirty-five-nation East-West conference in Madrid in 1980, Kampelman criticized détente as a one-way street and denounced the Soviet invasion of Afghanistan. He also took the Russians to task for arresting a "refusenik" leader who had sought to leave the Soviet Union. Reagan asked him to stay on in the incoming administration. Like other neocons, Kampelman believed in blunt talk. "Negotiation without confrontation was a charade," he said. While Jeane Kirkpatrick carried the offensive publicly at the United Nations, Kampelman was active in Madrid and elsewhere in pressing forward human rights issues.[57]

An important issue for him was the failure of the Soviet Union to abide by the human rights commitments of the 1975 Helsinki accord. He was especially bothered by the treatment of Soviet Jews, who were refused emigration, harassed, thrown into jail or shipped to Gulags, and frequently hospitalized as psychotics. During the Nixon–Ford years, the plight of Soviet Jewry was secondary to the overall strategy of détente. Kampelman identified closely with the indefatigable refusenik Anatoly Shcharansky, whose imprisonment came to symbolize for Jews around the world the desire of most Soviet Jews to escape Soviet oppression.

In emphasizing human rights, Kampelman and other neocons sought also to tarnish the image of the Soviet Union, which claimed a special relationship to persecuted peoples throughout the world. He was determined to emphasize the Reagan Doctrine. Later that year, Kampelman delivered a united Western position at Madrid. The Soviets had been arguing for three years in these talks (and in separate talks) that any discussion of human rights in their country was "interference in their internal affairs." They were now forced to move forward, at least in principle, in the direction of accepting the Western definition of human rights.

Among the Jewish liberals who came over to the neocon side, at least on national defense and international affairs, was Martin Peretz at *The New Republic*. A Harvard lecturer with roots in the civil rights movement, Peretz had married a wealthy millionairess, purchased the magazine in 1974, and became its editor-in-chief. He arrived at *The New Republic* as a thirty-five-year-old professor, with a scraggly beard and a reputation as a speaker at campus rallies and teach-ins. He was also a donor to left-wing causes, such as the radical San Francisco magazine *Ramparts* (edited by Peter Collier and David Horowitz, both of whom would later shift to the right), and to the presidential campaigns of Senators Eugene McCarthy and George McGovern.

By the 1970s, however, Peretz, a distant relative of the Yiddish writer I. L. Peretz, was undergoing a sense of Jewish renewal, largely as a result of Israel's battle for survival. He was becoming restless, also, with Great Society programs. He was fed up with the excesses of the race revolution and had come to believe that the American left was riddled with anti-Semitism.[58]

Peretz shifted the magazine's stance toward advocacy of a "muscular Judaism" and more conservative themes, even as it remained oriented to the Democratic Party. Unlike *Commentary*, which hewed to a consistent conservative posture, Peretz encouraged various points of view. The magazine's neoconservative wing was led by Fred Barnes, an evangelical Protestant; Morton Kondracke, the quintessential Jackson Democrat; and Charles Krauthammer, a student (like Perle) of Hans Morgenthau.

The New Republic became convinced, as Peretz later told a reporter, of "the idea that American power when successfully deployed is the best thing in the world and not the worst," a view that it is still advocating in the current Iraq war and its aftermath, despite the mistakes this country has made there. That point of view has distinguished *The New Republic* from the more leftist *The Nation*, to which it has often been compared over the years.[59] At luncheon tables in Washington and in hard-hitting articles, prominent Capitol Hill political figures were exposed to liberals and former liberals, like

Bernard Aronson, Robert Leiken, and Penn Kemble, who felt betrayed by the Sandinistas and their Marxist-oriented academic apologists.[60] Following briefings by Leiken, Aronson, and others, more centrist Democrats such as Nunn and Aspin began to reevaluate their position toward the Contras. On a visit to Nicaragua, Leiken and Aronson served as tour guides for Aspin, who would soon chair the House Armed Services Committee. Aspin came away disliking the Sandinistas and urged arming the Contras. *The New Republic* became a valuable addition to the neoconservative cause in the sense that it helped to shift the balance of power and isolated liberals.

In May 1989, just prior to its collapse, the Soviet Union was no longer able to provide assistance to the Sandinistas. The Sandinistas were faced with a dilemma. The Contras had not been able to overthrow them, but they, in turn, had been unable to wipe out the opposition. As a result of divided opinion in the United States, especially in Congress, Reagan alone could not take Ortega down. Criticism of the Ortega regime nevertheless was mounting. About the only thing that both sides could agree upon was the need for greater democracy in Nicaragua.

In the waning days of the Reagan administration, President Oscar Arias Sánchez of Costa Rica, one of the region's most respected leaders, recommended letting the people of Nicaragua decide the issue by popular vote. The Sandinistas were not enthusiastic, but they thought they could win. The Soviet Union was a nonplayer by this time, and the incoming Bush administration wanted the whole matter to disappear. Ortega scheduled the election for February 1990. One month earlier, leftists in San Francisco and Berkeley met to celebrate what they expected would be a big victory for the Sandinistas. But the celebration was premature. In a stunning upset, newspaper publisher Violetta Chamorro won the presidential election. The Sandinistas were voted out of power, and Nicaragua became a democratic nation, although not without continuing problems of great poverty and with remnants of the old Sandinistas remaining in important positions as a result of the amnesty they received. In three presidential elections following the one in 1990, the Sandinista party has never gained victory.[61]

With the end of the Cold War, a debate has continued on the role of the Reagan administration in bringing down the Soviet empire. Critics have argued that the Soviet system was fundamentally flawed and toppled of its own weight as a result of economic and other weaknesses and the revolt of its subject peoples. Credit is given also to the reform efforts of Mikhail Gorbachev, *Time* magazine's Person of the Year in 1991.

While conceding the important role of Gorbachev, Peter Schweizer asks important questions: "Why did the Kremlin feel the need to radically reform when it did? How did Gorbachev come to power? What are we to make of Gorbachev's continued insistence that his goal was to reform communism and not end it? Why did the Cold War end on Reagan's terms and not Gorbachev's?"[62]

Critics of Reagan and of the neocon policies that underlay the Reagan Doctrine tend to underplay or ignore outright the totalitarian nature of the Soviet system throughout its history. Police state methods kept the regime in power, despite the anger and desperation of its own people and subject peoples in other countries, and allowed it to mount a formidable military machine with the use of scarce resources. Totalitarian states have to be pushed hard to change. That attitude marked the difference between the Reagan Doctrine, on the one hand, and Nixon's and Kissinger's policy of détente and Carter's generally passive tactics on the other. U.S. allies in Nicaragua and the Soviet sattelites were also encouraged to break away from what Reagan called "the evil empire." Attempting to meet the Reagan build-up of military power indeed staggered the Soviet economy. The Soviet military's share of GNP rose "from 22 to 27 percent during Reagan's first term, while consumption by the civilian economy would drop to less that 45 percent."[63]

Whatever Reagan's critics then and now may have thought of his policies, both at home and abroad, in occupied and client Soviet states there were few individuals who did not see him as a liberator. Following the Soviet collapse, Reagan received invitations to go to Europe for victory celebrations. Arriving in Berlin in September 1990, he was hailed as "The Man Who Made Those Pussy Footers and Weaklings Feel Ashamed." He was led to the Berlin Wall, handed a hammer and chisel, and asked to break off a few pieces. Next, he was moved to the "death strip," where East German guards had once shot at those fleeing to the West. One German shouted, "Thanks, Mr. President." From there he traveled to Gdansk, where some 7,000 citizens waited to honor him. "Thank you, thank you," they shouted, as they sang "Sto Lat," a song honoring Polish heroes. While the crowd cheered, Lech Walesa's former parish priest handed him a sword "for helping to chop off the head of communism."[64]

10

Irving Kristol and a New Vision of Capitalism

As the neocons in and outside the Reagan administration began to strengthen the nation's resolve in confronting the Soviet Union, Irving Kristol and other neocons were searching for a new social/economic vision. In liberal circles, free markets had few friends. Some critics characterized capitalism as rapacious and dehumanizing. Statism was so strong that even President Nixon had sought to interfere with the national economy by imposing wage and price controls. "We're all Keynesians now," Nixon said in 1971, referring to the British economic theorist whose admirers argued that government was responsible not only for regulating modern capitalism but also for playing a leading role in guiding and stimulating the economy.[1]

Kristol's thinking was more nuanced. He recognized the pitfalls of runaway capitalism but saw great strengths in a system that, in his college days, he had denounced. His World War II stint in the army had convinced him that socialism was plain stupidity. As early as 1957, he wrote in *Commentary*, partly tongue-in-check, that it was time to say a good word for the Horatio Alger novels. "The moral of these stories," he said "is that even if one is born very poor, one can still end up rich and successful if one is good-looking, intelligent, healthy, diligent, ambitious and extremely lucky. I can think of no truer sociological observation."[2] Three years later he argued in *Encounter* that it was evident something as important as big business "should be managed by hard faced professionals rather than by, say the editors of *The New Left Review*."[3]

By the early and mid-1970s, Kristol was rounding to a more comprehensive support of the capitalist system. In an article in the *Wall Street Journal*, he professed that the skills of businessmen were as impressive as those of intellectuals, sometimes more so. Whereas he had once believed in the overriding importance of the public sector, he now recognized its limitations. He wrote that the "Post Office gets away with murder while AT&T is crucified for every fault because in the one case management's motives are assumed to be 'pure' while in the other they are by definition 'impure.'"[4]

Critics of the free market emphasized the gap between the rich and the poor, but they missed the point, Kristol insisted. Even though there are obvious disparities in wealth, the important thing to understand is that wealth is mobile. Fortunes are often dissipated and new ones created by hard-working, enterprising people. The ability to take advantage of market opportunities is not an "inherited human characteristic." Doubtless with the Jewish experience in mind, he noted that groups suffering discrimination are often the first to open up new areas of business.[5] Most important of all, as he and others observed in a special *Commentary* symposium, "Capitalism, Socialism, and Democracy" (April 1978), "there may be an inescapable connection between capitalism and democracy" and "something intrinsic to socialism" that makes it prone to the "totalitarian temptation."[6]

Kristol was hardly alone in defending capitalism. He had been preceded by Friedrich von Hayek, Milton Friedman, and even Ayn Rand, with their support of unfettered markets. But Kristol was among the first of the ex-Marxists to open up the philosophical discussion with a twist that was original among neocons (but not to Adam Smith, who originated the thought in *The Theory of Moral Sentiments*): capitalism must be linked with moral and social responsibility. In this respect, he was among the first of the ex-Marxists to put forward what might be called a modern or post-Marxist discussion of capitalism.

It was not long before others joined in what Mark Gerson calls "capitalist celebrations."[7] Michael Novak, Peter Berger, and William Barrett contributed to the *Commentary* symposium. "The true moral strength of capitalism," Gerson quotes Michael Novak as saying, "lies in the promotion of human creativity." In an essay in *Commentary* in 1989, Novak added that success came "in the burst of an idea" and the ability to translate it into a "marketable product."[8] Nathan Glazer added in the pages of *Partisan Review*, "A private landlord, if you look at all the figures, does a better job with old housing, better for the tenants in terms of the resources being put into it, than the public landlords do. He might do even better if he had part of those subsidies that we give to public landlords."[9]

The growing friendliness to market economics may have been the neocons' most important contribution to public policy, Mark Gerson suggests. Economics was the "last vestige of our liberalism," Midge Decter told him.[10]

Like many other neocons, Harvard philosopher Robert Nozick was an unlikely defender of capitalism. At Columbia, he had founded the leftist Students for a Democratic Society; but after reading Hayek and Friedman as a graduate student at Princeton, he switched sides. He later published *Anarchy, State and Utopia* (1974), which helped to spread pro-capitalist ideas in the United States as well as Great Britain.

His book directly attacked the redistributive ideas of the influential political theorist John Rawls. In *A Theory of Justice* (1971), Rawls held that all basic goods should be "distributed equally unless an unequal distribution created an advantage to the least favored." Supported by many liberals, this concept became the embodiment of the welfare state. Nozick took issue with Rawls's thinking, which, he said, favored material well-being over individual rights in ways that would turn the nature of capitalism on its head. Even if, theoretically, such equality could be achieved (it could come only through coercion, according to Nozick), most of the wealth would eventually be redistributed to those who were more aggressive and more talented.[11]

Perhaps the most surprising convert to the supply-side model was the liberal journalist Max Lerner. In the 1940s and 1950s, he was among *the* most forceful spokesmen for American liberalism. His columns in *PM*, a left-wing New York newspaper, were required reading for my generation growing up. By the 1980s, however, he had come full circle. Having once seen the country's economic institutions as "systematically rigged" against the working poor, he came to believe that Reagan's determination to overthrow Keynesian theory and replace it with free market economics (with tax cuts as its central pivot) was a bold and necessary approach. Supply-side economics might seem an eccentric cure for what ailed the society, he wrote in his columns (now for the *New York Post*), but it was important to remember that entrepreneurs "do produce wealth" and that one ought not to hamper their productive energies. The fact that tax cuts would favor the rich worried him little. The time had come "to try something new."[12] By the 1980s, Lerner had embraced the full range of neoconservative issues, from support of "star wars" to opposition to student rebellions.

The heart of the neocon case for a more benign view of capitalism lay less in economics than in its link to personal freedom. Indeed, the market economy, neocons felt, provided the essence of democracy. In "Capitalism, Socialism, and Democracy," Kristol summed up his strong feeling that capitalism was inextricably tied both to human freedom and to broader material well-being. "[N]ever in human history," he declared, "has one seen a society of political liberty that has not been based on a free market system – i.e. a system based on private property, where normal economic activity consisted of commercial transactions between consenting adults. Never, never, never. No exceptions."[13] Gertrude Himmelfarb observed that free enterprise fostered hard work, sobriety, thrift, and foresight. Such virtues, she said, "do not assume any special breeding or social status, or talent, or valor, or even money. They are common virtues within the reach of common people."[14]

Even as they came to celebrate capitalism, Kristol, Himmelfarb, and their neocon colleagues also recognized its limitations.[15] They knew that the older capitalist ethic had been replaced by a dangerous libertarianism and that a handful of corrupt corporate managers, hell-bent on boosting stock prices through deceit and deception, could debase the system. They would be disappointed but not surprised by the scandals that rocked the business world in the late 1990s.

In *Two Cheers for Capitalism* (1978), Kristol pointed out that material success created a climate of instant gratification that was often harmful. If you hear a banker moaning about the loss of the work ethic, he said, ask his opinion of making purchases on the installment plan. Invoking the stern economic code of his immigrant generation, Kristol recalled that "to buy now and pay later was the sign of corruption."[16] He agreed with David Reisman that we have witnessed the decline of the inner-directed man. Under the capitalist system, prosperity had transformed the average citizen into a mere consumer, hardly the highest form of social development.

J. David Hoeveler has suggested that Kristol believed that the "estrangement of capitalism from the moral code that legitimated it" had become "a central issue for America in the 20th Century."[17] Bell was similarly troubled by what he termed the cultural contradictions of capitalism. "When the Protestant ethic was sundered from bourgeois society," he wrote, "only the hedonism remained."[18] Kristol and the neocons differed also with the libertarians, who thought that capitalism should be free from regulation. For example, during the OPEC oil crisis of the 1970s, Kristol urged oil companies to cut their prices voluntarily. Such action would demonstrate evidence of political thinking and counter the ruthless image that capitalism often displayed.

Kristol and most of the neocons rejected the left's anticapitalist bias, which failed to recognize the essentially democratic character of the market system. Kristol said that the New Class, as it called itself, distrusted ordinary people, whose preferences, whether good or bad, it found vulgar.[19] Decter wrote in an angry outburst: "I can't remember when I last heard a millionaire, or a successful journalist, or a well-heeled academic, or even a politician of the so-called liberal persuasion say a genuinely kind word about the system that made possible his own considerable elevation in it. But what I would say is that they are spoiled rotten and cosmically greedy."[20] It was not to the market, however, that neocons looked, but to intermediate institutions and communities of memory – the home, religious bodies, and neighborhood or communal groups – for the moral regeneration of the society as well as for the overcoming of dependency.

Kristol was a "reluctant ideologue," or at least so he thought. Ideology, he suggested, according to Gary Dorrien, had been forced upon him by the "modern reality – economic, social, technological, intellectual, political." "Only in a static society can politics conform to its traditional pre-modern ideal: 'tending to the arrangement of society' (in Oakeshott's phrase) in a sober and prudent way, so as to achieve domestic tranquility, while conforming to traditional notions of just, official behavior," Dorrien adds. In a "world of scientific-technical innovation and economic growth . . . as well as the accompanying changes of values and habits," politics had to "assume another guise." Neocons had to transform the future "with at least as much energy as [their enthusiasm for] traditions of the past." In the modern world, "non-ideological politics was a politics disarmed."[21]

Kristol had come to believe that the most important event of the times was not the crisis of capitalism but the death of socialism. He saw the socialist ideal as linked to at least one wing of the Judeo-Christian tradition – the Gnostic or prophetic strain. The loss of any alternative as a practical choice left anticapitalism in the hands of the barbaric totalitarians, the makers of fascism and communism. Kristol saw it as essential that anticapitalist dissent should be freed from its socialist partner, which at one point in an American setting had been able to civilize dissent, mainly because it implicitly shared so many crucial values with the liberal capitalism it opposed. No longer could the left play that role.

Kristol's growing interest in economics and the free market in the mid-1970s coincided with a tax revolt that was spreading rapidly across the country. Its focus centered in California, where some 1.5 million signatures had been gathered in support of Proposition 13. Property taxes had been mounting, in part because of the rise in property values as a result of inflation. Some two-thirds of the California electorate had turned aside a moderate alternative in favor of a constitutional amendment to roll back property taxes and inhibit further tax increases. Kristol was in California during the passage of Proposition 13, and he realized something important was taking shape. It was a collision between middle-class people and those who ran the growing public sector. It represented for him a novel class war between the broader polity and the politicians and their "clients" in the public sector.[22]

In responding to the broader social currents and linking them with his new and growing vision of capitalism, Kristol played a key role in the development of a remarkable economic theory that would dominate the Reagan and both Bush administrations. The policy came to be known as "supply-side economics." While serving on the *Wall Street Journal*'s board of governors, Kristol began to cultivate a number of economists. One of the people he befriended was Jude Wanniski, an unorthodox journalist. Kristol was largely responsible for bringing him into the AEI, where he joined a brown-bag lunch group that included Kristol, Robert Bork, Antonin Scalia, and Lawrence Silberman.[23] Of Ukrainian-Lithuanian parentage, Wanniski, a non-Jew, had grown up in a Jewish environment in Brooklyn, where, he likes to recall, he was "a shabbos goy," a Christian youth hired for a coin or two to light the lights for Orthodox Jews on the Jewish Sabbath. In the course of his career as a journalist at the *Wall Street Journal*, he had become friendly with the economist Arthur Laffer and Laffer's close associate Robert Mundell (winner of a Nobel Prize in economics in 1999). After becoming familiar with their work, he judged that both men had arrived at a revolutionary idea, which he described initially in an op-ed piece in the *Wall Street Journal* under the bland title "It's Time to Cut Taxes."

At lunch in the fall of 1974, Kristol asked Wanniski to write an essay for *The Public Interest* on the gross ignorance of most journalists obout subjects relating to economics. When Wanniski demurred, Kristol offered him space to write on a subject of his own choosing. The piece appeared in the spring 1975 issue as "The Mundell-Laffer Hypothesis." The essay laid out a simple, almost elemental, thesis: people worked harder when they were allowed to keep more of their money. Although less revenue might be collected in the short run, the long run provided a greater advantage.[24]

This purported phenomenon came to be known later as the "Laffer curve," and it was actually developed at the Two Continents restaurant in Washington, D.C. Seeking to sell the idea, Wanniski arranged to have dinner with Laffer (and, as it turned out, Dick Cheney). During the dinner, Laffer drew a graph on a cocktail napkin to demonstrate how government revenues increase when tax rates are low but begin to decrease when rates hit a high point.

The concept challenged directly the Keynesian social spending model that had characterized the New Deal and Great Society programs. The Mundell–Laffer idea was to put more money in the hands of consumers. Through increased purchasing, they would help increase government revenues in spite of lower tax rates. Wanniski coined the term "supply-side economics" and set out to sell it. Among those drawn to the theory were Jack Kemp, a Republican congressman from Buffalo, who would later run unsuccessfully for vice president, and a Michigan congressman, David Stockman, soon to become President Reagan's budget chief. Jeffrey Bell, who had been Reagan's director of research in California, read Wanniski's piece in *The Public Interest* and urged him to expand it into a book. Kristol pushed this project along by obtaining through AEI and the Smith–Richardson Foundation a $40,000 grant for Wanniski to become a resident journalist at AEI.[25]

With a blurb by Kristol on the front cover ("The first economic primer since Adam Smith"), *The Way the World Works* (edited by Midge Decter) was published by Basic Books in 1978. Wanniski's book; George Gilder's *Wealth and Poverty* (1981), which drew some of its inspiration from Wanniski; and Michael Novak's *The Spirit of Democratic Capitalism* (1982) constituted a supply-side trilogy. *The Way the World Works* became the most popular book on economics since Milton Friedman's *Capitalism and Freedom*. It helped lay the basis for the Kemp–Roth tax cut, a bill that narrowly failed in Congress but later won the backing of Reagan during the 1980 presidential campaign and was signed into law in 1981.[26]

Supply-side economics quickly became the keystone of the Reagan administration's economic policy. Stockman, Reagan's budget director, who later recanted on the idea, writes in his memoir, "One day he [Kemp] handed me the manuscript of a book that would soon burst on the world in a blaze of illumination: Jude Wanniski's *The Way the World Works*. It reordered everything I had previously known or thought about economics."[27]

Wanniski gives Kristol credit for gaining wide attention for his ideas. "Critics could have dismissed me and Laffer and Mundell as wooly-headed were it not for Kristol's credibility," Wanniski said. "Irving is the invisible hand." George Weigel, then head of the conservative Ethics and Public Policy Center, would later explain that neoconservatism's infrastructure of policy institutes and magazines owed its success, in part, to the fact that "Irving understood historically how philanthropy and ideas and politics went together."[28]

Kristol published supply-side writers in *The Public Interest* and advised younger advocates on its "philosophical underpinnings." Whereas Wanniski and others focused on economics, Kristol insisted that it was simply a matter of common sense: it put more money into the hands of people. As he wrote in the *Wall Street Journal*:

> Economic growth, after all, is not a mystery of nature like black holes in distant galaxies. It is a consequence of purposive action by human beings very much like ourselves.... It is something that humanity has been intimately involved with for over two centuries now, and, if we are of a certain age, it is something we have personally witnessed and experienced in our lifetimes....[29]

Throughout the 1980s, *Commentary* joined in the supply-side crusade. It publicized the groundbreaking work of Novak, whose *The Spirit of Democratic Capitalism* provided the basis of a new moral and theological argument for the American economic system.[30] Podhoretz declared it was time to drag capitalism out of the closet.

There was a certain element of pragmatism in Kristol's promotion of supply-side economics. While pundits argued about its utility as an economic model, Kristol was conscious of the political utility of the idea. In *The Public Interest*, he confessed, "The task, as I saw it, was to create... a Republican majority – so political effectiveness was the priority, not the accounting deficiencies of government."[31] In 1982, he defended what he called a "conservative deficit," "one resulting from tax cuts" that would "put the welfare state in a moderately tight straight jacket."[32]

In fact, supply-side economics was subsequently blamed (along with the Reagan defense build-up) for creating extraordinary budget deficits that carried over into the administration of Bill Clinton. Between 1980 and 1992, the federal debt rose from $909 billion to more than $4 trillion.[33] In a series of interviews with William Greider in *The Atlantic*, a repentant Stockman blamed himself and his fellow supply-siders for the budget deficits.[34] It did not help matters either that Wanniski himself turned out to be an eccentric, later flirting with extremists like Lyndon LaRouche and Louis Farrakhan.

There was a brief recession starting in 1981 and stretching into 1982, which many pundits and politicians linked to "Reaganomics." The Reagan tax cuts, however, had not had time to take effect. Reagan was inaugurated in January, and the tax cuts did not go into effect until October. Kristol points out that Congress enacted much larger tax cuts in 1982 and spent more than Reagan had authorized, even as government revenues increased.[35]

Supporters of supply-side economics remained convinced. By 1983, real growth stood at 3.6 percent. A year later, it hit 6.8 percent. "Something must have worked," Kristol concludes.[36] There was nothing wrong with supply-side economics, Kristol maintains, only perhaps with some of the people who gravitated to the idea. Certainly, it was not a cure-all for society's problems.[37]

The big Reagan tax cut did not wipe out the welfare state, as some had feared. Most of the programs begun during the New Deal remained in place under his administration. After a hiatus during the first Bush administration and Bill Clinton's eight years in office, supply-side economics was revisited during the second Bush administration with the passage of his ten-year, $1.35 trillion tax cut package. This time, however, there were no promises that tax breaks to all working Americans would increase government revenues. Although its most fervent backers conceded that supply-side economics would likely lead to greater budget deficits, they nonetheless insisted that tax cuts would help to deliver steady economic growth, which is the basis for the survival of a modern democracy. What they may have failed to recognize is that while supply-side economics seems to function well in boom times, it is less effective when the national economy stumbles. While that may have been the case in the first years of the twenty-first century, the economic recovery of 2003 demonstrates that tax cuts may very well work again as planned.[38]

Keeping in mind the human casualties of the nation's economic fluctuations, the neocons were still wise to place their emphasis on economic expansion rather than on measures to limit such growth. Traditional conservatives have never been very good at reaching out to the great anonymous electorate. In calling for deep tax cuts and putting more money in the pockets of people, supply-siders identified with the average American and helped to create a conservative majority. In the early 1990s, former Clinton labor secretary Richard Reich, no friend of supply-side economics, conceded, "half of American households became investors, so the line between becoming an employee and an investor began to blur."[39]

Supply-side economics was more than a political ploy. It was part of a broader thrust that Kristol and other neocons hoped would enlarge the social vision of liberalism. Much as they had done in helping to define the central issues of the Cold War, they sought to resolve the tensions of capitalism and to define its broader role in society.

11

The Neoconservative Assault on the Counterculture

Neoconservatives viewed the collapse of the Soviet Union as their ultimate victory. A neoconservative ally, Francis Fukuyama, described the event as the "end of history." Midge Decter, seeing no further need for the Committee for the Free World, shut it down. Even as neocons celebrated, however, many remained uneasy. The counterculture, they felt, had become institutionalized on college campuses, in many sectors of the media, and in the politics of the nation. Writing in *The National Interest* in 1993, not long after Bill Clinton won election, Irving Kristol declared,

> There is no 'after the Cold War' for me. So far from having ended, my Cold War has increased in intensity, as sector after sector has been ruthlessly corrupted by the liberal ethos. Now that the other Cold War is over, the real Cold War has begun. We are far less prepared for this Cold War, far more vulnerable to the enemy, than was the case with our victorious war against a global Communist threat.[1]

Success in the Cold War, in short, had little meaning for neocons if the broader culture continued to spin out of control. It was less that the old rules and values were ignored or flouted than that the newer ethos seemed to suggest that there were no rules. Morality was simply a matter of individual choice, and moral relativism had become the new norm.

The counterculture sought acceptance for what neocons and many ordinary Americans considered to be bizarre ideas and behavior. In scholarly circles, Stanley Fish, most recently dean of the College of Liberal Arts and Sciences at the University of Illinois at Chicago, gained wide attention for the idea that there is no objective truth or transcendent ethical perspective. What passes for truth is only a response to power relationships in the society.

The most critical issue for neocons (and for Americans generally, regardless of political persuasion) was what they saw as the breakdown of the American family. Although Daniel Patrick Moynihan had already drawn national attention to the problem of the African-American family while serving in the Johnson administration in 1965, the family breakdown dilemma crossed racial lines. Throughout the United States, illegitimacy and single parenthood increased. Marriages failed in all income and ethnic groups. Divorce became the rule rather than the exception. Great numbers of young people postponed marriage or abandoned the institution altogether in pursuit of individual self-fulfillment. With the traditional family under attack, parental discipline weakened. Crime rates rose precipitously.

"Yet little was said or done to combat these conditions," wrote Mark Lilla, a former editor at *The Public Interest* and now a professor at the University of Chicago.

> The moral condition of the urban poor in pop music and advertising shames us, but we dare not say a word. Our new explicitness about sex in television and film, and growing indifference to what we call euphemistically "sexual preference," scares the wits out of responsible parents, who see sexual confusion and fear in their children's eyes. But ever since the Sixties they risk ridicule for raising objections that earlier would have seemed perfectly obvious to everyone.[2]

Kristol's benign view of capitalism nevertheless forced him to acknowledge that as societies became wealthier, they

> seem to breed all sorts of new social pathologies and discontents.... Crime and other forms of delinquency increase with increasing prosperity. Alcoholism and drug addiction also rise. Civic mindedness and public spiritedness are corroded by cynicism.... The emphasis is placed on the pleasures of consumption rather than the virtues of work. The ability to defer gratification... is scorned; "fly now, pay later" becomes not merely an advertising slogan, but also a popular philosophy of life.[3]

In *The Cultural Contradictions of Capitalism*, Daniel Bell found fault with the reigning economic system. He conceded that capitalism had been responsible for one of the world's greatest surges of creativity but argued that it had gotten out of hand. It seemed to promote change simply for the sake of change, thereby unsettling such traditional institutions as the family and the church.[4]

Podhoretz's break with the counterculture came about more slowly than Kristol's or Bell's. As we have seen, in his first years at *Commentary* he was very much a radical himself. His radicalism, however, was tentative and brief. He had hoped to reinvigorate liberal thought by creating intellectual challenges, not to demolish it. Indeed, by late 1964, partly as a result of student protests at Berkeley, he was coming to see that the New Left was "a far cry from the new radicalism I had been hoping might... emerge."[5]

A critical moment for him occurred when the *New York Review of Books* carried an essay supporting the student rebellion at Berkeley. Podhoretz responded by publishing a Nathan Glazer essay, "What Happened at Berkeley," in *Commentary* in February 1965 (originally rejected by the *New York Review of Books* as being "too long"), a piece critical of the

Berkeley "free speech" campus uprising. Podhoretz's break with radicalism accelerated when the *New York Review of Books* carried a letter by a former *Commentary* contributor, Staughton Lynd, asking, "May I inquire why it is immoral to desire a Vietcong victory?" Lynd went on to compare the Vietcong with this country's Founding Fathers, adding that communists were invoking the same demand, "Give me liberty or give me death."[6]

Not until 1970 did Podhoretz's doubts about radicalism coalesce into a conviction against a new kind of spiritual plague that was difficult to combat, a conviction he would spell out later in *Breaking Ranks*, in which he closed with a lament for the victims. "They had ... been inoculated against almost every one of the physical diseases which in times past had literally made it impossible for so many to reach adulthood. But against a spiritual plague like this one they were entirely helpless."[7]

It was bad enough that those whom Podhoretz had once called the "Know Nothing Bohemians" had begun to define American life and mores. What was even more galling to neocons was the capitulation of those in the centers of power to the New Class. The submission of the "old elite" was pithily analyzed later by David Gelernter, a younger Jewish neocon and professor of computer science at Yale, who had been maimed by the Unabomber. "Nothing compelled the Harvards and Yales to change their ways," wrote Gelernter in a scathing denunciation of the Ivy Leaguers. "They did it on their own; they kicked things off by volunteering to make room for a new elite."[8]

Podhoretz launched his full-scale attack on the counterculture in the June 1970 issue of *Commentary*, using what he would later call "the defiantly provocative style that would typify this phase of *Commentary*'s history."[9] He quickly followed up, "in equally harsh terms," with "Literary Revolutionism" and "Quackery in the Classroom." In the ensuing months came attacks on the New Left's response to the urban crisis, the widespread belief in certain quarters that the country was on the verge of fascism, the Black Panthers, as well as the counterculture's newest cause, women's lib. Podhoretz and his group of writers skewered not only the apostles of the new thought – Charles Reich, Theodore Roszak, and Kenneth Keniston – but also such " fellow traveling institutions" as the *New York Times*, the *New York Review of Books*, and the American Civil Liberties Union (ACLU). Podhoretz was determined now to become "the single most visible scourge of the Movement within the intellectual community."[10]

Neocons traced the origins of the cultural revolution to the New Class of academicians, artists, and literary and publishing figures (as well as anticapitalist intellectuals and welfare state bureaucrats) – those who had, in Moynihan's words, "defin[ed] deviancy down" by exempting from censure previously stigmatized conduct.[11] The phrase "New Class" itself came from the dissident Yugoslavian writer Milovan Djilas, who used it to describe communist elites in Eastern Europe who restricted thought in their countries, presumably as part of the effort to overcome social injustice.

Kristol believed that the New Class grew out of the expansion of higher education and the enormous increase in the number of college-educated individuals. He had identified this new elite even before it had been given a name, charging that it served its own self-interest rather than the common good, as it often proclaimed. The New Class, Kristol argued, wished to redistribute power to government (in which members of the New Class, as an intellectual and technical elite, would play a dominant role). The professional classes of modern bureaucratized societies are engaged in a class struggle with the business community for status and power, he wrote of New Class ideology. Its adherents encouraged the development of "new and hedonistic life styles" and "emphasized individualistic self expression which undermined communal and personal restraints, the essential elements for an orderly society and social progress."[12]

According to the neocons, these intellectuals could claim victory. William Buckley had once proclaimed famously that he would rather be governed by the first 2,000 names in the Boston phone book than by the faculties of Harvard and MIT. "Now that we are ruled by the combined faculties of Harvard and MIT, you can see what he meant," Gelernter later observed.[13] Once aimed upward at the "establishment," this animus was now directed downward at the public at large, according to Podhoretz.[14] New Class theory can be traced to the 1960s, although its fullest expression can be seen in a collection of essays, *The New Class* (1979), edited by B. Bruce Briggs.

The idea of a New Class (as Bell explained) was an extension of the thought of social critics Joseph Schumpeter and F. A. Hayek, who had written earlier of the role of intellectuals and writers in promoting a counterculture. Schumpeter observed that what distinguished intellectuals from other people was the power that they wielded, "the power of the spoken and written word." Most of them were outsiders with no "direct responsibility for practical affairs." Yet they gained followers because "the mass of people never develops definite opinions on its own initiative."[15]

Roger Kimball, one of the new group of neocon critics, traced the origins of the cultural revolution to the avant garde writers of the Beat Generation of the 1950s: "Their programmatic anti-Americanism, their avid celebration of drug abuse, their squalid, promiscuous sex lives, their pseudo-spirituality, their attack on rationality and their degradation of intellectual standards, their aggressive narcissism and juvenile political posturing: in all this and more, the Beats were every bit as 'advanced' as any Sixties radical."[16]

There was a certain irony, of course, in the neocon characterization of the New Class. Who were neocons, if not a new class? Were they not outsiders from immigrant Jewish backgrounds, hardly indifferent to gaining power and place? When I asked him about this, Kristol shrugged the question off. "We are dissidents from the New Class ideology," he said."[17]

In the late 1960s and 1970s, neocons, outraged by the excesses of the shattered society, created an intellectual underpinning for more traditional values. Their defense of the "bourgeois" lifestyle was led by James Q. Wilson, a public policy professor at UCLA, whose work was frequently featured in *Commentary* and *The Public Interest*, and the Victorian scholar Gertrude Himmelfarb. In their writings, one can witness the beginnings of the "family values" movement in the 1980s and 1990s.

In *The Moral Sense* (1993), Wilson reasserted the validity of morality in an age that lacked religious conviction. Wilson argued that traditional norms and values are part of human nature and grow out of the common experiences of ordinary human beings. While specific rules vary from culture to culture, every society has a "moral disposition." Good character "arises from the repetition of many small acts that began in a child's early development." The idea that the moral sense is innate but its practice learned stood at the center of his thought. The dominant liberal, cosmopolitan culture, by emphasizing virtually total openness, had worn away at the practice of morality.[18]

In one sense, however, Wilson dismissed the conventional wisdom of conservatives that the Great Disruption was a result of government policies or the effects of poverty and inequality. He believed that it grew out of the spread of information technology and a change in the status of women resulting from the availability of better jobs and the legalization of abortion. While these changes played a part, they were long in coming and grew out of the steady abandonment of the Victorian ethos of nineteenth-century England and America.

During the 1960s, Wilson argued, these changes speeded up. Along with his fellow neocons, he blamed "social elites who are easily drawn to new ideas and adventuresome practices." The tragedy of the poor was that, unlike the new elite, they lacked the resources – safeguards to protect their homes and drug treatment programs, for example – that would permit them to "cope with the destabilizing effects of contemporary society."[19]

Himmelfarb was an unlikely candidate for the role of social activist. She saw herself, at least initially, as a working mother, pursuing scholarly interests while raising her two children. Quiet in demeanor, she differed sharply from her outspoken husband. "Our styles are so different," she told an interviewer. "Irving makes these sharp, bold, assertive statements. Me, I would have to work up to it very tentatively."[20]

But Himmelfarb gained a following through her meticulous research and persuasive writing. Such books as *Poverty and Compassion* (1991), *The Demoralization of Society* (1995), and *One Nation, Two Cultures* (1999) made her one of the important voices in the attack on the counterculture. Like Wilson, Himmelfarb sought to clarify the distinction between liberty and license. These terms were not, as 1960s radical thought seemed to suggest, semantic siblings, but rather opposites, indeed bitter enemies. In *Poverty and*

Compassion, she wrote, "It was the welfare state that finally brought about the divorce of morality from social policy." The postmodern U.S had become, she added in *One Nation, Two Cultures*, something entirely new in American life.[21]

In op-ed pieces in the *Wall Street Journal*, articles in *Commentary* and the *American Scholar*, and most fully in *The Demoralization of Society: From Victorian Virtues to Modern Values*, Himmelfarb laid out the theme that lay at the heart of her work: the need to return to Victorian values. In her reading, the Victorians were far from the prissy, sanctimonious, uptight citizens for which that era is remembered. She applauded their values "of cleanliness, orderliness, obedience, thrift, sexual propriety centered in the family."[22]

Contrary to Marx's assertion that capitalism had transformed families into inanimate articles of commerce, Himmelfarb found working-class Victorians family-oriented and stable. She noted how "the poor in the almost impossible circumstances of their lives... conform[ed] to middle class standards of morality." By contrast, she was shocked by the incivility of young American radicals in the 1960s, who spurned their parents' values and hoped to overturn the social order. She believed it was America's welfare system, a system that was unknown in Victorian England, which "finally brought about the divorce of morality from social policy."[23]

Himmelfarb adopted Edmund Burke's dictum: "Men are qualified for civil liberty in exact proportion to their disposition to put moral chains upon their own appetites." She likened Victorian orderliness and self-restraint to the "Jewish ethic," as exemplified by Jewish free schools and Jewish free loan societies. In one chapter, "The Jew as Victorian," she quotes approvingly Beatrice Webb, a Fabian socialist, who found in such self-help institutions "a downward stream of charity and personal service, a benevolence at once so widespread and so thorough-going, that it fully justifies the saying, 'All Israel are brethren.'" The Jewish ethos, Himmelfarb declared, echoing her husband, was also the capitalist ethos. For that reason, it was not surprising that Margaret Thatcher, the most capitalist-minded of recent British prime ministers, had included a number of Jews in her cabinet. Himmelfarb quotes Thatcher's biographer, who wrote: "Judaism embodied many useful precepts and could produce many shining exemplars."[24]

A historian herself, Himmelfarb criticized the "new history," decrying the influence of the British Marxists and the French *Annalistes*. The latter focused on those groups previously excluded from serious examination. She had no problem with serious studies of the experiences of African-Americans, gays, women, and other hitherto outsider groups; but such studies, she said, should be part of a broader look at the society. Too often, she said, the history of such people and their cultures has been equated with "victimhood," as part of an assault on America as a failed society, and failed to mention the fact that society eventually opened up to these groups. She worried in *The New History and the Old* (1987) about "the current prejudice against greatness." Social historians, she said, explored "the lowest depths of life" while underplaying "the notable events, individuals, and institutions that have constituted our historical memory and our heritage."[25]

Himmelfarb's books generally downplayed the writings of traditional but advanced thinkers like Charles Darwin and John Stuart Mill and pressed forward less-favored conservatives, including Thomas Malthus and Edmund Burke. Her writings constituted a critical element in the culture wars, even as her husband carried the fight on other fronts. Over the years, the Kristols, along with their son, William, became America's "first family" of neoconservatism.

From the 1980s forward, publishing underwent significant changes. *Commentary, National Review*, and *The Public Interest* were joined by a new group of conservative magazines including *The National Interest, Public Opinion, This World* (later *First Things*), and *The New Criterion* (with Kristol often playing the role of the midwife).

In 1991, Martin Peretz installed Andrew Sullivan, a young English admirer of Margaret Thatcher's free market policies, as editor of *The New Republic.* The changes engineered by Peretz, a neocon on national defense and international issues, broke faith with the magazine's liberal tradition, at least to many longtime readers. Peretz himself did not vote Republican. "There is a big social gulf between the Republican Party and Jews," he said.[26]

In the 1950s, Regnery and Devin Adair were lonely outposts of conservatism in book publishing. In more recent years, Martin Kessler at Basic Books and Erwin Glikes at The Free Press helped level the playing field. Kessler, though not a conservative himself, was committed to the free market of ideas. Among the important and commercially successful conservative books he published were *Losing Ground* (1984) by Charles Murray, *The Tempting of America* (1990) by Robert Bork, *The End of History and the Last Man* (1992) by Francis Fukuyama, *Out of the Barrio* (1991) by Linda Chavez, and *Illiberal Education* (1991) by Dinesh D'Souza, one of the first neocons to challenge the rise of multiculturalism on the campus and in the broader society.[27]

The Belgium-born son of Jewish refugees from Hitler, Glikes studied at Harvard and then joined the faculty at Columbia University, where he taught English and served as an assistant dean. He seemed comfortably ensconced in academia until violent student demonstrations protesting the Vietnam War struck campuses across the country, including Columbia, in the 1960s. Infuriated, Glikes left Columbia for a career in publishing as a senior editor at Basic Books, where he worked for a while with Kristol. He soon moved to Simon and Schuster's trade book division. He encountered difficulty convincing his colleagues to publish more books by conservatives. When a sales representative told him that no one at Simon and Schuster would "lift a finger" to sell Norman Podhoretz's 1981 book *The Present Danger*, Glikes decided to go to The Free Press of Macmillan.[28]

Glikes viewed himself as a contrarian in a publishing world of liberal elitists. As a senior editor at Basic Books, he published the first book by George Will, then a little-known philosophy professor at the University of Toronto and not yet the popular conservative columnist he would become.[29] The books he did publish dealt with basic, often controversial, political ideas that could not be ignored by the dominant liberal culture. Glikes recognized the growing market for conservative books. Along with his young protégé Adam Bellow (Saul Bellow's son), he set out to capture the political center. He hoped to persuade the liberal or moderate reader that a conservative book's point of view was not only reasonable but might actually find a favorable review in the *New York Times* and elsewhere.[30]

In 1987, Glikes brought out a volume by a University of Chicago philosophy professor and translator of Plato and Rousseau, Allan Bloom. His new book, *The Closing of the American Mind*, seemed destined to gather dust in libraries and bookstores. Instead, it became a publishing sensation, remaining on the *New York Times* best-seller list for ten weeks. With more than one million copies of the book sold, its author's ideas suddenly came to dominate dinner party conversations in Georgetown and Manhattan.

Bloom argued that because American higher education was "open to all kinds of men, all kinds of lifestyles, all ideologies," it had become "closed" to the great truths found in classical writings, the basis of all learning. The result was the triumph of cultural relativism – the belief that all societies, beliefs, and values were equally worthy. In this construct, Western culture became "just another culture," no better or worse than any other. Yet he saw civilization, almost in a Darwinian sense, as a clash of cultures. "Cultures have different perceptions which determine how the world is," he wrote. "They cannot come to terms. There is no communication about the highest things.... Culture means a war against chaos and a war against other cultures."[31]

Bloom became a crusading general in the culture wars. He railed against the idea that truth is a social construct utilized by those in power to enhance their position and place. He attacked recent tendencies on campuses, such as black studies, women's studies, deconstruction, and the return of German philosophy as developed by the radical neo-Marxist Brandeis University philosopher Herbert Marcuse. Capturing and contributing to the neocon indictment of the counterculture of political correctness, Bloom believed that the real tragedy of the modern university lay in the surrender of college and university administrations and faculties to the demands of student, feminist, Black Power, and multicultural movements.[32]

Bloom, who died in 1992, laid out his arguments in a pungent, combative style, which made him especially effective. He compared radical feminism to the Reign of Terror in the French Revolution, dismissed the anthropologist Margaret Mead as a "sexual adventurer," and compared the Woodstock gathering to Hitler's Nuremburg rallies.[33]

Bloom stood in the tradition of legendary teachers of film and literature. He was a brilliant teacher and attracted the best students, whom he constantly challenged. Unmarried and gay, Bloom took a deep interest in their lives and subsequent careers. Paul Wolfowitz took one course with him. Bloom was also a resident faculty member in the unit in which Wolfowitz was living. "He had a lot to do with my coming to appreciate that the study of politics could be a serious business," Wolfowitz told an interviewer, "even though it wasn't science in the sense that I understood science to be. That was an eye opener." Bloom encouraged Wolfowitz to carry forward his childhood interest in world affairs, to the consternation of Wolfowitz's mathematics-teaching father, who considered political science to be much like astrology.[34]

Saul Bellow barely fictionalized him and these relationships in his novel *Ravelstein* (2000). His former students kept Bloom's telephone so busy with tidbits of inside information, Bellow muses in *Ravelstein*, that he must have been masterminding a shadow government.[35] At one point, Bellow has Bloom/Ravelstein returning from a phone call with a thinly disguised Paul Wolfowitz during the Persian Gulf War, reporting to his friends, "Colin Powell and Baker have advised the president not to send troops all the way to Baghdad.... They are afraid of a few casualties." Wolfowitz suggests, however, that this was exaggerated. Everyone knew Bloom could not keep a secret.[36]

The Closing of the American Mind was, in the final analysis, an updated version of the thought of Bloom's mentor and colleague at the University of Chicago, Leo Strauss. Largely through the influence of Bloom, a number of middle-level Reagan and Bush officials, among them William Kristol and Seth Cropsey (a speech writer for Caspar Weinberger) came to know the work of the German-born philosopher. Like Strauss, Bloom was obsessed with the ghosts of Weimar, Germany. He was convinced that America was embarked upon a similar downward path.[37]

Bloom was encouraged to write *The Closing of the American Mind* by his friend, the Nobel laureate novelist Saul Bellow, who shared many of his views and penned the Foreword to the book. Bellow was appalled by the effects of postmodernism. If there was to be a successful or at least coherent society, it had to be based on broader societal constraints.[38]

Although never easily categorized as a writer, Bellow became identified with the neoconservative movement in the 1970s and 1980s. In letters and symposia, he supported the view of neocons that the Soviet Union threatened American security and that of the West. And he agreed with them that the triumph of liberalism and the welfare state had resulted in moral laxity in this country. Like Kristol and such traditional liberals as Irving Howe, Bellow denounced the New Left as "political naifs" whose radicalism represented "a secession from the life of the mind." He opposed the creation of a black studies department at the University of Chicago, where he taught, demanded by the radical black writer Amiri Baraka (LeRoi Jones). Bellow's biographer, James Atlas, wrote that in the "women's movement, the Black Power movement, the students uprising on campuses across the land, [Bellow] saw an insurrection against all the things he valued. His whole identity as an intellectual, a representative of the high culture that had celebrated his work – indeed had made him one of its chief icons – had come under violent attack."[39]

Bellow wrote *Mr. Sammler's Planet* (1970), sometimes seen alongside *The Adventures of Augie March* (1953) to be among his finest novels, when his sense of Jewish identity had been inflamed by the Six Day War. *Mr. Sammler's Planet* is a story of a Polish Jew, an intellectual who escapes the Holocaust. He works as a journalist in London, where he knows a number of Bloomsbury intellectuals, including Lytton Strachey and John Maynard Keynes, before emigrating to the United States and taking residency on the Upper East Side of Manhattan. Here Mr. Sammler encounters instances of his new society's breakdown. He is accosted on one occasion by a black pickpocket, whom Sammler had earlier observed in the act on a bus. The pickpocket humiliates Sammler by exposing himself to him in the stairwell of his building. At another time, Sammler, while lecturing at Columbia on George Orwell's view of British radicals, is forced from the stage by hecklers. The university cannot or will not protect him. For Mr. Sammler, the experiences he had escaped from follow him to his new country.

"Like many people who had seen the world collapse once," Bellow writes, "Mr. Sammler entertained the possibility it might collapse twice. He did not agree with refugee friends that this doom was inevitable, but liberal beliefs did not seem capable of self defense, and you could smell decay."[40]

Some critics charged that in *Mr. Sammler's Planet*, Bellow "gave vent to an outburst of racism, misogyny, and puritanical intolerance." For Bellow, however, the novel was a metaphor for broader societal disruptions in the wake of the war and other catastrophes.[41] Along with many neocons who reached maturity in the postwar years, Bellow discovered an older America that was more congruent with the values and ideals of Mr. Sammler. Atlas describes a 1986 meeting of the PEN Congress, an international gathering of mainly left-wing leading writers in New York. The subject was "The Writer's Imagination and the Imagination of the State." Sitting on the dais with him were several notables, including German novelist Günter Grass. Bellow delivered an address that was unabashedly pro-American. "In America," Bellow declared, "we didn't start very high and we didn't rise very high, either." But if the United States had little to boast of in the way of high culture, he went on, it had at least provided its citizens with "shelter, protection and a certain amount of security against injustice." Clearly, Mr. Sammler would have welcomed Bellow's comments.[42]

A more surprising ally in the neocons' attack on the counterculture was novelist Philip Roth. In *Goodbye, Columbus* (1959), Roth had ridiculed

Jewish suburban arrivistes, and in *Portnoy's Complaint* (1969) he had celebrated the new sexual freedom of the 1960s. In his descriptions of middle-class conventions, he had hewed very close to New Left beliefs and to the counterculture of the 1960s. (Podhoretz later wrote scathingly that "Roth's great contribution [was] to bring masturbation, up to then one of the dirtiest and most secret of the dirty little secrets, into the realm of serious fiction.")[43]

In the Pulitzer Prize–winning *American Pastoral* (1997), however, Roth shifted gears in breathtaking fashion. His hero, Swede Levov, is a fully realized product of the bourgeois ethos. A football star in high school, a heroic marine in World War II, he acts out the American/Jewish postwar dream by marrying Miss Jersey, a non-Jewish, blond-haired beauty. Inheriting his father's business, he increases its profits through hard work and a heightened sense of responsibility. His love of America invests every aspect of his life. Tragically, however, he fails to teach these values to his daughter, an unhappy, stammering teenager, who (as with so many in her generation) resents the American bourgeois style of life and sets out to remake the world. Instead, she blows up a post office with a homemade bomb, killing a doctor and destroying her parents' marriage and her father's innocence.[44]

Roth was no neocon, as his next novel, *I Married a Communist* (1998), would demonstrate; however, in *The Human Stain* (2001) he focused on how a college professor is destroyed for being inadvertently politically incorrect, a story made all the more complex and interesting when the professor is revealed to be an African-American who has been passing for white and Jewish for most of his life.

What went wrong on college campuses, neocons believed, was unchecked student radicalism. Although only 13 percent of college students were "radically dissident" during the halcyon 1960s, according to a *Fortune* magazine poll, this minority managed to disrupt and paralyze mainly elite institutions throughout 1968 and 1969. The University of California at Berkeley was the first American school to be hit, and disruptions spread from there. San Francisco State University was shut down for three weeks.Harvard undergraduates invaded University Hall, threw out the deans, and rifled confidential files. At Columbia, students urinated on the carpet in President Grayson Kirk's office.[45]

Moynihan, then an aide to Richard Nixon in the White House, sent a member of his staff, Chester Finn, to study the mood on campus. Finn worried about "the prospect of... mutiny in the armed forces." Finn had talked to reasonable men like Irving Kristol, Moynihan added, who shared these fears.[46]

Nathan Glazer, then teaching at Berkeley, assailed the radicals' "increasing vituperation." He asked, "How does a radical – a mild radical, it is true, but still someone who felt closer to radical than to liberal writers and politicians in the late 1950s, end up by early 1970 a conservative, a mild conservative, but still closer to those who now call themselves conservatives than to those who call themselves liberals?"[47]

Multiculturalism was another special target of neocons. Working off ideas developed by Jewish civic agencies to improve intergroup relations in the 1950s, as well as Glazer's and Moynihan's *Beyond the Melting Pot* (1963), colleges and universities started out in the 1960s with the useful idea of deepening understanding of groups other than the white majority in this country and encouraging respect for the cultures of nonwhite peoples in other parts of the world. In the hands of racial and ethnic lobbies and victim groups, however, this curriculum was often transmogrified into an indictment of Western civilization. The latter came to be seen increasingly as a story of plunder, rapine, imperialism, exploitation, and slavery. Europe and America (to a much lesser degree) had been imperialistic and exploitative, but so had non-Western civilizations the world over. It was even less often noted that *anti-imperialism* began in the West, and that the antislavery and female equality movements arose there also. The West, in fact, had developed international systems that were created to discourage warfare.

To neocons, the campus rebellions despoiled cherished Western ways of learning. As Podhoretz notes, "Violence was committed against the distinction between democratic America and a tyrannical state and was then compounded by comparing the disciplines of an academic community – required courses and grades – to prisons and chains." He further charged that Berkeley radicals "were openly bent on demystifying and destroying" the "traditional values of American liberalism."[48]

Closely related to multiculturalism was what Diane Ravitch has called *The Language Police* (2003). A close ally of the neocons, Ravitch struck out at the growing trend in education to sanitize language. The argument was being made that students had a right *not* to be offended. Her book and her startling thirty-two-page glossary cited examples of words and phrases banished from texts – for example, "babe," chick," and "co-ed." Expurgated from texts also were portrayals of women as indecisive or of men as assertive. You were no longer permitted to say that Asians are studious and hardworking, that blacks stand out in sports and music, or that Jews once lived in tenements. Ravitch's words were aimed at the religious right and the multicultural left, but from the evidence she cited, her main target was the latter. The former might have some veto power; however, curricular materials were being created primarily by those who espoused ethnic and cultural diversity.[49]

Other neocons countered these trends by forming an organization to oppose "politically correct" multicultural education and racial preferences in college admissions and faculty hiring. The first mass meeting of what became the National Association of Scholars (NAS) was held in October 1982, with Irving Kristol as keynote speaker. Stephen H. Balch, a young Jewish neocon, had helped to develop the idea for NAS and became its dominant figure. He took a series of leaves from his faculty position at the John Jay College of Criminal Justice in New York to set up an office and hire staff. NAS planned to organize college professors and others interested in challenging the status quo on college campuses. Balch met also with Midge Decter, then executive director of the Committee for the Free World and editor of its publication, *Contentions*, who turned over her extensive mailing list to him. Initial funding (a grant of $210,000 spread over three years) came from Smith Richardson in 1986. Despite NAS's generally conservative orientation, its conferences included presentations by such academic luminaries as Yale historian C. Vann Woodward, Duke political scientist James David Barber (a former head of Amnesty International), Harvard sociobiologist Edward O. Wilson, and Columbia cultural historian Jacques Barzun, all of whom joined its board of directors. NAS, with the help of Irving Louis Horowitz at Transaction Publishers, published a journal, *Academic Questions*, which helped carry its ideas to a broader public. Its research center looked into and publicized stories of victims of academic abuses by (what Roger Kimball described as) "tenured radicals."[50]

By the 1990s, NAS had grown to include some four thousand members (faculty and graduate students); thirty-eight state chapters, campus chapters, and caucuses; and representatives in the American Sociological Association, the American Historical Association, and the Modern Language Association. Its membership was broadly based ideologically and included such prominent scholars as Gertrude Himmelfarb, Seymour Martin Lipset, and James Q. Wilson.[51]

Before long, NAS was no longer alone. It helped to spawn, formally or informally, a network of like-minded groups, such as the National Alumni Forum, the Association of Literary Scholars and Critics, and a new national accrediting body, the American Academy for Liberal Education. University of Pennsylvania history professor Alan Charles Kors, a founder of NAS, helped to establish the Foundation for Individual Rights in Education (FIRE), a nonprofit organization "devoted to free speech, individual liberty, religious freedom, the rights of conscience, legal equality, due process, and academic freedom on our nation's campuses."[52]

Gradually, NAS shed its reputation as a conservative vehicle. The *Chronicle of Higher Education*, marking NAS's ten-year history in 1997, reported that it had "earned a measure of respect – if not acceptance – in faculty circles." Gerald Graff, one of the founders of Teachers for a Democratic Culture, which was organized to counter NAS, made a similar point. Graff, an English professor at the University of Chicago, accused NAS of spreading misinformation, but he added: "I give grudging respect to a group that has demanded that professors explain themselves."[53]

Two leaders of the California Association of Scholars (CAS), Glynn Custred and Tom Wood – the former a professor at California State

University at Hayward and the latter CAS's executive director – induced Ward Connerly, a regent of the University of California and an African-American businessman, to head up a movement to win support for the California Civil Rights Initiative (CRI), known as Proposition 209. The measure, the wording of which was taken directly from the U.S. Civil Rights Act of 1964, declared, "The state shall not discriminate against or grant preferential treatment to any individual or group, on the basis of race, sex, color or ethnicity, or national origin in the operation of public employment, public contracting, or public education." The two men came to Connerly after the CRI had been written to ask him to serve as chairman of a statewide drive. Connerly, a proven fund raiser, had demonstrated earlier success in his effort to have the Board of Regents ban racial preferences at the University of California.[54]

Reluctant to take on the issue initially (he had been called an "Uncle Tom" once too often), Connerly changed his mind when it became clear to him that failure to enact the measure threatened the work he had done on the Board of Regents resolution. He got some 1.2 million signatures, enough to place the CRI measure on the November ballot. Bill Kristol told him that the measure would influence "the way America went about its racial business." Together they discussed how to give the initiative a national presence. Another important boost came from the late Eric Breindel, editorial page editor of the conservative *New York Post.* Breindel brought in important funding from *Post* publisher Rupert Murdoch. The measure won voter approval in 1996. "It was one of the most important things we did," Balch said.[55]

The attack on the counterculture has come from other directions as well. Conservatives have charged, according to *The Chronicle of Higher Education*, that the campuses, especially elite schools, have denied them opportunities to teach and other forms of recognition. (A survey developed by the Higher Education Research Institute reports that among over 50,000 faculty members and administrators during the period 2000 to 2002, some 48 percent described themselves as liberals or far left. Another 34 percent said they were middle of the road, and just 18 percent conservative or far right.) Leading the attack here has been David Horowitz, president of the California-based Center for the Study of Popular Culture. Horowitz is the son of parents who lost their school jobs during the McCarthy witch hunts for being members of the Communist Party. "If liberals and leftists were excluded from faculties to anything like the degree conservatives are," he says, "there would be a national howling going on." The issue, however, may be less overt discrimination than the culture of the contemporary campus, where conservatives just don't fit in.

Horowitz has pushed Congress and state legislatures to approve an "academic bill of rights," a body of ideas that he claims would provide greater diversity to varying points of view. He has been instrumental, the

Chronicle reports, in pressing forward legislation in nineteen states to support his proposal. Public universities in Colorado in the spring of 2004 agreed to abide by the spirit of the document. Conservatives have been backed up increasingly by well-organized and well-funded student groups.[56]

If Leo Strauss was the neocons' leading intellectual guru; James Q. Wilson the most persuasive advocate for the moral regeneration of society; Gertrude Himmelfarb the widely respected critic of New Age thought; and Alan Bloom the most devastating opponent of the contemporary university, Hilton Kramer, editor of *The New Criterion*, assumed the role of defender of the traditional culture on the battlefield of art and modernism. Born in Gloucester, Massachusetts, in 1928, Kramer was a descendent of Russian Jews and admirers of Franklin Roosevelt. He began with *Art Digest* in 1954, moved on to become managing editor of *Art Magazine*, and from 1958 to 1961 served as art editor of *The Nation*. Through his distinctive essays in *Commentary, The New Republic*, and *Commonweal*, Kramer gained recognition as a leading critical voice on behalf of modernism.

In 1965, he became art news editor of the *New York Times*. His articles often appeared in the paper's Sunday magazine. His first collection of essays, *The Age of Avant-Garde: An Art Chronicle of 1956–1972* (1973), consisted of essays dealing with Monet and Degas as well as current figures like Robert Motherwell, Willem de Kooning, and Ad Reinhardt.

In 1982, Kramer and the late Samuel Lipman, with $100,000 from several conservative sponsors, founded *The New Criterion*. In its first issue, the editors attacked what they saw as the politicization of art and the role of the left in its decline. "Not since the 1930s," they wrote, "have so many leftist pieties so casually insinuated themselves into both the creation and criticism of literature, and remained so immune to resistance or exposure." In their view, hostility toward bourgeois and capitalist society had continued unabated, and they saw no good reason for it. "Despite its many flaws," they declared, capitalism had shown itself to be "the greatest safeguard of intellectual and artistic freedom ... the modern world has given us."[57]

Kramer and his associate Roger Kimball pounded away at the radicals and defended the humanistic tradition they believed was being undermined by the New Class.[58] Kramer charged that art museums catered to every passing political whim, with exhibitions ranging from "Women and Politics" to "Art and Social Conscience" to examinations of racial chauvinism. He saw the politicization of art as obscuring its intrinsic aesthetic qualities. Grants made by the National Endowment for the Arts, Kramer wrote, following a review of its awards, went automatically to those who were opposed to every policy of the U.S. government, "except the one that put money in their own pockets."[59]

In an article in 1983 in *The New Criterion*, "American Art Since 1945: Who Will Write Its History?," Kimball sharply attacked Serge Guilbaut's book, *How New York Stole the Idea of Modern Art: Abstract Expressionsm, Freedom and the Cold War* (1983). A major theme of the book, according to Kramer, was that this country's intellectual classes cooperated inappropriately with U.S. propaganda efforts at the beginning of the Cold War. Kramer found this attack inexcusable. Modern art, he felt, was being implicated in "another unsavory aspect of capitalist bourgeois society," what the New Class deemed "its aggressive imperialism." He wondered just how far the political references of painting would detract from and obscure its intrinsic aesthetic qualities.

Kramer's important achievement was to link neoconservative thinking to the traditionalist defense of high culture. In the process, his magazine appealed not only to conservatives but also to liberals, who were restless with what they saw as the excesses of the counterculture.[60]

While Jewish neocons expressed themselves with great vehemence on numerous social issues and on foreign policy, they said little on the hot button issue of abortion. They were generally reluctant to join more traditional conservatives, including Catholic allies like Father Richard Neuhaus and George Weigel, on the pro-life side of the debate. *Commentary* ignored the issue, for the most part. One of the few articles it published, by James Q. Wilson, a Roman Catholic, in January 1994, rejected the argument that life begins with conception. Wilson argued that the death of a fifteen-day-old fetus should not be regarded as the death of a child. Irving Kristol, ever the pragmatist, was convinced that the United States would never criminalize abortion. Instead of fighting for that lost cause, he said, society should attempt to discourage abortion through regulations that might include prescribed waiting periods, spousal consent, and parental notification in the case of underage women.[61] This is exactly the direction that the abortion issue has taken, defusing some of its controversy.

Most of the Jewish neocons steered clear of writing about homosexuality as well, with the exception of Podhoretz and Decter, who were critical. More recently, in the light of the Supreme Court's ringing affirmation of sexual liberty in *Lawrence v. Texas* (2003), neocons have become more vocal. Even before *Lawrence*, Stanley Kurtz had argued that radical gays aimed to delegitimize historic understandings of the family and strike "at the heart of the organization of Western culture and societies."[62] After *Lawrence*, Kurtz suggested that the decision now opened the door to gay marriage and even polygamy.

In the main, neocons were not "a moralistic lot." They could be on both sides of the abortion and homosexuality issues, bringing them into collision with the paleoconservatives. Still, they were in revolt against the New Left's nihilistic attack against religious values and a traditional morality, which they saw as necessary to hold society together.

In the 1990s, the neocon attack on the counterculture broadened and began to gain support from prominent liberals. Arthur M. Schlesinger, Jr., warned of the dangers of fragmentation, re-segregation, and tribalization in *The Disuniting of America: Reflections on a Multicultural Society* (1992). Richard Bernstein, *New York Times* cultural affairs writer, supported the original purposes of multiculturalism in providing social justice for excluded sectors of society, but he cautioned against its excesses. Too often, he warned, it leads to a "Dictatorship of Virtues," the title of his 1994 book.

While entrenched on campuses and elsewhere, "politically correct behavior" became a term of opprobrium in some quarters. Harold Bloom, the literary scholar and author of *Shakespeare: The Invention of the Human* (1998), directed his barbs at university professors of Shakespeare: "I don't want a single person, with a few honorable exceptions, who ostensibly teach Shakespeare to even look at the book. They're hideous ideologues, pseudo Marxists, pseudo feminists, pseudo historians and disciples of Foucault [the deconstructionist writer]."[63]

A flood of books now trod the path that Alan Bloom had laid out in *The Closing of the American Mind.* They included *Profscam: Professors and the Demise of Higher Education* (1998) by Charles W. Sykes; *The War Against Intellect: Epistles in the Decline of Discourse* (1989) by Peter Shaw; *Tenured Radicals: How Politics Has Corrupted Our Higher Education* (1990) by Roger Kimball; and *Imposters in the Temple: American Intellectuals Are Destroying Our Universities and Cheating Our Students of Their Future* (1992) by Martin Anderson.

The left fought back, of course. Responding to Bloom's attack with his own book, *The Opening of the American Mind* (1996), historian Laurence W. Levine claimed that he could not recognize the portrait of the campus painted by conservative critics and their newfound allies, such as Bernstein and Schlesinger. The academic world, he argued, was "doing a more thorough and cosmopolitan job of educating a greater diversity of students in a broader and sounder array of courses covering the past and present... than ever before." Clearly, though, Levine and other defenders of new wave thought have been thrown on the defensive.[64]

Neocons have been criticized as having turned their back on the battle for civil rights. A more accurate reading, perhaps, is that they had moved on from their earlier support to another level of engagement. A considerable body of civil rights legislation had been enacted at city and state levels in the 1940s and 1950s. The Civil Rights Act of 1964 and voting rights legislation the following year made it clear that the civil rights revolution had been won. Most governmental disabilities had been removed. However, the condition of much of black America remained unchanged. Traditional civil rights measures, which had involved marches, sit-ins, and protests, could no longer ensure equality for those crippled by the effects of past prejudice, discrimination, and family disintegration.

When I served as vice chair of the U.S. Civil Rights Commission in the late 1980s, I became increasingly aware of such problems. Labor Department figures showed, however, that as the economy grew, the number of

African-American teenagers who found employment grew spectacularly. I wrote at the time that economic expansion would be the next stage of the civil rights revolution.[65]

In what might be termed the post–civil rights era, neocons have been joined by a significant group of African-American intellectuals, who were prepared to break with establishment civil rights thought. The writings of this new group of intellectuals appeared frequently in *Commentary* and other conservative journals and, more recently, in the mainstream media. Included among them are economists Glen Loury and Thomas Sowell; community activist Robert Woodson; San Francisco University English professor Shelby Steele; Yale law professor Stephen L. Carter; Clarence Thomas, former director of the Economic Opportunities Commission and now a Supreme Court justice; and John McWhorter, most recently a senior fellow at the Manhattan Institute. While differing sometimes with neocons (and among themselves), they echoed many neoconservative ideas.[66]

Like their white counterparts, these African-American intellectuals agreed that racial preferences and quotas were problematic. In an article in *Commentary* and in *One by One from the Inside Out* (1991), Glenn C. Loury criticized civil rights leaders for the debilitating rhetoric of victimization. He emphasized instead black self-help and moral renewal. Carter, who rejects being labeled a conservative, was also critical, in *Reflections of an Affirmative Action Baby* (1991), of government for having helped primarily middle-class blacks rather than those at the bottom and for having sought to buy "racial justice on the cheap." He recounted his rejection from Harvard Law School because admissions officials assumed that he was white. When they wanted to reconsider, Carter remarked, "I was good enough for a top law school only because I happened to be black."[67]

McWhorter has lashed out at what he has called the cult of victimology, separatism, and intellectualism he has witnessed on college campuses. When African-American reporter Jayson Blair was fired from the *New York Times* for fabricating stories, Blair fired back in the *New York Observer* that he was a victim of racism. McWhorter would have nothing of it. He reminded readers in the *Wall Street Journal* that prior to the mid-1960s, blacks who decried racism might have had genuine grievances. "But for many blacks today it has drifted into a recreational crutch," he noted. African-American students he had interviewed at Stanford in the late 1980s were disinclined to describe specific incidents of racism. They could say only that what they had experienced was "hard to explain."[68]

Though never an advocate of a color-blind society (as is Steele), Loury, in a 1985 essay in *The Public Interest*, saw the real poverty problem in the post–civil rights era as the "enemy within" (i.e., the weaknesses of communal institutions) rather than the "enemy without" (racism). The new black conservatives viewed dimly the paternalism of government policies. The idea that blacks cannot, as Steele put it, "run fast once they get to the 'starting line'" had resulted in programs that created and led to welfare dependency. The crisis, as black neocons saw it, was moral and cultural.[69]

African-American neocons, much like their white counterparts, have remained a minority voice in a minority culture. Still, they have been hard to ignore. Recently, disturbed by the publication by The Free Press of Charles Murray's and the late Professor Richard J. Herrnstein's *The Bell Curve* (1994), which described racial differences in intelligence, Loury, along with Woodson, were critical of the book.[70] Sowell, however, defended *The Bell Curve* as a "very honest book on a subject where sobriety, thoroughness and honesty are only likely to provoke cries of outrage." Following Supreme Court decisions in two Michigan cases in 2003 backing, in some circumstances, racial diversity in university admissions, Steele denounced the rulings as spurious and as placing American society on the threshold of legally sanctioned racialism.[71]

For Podhoretz and other neocons, the failure of many of the country's intellectuals to speak out against the excesses of the counterculture reflected their ambivalence about what was taking place. Podhoretz did not hesitate to name names. One person who disappointed him was Lionel Trilling.

In his memoir, *Ex Friends*, Podhoretz described the coldness that developed between the two friends. After what had been an amiable conversation, Trilling told Podhoretz that their mutual friend Sidney Hook had "*beschmutzed*" (the Yiddish term for soiled) himself by going too far to the right in his opposition to communism. Whatever the truth of Trilling's observation (Podhoretz doubted it), he felt that Trilling failed in making a more frontal attack on the New Left.

The subject arose again when the two participated in a September 1974 *Commentary* symposium, "Culture and the Present Moment," which featured also Cynthia Ozick and Hilton Kramer. Podhoretz accused the intellectual and academic communities of cowardice in the face of the radicalism that was damaging the culture, though he wrote later in a memoir that he was not attacking Trilling personally. In the roundtable discussion that followed, Trilling, who was ill and would live just another year, responded that Podhoretz had gone too far. "One has to conceive of it rather in terms of fatigue. Subjects and problems got presented in a way that made one's spirits fail. It wasn't that one was afraid to go into it, or afraid of being in opposition – I suppose I am speaking personally – but rather that in looking at the matter one's reaction was likely to be a despairing shrug."[72]

Trilling was internally conflicted, according to Podhoretz. Trilling believed in and celebrated "society and its restraints," he said, but "also wrote with great sympathy about the yearning for an 'unrestricted life.'"[73] In her candid memoir, Diana Trilling described her husband's private torment similarly. She said he had given over his career to the world of letters, restraint, and "gentle reasonableness" but was secretly drawn to a freer style of living. She added that he was unable to defend the traditional culture "because on some level he himself secretly resented or despised it, or at least he resented and despised that muted form of it that he himself embodied in his own writing and persona."[74]

Arguably, Trilling's inner torment might stand as a metaphor for the culture wars that engulfed the nation in the final decades of the twentieth century and continue to do so down to the present moment.

12

Jews and the Christian Right

Following the 1980 election, a major shift in Jewish political behavior appeared to be under way. For the first time in seventy-five years, a Democratic presidential candidate, Jimmy Carter, received less than a majority of the Jewish vote (45 percent). Reagan received a record 39 percent. (Independent candidate John Anderson got 15 percent.) Four years later, however, and despite his strong support for Israel, the Jewish vote for Reagan fell to 31 percent.[1] The return of Jews to their traditional Democratic moorings resulted mainly from growing fears of a reinvigorated Christian Right. Concerns about the impact of the New Left's and Jesse Jackson's influence within the Democratic Party had briefly shaken these loyalties but were soon trumped by an even more worrisome figure, according to one analyst: the Rev. Jerry Falwell.[2]

The rise of Falwell and the Christian Right had its origins in August 1978, when President Carter's director of the Internal Revenue Service ruled that any private schools set up after 1963 would be viewed as discriminatory and must forfeit their tax deductible standing. Since the vast number of private schools in the South were Christian, Southern Baptists and other fundamentalist bodies saw the ruling as troublesome. The threat forced them to do something they had avoided for many years: organize politically.

During the 1920s and 1930s, evangelicals and their fundamentalist wing had suffered a number of setbacks, including the Scopes "monkey trial" in Tennessee and the country's ill-fated experience with Prohibition. They felt the need to forgo activism and turn inward, focusing on personal salvation. Scholarly studies like Daniel Bell's *The New Radical Right* (1955) and Richard Hofstadter's *Anti-Intellectualism in American Life* (1962) reinforced a view of evangelicals as backward and bigoted. Cartoonist Al Capp satirized them in his popular cartoon strip, "Li'l Abner."[3]

Largely ignored by the broader culture, the evangelicals went underground. During their withdrawal, they built a massive network of independent organizations, youth ministries, evangelizing teams, Bible institutes, seminaries, missionary agencies, summer Bible conferences, and Bible distribution societies, all of which were quietly creating a major shift among the basic institutional carriers of American religious life.[4]

The evangelicals were ready to march. In an action led by the National Christian Action Coalition, almost half a million cards and letters poured into the IRS (more than the IRS had ever received for any proposed change) and the White House in protest. As a result, Congress held hearings to block the ruling. The episode was a political disaster for Democrats and a critical factor in bringing into existence a revived Christian Right.[5]

Howard Phillips, a Jew and a founder of Young Americans for Freedom, along with Paul Weyrich, a Melkite Catholic, and Ed McAteer, a businessman and Christian lay leader associated with Phillips's Conservative Caucus, persuaded Falwell to bring "the Christian perspective into politics." "The only way for conservatives to win," Philips said, "is to shift the focus from the national battleground to the grassroots where single conservative issues can win."[6] In a career spanning some twenty-two years, Falwell, an ordained Baptist minister, had built a congregation in Lynchburg, Virgina, encompassing some 17,000 members. At the time (early 1979), Falwell was convinced that God was calling him to bring the people of America together to battle against permissiveness and moral decay.[7]

During a strategy session in which New Right leaders were briefing Falwell on the current political situation, Paul Weyrich remarked, "Out there is what you might call a moral majority. They are politically and socially conservative. If we could get these people active in politics there is no limit to what we could do." Falwell was struck by the phrase. "That's it. That's the phrase I've been looking for," he said.[8]

Along with the Religious Round Table and the Christian Voice, Falwell's Moral Majority, founded on June 6, 1979, came to constitute the central core of the Christian Right.[9] Falwell was hardly alone. Other groups tapped nonfundamentalist evangelicals. The Christian Voice drew on Pentecostals. Pat Robertson, who had launched the Christian Broadcasting Network (CBN) in the early 1960s, mobilized charismatics through the Freedom Council and the Religious Round-Table; the National Christian Action Council organized others, including Southern Baptists.[10] According to Naomi Cohen, then a professor of history at Hunter College in New York, television evangelists reached an estimated 20 million viewers each week with their programs. By the middle of 1980, the Moral Majority would claim some 300,000 members.[11]

While the rise of the Christian Right as a social and political force caught many in the cosmopolitan culture by surprise, the reality is that religion has always been at the center of most of the country's major political issues down through the years, including support for and opposition to wars, slavery, corporate power, civil rights, and sexual codes. G. K. Chesterton once said that "America is a society with the soul of a church." In subsequent years, the Christian Right would become within the GOP what blacks and organized labor have been within the Democratic Party, a core constituency without which political success would be doubtful.[12]

Falwell was a curious mixture of the contradictary impulses now flowing in the evangelical world. He liked to see himself as a moderate. His "Ninety-Five Theses for the 1980s" focused on strengthening the family, hence the Moral Majority's opposition to abortion; homosexuality; drug abuse; adultery and premarital sex; pornography; and the Equal Rights Amendment. While it sought voluntary prayer and Bible reading and Easter and Christmas celebrations in public schools, it concurred in the separation of church and state. In paid advertisements (one million of its three-million-dollar first-year budget came from Falwell's *Old Time Gospel Hour*), the Moral Majority explained that it supported equal rights for women (although the Equal Rights Amendment went about it improperly) and that it did not attempt to take away the civil rights of homosexuals. The platform lacked a social justice component including any discussion of civil rights, poverty, or urban decay, but it included five planks in support of Israel.[13]

Jews have always been of special interest to evangelicals because of their perceived relationship to God. Indeed, as "people of the book," Falwell naïvely hoped to involve them in his movement. Shortly after the formation of the Moral Majority, Falwell encouraged meetings with representatives of Jewish agencies, in order "to make the Jewish community aware that we are not an anti-Semitic group and that we probably are the strongest supporter of Israel in the country." "God," he said, "has blessed America because America has blessed the Jew." Such friendliness, however, did not prevent him from making foolish remarks about Jews, including telling a Kingsport, Tennessee, audience in 1999 that the anti-Christ was alive today and was a male Jew.[14]

The 30 to 60 million evangelicals introduced a wild card into American social and political life. By 1980, Seymour Martin Lipset and Earl Raab reported that between 20 and 25 percent of Americans (some 30 million adults) were evangelicals. This figure included a number of Roman Catholics and blacks.[15] Earlier, *Time* had reported that evangelical churches numbered some 45 million, whereas the "cultured Protestant Establishment" affiliated with the National Council of Churches was declining to some 33.5 million.[16] Demographer Barry Kosmin estimates the most recent reliable figure, excluding Catholics and African-American evangelicals, at 60 million Americans, a quarter of the population.[17]

Many Jews have been suspicious of – when they are not outrightly hostile toward – evangelicals. Historian David Hollinger has described most Jews as "cosmopolitans"; part of their ethos stresses "the virtues of tolerance, relativism, and rationalism joined together with a strong contempt for the backward, 'provincial' mind."[18] This image was reinforced in the 1930s and

1940s by a number of fundamentalist preachers, including the Revs. Gerald Winrod and Gerald L. K. Smith, and a Roman Catholic priest, Father Charles Coughlin, who spewed forth a steady stream of anti-Semitism. Simultaneously, Jews found themselves more comfortable with liberal church bodies, with whom they could join on a wide range of social policy issues.

Like evangelical Protestants, neocons were involved also in a battle against the counterculture and "militant liberalism." In fact, the two groups had more in common with each other than with traditional conservatives. The latter placed a heavy emphasis on economics (a science of limits), and they were anti-statist, as Irving Kristol wrote in an article in *The Public Interest*. The neocon criticism of welfare (a favorite topic of traditional conservatives) was more centered on the ways in which it corrupted the souls of its recipients and crippled their ability to participate fully in American life. Moreover, both Jews and evangelicals expressed concern about the troubled condition of the modern American family.[19]

Neocons realized early on that evangelicals differed only slightly in their social and political behavior from other Americans. They were not necessarily bigots or reactionaries. They reflected the American consensus on many economic and political issues and remained divided on several others. Lipset and Raab addressed the question of whether government should be more or less involved in dealing with social problems: just over 50 percent of evangelicals answered that it should, according to a Gallup poll in August 1980. On such litmus-test issues as firearms registration and support for the Equal Rights Amendment, again slightly over half responded in the affirmative. "One lesson to be drawn from these figures," the two social scientists concluded, "is that the term 'evangelical' is rather meaningless when intepreting reactions to general political issues."[20]

Nathan Glazer sees the newfound activism promoted by Falwell and others in the fundamentalist wing of the evangelical movement as a kind of defensive reaction, rather than as an attempt to force a Christian way of life on the broader society. He sees the evangelicals as trying to defend their own values, which throughout much of American history had been widely accepted, against the largely successful efforts of New Age activists to change traditional patterns of American thought and behavior. Such activism has included aggressive and successful campaigns to overturn abortion laws, remove Bible reading and prayer from the public schools, redefine marriage, and bar virtually any reference to religion from the public sector.

Even as they challenged these efforts, evangelicals continued to hold philo-Semitic beliefs. A poll taken by the ADL of some 1,000 religiously conservative Christians in the late 1980s reported that most evangelicals do not "consciously use their deeply held faith and convictions as justification for anti-Semitic views of Jews." Nathan Perlmutter, the League's director and a neoconservative, considered that a marked improvement over previous studies done in the mid-1960s.[21]

Throughout the 1970s and 1980s, polls confirmed that fundamentalist as well as evangelical Christians were more supportive of Israel than liberal church bodies, such as the Quakers, Presbyterians, and Episcopalians. Critics charged that this support had mainly to do with their theology – that the second coming of Jesus was linked to the return of Jews to the Holy Land. A poll (released on October 2002) taken for the International Fellowship of Christians and Jews, a group seeking closer ties between Jews and evangelicals, however, indicated that the reasons were not necessarily theologically based. More than half said they supported Israel because of its democracy and its unequivocal friendship to the United States.[22] Falwell offered practical reasons for such support as well. Israel was America's only democratic ally in the Middle East and stood as a bulwark against the spread of communism. In 1980, in a move that shocked many Jewish liberals, Israeli Prime Minister Menachim Begin presented Falwell with Israel's prestigious Jabotinsky Award. The following year, when the National Council of Churches condemned Israel's bombing of a nuclear reactor in Iraq, Falwell, at the request of the Israeli government, spoke out against this criticism.[23]

As a result of such hard data, and as fears for Israel's safety and security mounted following the Six-Day War in 1967 and the Yom Kippur War in 1973, several Jewish civic agencies, including the American Jewish Committee, began reaching out to evangelicals. By the mid-1980s (in spite of such reckless statements as Rev. Bailey Smith's "God does not hear the prayer of a Jew"), both Irving Kristol and Lucy Dawidowicz, a historian of the Holocaust and a neocon, were writing articles in *Commentary* downplaying the importance of evangelical theology. "Why should Jews care about the theology of a fundamentalist preacher who speaks with no authority as to God's intentions?" Dawidowicz asked. And what do such "theoretical abstractions" matter anyway when the preacher is "vigorously pro-Israel"?[24]

Kristol made much the same point. He believed that the real reason Jews were concerned about the Moral Majority was because of the Jewish commitment to secular political [liberal] religion. Nonetheless, he observed, "The fact that the Moral Majoirty is pro-Israel for theological reasons that flow from Christian belief is hardly a reason for Jews to distance themselves from it. Why would it be a problem for us? It is their theology, but it is our Israel."[25]

An early pioneer in the movement to reach out to evangelicals was the AJC's director of interreligious affairs, Rabbi Marc Tanenbaum. In the 1970s and 1980s, he began a dialogue with mainstream evangelicals, including the prominent Baptist leader Billy Graham. According to Naomi Cohen, Graham "actively supported Israel during the 1967 war, publicly condemned anti-Semitism in the 1970s, and backed the cause of Soviet Jewry." The influential Graham also opposed organized conversional activities focusing on Jews. Jews, he declared, enjoyed a permanent covenant with God.[26] According to Ralph Reed, the late Nathan Perlmutter (the ADL's national executive head) was another Jewish leader who encouraged dialogue with evangelicals. In the mid-1980s, he invited Robertson to New York to meet with the ADL's executive board, a meeting that came to a close with the group joining hands to pray together and pledge mutual friendship.[27]

In 1983, Yechiel Eckstein, a young Orthodox rabbi who had once worked at the ADL, created an organization called the International Fellowship of Christians and Jews (IFCJ) in Chicago, in an effort to cement ties with evangelicals. Working with both groups, he attempted to teach his listeners and readers, through seminars and his own writings, about the convictions and sensitivities of the different religions. Claiming that "true Christians are the Jews' best friends," Eckstein also inaugurated the Center for Judeo Christian Values in Washington, D.C., a group dedicated to finding common religious ground in order to establish moral standards and a greater sense of personal accountability in society. Senators Joseph Lieberman (D. Conn.) and Dan Coats (R. Ind.) served as cochairs of the organization.[28]

By 1998 and 1999, IFCJ was the largest donor to the United Jewish Appeal (outside its system of community-based Jewish federations). In 1999, it gave $6.5 million – funds raised through television and radio appeals and direct-response mail marketing to evangelical Christians in America – to Israel through the UJA, which sends about $270 million to Israel annually.[29] By 2002, Eckstein reported that American evangelicals had quietly given more than $100 million over the previous seven years in humanitarian assistance to Jews in need worldwide, including resettlement costs, housing, food, and medical aid.[30]

Despite these efforts, the rise of the Christian Right continued to cause anxiety in the broader Jewish community. Eckstein said he "felt like a pariah here in the American Jewish community."[31] Public opinion polls indicate that Jews are eager to keep religion out of politics. Indeed, such feelings have increased recently, one study suggests. When Joseph Lieberman was nominated by the Democratic Party to run as vice president in 2002, Jews were pleased at his selection; but they did not wholly agree with his sentiment that religion ought to play an important role in shaping American values. In 2000, Abe Foxman, Perlmutter's successor at ADL, sent him a letter urging him to deemphasize the religious content of his speeches.[32]

Many Jews saw the rise of the Moral Majority as a continuing attempt by evangelicals and fundamentalists to Christianize them. Eckstein felt he needed to accompany Rev. Smith to Israel, in a hastily arranged "educational tour," after which Smith backed off his earlier slur, insisting, still, that evangelicals had to remain true to their mission to spread the word of Christ. A national survey of Jews by AJC in 1984 reported that some 46 percent of Jews listed "most" or "many" fundamentalist as anti-Semitic.[33]

Jewish concerns were exacerbated further at the 1984 Republican convention. Eight Jewish organizations appealed to the Republican platform committee to broaden its strong condemnation of bigotry by rejecting the current divisive assault on the separation of church and state. The Republican leadership, however, was not about to turn aside from what was becoming a core constituency, gambling that Jewish voters, a very small part of their constituency, could be placated by the platform itself and that they would be influenced by fears about Jesse Jackson's rise as a prominent figure in the Democratic Party (he had only recently referred to heavily Jewish New York City as "Hymietown"). At the convention, Falwell and other evangelical leaders delivered invocations. Delegates arriving there found copies of the New Testament in their kits. Following the convention, Reagan compounded the problem when, at a prayer breakfast, he declared that religion and politics were inevitably related and that proponents of church-state separation were "intolerant of religion."[34]

Despite Falwell's efforts to reach out to Jews, he was awkward and inexperienced. The late Rabbi Tannenbaum told me of a forty-five-minute visit he had with Falwell, at the conclusion of which the evangelical minister said, as he was leaving, that this was the longest conversation he had ever had with a Jew.[35] Falwell became what one reporter called "that man Jews love to hate." He declared that AIDS was a sign of God's punishment on those who did not heed Him. One of his leaders on the West Coast suggested that homosexuals be executed.[36]

The Reagan years marked the high point of the Moral Majority's influence but underscored its many weaknesses. It subordinated local organizing to direct-mail fund raising, which resulted in a large mailing list of relatively little strength. Conservative religious activist Ralph Reed, who met Falwell in 1984, remarked that Falwell liked publicity but "rarely did the heavy lifting." He never got around to "doing the dirty work of grassroots organization and training workshops."[37] When the financial and sexual misdeeds of evangelists Jim Bakker and Jimmy Swaggart became widely known, the movement turned into an object of ridicule and collapsed. In June 1989, Falwell closed down the Moral Majority.

A "second wave" of the movement, however, remained alive. One wing of "pragmatists" argued that it needed to build grassroots organizations in order to mobilize voters more effectively. It stressed that lobbying and litigation were best tied to influence in the voting booth and shifted the movement's agenda away from moral traditionalism to a focus on family values and the rights of traditionalists in a secular culture.[38] Televangelist Pat Robertson, whose grassroots army and television empire had a wide network of viewers, attempted to step into the breach by making a bid for the Republican presidential nomination in 1988, coming in second in the Iowa caucuses.

Robertson, like Falwell, was an odd mixture of the old and the new in the newly aroused religious conservative movement. He had been a lifelong Democrat in the old Southern New Deal tradition and had once campaigned for Adlai Stevenson. He had helped integrate churches in Tidewater, Virginia, and also campaigned against former Klan leader David Duke during the latter's gubernatorial race in Louisiana. Robertson viewed Duke as a racist and neo-Nazi. At a critical point in the 1976 campaign, he endorsed Jimmy Carter, a "born again Christian." Later, he became disenchanted when Carter was unwilling to support the agenda of the Christian Right.[39]

Following Robertson's political defeat, he convened a meeting of "pro-family" elements in Atlanta. Republican leaders (even Ronald Reagan), he told the group, had taken their support for granted. There was a need to build a permanent political infrastructure to give Christians a voice in government. Robertson invited to the meeting a twenty-seven-year-old Republican activist who was earning a doctorate in history at Emory University. At Robertson's request, Ralph Reed, who had been involved in Republican politics for quite some time, prepared a memorandum on how to organize a grassroots organization. The memo recommended that the new group focus on building a state-by-state, county-by-county organization, right down to the neighborhood level.[40]

Reed was an inspired choice. Reed, however, was preparing himself for a career in college teaching after finishing his doctoral dissertation (on the history of Southern evangelical colleges). Robertson waited until this was done before moving to Virginia Beach to set up the headquarters of the Christian Coalition.

Reed is one of the most unusual individuals to emerge in the new phase of the religious conservative movement. Older figures like Graham, Falwell, and Robertson, while attempting to give leadership to newer forces developing among modern evangelicals, reflected older ways of thought and behavior. Reed spoke to, or at least attempted to speak to, the newly emerging generation of evangelicals, while balancing the message with the older tradition. With Robertson's acquiescence, Reed, who was theologically flexible, was willing to compromise on key issues. For example, he reached out to economic conservatives by integrating tax reduction and smaller government into the group's agenda as part of its stress on individual responsibility, without turning the clock back on race relations, equal opportunity for women, or religious freedom.[41]

Reed grew up in Miami, in what he told me was a "Jewish atmosphere." Given a choice of associating with more rambunctious youngsters in high school, he "ran" with more middle-class Jewish students. (Mischievously, he said this was natural, since his father was a doctor.) He had hoped to fashion an academic career, but politics always attracted him. His baptism in politics occurred at the University of Georgia, where he headed the Young Republican Club. There he papered the campus with leaflets in an election to unseat Senator Herman Talmadge on behalf of a Republican candidate, who won.[42]

Jack Abramoff, an attorney in Washington, and earlier a conservative firebrand at Brandeis University, gave Reed his first job as a political intern in Washington in 1981, when Abramoff, an orthodox Jew, became national chairman of College Republicans. Reed lived in his home, attended services with him, and introduced Abramoff to his wife, who came from Georgia. Abramoff found Reed "incredibly philo-semitic." When an anti-Semitic incident occurred in the organization, Reed told him, "I took care of it."[43]

In 1983, Reed became executive director of the National College Republicans, mobilizing the youth vote for Reagan and working with top GOP operatives like Lee Atwater and Ed Rollins. At about this time, he felt the first stirrings of a personal religious awakening. Raised as a Methodist, he had gradually drifted away from the church. He now felt the need for spiritual roots. In 1984, he founded a political organization of campus evangelicals, Students for America, a kind of YAF for the 1980s. In his memoir, *Active Faith*, he concedes that he was "a bare knuckle political operative" in the rough-and-tumble of politics. Like his mentor, Atwater, who found in his unsuccessful battle with brain cancer a more humane mode of thought and behavior, Reed writes that his heart "was softened" and his "political style changed by a faith experience." Shortly thereafter, he began attending evangelical church services in Washington.[44]

The contrast between Reed and Robertson, to whom Reed gave unswerving loyality, and who in turn allowed him to become the public face of the Coalition, could hardly be sharper. Reed reflected the pragmatic and more progressive side of the religious conservative movement. Robertson was a product of what Richard John Neuhaus has called its Reconstructionist phase. Sometimes known as Theonomy or Dominion Theology, "it [is] a bastard form of Calvinism," Neuhaus writes, contending that "the American constitutional order must be replaced by a new order based on 'Bible Law.'"[45]

Reed rejected this ideology. "Reconstructionism is an authoritarian ideology that threatens the most basic civil liberties of a free and democratic society," he declared. The pro-family movement "must unequivocally dissassociate itself from Reconstructionism and other efforts to use the government to impose biblical law through direct political action. It must firmly and openly exclude the triumphalist and authoritarian elements from the new theology of Christian, political, involvement."[46] Like Frank Meyer earlier, Reed helped to create a "fusionist strategy," and even a populist mandate, based on his belief that "the health of the larger society depends not only on their winning what to them is the most urgent item on their agenda – ending legalized abortion – but also on a sound economy, good schools, and a functioning social welfare system."[47]

In his attempt to make over the Christian Right, Reed "appealed to those evangelicals eager to demonstrate that wanting to protect the unborn and defend traditional values didn't make them racist or intolerant or hateful."[48] Reed, in short, was determined to become the religious conscience of the Christian Right, linking it to its progressive, evangelical history, which included strong support of separation of church and state and, in the nineteenth century, abolition of slavery. In moving in this direction, he did not minimize the group's failures. "It is a painful truth," he pointed out, "that the white evangelical church was not only on the sidelines, but on the wrong side, of the most central struggle for social justice in this century" – the civil rights movement.[49] When a spate of firebombings of churches (more than half of them black) broke out in the South and other parts of the country in 1996, he called on the Republican Congress to hold hearings and offered a $25,000 reward for information that would lead to the arrest of the perpetrators. Later, he announced before a small group of pastors and civil rights leaders in Atlanta that the Coaliton planned to raise $1 million to rebuild the burnt churches. Early in January 1997, he announced a plan (the Samaritan Project) to raise $1 million for African-American and Hispanic churches in the inner cities, to work with black children at risk. Robertson reportedly was furious that he had not involved the board of the Coalition.[50]

Reed's less doctrinaire approach reflected the profound changes taking place among evangelicals nationally. Whereas the image persisted of a movement dominated by southern rednecks, it had become far more diverse, both geographically and socially. Historian Alan Brinkley points out that evangelicals now include "people who have shared the fruits of the consumer culture; people who have become part of the bureaucratized world of the organizational society . . . people from urban areas . . . whose new affluence has not weakened their powerful religious beliefs. If anything, it may have strengthened them."[51]

Critic Alan Wolfe, writing in *Atlantic Monthly*, has called attention to "the opening of the evangelical mind" and to "a rich, intellectual tradition that has been developing among scholars in a number of evangelical, educational institutions like Wheaton and Calvin Colleges and Fuller Theological Seminary." The tradition is best represented, he wrote, in the publication *Books & Culture*, modeled on the *New York Review of Books*. In addition to articles by evangelical scholars, it has featured discussions on Jean-Jacques Rousseau and popular films as well as interviews with Stanley Crouch, Adam Michnik, and Francis Fukuyama. A sizable portion of modern evangelicals have been Democrats who are economic liberals. Many others are more liberal on social and economic issues than most mainline Protestants. In Brinkley's opinion, Stephen L. Carter, a Yale law professor and best-selling novelist, is as representative of modern-day evangelicalism as Jerry Falwell.[52]

This trend has been largely missed by the media, as *New York Times* columnist Nicholas D. Kristof has noted. He writes that "nearly all of us in the news business are completely out of touch with a group that includes 46 percent of Americans." Kristof could not think of a single evangelical working for a major news organization.[53]

While taking the high road, Reed, nevertheless, remained a gut fighter. He once described himself as "a bare knuckle political operative" who believed in winning at any price. Social scientists Mark J. Rozell and Clyde Wilcox quoted Reed. "I do guerrila warfare. I paint my face and travel at night. You don't know it's over until you're in a body bag."[54] Clearly, the two tendencies of idealism and playing to win warred within him.

Even so, Reed used his influence to prevent the more extreme elements within the conservative movement from taking over the GOP. Always the pragmatist, he knew that the movement would go nowhere if it became known as a haven for zealots. Behind the scenes (the Coalition would lose its tax-exempt status if it openly endorsed political candidates), Reed blocked Pat Buchanan's bid for the Republican nomination in 1996. Buchanan's George Wallace–like populism, his isolationism, and his attacks on neocons for their strong support of Israel outraged Jews (who saw behind the façade); his isolationism also turned off mainstream conservatives. Quietly, Reed threw the weight of the Christian Coalition behind moderate Senator Bob Dole in the crucial South Carolina primary. Buchanan's loss there dealt a fatal blow to his campaign, and Reed was widely credited with causing his defeat.[55]

By 1995, the Christian Coalition claimed some seventeen hundred local chapters in all fifty states and a database of some 1.7 million members, making it the largest umbrella group on the religious right. Its numbers were exaggerated, according to Reed's biographer, but there was little doubt about its ability to get out the vote and groom candidates to run. The high point of these electoral activities came in 1994, when the Christian Right joined a broad conservative coalition to help the Republicans take control of both houses of Congress for the first time in forty years and brought Newt Gingrich, with his Contract with America, to power in Washington. Hitherto seen as being at the fringe of the political process, evangelical Protestants and the Christian Right now stood at its center.

In June 1994, the ADL released a report, *The Religious Right: The Assault on Tolerance and Pluralism in America.* The 193-page report conceded that it was legitimate for conservative Christians to defend their values in the political process, but the weight of the document excoriated the religious right for its "sectarian, absolutist declarations"; for "bring[ing] to cultural disagreements a rhetoric of fear, suspicion, even hatred"; and for "trafficking with bigots and conspiracists." The ADL labeled the religious right an "exclusionist religious movement," which would destroy the wall of separation of church and state, and was abetted sometimes "at the highest levels by figures who have expressed conspiratorial, anti-Jewish and extremist sentiments."

In its report, the ADL singled out for attack Falwell; Weyrich (of the Free Congress Foundation); Donald W. Wildmon, founder of the American Family Association; and the Christian Coalition, including Robertson. It cited reports that Robertson had charged Jews in general with being "spiritually deaf" and "spiritually blind" and had singled out liberal Jews for engaging in "an ongoing attempt to undermine the public strength of Christianity."[56]

The attack on Robertson quickly escalated. In an article in the *New York Review of Books*, "Rev. Robertson's Grand International Conspiracy

Theory," Michael Lind called attention to Robertson's *The New World Order* (1994), published during the Gulf War. Robertson described a broad conspiracy to take over society led by a secret group, the Order of the Illuminati, allegedly founded in 1776 by European and other bankers, which later came to include the "Rothschild interests" and bankers Jacob Schiff and Paul Warberg. They were described as having planned the French Revolution, subsequently backing Marx and Engels, and creating havoc with the United States' economic system through the Order's instrument, the Federal Reserve Board.[57] Other critics soon joined in, pointing out that some of Robertson's sources in an earlier book, *The New Millennium* (1990), were writers of anti-Semitic tracts. The implications of Jewish conspiracy were clear.

The attacks on the Christian Right by Jews and others now grew even more impassioned. Rabbi Balfour Brickner, rabbi emeritus of the Stephen S. Wise Free Synagogue of New York, told the *National Jewish Post & Opinion* that religious conservatism for the foreseeable future is defined not by arguments but "only hatreds." *Washington Post* syndicated columnist Richard Cohen wrote that in order to gain the support of the Christian Coalition, the GOP had made a pact with the devil. The April 17, 1995, issue of *The New Republic* described Robertson's ideology as "crypto-fascist." In subsequent months, liberal columnists Frank Rich and Anthony Lewis poured out column after column in the *New York Times*, describing the threat posed to society by Robertson, his lieutenant Ralph Reed, and the Christian Right.

In response, Robertson and Reed released a fact sheet accusing the ADL of inaccuracies (Robertson denied making the "spiritually deaf and spiritually blind" remark, and the ADL apologized, while standing by its statement).[58] In a letter to the ADL and in a 500-word statement to the *Times*, Robertson insisted that the views expressed in *The New World Order* were not anti-Semitic, and he repudiated the claim of a worldwide conspiracy. He pointed to the Christian Coaliton's pro-Israel posture. He regretted that his description of international bankers with Jewish names was seen as anti-Jewish, and he said his statements "were misunderstood." As evidence of his goodwill, he cited in an interview a passage from the book predicting that the next objective of "the presently constituted new world order" at the United Nations would be to target Israel. He said that he named his political organization the Christian Coalition because his base was largely among conservative evangelicals.[59]

Robertson cited his record of condemning the UN statement equating Zionism with racism. He said he had consistently attacked anti-Semitism and had rejected the candidacy of neo-Nazi David Duke in Louisiana's 1991 gubernatorial election. He also insisted that only his "most personal beliefs and . . . most fundamental convictions" supported church-state separation.[60]

What happened next must have stunned the ADL, for it came under attack from a number of Jews. Seventy-five Jews signed an advertisment, "Should

Jews Fear the 'Christian Right'?," on the op-ed page of the *New York Times* on August 2, 1994, attacking the Jewish civil rights organization. Organized by Rabbi Daniel Lapin, an orthodox rabbi, who two years earlier had created a politically conservative Jewish organization, Toward Tradition, in Seattle, Washington, and by Midge Decter, who had helped raise the money for the advertisement and collected the signatures, the statement declared that the ADL report used a few marginal extremists to impeach individuals and groups who acted out publicly their Christian beliefs. It concluded, "Judaism is not, as the ADL seems to suggest, co-extensive with liberalism."[61]

Along with Kristol, Decter, and Gertrude Himmelfarb, several young Jewish intellectuals, including historians Jonathan D. Sarna (the Joseph H. and Belle R. Braun Professor of American History at Brandeis University) and David Dalin, journalist David Klinghoffer (literary editor of *National Review*), and columnists Mona Charen and William Kristol also signed the ad. In an interview with the *Forward*, Sarna said that he "lamented that the report was not more nuanced with a better understanding of the history of evangelism and the understanding that it is not a unified movement." The report, he added, did not deal with the religious right's view of Jews and Judaism "on its own terms [and] from their theological viewpoint." Charen, in the same interview, was more harsh: "The ADL report contains no footnotes or supporting materials but is littered with characterizations like 'prophets of rage,' 'paranoia,' and 'hysteria' – words that suit the report itself perfectly."[62]

Several other Jewish public figures, including former senator Rudy Boshwitz of Minnesota, a moderate Republican, also claimed that the ADL had gone too far. Boshwitz denied that there was any anti-Semitism among Christian Right leaders he knew. Two Southwest regional board ADL leaders resigned from the organization, and its chairman was forced out. In an op-ed piece in the *Forward*, former U.S. ambassador to the United Nations and chair of the Conference of Presidents of Major Jewish Organizations Morris B. Abrams contrasted the attitudes and behavior toward Israel of Christian fundamentalists with those of liberal, Christian bodies – to the detriment of the latter.[63]

Norman Podhoretz undertook the most comprehensive defense of Robertson. While sharply critical of Robertson's "crackpot theory" that the Rothschilds, Warburg, and Schiff were attempting to take over the world, Podhoretz accepted Robertson's denial and apology, suggesting that Robertson may not have been aware of the anti-Semitic implications of some of the ideas to which he subscribed. He was hardly convincing here, but he was willing to give friends of Israel the benefit of the doubt. He dismissed arguments that Robertson's support of Israel was based on an apocalyptic theology about the second coming of Christ, arguing that the center of his attack was on the tenets of liberalism (to which so many Jews subscribe) rather than on Jews as such. Along with other defenders of the Christian

Right, Podhoretz wondered why Jewish agencies had not subjected liberal church bodies (like the National Council of Churches, who were hostile to Israel and supported the Arab cause) to such fierce criticism.[64]

By this time, it seems clear, neocons seemed more at home with Christian conservatives than with liberal Jews. They believed that the spread of secularism and relativism was far more dangerous than occasionally outrageous statements of the religious right. There is no small irony here. For most of their lives, Jewish neocons had been relatively indifferent to traditional Judaism; they were themselves a part of the secular culture. "I've always been a believer," Irving Kristol told an interviewer in 1996. "Don't ask me in what. That gets too complicated. The word 'God' confuses everything."[65] Only Midge Decter, among the original neocons, came close to dealing with religion in more traditional, faith-based terms. In an article that appeared in *First Things*, she appealed to Jews to return to God. For Jews, she declared, the "real questions are not or rather ought not to be, does he exist and if so, who is he, but rather, only what is it that He wants of us."[66]

Despite the specter of anti-Semitism aroused by the Christian Right, neocons identified with the evangelicals' criticism of the counterculture and their determination to rid the world of communism. In these things, neocons found common cause with the Christian Right. "The plain truth," Irving Kristol declared,

> is that if we are ever going to cope with the deficit and the social programs that inflate it, we are going to have to begin with a very different view of human nature and human responsibility in relation to such issues as criminality, sexuality, welfare dependency, even medical insurance. Only to the degree that such a new – actually very old – way of looking at ourselves and our fellow citizens emerges can a public opinion be shaped that will candidly confront the fiscal crisis of the welfare state.... Presidential calls for "sacrifice," meaning a willingnesss to pay higher taxes, are a liberal cop-out. Why don't we hear something about self-control and self-reliance? It's the traditional spiritual values that we as individuals need, not newly invented, trendy ones.[67]

Simultaneously, there was developing among neonconservatives a growing interest in religion. Kristol had been writing on the subject on and off for many years. In the Foreword to the twentieth-anniversary edition of *The Cultural Contradictions of Capitalism*, Daniel Bell wrote:

> My interest in religion goes back... to [an] awareness in men of their finiteness and the inexorable limits to their power... and the consequent effort to find a coherent answer to reconcile them to the human condition.... The exhaustion of Modernism, the aridity of Communist life, the tedium of the unrestrained self, and the meaninglessness of the monolithic political changes all indicate that a long era is coming to a slow close.... I believe that a culture which has become aware of the limits in exploring the mundane will turn at some point, to the effort to recover the sacred.[68]

Unlike Neuhaus, a Lutheran minister who converted to Roman Catholicism and became a neocon ally, Jewish neocons had rediscovered religion through reason and practical necessity, indeed as an adjunct to their quarrel with the counterculture. "Irving [Kristol], God bless him, has a very different understanding of religion than I do," Neuhaus said. "We agree on many things, but [his view on religion], how should I put it accurately, is more of an instrumental view, grounded less in any devotional purposes than as a stabilizing force in society."[69]

In *Commentary*, Kristol acknowledged that Jews belonged to Jewish institutions and proudly identified themselves as Jews, but their religion, he explained, was "only Jewish in its externals." Jews are at heart secular humanists, he wrote, which may be "why American Jews are so vigilant about removing all the signs and symbols of traditional religions from 'the public square,' so insistent that religion be merely a 'private affair,' so determined that separation of church and state be interpreted to mean the separation of all institutions from any signs of a connection with traditional religions."[70] Despite their growing unreliability on Israel, Kristol argued in another article in *Commentary*, the liberal church bodies were the favorite churches of the institutional Jewish community, because they are "less aggressively Christian."[71]

Secular humanism had been "good for Jews," Kristol conceded. It accounted for an "unparalleled degree of comfort and security"; but given the moral disarray in American life, the force of moral tradition grounded in religion and religious teachings needed reassertion. Taken together with the fact that the Christian Right was a staunch supporter of Israel, it became even more critical that Jews not turn their back on these putative allies.[72]

In the wake of the ADL report on the Religious Right, Ralph Reed played the role of a healer. In a speech before the ADL's national leadership on April 3, 1995, he acknowledged that "religious conservatives have at times been insensitive and have lacked a full understanding of the horrors experienced by the Jewish people" – horrors for which, he conceded, "Christians bear a measure of culpability." Support for Israel, he added, did not mean that Christian conservatives were freed from any responsibility for anti-Jewish feeling. Reed met head-on the charge that his organization sought to promote a "Christian nation." He told his listeners that the Christian Coalition believes in a nation that is not officially Christian. It supported only a broad constitutional amendment that would expand the right of free religious expression in public settings, not a measure specifically permitting school prayer.[73]

Reed repeated this message one month later before the American Israel Public Affairs Committee (AIPAC), the primary pro-Israel lobbying group in Washington. He declared that the widespread stereotype of gun-toting anti-Semites riding around in pickup trucks was unfair. "Just because we don't share the same political agenda as liberal Jews, it should not mean we can't cooperate."[74]

Elliott Abrams, who attended the AIPAC meeting, was impressed. He did not know whether Reed needed Jews, he said, but "we need Ralph Reed."[75] In other quarters, however, Reed's message was received with skepticism. *New York Times* columnist Frank Rich, who is Jewish, conceded that Reed's positions were more attractive than Robertson's, but to Rich, this meant only that Reed was more clever. He believed the two were playing out the classic "good cop, bad cop" game. Columnists at the *Wall Street Journal* and *Los Angeles Times* agreed with Rich.[76] In turn, the right-wing *Washington Times* dismissed his ADL speech as an "act of groveling."[77] Writing in *The Nation*, Christopher Hitchens, alluding to Reed's youthful, slender appearance and his Ph.D., said that Reed combined a "gender-free appearance" with "a seductive line in Insincerity 101."[78]

Reed had assigned himself a difficult task – the modernization of Christian conservatism. In eight years as the Christian Coalition's principal spokesman, he had moved it beyond its traditional opposition to abortion and homosexuality into areas of general concern. Under Reed's guidance, the Christian Coalition in 1995 urged the new Republican Congress to shelve attempts to secure a school prayer amendment and to work instead for a "Religious Liberty Amendment," which would guarantee rights of religious expression and equal access to facilities in public schools and other public settings.[79]

Spokesmen for the religious right were now abandoning a school prayer amendment and opting for something like a religious equality amendment. While such an amendment was never enacted, President Clinton moved in this direction. In 1995, he released guidelines (based on the research of several groups, including Jewish bodies) on religion in the schools, which helped to clarify the distinction between public schools' endorsing one faith, which the Constitution clearly bans, and students expressing their faith *within* certain limits inside schools. The guidelines read, in part, "Students may express their beliefs about religion in the form of homework, artwork and other written and oral assignments, free of discrimination based on the religious content of their submissions." Clearly, the Christian Right under Reed's tutelage was affecting not just the political climate but also the social climate of the times. Reed's lasting legacy "was to show religious Right activists a path out of their political ghetto and into mainstream politics."[80]

The Christian Right reached perhaps the high point of its influence in 1994. That year saw the Republican Party gain control of both houses of Congress. Reed, perhaps self-servingly, estimated that forty-four of the seventy-three freshmen Republicans elected to the House had close ties with conservative religionists.[81]

Riding the tide, the Christian Coalition released its "Contract with the American Family" in May 1995, which even critics found suprisingly mild. It called for local control of education; vouchers or choice in education, including their use in parochial schools, which some liberals supported; a $500 tax credit for children; elimination of the marriage tax penalty; and restrictions on pornography. According to neocon David Brooks, the Christian Coalition's contribution to Gingrich's "Contract with America" was the $500-per-child tax credit, a pocketbook issue.[82] Significantly, the "Contract with the American Family" aimed to limit only late-term abortions and did not mention anything about opposition to civil rights protections for homosexuals. Most of these objectives were not adopted, but they were evidence of a milder approach. Not surprisingly, Pat Buchanan denounced the contract as timid.[83] Other critics argued that the Christian Coalition had not changed but, under Reed's direction, had become shrewder in seeking to accomplish its purposes.

Even with its impressive mobilization of religious activists, the Christian Coalition began to lose ground at about this time. During the 1980s and 1990s, only about 10 to 15 percent of evangelicals reported in a survey that they supported religious right organizations, although a somewhat larger proportion favored specific issues on its agenda. In Virginia, the home of Falwell and Robertson and the national headquarters of the Christian Coalition and other religious right organizations, only 15 percent of voters said they would increase their support for a candidate endorsed by the Coalition. The Christian Right's strength lay only in certain geographic areas of the country, such as the South, and its veto power in the GOP.[84]

The religious right also faced the deep antipathy of the media. It did not have the firepower or the troops for the long fight that organizations like the ACLU, the Sierra Club, the National Organization for Women, and Ralph Nader's network of consumer lobbies had, according to Jeffrey Berry's study of citizens' groups.[85] The Christian Coalition was also heavily in debt. In 1997, Reed, a young man with a growing family, resigned to begin a career as a conservative political consultant.

With Reed's departure, the Christian Coalition became a skeleton of its former self. The disappointments that it and other right-wing religious groups had suffered resulted in Weyrich and others urging conservative Christians to redirect their energy away from politics "to saving souls."[86] Despite this setback, the broader evangelical movement remained a strong force, intensifying its support for Israel, especially after September 11, 2001. As another Intifada took a heavy toll on Israel's economy, evangelicals stepped up financial support for the embattled Jewish state. In the spring of 2003, Rabbi Eckstein announced that the International Fellowship of Christians and Jews was donating $2.5 million dollars to the social service budgets of eighty-one Israeli cities.[87] A year earlier, Reed, now a political consultant in Atlanta and chairman of the Georgia Republican Party, joined with Eckstein in the formation of a new organization called Stand for Israel to mobilize the nation's evangelical Christians in support of Israel, "a sort of Christian AIPAC," Eckstein noted.[88] Early in July 2003, Republican Tom DeLay, the House majority leader and a leading evangelical, visited Israel and spoke before the Knesset. He pledged continued support for Israel and opposition to President Bush's "road map" for peace if it meant coercing the Jewish state to make concessions that would harm its security.[89]

At this point, a remarkable and unprecedented shift on the part of Jewish civic agency leadership took shape. Despite the willingness of neocons to enter into dialogue with the Christian Right, the broader Jewish community had always held back; but early in 2002, Jewish civic groups began to reach out. In the summer of that year, a regional branch of the Zionist Organization of America (ZOA) in Chicago honored Pat Robertson at its annual Salute to Israel Dinner. On May 2, 2003, the ADL took out an ad in the *New York Times*, in which Reed hailed the Jewish state's continued survival as "proof of God's sovereignty."

Although criticized, Foxman was not apologetic. "I am proud to have Ralph Reed as a friend and as an advocate on Israel," he said; he was sorry only that politically liberal Christians tended to be weaker in their support of the Jewish state. Similar statements calling for increased dialogue with evangelicals were forthcoming, not only from the right-wing ZOA but also from the liberal Jewish Council for Public Affairs, a representative group of Jewish community relations agencies. The effort to connect with the Christian Right on Israel took on greater force in 2004 as liberal church groups such as the Presbyterian Church (USA) and Anglican officials moved for consideration of a plan to cut off investment to protest Israel's behavior with regard to the Palestinians. As the nation moved into a new century, the neocons appear to have won the argument within the Jewish civic agency community that it should develop closer ties to evangelicals and the Christian Right.[90]

13

Epilogue

What is the legacy of neoconservatism? If we date this movement to the late 1940s and early 1950s, as I do, it is now almost sixty years old. What brought it into existence and held it together for decades was the crusade against the spread of international communism. With the collapse of the Soviet empire in 1991, it appeared to have ended. Indeed, Norman Podhoretz, writing in the March 1996 issue of *Commentary*, declared that it had "disappeared into the broader conservative movement."[1]

Its obituary, however, was premature. The destruction of New York's World Trade Center on September 11, 2001, alerted Americans to the threat of international terrorism and gave neocons a new lease on life. They were among the first to recognize the imminent danger long before 9/11, and they were among the strongest advocates of the invasion of Iraq. As we have seen, angry critics accused them of pushing a naïve and inexperienced president into an unnecessary imperial adventure.

The role of the neoconservatives in influencing the Bush administration's policies has undoubtedly been exaggerated. Such figures as Defense Secretary Donald Rumsfeld, former national security adviser and now Secretary of State Condoleeza Rice, and, of course, the president himself are *not* neoconservatives but rather advocates of a strong national defense, and they are capable of making up their own minds. This said, the influence of the neocons on America's foreign and domestic policies, both during the Cold War and more recently, has been significant. Although they have been few in number, at least until comparatively recently, their writings in newspapers, magazines, and books, their appearances on television, and their positions in government have made them important figures.

They were among the first to point out flaws in the nation's welfare system and the first to recognize, following World War II, the threat posed by Joseph Stalin and the Soviet Union, against which they mounted a crusade within left-wing circles and the broader public. They questioned whether government should remain the primary vehicle for progressive social change, which they generally supported, and recommended larger roles for religious and neighorhood groups in order to supplement government activities.

It was a measure of their persuasiveness, in part, that welfare reform is now a widely accepted principle of both political parties. As their thinking evolved, these former liberals and socialists grew increasingly respectful of capitalism, bringing many in and outside of the left to a wider acceptance of the critical role of the free market in increasing material well-being and the freedoms that come with it. The effectiveness of supply-side economics, which they enthusiastically promoted, remains controversial; but for better or worse, the economic policy of the Reagan administration has become the economic policy of the second Bush administration.

Even in the assault on the counterculture, where neocons felt they had failed, there is a new sobriety among Americans. A Zogby poll released in November 2002 found that Americans generally are becoming more conservative on abortion. A November 2003 Gallup poll concurred that as many as 32 percent of teenagers – almost twice the percentage of adults – believe abortion should be outlawed.[2] In 2003, Congress passed (and President Bush signed into law) a ban on what critics of the procedure call "partial birth abortion." Divorce and out-of-wedlock births, while still prolific, are down, as are teenage pregnancies.[3]

One of the most thoughtful critics of the neocons, sociologist Alan Wolfe, has pointed out that neocons came on the scene at a critical moment.

> The 1960s, after all, were truly a destabilizing period in which institutions and traditions of all kinds were asked to justify themselves – and many could not. Since they represented a cultural revolution, the decades of the 1960s and 1970s demanded a stabilizing reaction and this is what the neoconservatives were the first to understand and to offer. One need not agree with everything that they said to acknowledge the distance that had developed between it [the cultural revolution] and the larger body of Americans and the debt to the neoconservatives for helping to stop certain destructive social trends in their tracks.[4]

"They did not convert existing conservatism," historian Gary Dorrien susgests,"but rather created an alternative to it."[5] Fueling the "marriage" has been what George Nash calls "idea power." The participation of intellectuals in shaping public policy had always been associated with the other side of the political spectrum. Franklin Roosevelt had his "brain trust"; John F. Kennedy, his Harvard professors; and Lyndon Johnson, his Great Society strategists. The recent "intellectualization of American politics" has taken shape within the conservative camp, largely through the impact of the neocons.[6] The neoconservative intellectuals completed the modernization that William F. Buckley had begun when he created *National Review* in 1955. They not only enlarged its vision but helped make it acceptable to larger numbers of Americans. In doing so, they provided many of the ideas and arguments that allowed it to compete with and triumph over the prevailing liberalism of the previous half-century. And from the neocons, conservatives learned that one of the most effective arguments against racial preferences was Martin Luther King's appeal to judge people not by the color of their skin but by the content of their character.[7]

What marked off the neocons from most older right-wing conservatives was their clearer understanding of the void that existed in American politics. Restless as Americans had become with the welfare state, they were not prepared to wipe out social reforms dating from the days of the New Deal. The neocons transformed the nature of the debate from an emphasis on welfare cheating, a favorite conservative shibboleth, to what Irving Kristol termed "the demonstrated corruption of body and soul experienced by recipients of welfare."[8]

Old-line conservatives opposed school integration by appealing to the original meaning of the Fourteenth Amendment and to states' rights. The neocons supported school desegregation but stressed what virtually everyone, including many African-Americans, came to understand: busing to achieve integration did not work; it did not bring about increased racial harmony, and it did not improve the scholastic achievement of black or white children.

The neocons, of course, did not win kudos among older-style conservatives for their pains. They found themselves under sharp attack from paleoconservatives, as well as those on the liberal left. The paleos, in fact, often accused neocons of leading the conservative movement astray.[9] In more recent years, the paleos came to center around Pat Buchanan, a speech writer for Nixon and Reagan turned politician, who vowed to "take back" the conservative movement from the "neocon cabal." Buchanan, a throwback to an old-style, anti-Semitic, and extreme form of conservatism, has questioned aspects of the Holocaust, including the number of Jews who were murdered, and insisted that Jews wield an unhealthy influence on this country's policies with regard to Israel. Following his unsuccessful attempt to gain the Republican nomination in 1992, however, he has virtually disappeared from American political life. His 1992 campaign may well have been the "last hurrah" of the old right.

In the cultural arena, neocons barely disguised their contempt for older-style conservatives, whom they viewed as philistines. The late Samuel Lipman, *Commentary*'s one-time music critic, observed that traditional conservatives placed their emphasis on national elections, battling communism, and running businesses, leaving the culture – where ideas are generated and disseminated – to the left. "Culture shapes our lives," Lipman wrote, "and affects every action we take." This was another lesson that neoconservatism taught more traditional conservatism.[10] Jewish neocons, in short, led the way in smoothing out conservatism's rough edges. Buckley acknowledged the debt, noting that the neocon's social scientific expertise helped butress his conservative ideology.[11] In a sense, President George W. Bush's administration, with its slogan of "compassionate conservatism," reflects neoconservative ideology.[12]

The various shades of left have also been forced to review their strategies and tactics. In a 2002 article in the left-wing journal *Dissent*, Michael Walzer asked, "Can There Be a Decent Left?" He found that the left's reaction to the September 11 terrorist attack manifested a "barely concealed glee that the imperial state had finally gotten what it deserved." The left had become alienated from Americans, Walzer added, and he urged it to abandon its current "rag-tag Marxism" and "stop blaming America first."[13] The 1960s activist Todd Gitlin, in *Mother Jones*, and the liberal historian Michael Kazin, in *Dissent*, have expressed similar sentiments. And in *Terror and Liberalism* (2003), Paul Berman called for resurrecting the anti-totalitarian, liberal alliance of old that stood up to Hitler and Stalin.[14] Observing these shifts, critic David Brooks, himself a neocon, exults, "We're all neoconservatives now."[15] To be sure, as U.S. troops became bogged down in Iraq and violence there grew, there has been a decline in the image of neocons, but the reelection of Bush in 2004 and the failure of the Democratic Party has underlined the neocon argument. Indeed, much of the public policy discussion under way in American life in recent years has revolved around issues raised by neoconservatives.

The most enduring legacy of neoconservatism, however, has been the creation of a new generation of highly influential younger conservative Jewish intellectuals, social activists, and allies. When Irving Kristol, Podhoretz, Sidney Hook, Nathan Glazer, Daniel Bell, and Erwin Glikes at The Free Press set out to reshape the thought of many on the left and the broader public, the movement consisted of perhaps two dozen individuals. Their numbers today have increased to hundreds of individuals threaded throughout the news media, think tanks, political life, government, and the universities. Among the leading figures are Bill Kristol, editor of *The Weekly Standard*; Neal Kozodoy, editor of *Commentary*; and columnists and writers David Brooks, Charles Krauthammer, Mona Charen, Lisa Schiffren, Wendy Shallit, Kay Heimowitz, Seth Lipsky, Don Feder, David Frum, Daniel Pipes, John Podhoretz, Jeff Jacoby, Adam Wolfson, and the late Eric Briendel, among others. Wolfson succeeded Irving Kristol as editor of *The Public Interest* in 2002.

Their articles appear in mainstream publications as well as in the "little" magazines. Academic neocons include Leon R. Kass, who taught at the University of Chicago and now heads the President's Council on Bioethics; Robert Kagan, Alexander Hamilton Fellow at American University; David Novak, professor of modern Judaic studies at the University of Virginia; and David Gelernter, professor of computer science at Yale. Gelernter is unusually wide-ranging in his writings, which cover art, literature, religion, and other cultural topics; his articles often appear in the *New York Times* and other prestigious journals.

Some, like John Podhoretz and Bill Kristol, are children of the original neocons. Others, like Elliott Abrams, a son-in-law of Podhoretz, along with

Richard Perle and Paul Wolfowitz, were young neocons in the 1970s and 1980s who have now moved to the top rung of the movement. Joshua Muravchik at the American Enterprise Institute and Robert Kagan are relative newcomers. Their influence has been felt everywhere. Brooks, a former journalist at the *Wall Street Journal* and senior editor at *The Weekly Standard*, now writes a regular column on the op-ed page of the *New York Times*. Dennis Prager and Michael Medved host radio talk shows on the West Coast. The latter authored *Hollywood vs. America* (1992), which helped to launch the recent public discussion of the emphasis on violence in the nation's film capital. And Frank Luntz, a Republican pollster, reportedly helped to develop and publicize former Congressman Newt Gingrich's Contract with America, which has been credited with giving the GOP control of the House and Senate in 1994.[16]

Lisa Schiffren, a speech writer in the first Bush administration, wrote Vice President Dan Quayle's "Murphy Brown" speech, criticizing television star Candice Bergen's portrayal of a television celebrity giving birth to a child out of wedlock. David Frum served as a speech writer in the second Bush administration, where he coined the phrase "axis of evil" – originally "axis of hatred" – referring to Iran, North Korea, and Iraq as terrorist nations.[17] As editorial director of The Free Press, Adam Bellow, a protégé of Glikes, published such controversial works as Dinesh D'Souza's *The End of Racism* (1995), Charles Murray and Richard Hernstein's *The Bell Curve* (1994), and David Brock's *The Real Anita Hill* (1993). The neocons can also boast highly acclaimed novelist Mark Helprin (*A Soldier of a Great War, A City in Winter*) And through Myron Magnet, head of the Manhattan Institute's *City Journal*, much of Rudy Giuliani's conservative agenda as mayor of New York was put in place.[18]

Seth Lipsky is one of the more interesting figures among the new breed of neocons. A former reporter, news editor, and member of the *Wall Street Journal* editorial board, he was a Reagan admirer. Lipsky came up with the idea of taking over the old-labor socialist Yiddish-language newspaper *Forverts*, whose older readership had mostly died off. Lipsky approached the guardians of the legendary newspaper in 1987 to set up a weekly English version. It took three years before he found the funding, and he was named editor of the *Forward* in 1990.

The small, balding, fiftyish Lipsky hired one or two liberal columnists, but he generally made the *Forward* into a neoconservative organ, winning admirers on both the left and the right for the quality of its writing, especially its cultural features. *New York Times* liberal columnist Frank Rich hailed its "fearlessness and good writing."[19] The *Forward* defended the *Dartmouth Review*, a satirical right-wing underground student newspaper, when it felt, after conducting its own investigation, it had been unfairly tarred with an anti-Semitic brush; it carried an article just a few months into publication by Ariel Sharon, the Israeli right-winger and now prime minister; it supported Supreme Court Justice Clarence Thomas's right to speak when an

African-American organization sought to cancel his appearance; and, following the Senate vote to reject the impeachment of President Clinton, with which it agreed, it went on to congratulate the press, including the *Wall Street Journal* and *American Spectator*, for grasping early on the flawed character of President Clinton and educating the public to it.[20] By 1999, however, at the tenth anniversary of its founding, internal contradictions and pressures had become too strong, and Lipsky resigned. He went on to create a new conservative newspaper, *The New York Sun*, which joins the *New York Post*, once a journal of the left, in bringing more conservative thought and activities to New Yorkers.

The most influential of the new generation of Jewish conservatives, however, is Bill Kristol. Born in 1953, Kristol first gained attention when he served as an aide to Secretary William Bennett at the Education Department during the first Bush administration; he was later Vice President Dan Quayle's chief of staff. He quickly established himself as a favorite conservative commentator with his frequent appearances on CNN, *Nightline*, and *Meet the Press*.

Growing up in the New York Upper West Side home of his parents, Gertrude Himmelfarb and Irving Kristol – "Great DNA there," says Bennett – was an intellectual adventure. As a teenager, young Bill greeted guests at the door of their home and remembers getting into an argument with Lionel Trilling. Kristol says he rebelled against his generation, not his parents.[21]

Kristol entered Harvard in 1970 as the Vietnam War raged. He sported a Spiro T. Agnew sweatshirt and announced himself as a backer of Richard Nixon. At Harvard, he joined a small circle of neoconservatives, "Straussian" intellectual types who studied under conservative professors Harvey Mansfield and Samuel Huntington. An insight he took away from Mansfield was the importance, especially in a democracy, of reasonable men and women being able to change their mind when circumtances changed.[22]

Initially, he planned a career as an academic (Kristol earned a Ph.D. from Harvard), but he decided he was not cut out for the Halls of Ivy. He spent two years at the Kennedy School of Government at Harvard, after which he joined Bennett in Washington. As Quayle's chief of staff, he vetted Quayle's attack on the cultural elite, bringing to Schiffren's speech his mother's ideas about the decline of virtue and his father's ideas on the alleged malignant influence of the New Class.[23]

During the Clinton years, Kristol became the "keeper of the neoconservative flame" in Washington.[24] Like his father, Kristol proved to be an institution builder. In November 1993, a year after Clinton's election, Kristol founded a think tank, the Project for the Republican Future. In effect, he established what his biographer has called a "new, political art form," appointing himself the guardian of the GOP. With his father's chutzpah, he faxed, to a list of hundreds, a presumably confidential and unsolicited memo (nevertheless summarized in the *Washington Times*) announcing his opinions on a wide range of public policy issues. In what would be the first of many such memos, Kristol chose as his target the president's health care plan.

Clinton had argued, as many people believed, that the health system was in crisis. Some Republicans accepted this premise because of what was seen as the popularity of health care reform. Kristol felt otherwise. He counseled that Republicans should reject the idea of a crisis. He recognized how popular the administration's approach might be, but, Straussian that he was, he felt popularity was not truth. He rejected the president's plan as socialized medicine that would be disruptive and harmful to a flawed but essentially workable U.S. health care system. The problems in the system could be dealt with incrementally, by changing the tax code to make insurance less expensive and by modifying regulations in order to help people with preexisting conditions. Party leaders resisted. Even House minority whip Newt Gingrich felt that Kristol's "no crisis" line sent the wrong signal to the American people.

Kristol's campaign got a lift, his biographer writes, when early in February 1994 an article in *The New Republic* pointed out that Clinton's health care plan would wipe out personal medical choices and threatened individual privacy. The insurance industry similarly weighed in. By summer, sentiment on Capitol Hill had shifted. Many credited Kristol's sustained campaign with playing a key role in averting a national health care disaster.[25]

Kristol played a critical role, also, in destroying a Clinton initiative on welfare reform early in his adminstration with another barrage of memos, close observers have noted. He was joined by Charles Murray and William Bennett as well as by the Heritage Foundation, all of whom argued before legislators that out-of-wedlock children were the central issue, not jobs. There was a huge gap on the welfare roles between single-parent homes (some 35 percent in 1994) and married-couple families. The welfare reform legislation that Clinton signed into law called for strict time limits to move welfare recipients off the dole and ultimately ended welfare entitlements. "Murphy Brown was not a joke any more," Easton, his biographer, writes.[26]

Kristol's importance most recently, however, has been as editor of *The Weekly Standard*. The idea for the magazine was John Podhoretz's (suggested, curiously, in a coffee shop named Utopia on the Upper West Side of New York).[27] Kristol took the proposal to Rupert Murdoch, the conservative media tycoon. When Murdoch assured him that the magazine would have editorial freedom, and that he would cover its losses until it got on its feet, Kristol went ahead. *The Weekly Standard* shares much the same viewpoint as *Commentary*, but its articles are usually shorter and its style lighter. It is also somewhat less predictable. It supported Senator John McCain, the champion of campaign finance reform, in the Republican primaries in 2000.

The magazine quickly moved to a level of influence enjoyed previously by *Commentary* and *The Public Interest*, serving as a primary vehicle of neoconservative thought. At the start of 2001, it had just over 76,000 subscribers. *Commentary*, while still edited with great skill and thoughtful intelligence by Podhoretz's successor, Neal Kozodoy, reached its greatest influence during the Cold War. *The Weekly Standard* reflects another and different era.[28] In a sense, what *Commentary* was to Reagan and the Cold War,

The Weekly Standard is to George W. Bush and the war on terrorism. As a result, it has become a major player in Washington. The headline of a March 11, 2003, story in the *New York Times* proclaimed, "White House Listens When Weekly Speaks."

Kristol, in his early fifties, was hardly a newcomer to the idea of aggressive national and defense policies, having grown up in the Himmelfarb/Kristol home. In 1996, he and political scientist Robert Kagan published an article in *Foreign Affairs*, "Toward a Neo-Reaganite Foreign Policy." The two men argued that under President Clinton, a time of passivity existed toward the threat of terrorism. On December 1, 1997, a special issue of *The Weekly Standard* was headlined "Saddam Must Go." Finally, in 1998, Kristol started the Project for a New American Century, a think tank set up to project these ideas to a larger public.

While sharing most of the ideas of their fathers and mothers, the younger neocons differ from their elders in several ways. The latter grew up in an immigrant environment suspended between two worlds. They were not fully assimilated and were driven, in some measure, by the insecurities of arrivistes. For much of their adult lives and careers, the earlier generation believed themselves to be in an uphill and losing struggle against communism and Soviet expansionism. Like Whittaker Chambers, they saw themselves fighting on the wrong side of history, which probably accounts for some of their prickliness. With the older neocons in mind, Brooks remarked, "political movements that perceive themselves in the wilderness often generate courage, clarity, and brilliance; but they do not emanate 'good cheer.'"[29]

Conservatism has been bred into the bone of the younger neocons. Not having encountered the searing battles of the Cold War, they tend also to be more confident. Brooks often writes about broader topics in a more lighthearted vein, as can be seen in his bestseller *Bobos in Paradise* (2000), which describes that class of Americans who have combined the bourgeois world of capitalist enterprise with bohemian counterculture.

Younger neocons also differ from their fathers and mothers in their response to religion. The older generation's early attraction to modernism and leftist politics, coupled with a fierce desire to move up in the society, inclined them in more secular directions. "I felt no passionate attachment to Judaism, or to Zionism, or even to the Jewish people," Irving Kristol admits in his fragmentary memoir. "I had read nothing on any of these matters, and the only magazine that entered our house was *The New Masses*."[30]

Throughout much of the 1960s, Gary Dorrien writes, *Commentary* dealt with the Jewish question, with articles on Jewish culture and history that were not especially religious.[31] Starting in the 1970s and 1980s (though for Irving Kristol earlier), the writings of the elders began to warm toward religion. Norman Podhoretz's most recent book, *The Prophets: Who They Were, What They Are* (2003), is the culmination of several years of study.

The older generation's interest in religion, however, tended to be more instrumental; that is, it has not been a deeply personal experience. Religion is necessary, they insisted, in order to ensure greater order and stability in society. Strengthening Judaism, especially among the young, would counter the effects of assimilation and provide support for the embattled state of Israel. It was only in recent years, for example, that the Kristols joined a synagogue.[32]

By contrast, a number of the younger generation neocons are – or have become – traditional or even orthodox Jews. They seek a spiritual dimension in their lives. They include Feder, Prager, Medved, David Klinghoffer, and Daniel Lapin, an Orthodox rabbi active in public policy issues through a group called Toward Tradition, which he founded. "Like a lot of people these days," Brooks wrote in the *Atlantic Monthly*, "I am a recovering secularist."[33] He and his wife, a converted Jew, are members of a synagogue. David Gelernter, who was seriously injured by the Unabomber, sends his children to a Jewish day school in New Haven. He has written five articles (under the general title "Judaism beyond Words") in *Commentary*, most recently on the centrality of God in Judaism and its meaning for society.

William Kristol, Brooks, and Elliott Abrams (who started a kosher home several years ago) attend temple services with their families and are active in their congregations. Kozodoy was a founder and acts as *gabbai* (or leader) of Congregation Or Zarua in New York. Klinghoffer has written poignantly in *National Review* (where he served as literary editor) and later in his book, *The Lord Will Gather Me In: My Journey to Jewish Orthodoxy* (2002), of his evolution from Reform Judaism to religious orthodoxy following his bar mitzvah in southern California in 1977.

In *Faith or Fear: How Jews Can Survive in Christian America* (1997), Abrams, who stands somewhere between the older and newer neocons in age, points out that for most of their historical experience, Jews were governed by a religious tradition that placed God and his commandments at the center of their universe. Following the Enlightenment, Jewish elites embraced a new definition of Judaism, Abrams notes. The traditional faith was replaced by a civil religion, emphasizing social justice, philanthropy, and the liberal agenda, put forward in twentieth-century America by the Democratic Party and a panoply of civic and communal organzations. Driven by a fear of anti-Semitism, "we tried to push religion out of American public life," Abrams asserts, concluding that Jews should make religion the center of their lives again.[34]

The new focus on religion is driven also by a growing recognition that the most important force shaping the society and individuals is not government but the broader culture. Neocons see the latter as becoming more and more degrading. Wendy Shalit, a frequent contributor to *Commentary*, has urged a return to modesty, the title of her book published in 1998. Young women have been encouraged by cultural pressures to engage in sex prematurely, she writes. "For the woman who doesn't want to have sex, the ground had completely dropped under her; there is no social support for the right to say 'no.' Women who do so are viewed as repressed or just plain weird."[35] In the same vein, Kay S. Hymotitz chides child-rearing books that eschew "the sturdy image of youth" found in classic works by Louisa May Alcott and Laura Ingalls Wilder in favor of "children as vulnerable dependents who require classes to bolster their tender psyches and a panoply of protective gear for their fragile bodies."[36]

The heightened interest in religion has brought young neocons closer to Christian evanglicals. The unlikely alliance and friendship of Gary L. Bauer, the Christian conservative who grew up a janitor's son in Kentucky, and William Kristol has not been forged solely by evangelical support for Israel; equally important has been their joint acceptance of what historian Mark Gerson terms "the Judeo-Christian and bourgeois virtues that stem from the Ten Commandments and the Bible."[37] They are united in fighting what Irving Kristol calls "the upsurge of anti-biblical barbarism."[38] Aware of the deep fear of the Christian Right, Irving Kristol suggests that Jews should worry less about Christians converting them and more about Christians marrying them.[39]

In answer to critics who accuse neocons of underplaying the dangers posed by the Christian Right, neocons lean heavily on recent studies indicating that modern-day evangelicals do not view Jews with hostility and that only a small number remain focused on trying to convert them. The neocons argue that the Jewish community's visceral reaction to the religious right is driven more by its secular and liberal ideology than by its Jewishness. Bill Kristol suggests that the growth of the Christian Right "will make people for whom perfect assimilation into America is their goal a little bit uncomfortable," but that this is better for everyone.[40]

"One of the functions of a liberal government," Irving Kristol suggests, "was to see that religious institutions prospered." In his view, the state should encourage religion, because a secularist philosophy "could not by itself supply . . . a sense of moral responsibility."[41]

The growth of the "new paganism" (as the late political scientist Daniel Elazar called the breakdown of traditional norms and values) has led such writers as Jerold S. Auerbach, Alan Mittelman, David Novak, David Dalin, Dennis Prager, and Jonathan D. Sarna, the Joseph H. and Belle R. Brawn Professor of American Jewish History at Brandeis, to join with their elders in questioning the usefulness of Jefferson's "wall of separation," so eagerly supported by Jewish civic agencies like the American Jewish Committee and the American Jewish Congress. Much of what passes for fact about "American Jewry's long-standing historic embrace of separatism," Sarna and his historian colleague Dalin write in their sourcebook, *Religion and State in the American Jewish Experience* (1997), "turns out upon careful examination to consist of half-truths and sometimes pure fantasy."[42] Echoing Irving and Bill Kristol, Auerbach adds, "For Jews, strict separation became a convenient constitutional rationale for strict secularism."[43]

"I grew up believing this 'Wall of Separation' so much so that I was convinced it had been written into the Constitution itself," Sarna adds. As a historian reviewing the vital role played by religion in American life on issues such as Progressive-era reform, civil rights, and the anti-Vietnam movement, he came to realize the important role of religion in the public arena. "Were these, I asked myself, the kinds of activities that I wanted now to curtail by restricting religion to home and Church?"[44]

Sarna and Dalin remind Jews that for much of their history in this country they did not seek to divorce religion from public life; they sought instead to be free from discrimination because of their beliefs and practices. Rather than attacking Sunday closing laws as a manifestation of a religious establishment, for example, they pressed for exemptions for Jews and others who observed their sabbath on Saturday. The turn to separation came only later, they indicate, at the close of the nineteenth century, when Christian missionary efforts and attempts to declare America a "Christian nation" accelerated. In their sourcebook, Sarna and Dalin set out to recover "divergent voices and opinions," concluding that "American Jewish views on religion and state issues have never in the past been monolithic, just as they are not monolithic now."[45]

Sarna, however, remains nervous about "state-sponsored Christianity." He worries that many Americans, including the Southern Baptist Convention and the Christian Coalition, as well as the Rev. Pat Robertson, if given a chance, might write their religion into American law. Nevertheless, he agrees with Abrams that "religion of every sort needs to be nurtured in America."[46]

It may be a measure of the impact of this new thought on separatism, spearheaded by neoconservatives, that Marc Stern, general counsel of the American Jewish Congress, which in the post–World War II years did so much to promote the principle of strict separation, wrote an article in the *Forward* on November 14, 2003, calling upon the Jewish community to reevaluate its position. Significantly, the Supreme Court has been moving in this direction, arguing that religious bodies should not be discriminated against. In 1995, the High Court ruled that a university could not deny funds drawn from student fees to a campus religious newspaper when such funds were being offered to a broad class of participants. In *Agostine v. Felton*, the court, overruling two previous decisions, upheld the financing of remedial education and counseling services in parochial schools with public monies as long as these services were "secular, neutral and non-ideological." And in 2002, the court ruled that the Cleveland school district could provide educational vouchers – a posture supported by the second Bush administration and neocons – permitting schoolchildren to attend religious as well as nonreligious schools in the district.[47]

The neocons, in short, have been remarkably prescient in identifying the central issues of the times and supporting approaches that have found favor with many of their countrymen. I do not mean to suggest here that the neocons got it all right. In extolling the beneficent effects of capitalism, they have been caught short as the nation witnessed the corporate scandals involving

Enron, WorldCom, and others. While neocons never opposed government regulation of business – and even spoke out against the corrupting effects of capitalism in the form of consumerism – they hardly anticipated the broader corruption of recent years. Forced somewhat to retreat, Irwin M. Stelzer has suggested, vaguely, in *The Weekly Standard* and *The Public Interest*, a "pragmatic mixture" of "legislation, regulation competition in the markets for products and companies, and reinforcement of less self-interested behavior through enhanced transparency."[48]

Nor has the older or new generation of neocons come to grips with the wide economic disparities in American life. Approximately thirty-five million people, many of them working, live in poverty in the United States, according to David K. Shipler in *The Working Poor* (2004). The neocons have only partially sought to address this problem, through educational vouchers and charitable choice, which seek to enlist the religious communities in local solutions. As the Bush administration encourages tax cuts, in part to spur the economy out of recession, critics argue that this policy aids only the rich; cash-strapped states struggle to balance budgets and Medicaid coverage. The Bush tax cuts may have played a part in stimulating the economy – by the close of 2003, the economy had had its highest quarterly growth in twenty years (8.2 percent); but one wonders whether more jobs might have been created if the tax cuts had been aimed at low- and moderate-income households, since those classes are more likely to spend their tax savings than the well-to-do. While it is also true that opposition from congressional Democrats and teachers unions has stymied the extension of such programs, the neocons have not said much about the failure of the administraton to put the full force of the president's office behind vouchers or charitable choice. Many Americans, in short, never feel the results of "compassionate conservatism."[49]

In part because of such failures, or more accurately indifference, neoconservatism has sustained casualties over the years. The movement was never as unified as it sometimes appeared. Strains and conflicts developed early on and sharpened in the ensuing years. Seymour Martin Lipsett and Daniel Bell were early dropouts. As we have seen, Bell, a self-described "socialist in economics, a liberal in politics, and a conservative in culture," resigned in 1972 from *The Public Interest* when Irving Kristol declared for Richard Nixon. Indeed, he denies today that he ever was a neocon.[50]

Daniel Patrick Moynihan's disaffection was especially disappointing. He had worked closely with Kristol and Podhoretz as the movement was taking shape. Podhoretz credits himself with helping to launch Moynihan's political career by publishing his articles in *Commentary*. Moynihan, nonetheless, remained independent in his thought. Although he opposed President Clinton's health care program, he also opposed Robert Bork's nomination to the High Court and opted against welfare reform, signed into law by President Clinton, becoming, as a result, an "unreliable neoconservative." He also had little use for Ronald Reagan. While firmly anticommunist, he did not join in the hawkish views of the neocons in the latter phase of his career, and, in fact, he opposed the first Gulf War.[51]

On social issues, however, his positions remained closely aligned with those of the neocons, perhaps because of his Irish-Catholic background and his sense that the nation was in the midst of a moral and cultural crisis. Following his retirement from the Senate and shortly before his death in 2003, he said it was regrettable that the first time the Democratic presidential hopefuls got together it was only to endorse an abortion rights agenda rather than to take a position that might reach out beyond the party base. Defense of partial-birth abortion, he said, "was not right with the American people." He favored also some form of privatizing social security. While drafting the final report as cochair of the President's Commission on Social Security, Moynihan worked in George W. Bush's plan to let ordinary people build wealth.[52]

The defection of Nathan Glazer, the quiet-mannered and scholarly early ally, reflected fundamental deeper divisions within the group. His movement away from neoconservatism was gradual. His strong anticommunism and democratic stance remained throughout the 1970s and 1980s, but what he calls his "less energetic social style" was not a good fit as the neocons moved in more conservative directions. In addition to his unwillingness to wage war in the *Commentary* manner against the Soviet Union, he also came to differ with its strong support for the right-wing government of Menachem Begin, who became prime miniser of Israel in 1977. A member of Breira (Hebrew for "alternative"), a left-oriented group in this country, Glazer favored Israeli withdrawal from the territories it had occupied following the Six-Day and Yom Kippur Wars.[53]

Although a leader in the movement opposed to quotas and the author of an influential study, *Affirmative Discrimination* (1975), which became a textbook for neocons and others, Glazer became, over time, concerned that color-blindness in college admissions, as favored by the neocons along with many other Americans, would greatly reduce the proportion of African-Americans in higher education. He questioned whether the nation was willing to accept this result, with its damaging consequences for race relations and for the ultimate goal of a decent multiracial society.

Early in 2003, Glazer joined in a friend-of-the-court brief defending the University of Michigan's affirmative action policies in a suit brought by the Bush administration and backed by many neocons. He came under heavy fire from neoconservatives.[54] In June 2003, the Supreme Court found along the lines Glazer had suggested, focusing heavily on the importance of diversity in admissions rather than racial preferences as a practical need in a multigroup society. Glazer has rarely written for *Commentary* in recent years.

Even as the neocons helped to shape the thinking of many Americans, they had little impact on the political behavior of Jews. There is much truth in Milton Himmelfarb's observation that the Jewish arm grows paralyzed when it reaches to pull the Republican lever. Jews gave Democrat Al Gore some 79 percent of their vote in 2000.

There are signs, nonetheless, that the Democratic hammerlock on the Jewish vote has begun to weaken somewhat, especially at city and state levels. In his first two runs for mayor of New York against Mayor David Dinkins, which he lost, Giuliani, generally seen as a conservative Republican at the time, received some two-thirds of the Jewish vote. In his third try against an all-out liberal, Ruth Messinger, a Jew, the figure rose to three out of four Jewish voters, an unprecedented figure in New York. (This was before 9/11, after which Giuliani gained much acclaim for his solid performance.) Republican Richard Riordan in Los Angeles, the second-largest center of Jewish population in the United States, split the Jewish vote in his first race for mayor, and in his successful bid for reelection in 1997 (against former student radical Tom Hayden) his share of that vote rose to 71 percent. Similarly, Republican candidates including George Pataki in New York and Christie Whitman in New Jersey received between 40 and 50 percent of the Jewish vote in their successful campaigns for governor.[55] More recently, however, Jews voted heavily for Senator Frank Lautenberg for the U.S. Senate in New Jersey and for Ed Rendell for governor in Pennsylvania.

The new breed of GOP politicos, however, are a far cry from the old-line Republican conservatives, who since the days of Franklin D. Roosevelt have stirred Jewish fears. The former are seen as moderates or, in the case of Giuliani, a conservative who moved to the center. Giuliani, for example, has supported gay and abortion rights and freer immigration to this country.

It is true, as public opinion surveys indicate, that in contrast to the neocons, most American Jews are willing to spend more on government programs and to cut less. They are more liberal than the general population on issues of sexual morality and on a broad range of civil rights issues, including abortion rights. But recent polls also show that Jews worry about crime and violence and racial preferences or quotas. An American Jewish Committee survey in 1997 showed that 80 percent of respondents favored the death penalty for persons convicted of murder. On welfare, Jewish respondents are similar to other whites in asserting that past government programs have been detrimental to welfare recipients. Although historically supportive of civil liberties, Jews said little – initially, at least – about President George W. Bush's counterterrorism legislation. Indeed, his call for an identification system for all American citizens won the backing of 70 percent of American Jews, according to a survey by Market Facts for the American Jewish Committee.[56]

What may be new and significant is that the Jewish move to the right (if we can call it that) seems to be more evident among younger Jewish voters. "This is the Reagan generation, a generation that knows not FDR or JFK," political scientist Alan M. Fisher has written. "It is three generations away from the ferment of the Jewish labor movement... even the civil rights and student anti-Vietnam movements of the 1960s coincide with their birth and infancy but not with their political experience."[57] An exit poll of

Jews in Philadelphia taken during the 2000 election by Zogby International found them, as expected, voting heavily for Gore. Within the eighteen- to twenty-nine-year-old cohort, however, Bush came out ahead, 59 percent to 34 percent. Zogby found a similar pattern in New Jersey.[58]

Noting these trends, George Nash has written, "*Commentary* [and the neocons] under Podhoretz "did not convert the majority of American Jews to its brand of conservatism.... [W]hat it did accomplish was something almost as momentous: it made conservatism a respected and unignorable presence in the Jewish community."[59]

The build-up to the Iraq War, along with the war's aftermath, have posed special problems for neocons. Here a split within their ranks developed early on. Although neocons backed the Persian Gulf War in 1991, Irving Kristol felt that the United States should intervene abroad only when our interests as a nation are directly involved. Once Iraq was clearly defeated, he supported the first President Bush's decision not to go all the way to Baghdad. He favored instead the "cautionary non-interventionist" course that the administration followed.[60] As the second Bush administration edged closer to war in Iraq, some neocons opposed intervention if the sole purpose was to be the spread of democracy in the region, a policy frequently advocated by William Kristol and scholar Robert Kagan in the pages of *The Weekly Standard*. Richard Pipes had no problem with attempting to eliminate Saddam Hussein from power, he writes in a memoir, but he felt that democratization was too ambitious as a rationale.[61] Charles Krauthammer was opposed also initially to American involvement in Kosovo and Liberia. Neither one involved, he felt, American interests directly. Here he stood with conservative columnist George Will, who has been critical of neocons for their crusading zeal.[62] Often a globalist himself, Kristol declared in 1991 "the prospect of American military intervention and occupation to 'make democracy work'... in short... is not and cannot be a serious option for American foreign policy."[63]

In the aftermath of 9/11, however, the younger neocons in and out of government – Podhoretz was an exception – who had displaced their elders, had come to believe the former had failed to factor into their thinking the war on terrorism. They believed especially that it was this nation's responsibility to engage in an economic, political, and military crusade for world democracy if we were to succeed in the war on terrorism. When renegade nations are led by tyrants, they argued, terrorism and encouragement of terrorism is often built into their behavior. This, along with thinking themselves democratic idealists in the tradition of Woodrow Wilson, made them feel that a conservative Wilsonian moment had finally arrived.[64]

As secretary of defense in the first Bush administration, Dick Cheney, along with Norman Podhoretz, believed that Gorbachev would not deliver on his promises of reform and that he continued to remain a threat. A month into his role, Cheney convened a planning committee, led by his undersecretary of defense, neocon Paul Wolfowitz, to draft a new Defense Planning

Guidance (DPG) document, intended to push for regime change that would lead to a democratic Soviet Union. The scope of the document went through various changes in examining situations where U.S. interests were threatened, including later an invasion of Iraq if Saddam Hussein rebounded from his defeat in 1991. An early draft recommended that the United States should be prepared to act independently when international approval for collective action could not be obtained. The language was seen as too warlike and the document ended up on the shelf, only to be revived after 9/11.[65]

The issue came up again following the decision to leave Saddam Hussein in power after driving him out of Kuwait in 1991. Once more the Pentagon, with Wolfowitz in the lead, produced the Defense Planning Guidance to be employed during a second Bush administration, if he were reelected. By this time, Wolfowitz, whose skill lay in connecting things, had emerged as the central figure in designing and pressing forward the more aggressive designs for dealing with the later war on terrorism.

Wolfowitz is the son of a Jewish family that had migrated from Warsaw and settled in New York City. His father took his B.A. degree at City College and went on to a career as one of this country's preeminent scholars on statistical theory, later joining the faculty at Cornell. Young Wolfowitz won a scholarship at that prestigious university and became a member of the Telluride Association, a group devoted to practicing democracy on campus by living it in their day-to-day lives. In 1963, Allan Bloom came to Cornell, and Wolfowitz quickly became part of his circle.[66]

Following undergraduate school, Wolfowitz attended Harvard and later the University of Chicago, where he obtained his Ph.D. Strauss's ideas of a strong-willed leader with clear direction and beliefs and the willingness to implement them against strong opposition proved attractive to Wolfowitz. Though he did not like being categorized in any way, Wolfowitz went on to midlevel posts in the Carter, Reagan, and senior Bush administrations. Nonetheless, he remained a leading Straussian, according to Jeane Kirkpatrick.[67]

Wolfowitz is an unlikely figure to play the part of an extremist, as many of his critics charge that he has. As James Mann writes in *The Rise of the Vulcans* (2204): "While never abandoning his principles, he regularly worried about doing what was politically prudent." When he did come to "strong positions," it was usually over a period of time. In the early 1990s, he did not favor overthrowing Saddam Hussein. By 1997, however, his position had hardened. He was critical of the Clinton administration and of Democrats generally for what he felt was their inadequate response to the Iraq leader's stonewalling of UN resolutions and weapons inspectors. In a piece he wrote for a book about Iraq's future, he called for replacing the Iraqi government. And by the close of 1997, in an article for *The Weekly Standard* coauthored by Zalmay Khalilzad, an aide, he was urging the overthrow of Saddam: "It must be part of an overall political strategy that sets as its goal not merely containment of Saddam but the liberation of Iraq from his tyranny."[68]

One of the early drafts of the DPG declared that U.S. policy ought "to encourage the spread of democratic forms of government" in order to ensure our safety. By this time, the UN had discovered an advanced Iraqi nuclear weapons program, beyond what the intelligence community had thought possible. Throughout the 1990s, UN inspector Hans Blix had agreed that Saddam Hussein not only had large amounts of chemical and biological toxins but also had not hesitated to use them against Iran and his own people.[69]

As the first Bush administration left office early in January 1993, the Wolfowitz planning staff revised the document, whose main point was that American leadership was required to create an international environment conducive to this country's values. Thus, as early as a decade before the Bush Doctrine was formulated, the DPG and Wolfowitz had already raised the question of making a peremptory military strike against Iraq – even unilaterally, if necessary.

As we have seen, even before George W. Bush set foot in the White House, William Kristol had laid out a new, more militant course the future president might follow. In 1996, he and political scientist Robert Kagan published an article in *Foreign Affairs*, "Toward a Neo-Reaganite Foreign Policy," warning of Clinton's passivity toward a terrorist threat. On December 1, 1997, a special issue of *The Weekly Standard* was headlined, "Saddam Must Go." And in 1998, Project for the New American Century staffer Gary Schmitt prepared a letter to President Clinton, signed by eighteen national security hawks, including Wolfowitz, Donald Rumsfeld, and Richard Perle. The letter called for precisely the kind of preemptive invasion of Iraq that Bush would undertake five years later. It gave as the reason for such an invasion the same justification that Bush would later cite: "The only acceptable strategy is one that eliminates the possiblity that Iraq will be able to use or threaten to use weapons of mass destruction. In the near term this is a willingness to undertake military action.... In the long term, it means removing Saddam Hussein and his regime from power."[70]

The neocons initially viewed the incoming Bush administration as a return to what they saw as the wishy-washy policies of Clinton and George H. W. Bush, who had held back from finishing the job in the Persian Gulf War. To their surprise, however, half of the signatories of the letter to Clinton wound up with jobs in that administration. Although kept at arm's length during the early days of the second Bush administration, prior to 9/11, neocons remained important, particularly at Bill Kristol's Project for the New American Century. An observer noted that its Tuesday morning briefings found administration staff moving freely from these briefings to their various government roles.[71]

President Bush's "axis of evil" speech gave their ideas a further push, as did his West Point speech in the summer of 2002. Bush followed up these statements on November 7, 2003, in a major address before the National Endowment for Democracy. Here he challenged Iran, Syria, and two Middle Eastern allies, Saudi Arabia and Egypt, to embark upon democratic reforms and to view the overthrow of Saddam Hussein as "a watershed event in the global democratic revolution." Bush compared this "forward strategy of freedom in the Middle East" to President Reagan's 1982 speech in England, in which the latter had described the failures of communism.[72]

Following the early successes of the invasion of Iraq and citing Reagan's moral clarity, William Kristol triumphantly told an interviewer, "We saw, earlier than most people, that the world was very dangerous, that America's drift during the 1990s was very dangerous. We were alarmed; we tried to call attention to all that. So I don't want to say we felt vindicated, but we do feel our analysis was right."[73]

By the end of 2003, however, following setbacks in the aftermath of the Iraq occupation, neocons came to worry that the political and policy leadership in Washington seemed no longer interested in maintaining the battle against terrorism. Neoconservatives David Frum and Richard Perle published *An End to Evil: How to Win the War on Terror* (2003) as a means of trying to summon Americans back to the mood of determination and resolution of 9/11.[74] Mark Helprin, in a *Wall Street Journal* article criticizing the administration's handling of the war, observed also that the Democratic party's "ideological keel is a leaden and unthinking pacificism, a pretentious and illogical deference to all things European."[75]

In the final analysis, the legacy of neoconservatives will rest on the results of the Iraq war and its aftermath. American casualties and growing insurgencies have put neocons on the defensive. They have been only slightly less critical than the left and other critics in attacking the Bush administration for its mistakes, including insufficient planning for the aftermath of the war and the inadequate numbers of troops to deal with the situation.

At this writing, it is still too early to make any predictions. The invasion of Iraq may well be the disaster that critics of the war have charged. "There is no way to militarily lose in Iraq," the chairman of the Joint Chiefs, Richard Myers, grimly said, with Rumsfeld at his side in May 2004. "There is also no way to militarily win in Iraq."[76] The religio-ethnic divisions within Iraq and the people's inexperience with democracy may prove to be beyond the immediate capabilities of the Iraqis, or at least may require a lengthy process of accommodation.

Looking beyond the many serious mistakes that have been made, however, perhaps a different scenario is taking shape. Starting in 1979, it should be recalled, the political order in the Middle East had begun to fall apart. The shah had given way to Ayatollah Khomeini in Iran, the Soviets had invaded Afghanistan, and Saddam Hussein had seized power in Iraq. Indeed, without seeming to realize it, the United States was now at war with terrorism in the Middle East. During this period and prior to 9/11, we had surely been under attack: Iran took American hostages during the Carter administration with impunity; Al-Qaeda and other terrorist groups staged destructive and often deadly attacks in 1983 on our Marine barracks in Beirut, which killed

241 of our servicemen, and on the U.S.S. *Cole*, which took seventeen lives. September 11 was the culmination of these attacks. As Stephen F. Hayes has pointed out, extensive ties also existed between Al-Qaeda and Iraq, even as there is no evidence that Iraq colluded with Al-Qaeda in the 9/11 attacks.[77]

What was new and bold about the Bush Doctrine and the neocon advisors who pressed it forward was that it recognized that this country was already at war – a new kind of war that we had never experienced before. The underlying premise of that war, which the debate over weapons of mass destruction tended to obfuscate, was that we had set out to change the basic dynamic in the Middle East, which was responsible for most of the terrorism we were facing. The decision to launch a preemptive strike, although it offended some of our putative allies, resulted in a humanely and successfully fought war. Saddam, his murderous sons, and their henchmen are imprisoned or dead. Although there are various insurgencies continuing to destablize the area, there has been no countrywide civil war. On June 28, 2004, two days sooner than planned, this country began the process of handing over internal governance to the Iraqis themselves. In January 2005, Iraq held a free election despite widespread insurgencies. There are indications that the Iraqis will continue to gain greater sovereignty and that the United States will ultimately depart the region, with the hope that our main objectives have been achieved. "No one expected the long range policies of the Bush administration to be a cakewalk," David Brooks writes. "The challenges turn out to be tougher than we imagined. Our excessive optimism is exposed. New skills are demanded. But nothing important was ever begun in a prudential frame of mind."[78]

Indeed, the policies put in place have already had some wider effects. The Taliban in Afghanistan were defeated by American-led military action, and that country held its first free elections in October 2004, with women voting. On December 19, 2003, to everyone's surprise, Col. Muammar al-Qaddafi, long a threat of terrorist activity, agreed to give up all of his nuclear, chemical, and biological weapons and to permit inspections in order to ensure this outcome. The decision came after nine months of secret negotiations with the United States and Britain, undertaken as the invasion of Iraq got under way. And even the UN, which many thought should have had a more central place in dealing with the threat from Iraq, has been brought into the process of stablizing the situation. Admittedly this is an optimistic scenario, but it is as likely as its reverse: the total disaster theory. The neocons may have gotten it right after all.

With a majority of some three and a half million votes and further gains in the Senate and House, the reelection of President Bush in 2004 underlines this observation. Not only does it seem congruent with the central premise of this book that we are presently living in an age of conservatism, it further acknowledges the role of the neocons in shaping the strategies and ideas of our times. The major issue of the campaign was the war on terrorism, which appeared to resonate with the voters.[79]

What seems apparent as well is the continued failure of liberal, cosmopolitan culture as reflected in major segments of the media and the Democratic Party – Bill Clinton proved to be an exception during his second term – to understand and identify in any meaningful way with the social and cultural changes that have reshaped the nation in the last thirty to forty years.[80] Indeed, it often seems contemptuous of the ideas and behavior of the main body of Americans. ("How do you make a rational pitch to people who have put that part of the brain on hold," *New York Times* columnist Bob Herbert wrote in his postmortem on the election on November 4.) Efforts to get out the vote in the days just before the election, many observers believed, favored the Democrats; they showed little understanding that conservatives brought their own sense of passion and idealism and probably outnumbered the liberal-left in registration.

As for Jewish voting patterns, Republicans scored only a small gain, according to postelection surveys, from 19 percent in 2000 to 23 or 24 percent. Whatever the changes in political patterns at state and local levels in recent years, Jews continue to be reluctant to attach themselves to more conservative politics at the national level.[81]

Neoconservatism (or, as Irving Kristol has called it, "the neoconservative persuasion") is still a work in progress.[82] It falls to the new generation of neocons to redefine and deal with the newer issues of our times, both at home and abroad. In recent years, with the Democratic Party ideologically divided and an older-style liberalism searching for a new focus, new policy initiatives have been played out largely within the conservative camp. Social critic A. J. Bacevich asks whether it will be able to match "the negative achievement of undoing liberalism with the constructive one of articulating a compelling vision for the renewal of society."[83]

The question is a compelling one. The idea that Jews have been put on earth to make it a better, perhaps even a holy, place continues to shape their worldview and that of many of their co-religionists. David Gelernter puts it succinctly: "Conscience . . . the devil once said, is a Jewish invention, too . . . and he was right."[84]

Like most Americans, Jews will reject calls for "family values," self-discipline, self-reliance, and "compassionate conservatism" if they turn out to be only empty slogans. Irving Kristol seemed always to understand that while conservative Republicans continually denounced the welfare state, they rarely offered an alternative vision of how Americans should be governed in domestic affairs: "In America all successful politics is the politics of hope," he declared, "a mood not noticeable in traditional American conservatism."[85]

This book suggests that Jews and non-Jews alike are becoming more conservative, in part because of their neoconservative guides, who have made it more respectable to think in these terms. If I am correct, the task for neoconservatism is clear. It must infuse American life with a new vision that will strengthen democracy at home and abroad, increase the social and economic well-being of all Americans, and set an example for the rest of the world.

Notes

Introduction

1. Robert Kagan and William Kristol, "Why We Went to War," *The Weekly Standard*, October 20, 2003, 7–11. Two other important articles dealing with younger neoconservatives are Bill Keller, "The Sunshine Warrior," *New York Times Magazine*, September 9, 2002, 48–55, 84, 96–7; and Joshua Muravchik, "The Neoconservative Cabal," *Commentary*, September 2003, 26–33.
2. The full text of President George W. Bush's January 29, 2002, State of the Union address is available on the Government Printing Office website at <http://www.gpo.gov/congress/sou/sou02.html>.
3. As quoted in James Hamill, "The U.S., Iraq, and International Relations, Part Two: A Pyrrhic Victory," *Contemporary Review*, July 2003, 9–10.
4. Jack Shafer, "Richard Perle Libel Watch, Week 24: Sympathy for the Foreign-Policy *Macher*," *Slate*, Microsoft Network, <http//slate.msn.com/id/2087851>. On Lewis, see History News Network, November 4, 2002. See also Gaddis, *Surprise, Security, and the American Experience* (Cambridge, MA: Harvard University Press, 2004).
5. Murray Friedman, "Let's Pray for Peace in Iraq and Elsewhere," *Jewish Exponent* (Philadelphia), September 23, 2004; *New York Times*, September 4, 2004. A special target has been Douglas Feith, undersecretary of defense for policy. Feith came under scrutiny in stories that appeared the *New York Times*, *The Wall Street Journal*, and other newspapers as the Defense Department official most responsible for the formation and execution of policy in postwar Iraq. He has been blasted also for what is seen as his faulty strategic vision. Almost always, the attacks have been anonymous and emphasize his sympathies for Israel. In the spring of 2004, stories appeared the *New York Times*, the *Wall Street Journal*, and other newspapers that the FBI was investigating a member of his staff for allegedly turning over memos to the Jewish state through an Israel lobbying group. The rumors continued throughout the summer and fall. However, there has been no substantiation at this writing of the charge, nor an indictment handed down. Feith has been left to twist in the wind. Steve Goldstein, "As Iraq Struggles, Critics Zero in on Pentagon Aide, *Philadelphia Inquirer*, September 28, 2004.

6. The full text of the National Security Strategy of the United States of America is available on the White House website at <http://www.whitehouse.gov/nsc/nss.html>.
7. See Joshua Muravchik, "The Bush Doctrine," *Commentary*, December 2002, 23–30; Arthur Schlesinger, Jr., "Eyeless in Iraq," *New York Review of Books*, October 23, 2003, 24.
8. Eliot Cohen, "World War IV," *Wall Street Journal*, November 20, 2001, sec. 1.
9. Ivo H. Daalder and James M. Lindsay, *America Unbound: The Bush Revolution in Foreign Policy* (Washington, DC: Brookings, 2003).
10. Charles Liebman, *The Ambivalent Jew: Politics, Religion, and Family in American Jewish Life* (Philadelphia: Jewish Publication Society of America, 1973), 140–2.
11. David Dalin, "Judaism's War on Poverty," *Policy Review* 85 (September–October 1997): 30.
12. Ibid.
13. Edward S. Shapiro, "Jews with Money," *Judaism* 36, no. 1 (Winter 1987): 12
14. Quoted in Hillel Halkin, "Unraveling the Mystery of a Proud Christian's Jewishness," *Forward*, December 20, 1996. See also Paul Smith, *Disraeli: A Brief Life* (New York: Cambridge University Press, 1996).
15. Cited in Dalin, "Judaism's War," 31.
16. Jerold S. Auerbach, *Rabbis and Lawyers: The Journey from Torah to Constitution* (Bloomington: Indiana University Press, 1990), 81–2. On the Pittsburgh Platform, see the Appendix in Michael A. Meyer, *Response to Modernity: A History of the Reform Movement in Judaism* (New York: Oxford University Press, 1988), 387–8.
17. Jonathan D. Sarna, "Church-State Dilemmas of American Jews," in *Jews and the American Public Square*, ed. Alan Mittleman, Jonathan D. Sarna, and Robert Licht (Lanham, MD: Rowman and Littlefield, 2002), 58.
18. See Edward S. Shapiro, "Right Turn? Jews and the American Conservative Movement," in L. Sandy Maisel and Iran N. Forman, eds., *Jews in American Politics* (Lanham, MD: Rowman and Littlefield, 2001), 199; Ralph De Toledano, *Lament for a Generation* (New York: Farrar Straus and Cudahy, 1960), 196; and Geoffrey Braham Levey, "Toward an Adequate Explanation of American Jewish Liberalism," paper presented at the annual meeting of the American Political Science Association, Washington, DC, August 29–September 1, 1991, 3.
19. See Laurence H. Fuchs, "American Jews and the Presidential Vote," in Laurence H. Fuchs, *American Ethnic Politics* (New York: Harper and Row, 1968), 52.
20. Arthur Goren, "Orthodox Politics, Republican and Jewish," in *Proceedings of the Eighth World Congress of Jewish Studies: Jewish History* (Jerusalem, 1983), 63–7.
21. See Ira Katznelson, "Between Separation and Disappearance: Jews on the Margins of American Liberalism," in Pierre Birnbaum and Ira Katznelson, *Paths of Emancipation: Jews, States and Citizenship* (Princeton, NJ: Princeton University Press, 1995), 200.
22. As quoted in David G. Dalin, "Louis Marshall, the Jewish Vote, and the Republican Party," *Jewish Political Studies Review* 4, no. 1 (Spring 1992).
23. See Stephen D. Isaacs, *Jews and American Politics* (Garden City, NY: Doubleday, 1975), 151.

24. See Ira N. Forman, ed., "The Politics of Minority Consciousness: The Historical Voting Behavior of American Jews," in Maisel and Forman, eds., *Jews in American Politics*, 152–3.
25. As quoted in Garry Dorrien, *The Neoconservative Mind: Politics, Culture, and the War of Ideology* (Philadelphia: Temple University Press, 1993), x. Much the same evaluation has been made by Alan Wolfe, "The Revolution That Never Was," *The New Republic*, June 7, 1999, 34–42, and by Sam Tanenhaus, "When the Left Turns Right, It Leaves the Middle Muddled," *New York Times*, September 16, 2000, sec. B.
26. See, for example, Daphne Merkin, "Getting Even," *The New Yorker*, February 22, 1999, 166–71. Christopher Lehmann-Haupt refers to Podhoretz's "deliciously gossipy and scintillating recollections of our times" in his review of the book in the February 15, 1999, *New York Times*.
27. Wolfe, "The Revolution," 36. On Dollup, see John Micklethwait and Adrian Wooldridge "For Conservatives, Mission Accomplished." *New York Times*, May 18, 2004.
28. Jason Zengerle, "Fiddling with the Reception," *New York Times Magazine*, August 17, 2003, 40. Fox news channel won more viewers during the 2004 Republican convention than the major broadcast networks. Some 7.3 million watched Bush's speech there, compared to 5.9 million who watched it on second-place NBC. The day before, Fox's 5.9 million viewers roughly equalled the audience for ABC and CBS combined. *Wall Street Journal*, September 7, 2004.
29. Michael Kazin, "The Grass Roots Right: New Histories of U.S. Conservatism in the Twentieth Century," *American Historical Review* 97 (February 1992): 136.
30. Alan Brinkley, "The Problem of American Conservatism," *American Historical Review* 99, no. 2 (April 1994): 409–29.
31. Leo P. Ribuffo, "Why Is There So Much Conservatism in the United States and Why Do So Few Historians Know Anything About It?," *American Historical Review* 99, no. 2 (April 1994): 438–49. See also Patricia Cohen, "Leftist Scholars Look Right at Last and Find a History, *New York Times*, April 18, 1998, sec. B.
32. Joseph Epstein, "A Virtuecrat Remembers," in John H. Bunzel, *Political Passages: Journeys of Change through Two Decades, 1968–1988* (New York: The Free Press, 1988), 39.
33. Stephen J. Whitfield, *In Search of American Jewish Culture* (Lebanon, NH: Brandeis University Press/University Press of New England, 1999), 85.
34. As quoted in Richard Bernstein, "A Thinker Attuned to Thinking: James Q. Wilson Has Insights, Like Those on Cutting Crime, That Tend to Prove Out," *New York Times*, August 22, 1998, sec. B.

Chapter 1

1. *Arguing The World*, video directed by Joseph Dorman (1998; New York: First Run Features, 2000).
2. "E. Digby Baltzell Dies at 80; Studied WASP's," *New York Times*, August 20, 1996, sec. B. See also Norman Podhoretz, "Heroism in a Politically Correct Age," *National Review*, January 26, 1998, 45–7.

3. As quoted in David Hollinger, *Science, Jews and Secular Culture: Studies in Mid-Twentieth Century Intellectual History* (Princeton, NJ: Princeton University Press, 1996), 28.
4. Ibid.
5. David Brooks, "Looking Out, and In," *New York Times*, September 20, 2003, sec. A.
6. See Edward S. Shapiro, *A Time for Healing: American Jewry since World War II* (Baltimore: Johns Hopkins University Press, 1992), 29.
7. Dan A. Oren, *Joining the Club: A History of Jews at Yale* (New Haven, CT: Yale University Press, 1986), quoted in Hollinger, *Science, Jews*, 158.
8. Hollinger, *Science, Jews*, 8.
9. Ibid., 28.
10. H. Stuart Hughes, *The Sea Change: The Migration of Social Thought, 1930–1965* (New York: Harper and Row, 1975), 1–4.
11. Shapiro, *A Time for Healing*, 32.
12. Henry L. Feingold, *Time for Searching: Entering the Mainstream, 1920–1945* (The Jewish People in America Series, vol. 4) (Baltimore: Johns Hopkins University Press, 1992), 78.
13. See Irving Howe, *A Margin of Hope: An Intellectual Biography* (San Diego, CA: Harcourt Brace Jovanovich, 1982); Alexander Bloom, *Prodigal Sons: The New York Intellectuals and Their World* (New York: Oxford University Press, 1986); Carole S. Kessner, *The "Other" New York Intellectuals* (New York: New York University Press, 1994). Glazer did earn a Ph.D. on his own some years later.
14. Joseph Berger, "William Phillips, Co-Founder and Soul of *Partisan Review*, Dies at 94," *New York Times*, September 14, 2002, sec. A.
15. Eli Lederhendler, *New York Jews and the Decline of Urban Ethnicity, 1950–1970* (Syracuse, NY: Syracuse University Press, 2001), 16.
16. Ibid., 32.
17. Irving Howe, "The New York Intellectuals: A Chronicle and a Critique," *Commentary*, October 1968, 29–51. For a discussion of this piece, see Edward Alexander, *Irving Howe: Socialist, Critic, Jew* (Bloomington: Indiana University Press, 1988), 31–3.
18. Feingold, *Time for Searching*, 78.
19. Joseph Dorman, *Arguing the World*. Film documentary directed by Dorman, 1999.
20. Terry A. Cooney, *The Rise of the New York Intellectuals: Partisan Review and Its Circle* (Madison: University of Wisconsin Press, 1986), 242–3.
21. Liebman, *The Ambivalent Jew*, 158.
22. Wilbor Hampton, "Alan Ginsberg, Master Poet of the Beat Generation, Dies At 70," *New York Times*, April 6, 1997, sec. 1.
23. Ann Douglas, "City Where the Beats Were Moved to Howl," *New York Times*, December 26, 1997, sec. E.
24. Morris Dickstein, *Leopards in the Temple: The Transformation of American Fiction, 1945–1970* (Cambridge, MA: Harvard University Press, 2002), 5.
25. Norman Mailer, *The White Negro* (San Francisco: City Light Books, 1958).
26. Andrew R. Heinze, "Jews and American Popular Psychology: Reconsidering the Protestant Paradigm of Popular Thought," *Journal of American History* 88, no. 3 (December 2001): 951.

27. Hollinger, *Science, Jews*, 24.
28. Ibid., 66.
29. James H. Jones, "Dr. Yes," *The New Yorker*, August 25 and September 1, 1997, 100–3. See also Alan Wolfe, "The Professor of Desire," *The New Republic*, November 24, 1997, 32. Funded by the Rockefeller Foundation, Kinsey's *Sexual Behavior in the Human Male* was brought out in January 1948 by W. B. Saunders Company of Philadelphia, a respectable publisher of scientific books. *Sexual Behavior in the Human Female* appeared in 1953.
30. Feingold, *Time for Searching*, 78.
31. Interview with the author, March 26, 1998. On *Commentary*'s relative indifference to the Jewish state during these years, see also Steven J. Zipperstein, "*Commentary* and American Jewish Culture in the 1940s and 1950s," *Jewish Social Studies* 3, no. 1 (Winter 1997): 20.
32. As quoted in Alexander Bloom, *Prodigal Sons: The New York Intellectuals and Their World* (New York: Oxford University Press, 1986), 292; see also Cooney, *Rise of New York Intellectuals*, 241.
33. Mary McCarthy had argued at the time of the production that Miller's characters had all the semblances of Jews, although Willy, in particular, "could not be Jewish because he had to be 'America.'" See Mary McCarthy, *Sights and Spectacles, 1937–1958* (New York: Farrar Straus and Cudahy, 1956), xxiii. See also Robert Brustein, "Arthur Miller at 87," *The New Republic*, October 14, 2002, 27.
34. As quoted in Susanne Klingenstein, *Jews in the American Academy, 1900–1940: The Dynamics of Intellectual Assimilation* (Syracuse, NY: Syracuse University Press, 1998), 142. See also Hollinger, *Science, Jews*, 66.
35. Richard Bernstein, "Critic's Notebook: 50 Years Later, the Jewishness of Anne Frank Blossoms," *New York Times*, December 24, 1997, sec. E. "Garson Kanin, the director of the earlier version, went so far as to take out lines about historical persecution of Jews because it represented what he called 'an embarrassing piece of special pleading.'"
36. Klingenstein, *Jews in the American Academy*, 11.
37. As quoted in Cooney, *Rise of New York Intellectuals*, 244–5.
38. Ibid., 231.
39. Stuart Svonkin, *Jews against Prejudice: American Jews and the Fight for Civil Liberties* (New York: Columbia University Press, 1997), 79.
40. Lederhendler, *Decline of Urban Ethnicity*, 15, 26.
41. Svonkin, *Jews against Prejudice*, 7.
42. J. J. Goldberg, *Jewish Power: Inside the American Jewish Establishment* (Reading, MA: Addison-Wesley, 1996), 128.
43. Murray Friedman, *What Went Wrong: The Creation and Collapse of the Black-Jewish Alliance* (New York: The Free Press, 1995), 134–5; Shapiro, *Time for Healing*, 31.
44. Friedman, *What Went Wrong?*, 150; Svonkin, *Jews against Prejudice*, 184. Also useful in the battle against segregation was a survey of over five hundred anthropologists, sociologists, and social psychologists conducted by Isidor Chein and Max Deutscher, two members of the congressional Commission on Community Interrelations, which suggested that even if facilities were equalized, segregation would still cause psychological damage to black children.

45. Friedman, *What Went Wrong?*, 151. Later, the High Court would be criticized for using social science data in striking down segregation rather than resting the decision on the equal protection clause of the Constitution. Suppose such studies showed that the reverse were true and children were not damaged? Would segregated schools be any less unconstitutional? Clark's research was flawed in other ways. The sample was too small. Clark himself had warned the NAACP that it was impossible to isolate the psychological impact of prejudice and discrimination on black children from school segregation alone. Broader patterns of discrimination in the society were implicated as well. See Kenneth B. Clark, *Prejudice and Your Child*, 2nd ed. (Boston: Beacon Press, 1995), 210; and Hadley Arkes, "The Problem of Kenneth B. Clark," *Commentary*, November 1974, 22.
46. Quoted in Svonkin, *Jews against Prejudice*, 42.
47. Ibid., 61; Friedman, *What Went Wrong?*, 140.
48. Friedman, *What Went Wrong?*, 141.
49. Quoted in Goldberg, *Jewish Power*, 12.
50. Quoted in Lenora E. Berson, *The Negroes and the Jews* (New York: Random House, 1971), 109–10.
51. Goldberg, *Jewish Power*, 128. Shortly after I arrived in Philadelphia to head the Committee in 1959, I became secretary of the Pennsylvania Equal Rights Council, a group of forty church, labor, and civic groups that sought to enact fair housing legislation. A photograph hung on the wall of my office for many years showing the leaders of the group smiling as Governor David Lawrence signed the bill into law. Earlier, the local director of the ADL had served as secretary of the group and helped to push through fair education and fair employment practices legislation.
52. Jack Wertheimer, "Breaking Ranks: Jewish Conservatives in Post-War America," paper presented at the annual meeting of the American Historical Association, Washington, DC, January 5, 1997, 2.
53. Lawrence Grossman, "Mainstream Orthodoxy and the American Public Square," working paper, August 2001, 4.
54. Naomi W. Cohen, *Jews in Christian America: The Pursuit of Religious Equality* (New York: Oxford University Press, 1992), 175.
55. Lederhendler, *New York Jews*, 114.
56. Hollinger, *Science, Jews*, 20.
57. Alan Mittleman, "From Jewish Street to Public Square," *First Things*, August/September 2002, 34.
58. The phrase "equal footing" is taken from a petition of Jonas Phillips, a revolutionary-era Jewish leader in Philadelphia, who addressed a petition to the representatives of the thirteen states as they met in Philadelphia in 1789 to draft a new frame of government for the United States. He noted that the test oath in the Pennsylvania Constitution stood in contradiction to its Bill of Rights and begged the delegates not to repeat this error. "The Israelites," Phillips explained, "will think themselves happy to live under a government where all Religious societies are on an Equal footing." See Jonathan D. Sarna and David Dalin, *Religion and State in the American Jewish Experience* (Notre Dame, IN: Notre Dame University Press, 1997), 70–4.

59. Edwin Wolf II and Maxwell Whiteman, *The History of the Jews of Philadelphia from Colonial Times to the Age of Jackson* (Philadelphia: Jewish Publication Society, 1956), 150.
60. Sarna and Dalin, *Religion and State*, 21.
61. Ibid., 195–7.
62. Ibid., 236–7. The U.S. Constitution, according to the University of Chicago legal scholar Philip Hamburger (and others), says nothing about a wall of separation, which was Jefferson's metaphor in a private letter written to the Danbury Baptist Association in 1802, years after the adoption of the Constitution and Bill of Rights. See Philip Hamburger, *Separation of Church and State* (Cambridge, MA: Harvard University Press, 2002), 479–92.
63. Sarna and Dalin, *Religion and State*, 233. See also James E. Wood, Jr., ed., *Religion and the State: Essays in Honor of Leo Pfeffer* (Waco, TX: Baylor University Press, 1985).
64. As quoted in Sarna and Dalin, *Religion and State*, 234.
65. Ibid., 235–6.
66. Goldberg, *Jewish Power*, 122.
67. See Will Herberg's discussion of this in Sarna and Dalin, *Religion and State*, 254. Herberg notes that this view of religion in the public sphere is embodied in the Northwest Ordinance passed by Congress in 1787, Article 3 of which reads, "It can be found also in 'Jeffersonian' Georgia's charter of the University of Georgia two years earlier, which declared, it is 'among the first objects of those who wish well to the national prosperity, to encourage and support the principles of religion and morality. . . .' "
68. For a discussion of the nativist origins of Everson, see Hamburger, *Separation of Church and State*, 455–8.
69. As cited in Sarna and Dalin, *Religion and State*, 22.
70. Gregg Ivers, *To Build a Wall: American Jews and the Separation of Church and State* (Charlottesville: University Press of Virginia, 1995), 4.
71. Stephen V. Monsma and J. Christopher Soper, eds., *Equal Treatment of Religion in a Pluralistic Society* (Grand Rapids, MI: William B. Eerdmans, 1998), 164.
72. As quoted in Goldberg, *Jewish Power*, 124.
73. Ivers, *To Build a Wall*, 2.
74. Ibid., 139.
75. The Jewish involvement with such causes has been discussed by Irving Howe, Moses Rischin, Arthur Liebman, and Lawrence Fuchs and need not be described in great detail here. In the most recent major discussion, in Marc Dollinger, *Quest for Inclusion: Jews and Liberalism in Modern America* (Princeton, NJ: Princeton University Press, 2000), Dollinger argues that Jewish liberalism has been a practical device for Jews' gaining entrance into mainstream society and upward mobility, a theme the reader will find voiced throughout this book.
76. See Sidney Blumenthal, *The Rise of the Counterestablishment: From Conservative Ideology to Political Power* (New York: New York Times Books, 1986); Shapiro, *A Time for Healing*, 28; Svonkin, *Jews against Prejudice*, 272.
77. Richard Gid Powers, *Not without Honor: The History of American Anti-Communism* (New York: The Free Press, 1995), 256–7. See also Daniel Bell, ed., *The New American Right* (New York: Criterion Books, 1963), 33–55.

Chapter 2

1. Howe, *A Margin of Hope*, 64. For a broader discussion of the City College influences, see Mark Gerson, *The Neoconservative Vision: From Cold War to the Culture Wars* (Lanham, MD: Madison Books, 1996), 20–1.
2. Jacob Weisberg, "Profile – The Family Way," *The New Republic*, October 21, 1996, 180–9. See also Daniel Bell's letter to the editor in the February 23, 1998, issue of *The New Republic.*
3. Howe, *A Margin of Hope*, 64–5.
4. Bloom, *Prodigal Sons*, 40.
5. Irving Kristol, "Memoirs of a Trotskyist," *New York Times Magazine*, January 23, 1977, 51.
6. Howe, *A Margin of Hope*, 62.
7. Sidney Hook, *Out of Step: An Unquiet Life in the 20th Century* (New York: Harper and Row, 1987), 66; Bloom, *Prodigal Sons*, 39.
8. Edward Shils, "Totalitarians and Antinomians," in Bunzel, ed. *Political Passages*, 12.
9. Bloom, *Prodigal Sons*, 41; Nathan Liebowitz, *Daniel Bell and the Agony of Modern Liberalism* (Westport, CT: Greenwood Press, 1985), 71.
10. David Hoeveler, Jr., *Watch on the Right: Conservative Intellectuals in the Reagan Era* (Madison: University of Wisconsin Press, 1991), 82.
11. As quoted in Dorrien, *The Neoconservative Mind*, 70.
12. As quoted in Norman Podhoretz, *Making It* (New York: Random House, 1967), 42–3.
13. Irving Kristol, *Neo Conservatism: The Autobiography of an Idea* (New York: The Free Press, 1995), 13.
14. Ibid.
15. Liebowitz, *Daniel Bell*, 71.
16. Wolfgang Saxon, "Lewis Feuer, 89, Scholar in Sociology and Government," *New York Times*, November 30, 2002, sec. A.
17. Edward S. Shapiro, "The Jew as Patriot: Herman Wouk and American Jewish Identity," *American Jewish History* 84, no. 4 (December 1996): 336. In the climactic scene, the officers who had mutinied against the dictatorial Captain Queeg are celebrating their exoneration by the military court. At the height of the celebration, Barry Greenwald, who had defended them in the court martial and destroyed Queeg through his devastating questioning, stumbles into the room half-drunk. Instead of joining in the festivities, he berates himself and the other officers. He tells them that he is a Jew and that if the country had not won the war, his mother would have been boiled down to a bar of soap. While they were enjoying civilian life and looking down on Queeg and the other "stuffy, stupid Prussians in the Navy and the Army," the latter were preparing to defend Western freedom against the Nazis (ibid., 339).
18. Dorrien, *The Neoconservative Mind*, 351.
19. Norman Podhoretz, *Breaking Ranks: A Political Memoir* (New York: Harper and Row, 1979), 164–5.
20. "Our Country and Our Culture," *Partisan Review* 19, no. 3 (May/June 1952): 282. See also Godfrey Hodgson, *The World Turned Upside Down: A History of the Conservative Ascendancy in America* (Boston: Houghton Mifflin, 1996), 134; and

Edward Rothstein, "Cultural Soul-Searching: In 50 Years It's Emigrated Back to Europe," *New York Times*, May 18, 2002, sec. B.

21. Sanford Pinsker, "Our Cultures and Our Countries," *Forward*, May 24, 2002, 11. For a fifty-year retrospective of this seminal series, see "Our Country, Our Culture: The Changing Role of Intellectuals, Artists, and Scientists in America, 1952–2002," a special issue of *Partisan Review* 69, no. 4 (Fall 2002).
22. See Lucas A. Powe, Jr., *The Warren Court and American Politics* (Cambridge, MA: Harvard University Press, 2000).
23. *West Virginia State Board of Education v. Barnette,* 319 US 624 (1943).
24. Max Lerner, *Nine Scorpions in a Bottle: Great Judges and Cases of the Supreme Court*, ed. Richard Cummings (New York: Arcade, 1994), 161, 279; Bruce Allen Murphy, *The Brandeis/Frankfurter Connection: The Secret Political Activities of Two Supreme Court Justices* (New York: Oxford University Press, 1982), 9. For an overview of Frankfurter's career, see James Grossman, "A Note on Felix Frankfurter," *Commentary*, March 1996, 59–64.
25. Bloom, *Prodigal Sons*, 142–3.
26. Irving Kristol, "How Basic Is 'Basic Judaism'?," *Commentary*, January 1948, 27.
27. Irving Kristol, "God and the Psychoanalysts," in Kristol, *Neo Conservatism*, 389–404.
28. Ibid., 390–2.
29. Kristol, *Neo Conservatism*, 405–19.
30. Bloom, *Prodigal Sons*, 142–5.
31. Liebowitz, *Daniel Bell*, 70.
32. Naomi Cohen, *Not Free to Desist: The American Jewish Committee, 1906–1966* (Philadelphia: Jewish Publication Society of America, 1972), 263.
33. Daniel Bell, "Reflections on Jewish Identity," *Commentary*, June 1961, 472.
34. Ruth R. Wisse, *The Modern Jewish Canon: A Journey through Language and Culture* (New York: The Free Press, 2000), 25, 34.
35. Gerson, *The Neoconservative Vision*, 86–7, 91. See also Nathan Glazer, "New York's Puerto Ricans," *Commentary*, November 1958, 471.
36. Gerson, *The Neoconservative Vision*, 86.
37. Norman Podhoretz, *My Love Affair with America: The Cautionary Tale of a Cheerful Conservative* (New York: The Free Press, 2000), 7, 33; Thomas L. Jeffers, "Podhoretz's Discourses on America," *Hudson Review* 54, no. 2 (Summer 2001): 204.
38. Jeffers, "Podhoretz's Discourses," 205.
39. Norman Podhoretz, *Doings and Undoings: The Fifties and After in American Writing* (New York: Farrar Straus, 1964), 106–7.
40. Jeffers, "Podhoretz's Discourses," 203.
41. Ann Charters, ed., *Jack Kerouac: Selected Letters, 1957–1969* (New York: Viking, 1997), 121.
42. Norman Podhoretz, "My War with Allen Ginsberg," *Commentary*, August 1997, 32.
43. See Diana Trilling, "The Other Night at Columbia," *Partisan Review* 26, no. 2 (Spring 1959): 214–30. See discussion of this episode in Morris Dickstein, *Gates of Eden: American Culture in the Sixties* (Cambridge, MA: Harvard University Press, 1977), 3–4.

44. Michael Norman, "Diana Trilling, a Cultural Critic and Member of a Select Intellectual Circle, Dies at 91," *New York Times*, October 25, 1996, sec. A.
45. As quoted in Shapiro, "The Jew as Patriot," 334.
46. As quoted in Gerson, *The Neoconservative Vision*, 200.
47. Irving Kristol, "Class and Sociology: The Shadow of Marxism," *Commentary*, October 1957, 353.
48. Gerson, *The Neoconservative Vision*, 166.
49. Alan M. Wald, *The New York Intellectuals: The Rise and Decline of the Anti-Stalinist Left from the 1930s to the 1980s* (Chapel Hill: University of North Carolina Press, 1987), 30–1.
50. Kristol, *Neo Conservatism*, 17; Podhoretz, *Breaking Ranks*, 33; Zipperstein, "*Commentary* and American Jewish Culture," 19; George Nash, "*Commentary, The Public Interest*, and the Problem of Jewish Conservatism," *American Jewish History* 87, nos. 2 and 3 (June 1999 and September 1999), 160.
51. Zipperstein, "*Commentary* and American Jewish Culture," 18–20.
52. Bloom, *Prodigal Sons*, 243.
53. Podhoretz, *Breaking Ranks*, 207; Liebowitz, *Daniel Bell*, 126; Nathan Abrams, "America Is Home: *Commentary* Magazine and the Refocusing of the Community of Memory, 1945–1960," *Jewish Culture and History* 3, no. 1 (Summer 2000), 46–7.
54. Clement Greenberg, "The Plight of Our Culture," *Commentary*, June and July 1953, 28–30.
55. Ibid.
56. As quoted in Abrams, "America Is Home," 47.
57. Ibid., 54, 57, 61.
58. Ibid., 50. Although *Partisan Review* became indignantly anticommunist, it remained an independent Marxist-Trotskyite journal. It soon gravitated toward modernism, which, according to Abrams, focused on "the outsider, autonomy and critique of bourgeois society."
59. Podhoretz, *Breaking Ranks*, 89.
60. Kristol, *Neo Conservatism*, 6.
61. Ibid.; Wald, *The New York Intellectuals*, 33–7.
62. Bloom, *Prodigal Sons*, 384.
63. As quoted in Edward Rothstein, "As Culture Wars Go On, Battle Lines Blur a Bit," *New York Times*, May 27, 1997, sec. C.
64. Dorrien, *The Neoconservative Mind*, 96
65. Podhoretz, *Breaking Ranks*, 280.
66. As quoted in Susanne Klingenstein, *Enlarging America: The Cultural Work of Jewish Literary Scholars, 1930–1990* (Syracuse, NY: Syracuse University Press, 1998), 30.
67. Podhoretz, *Breaking Ranks*, 220–1.
68. Klingenstein, *Enlarging America*, 33.
69. Marc Blitz, "Government Practice and the School of Strauss," in Kenneth L. Deutsch and John A. Murley, eds., *Leo Strauss, the Straussians, and the American Regime* (Lanham, MD: Rowman and Littlefield, 2000).
70. Allan Bloom, *Giants and Dwarfs: Essays, 1960–1990* (New York: Simon and Schuster, 1990), 235–6, 242. See also Nina J. Easton, *Gang of Five: Leaders at the Center of the Conservative Crusade* (New York: Simon and Schuster, 2000),

39; Gregory Bruce Smith, "Who Was Leo Strauss?," *American Scholar* 66, no. 1 (Winter 1997): 96; Kenneth Hart Green, *Jew and Philosopher: The Return to Maimonides in the Jewish Thought of Leo Strauss* (Albany: State University of New York Press, 1996).

71. Leo Strauss, *Natural Rights and History* (Chicago: University of Chicago Press, 1953), 5–6.
72. See Strauss's introductory essay in Moses Maimonides, *A Guide to the Perplexed*, vols. 1 and 2, trans. Shlomo Pines (Chicago: University of Chicago Press, 1963).
73. Ted V. McAllister, *Revolt against Modernity: Leo Strauss, Eric Voegelin, and the Search for a Post-Liberal Order* (Lawrence: University of Kansas Press, 1996).
74. George Nash, *The Conservative Intellectual Movement in America since 1945* (Wilmington, DE: ISI Books, 1996).
75. Kristol, *Neo Conservatism*, 7.
76. Bloom, *Giants and Dwarfs*, 254.
77. David G. Dalin, *From Marxism to Judaism: The Collected Essays of Will Herberg* (New York: Markus Wiener, 1989), xv; Kessner, *The "Other" New York Intellectuals*, 356.
78. Kessner, *The "Other" New York Intellectuals*, 356.
79. John P. Diggins, *Up from Communism: Conservative Odysseys in American Intellectual History* (New York: Harper and Row, 1975), 283–4.
80. Will Herberg, *Judaism and Modern Man: An Interpretation of Jewish Religion* (1951; reprint, with an introduction by Neil Gilman, Woodstock, VT: Jewish Lights Publishers, 1997), vi; Kessner, *The "Other" New York Intellectuals*, 356.
81. Cohen, *Jews in Christian America*, 167.
82. Will Herberg, "The Sectarian Conflict over Church and State," *Commentary*, November 1952, 450–62;
83. Sarna and Dalin, *Religion and State*, 26; Cohen, *Jews in Christian America*, 179; Richard John Neuhaus, "Serving a Jealous God," *National Review*, July 14, 1989, 50–3.

Chapter 3

1. David Halberstam, *The Fifties* (New York: Villard Books, 1993).
2. See Jeffrey O. Nelson, "1953: The Year Liberals Began to Listen," *Intercollegiate Review* 29, no. 1 (Fall 1993): 28–9.
3. See Jerry Z. Muller, *The Mind and the Market: Capitalism in Modern European Thought* (New York: Knopf, 2002).
4. Charles W. Dunn and J. Woodard, *The Conservative Tradition in America* (Lanham, MD: Rowman and Littlefield, 1996), 5.
5. Nash, *The Conservative Intellectual Movement*, 65; Nelson, "1953," 29.
6. See James E. Person, Jr., *Russell Kirk: A Critical Biography of a Conservative Mind* (Lanham, MD: Madison Books, 1999).
7. Nash, *The Conservative Intellectual Movement*, xiii, 5, 35, 80. For a fuller discussion of the articulation of conservative principles that was well under way in the early years of the Cold War, see Gregory L. Schneider, *Cadres for Conservatism: Young Americans for Freedom and the Rise of the Contemporary Right* (New York: New York University Press, 1999), 9–17.

8. Stephen Goode and Eli Lehrer, "Keeping Books: Conservative Publishers Enjoying Success," *Insight on the News*, August 31, 1998, 8–11. See also Henry Regnery, *Memoirs of a Dissident Publisher* (New York: Harcourt Brace Jovanovich, 1979).
9. As quoted in Bloom, *Prodigal Sons*, 314.
10. George Nash, "Forgotten Jewish Godfathers: Premature Jewish Conservatives and the Rise of *National Review*," *American Jewish History* 87, nos. 1 and 2 (June and September 1999): 138.
11. Ibid., 132.
12. Dorrien, *The Neoconservative Mind*, 39; Nash, *The Conservative Intellectual Movement*, 86–7; Daniel Aaron, *Writers on the Left: Episodes in American Literary Communism* (New York: Columbia University Press, 1992), 231.
13. Nash, "Forgotten Godfathers," 135; de Toledano, *Lament for a Generation*, 37.
14. John A. Andrews, *The Other Side of the Sixties: Young Americans for Freedom and the Rise of Conservative Politics* (New York: Columbia University Press, 1997), 43. When a friend of de Toledano's was allegedly murdered "on the orders of Moscow" in 1943, "my war against Communism," he wrote, "suddenly acquired a very personal dimension" (see de Toledano, *Lament for a Generation*, 61–4).
15. Nash, "Forgotten Godfathers," 136.
16. Ibid., 131, 136–7. The threat to freedom of expression long associated with McCarthyism also applied to others who failed to toe the line maintained by the left. In 1947, Arthur M. Schlesinger, Jr., the historian, took a copy of George Orwell's *Animal Farm* (1945) to his publishing house, Little, Brown, for consideration. A harsh indictment of the Soviet Union, Orwell's book was rejected. Schlesinger, a strong anticommunist and a liberal, blamed the decision on Angus Cameron, the editor-in-chief, whose leftist sympathies forced him to resign during the anticommunist fervor of the 1950s (see Douglas Martin, "August Cameron, 93, Editor Forced Out in McCarthy Era," *New York Times*, November 23, 2002, sec. A).
17. William F. Buckley, Jr., *The Jeweler's Eye: A Book of Irresistible Political Reflections* (New York: Putnam, 1968), 343.
18. Ibid.; Regnery, *Memoirs*, 35; Paul Gottfried, *The Conservative Movement*, rev. ed. (New York: Twayne, 1993), 15. Nock, who died in 1945, was one of the seminal figures in the conservative revival then under way. He is best remembered for his *Memoirs of a Superfluous Man* (1943). During World War II, Robert Nisbet, soon to be one of the important social theorists of the new conservatism, "practically memorized" Nock's book. Kirk also corresponded with Nock, who was a frequent visitor to the Buckley home in Sharon, Connecticut. Nockean libertarianism would be a formidable influence on the future editor of the *National Review*.
19. As quoted in Charles H. Hamilton, ed., *Fugitive Essays: Selected Writings of Frank Chodorov* (Indianapolis: Liberty Press, 1980), 20–1.
20. Nash, *The Conservative Intellectual Movement*, 348.
21. Regnery, *Memoirs*, 35–6; Nash, *The Conservative Intellectual Movement*, 16–18; Hamilton, *Fugitive Essays*, 18.
22. Edward S. Shapiro, "Waiting for Righty," *Michael* 25 (2000): 170.
23. James T. Baker, *Ayn Rand* (Boston: Twayne, 1987), 16; Hodgson, *The World Turned Upside Down*, 31–2. See also David Harriman, ed., *Journals of Ayn Rand*

(New York: Dutton, 1997). According to the website <forum.objectivismonline.net>, sales of *Atlas Shrugged* as of 2004 have probably exceeded five million copies.

24. As quoted in John B. Judis, *William F. Buckley, Jr.: Patron Saint of the Conservatives* (New York: Simon and Schuster, 1988). See also Paula E. Hyman and Deborah Dash Moore, *Jewish Women in America*, vol. 2 (New York: Routledge, 1997), 1124.
25. Ayn Rand, *The Fountainhead* (Indianapolis: Bobbs-Merrill, 1943), 741–2.
26. Hodgson, *The World Turned Upside Down*, 34, 45.
27. Ayn Rand, interview by Alvin Toffler in *Playboy*, March 1964, 36.
28. As he advanced on the national scene, Greenspan has said little about his ties to the controversial Rand. He still describes himself as a libertarian and considers his friendship with Rand very important in the development of his thinking. An ideological conservative, he believes strongly that reducing taxes helps to improve the economy's ability to grow. He is also instinctively squeamish about using government money and power to fight battles in the private markets. (Keith Bradsher, "The Art and Science of Alan Greenspan: How to Stay Popular in a Divided Washington, and Keep Inflation in Check," *New York Times*, January 4, 1996, sec. D) See also Bob Woodward, *Maestro: Greenspan's Feds and the American Boom* (New York: Simon and Schuster, 2000); and Justin Martin, *Greenspan: The Man behind the Money* (New York: Perseus, 2000).
29. As quoted in Bill Goldstein, "Greenspan Shrugged: When Greed Was a Virtue and Regulation the Enemy," *New York Times*, July 21, 2002, sec. 4.
30. A psychotherapist, Branden was given the task of "liberating" Greenspan and other members of the group from their "residual subjectivism" through therapy sessions (see Gottfried, *The Conservative Movement*, 45–6).
31. Justin Raimondo, *An Enemy of the State* (Amherst, MA: Prometheus Books, 2000). See also Murray N. Rothbard, "Life in the Old Right," *Chronicles*, August 1994, 15–19.
32. Paul Samuelson, "The Friedman Age," *The Economist*, June 10, 1998.
33. Nash, *The Conservative Intellectual Movement*, 88.
34. Milton Friedman and Rose D. Friedman, *Two Lucky People: Memoirs* (Chicago: University of Chicago Press, 1998).
35. See Robert L. Bartley, "About Freedom in the Free World," *Wall Street Journal*, October 14, 2002, sec. 1.
36. Nash, *The Conservative Intellectual Movement*, 21; Ralph Harris, "The Plan to End Planning," *National Review*, June 16, 1997, 23–4; Friedman and Friedman, *Two Lucky People*, 158–9.
37. See Jim Powell, *FDR's Folly: How Roosevelt and His New Deal Prolonged the Great Depression* (New York: Crown Forum, 2003).
38. Milton and Rose Friedman, interview by Michael Robinson in *The American Enterprise*, January/February 1999, 18.
39. Milton Friedman (with Rose D. Friedman), *Capitalism and Freedom* (Chicago: University of Chicago Press, 1963), 89, 91, 93.
40. Gottfried, *The Conservative Movement*, 70; Nash, *The Conservative Intellectual Movement*, 184–7, 288; Friedmans interview, 20.
41. Blumenthal, *The Rise of the Counterestablishment*, 107.

42. As quoted in Kevin J. Smant, *Principles and Heresies: Frank S. Meyer and the Shaping of the American Conservative Movement* (Wilmington, DE: ISI Books, 2002), 94.
43. Ibid., 3.
44. William C. Dennis, Foreword to *In Defense of Freedom and Related Essays* by Frank S. Meyer (Indianapolis: Liberty Fund, 1996), xii.
45. Edward Shils, Introduction to Bunzel, *Political Passages*, 11–12.
46. Smant, *Principles and Heresies*, 25, 28.
47. Ibid., 11, 20–2, 28.
48. Frank S. Meyer, *In Defense of Freedom: A Conservative Credo* (Chicago: Regnery, 1962), 60.
49. As quoted by William C. Dennis, Foreword to *In Defense of Freedom and Related Essays* (Indianapolis: Liberty Fund, 1996), xviii.
50. Meyer, in Dennis, *In Defense of Freedom*, xviii.
51. See Gottfried, *The Conservative Movement*, 24; Regnery, *Memoirs*, 190; Nash, *The Conservative Intellectual Movement*, 184.
52. Meyer, *In Defense of Freedom*, 229–32.
53. Hodgson, *The World Turned Upside Down*, 89–90; Schneider, *Cadres for Conservatism*, xv, xvii, 128.
54. Nash, *The Conservative Intellectual Movement*, 164.
55. Smant, *Principles and Heresies*, xxii.
56. Nash, "Forgotten Godfathers," 130.
57. Ibid., 131.
58. Ibid.
59. Strauss voiced this idea in a lecture, "Why We Remain Jews," delivered at the University of Chicago Hillel House in 1962.
60. Kenneth Hart Green, *Jew and Philosopher: The Return to Maimonides in the Jewish Thought of Leo Strauss* (New York: New York University Press, 1993), ix; Peter Berkowitz, "The Reason of Revelation: The Jewish Thought of Leo Strauss," *The Weekly Standard*, May 25, 1988, 32. I am grateful to my colleague Martin Plax at the American Jewish Committee for bringing the Green material to my attention.
61. Shadia B. Drury, *Leo Strauss and the American Right* (New York: St. Martin's Press, 1997), 5; Nash, "Forgotten Godfathers," 29–30; Berkowitz, "The Reason of Revelation," 29–30.
62. De Toledano, *Lament*, 244.
63. Conservative funder Alfred Lilienthal wrote for the September 1949 issue of *Reader's Digest* an essay, "Israel's Flag Is Not Mine." When Regnery asked Schlamm to read Lilienthal's anti-Zionist manuscript *What Price Israel?*, Schlamm strongly recommended publication of the tract (see Regnery, *Memoirs*, 119).
64. De Toledano, *Lament*, 213. For a full discussion of de Toledano's relationship to Judaism, see Nash, "Forgotten Godfathers," 33, 150–1.
65. Buckley, *The Jeweler's Eye*, 343.
66. Marvin Liebman, *Coming Out Conservative: An Autobiography* (San Francisco: Chronicle Books, 1992), 13; Eric Pace, "Marvin Liebman, 73, Dies; Conservative for Gay Rights," *New York Times*, April 3, 1997, sec. D.
67. Buckley, *The Jeweler's Eye*, 343; Gottfried, *The Conservative Movement*, 34.

68. Smant, *Principles and Heresies*, 1, 340.
69. William F. Buckley, "R.I.P.: Frank S. Meyer," *National Review*, April 28, 1972, 466–7; Gottfried, *The Conservative Movement*, 34; Smant, *Principles and Heresies*, 341.
70. Andrews, *The Other Side of the Sixties*, 164.
71. De Toledano, *Lament*, 216.
72. Ibid., 179.
73. John Chamberlain, *A Life with the Printed Word* (Chicago: Regnery Gateway, 1982), 127.
74. Powers, *Not without Honor*, 262.
75. Nash, "Forgotten Godfathers," 24.
76. Leo Strauss, letter to the editor, *National Review*, January 5, 1957, 23.
77. Andrews, *The Other Side of the Sixties*, 107–8.
78. Nash, "Forgotten Godfathers," 27.
79. Liebman, *Coming Out Conservative*, 156.
80. Schneider, *Cadres for Conservatism*, 50.
81. Liebman, *Coming Out Conservative*, 153–7.

Chapter 4

1. Sam Tanenhaus, *Whittaker Chambers: A Biography* (New York: Random House, 1997), 192. The title of this chapter was taken from Jim Tuck, *The Liberal Civil War: Fraternity and Fratricide on the Left* (Lanham, MD: University Press of America, 1998).
2. Tanenhaus, *Whittaker Chambers*; Tony Judt, "Why the Cold War Worked," *New York Review of Books*, October 9, 1997, 40. The role of the Soviet Union in the Korean War is now widely accepted by historians. See William Stueck, *Rethinking the Korean War: A New Diplomatic and Strategic History* (Princeton, NJ: Princeton University Press, 2002).
3. John Lewis Gaddis, *We Now Know: Rethinking Cold War History* (New York: Oxford University Press, 1997), 25, 292–3; Melvyn P. Leffler, review of *We Now Know: Rethinking Cold War History* by John Lewis Gaddis, *American Historical Review* 104, no. 2 (April 1999): 501–24.
4. John Lewis Gaddis, "The New Cold War History," *Footnotes: Newsletter of the Foreign Policy Research Institute's Marvin Wachman Fund for International Education* 5, no. 5 (June 1998): 1. "This essay is based on the keynote address delivered by Professor Gaddis at the Foreign Policy Research Institute's History Institute on 'The Cold War Revisited,' May 1–2, 1998." See also Norman Friedman, *The Fifty-Year War: Conflict and Strategy in the Cold War* (Annapolis, MD: Naval Institute Press, 2000). Friedman argues that Stalin's commitment to communist expansion can be traced back to Soviet involvement in the Spanish Civil War in the 1930s. Gaddis has been disputed on the origins of the Cold War and on the scope of Soviet global expansion by Arnold A. Offner, *Another Such Victory: President Truman and the Cold War, 1945–1953* (Stanford, CA: Stanford University Press, 2002).
5. Murray Friedman and Albert D. Chernin, *A Second Exodus: The American Movement to Free Soviet Jews* (New York: Brandeis University Press, 1999), 70.

6. Jonathan Mahler, "Lozovsky's Last Stand," *Forward*, February 27, 1998; Tuck, *The Liberal Civil War*, 16–19.
7. On Stalin's war on Jews and his execution of Soviet Jewish literary and intellectual figures, see Vladimir Naumov and Joshua Rubenstein, eds., *Stalin's Secret Pogroms: The Postwar Inquisition of the Jewish Anti-Fascist Committee*, trans. Laura E. Wolfson (New Haven, CT: Yale University Press, 2001).
8. Vladislav Zukok and Constantine Pleshakov, *Inside the Kremlin Cold War: From Stalin to Khrushchev* (Cambridge, MA: Harvard University Press, 1996), 28.
9. Ronald Radosh, "The Red Scare Was Real," *New York Post*, July 10, 2002. See R. Bruce Craig, *Treasonable Doubt: The Harry Dexter White Spy Case* (Kansas City: University Press of Kansas, 2004). Craig concludes that White engaged in a "species of espionage."
10. John Earl Haynes and Harvey Klehr, *Venona: Decoding Soviet Espionage in America* (New Haven, CT: Yale University Press, 1999), 9. Between them, Haynes and Klehr have produced some eleven books on American communism and Soviet espionage. The decoded cables of the Venona Project in 1948 identify some 349 individuals who were feeding information to Soviet intelligence agencies. Nor was this the extent of penetration. Many agents could not be identified by American cryptanalysis. Boris Bykov, the resident Soviet spy master in Washington, admitted, "We have agents at the very center of government influencing policy." See Harvey Klehr and Ronald Radosh, *The Amerasia Spy Case: Prelude to McCarythyism* (Chapel Hill: University of North Carolina Press, 1996), 6. More recently, a revisionist attack on these findings that takes a sympathetic view of those who had engaged in espionage has been under way. Typical is Yeshiva University Professor Ellen Schrecker's *Many Are the Crimes: McCarthyism in America* (New York: Little, Brown, 1998). Schrecker, along with Victor Navasky, editor of *The Nation*, argues that the spies had laudable purposes, since the Soviets in the 1930s appeared to be battling the Nazis while Western states were engaged in appeasement. They also contend that the harm done to this country by Soviet espionage was minimal in comparison to the McCarthy "purges." See also John Earl Haynes and Harvey Klehr, *In Denial: Historians, Communism and Espionage* (New York: Encounter, 2003).
11. Haynes and Klehr, *Venona*, 9, 22.
12. It should be noted that Adolph Hitler also twice graced the cover of *Time* as its "Man of the Year." That designation had less to do with approval of the person than the fact that the cover figure had dominated world events in the previous year.
13. Tuck, *The Liberal Civil War*, 1–2, 12.
14. Doris Lessing, *Walking in the Shade: My Autobiography, 1949–1962* (New York: HarperCollins, 1997).
15. Tuck, *The Liberal Civil War*, 12.
16. As quoted in Graham White and John Maze, *Henry Wallace: His Search for a New World Order* (Chapel Hill: University of North Carolina Press, 1995); Gerson, *The Neoconservative Vision*, 46; Hook, *Out of Step*, 324.
17. Tuck, *The Liberal Civil War*, 209; Richard Helms, *A Look over My Shoulder: A Life in the CIA* (New York: Random House, 2003), 350.

18. Ibid., 12. See also Todd Bennett, "Culture, Power, and Mission to Moscow: Film and Soviet-American Cultural Relations during World War II," *Journal of American History* 88, no. 2 (September 2001), 489–518.
19. Robbie Lieberman, *The Strangest Dream: Communism, Anticommunism, and the U.S. Peace Movement, 1945–1963* (Syracuse, NY: Syracuse University Press, 2000).
20. Tanenhaus, *Whittaker Chambers*, 192.
21. Powers, *Not Without Honor*, 198.
22. Klehr and Radosh, *The Amerasia Spy Case*, 7; Hilton Kramer, *The Twilight of the Intellectuals: Culture and Politics in the Era of the Cold War* (Chicago: Ivan R. Dee, 1999), 139. See also Barrie Penrose and Simon Freeman, *The Secret Life of Anthony Blunt* (New York: Farrar, Straus, and Giroux, 1987).
23. Chamberlain, *Printed Word*, 135.
24. Hollinger, *Science, Jews*, 68.
25. Tuck, *The Liberal Civil War*, 9.
26. As quoted in John Burkhart Gilbert, *Writers and Partisans: A History of Radicalism in America* (New York: Wiley, 1968), 264–5.
27. *Encyclopedia Judaica*, s.v. "Arendt, Hannah."
28. Dorrien, *The Neoconservative Mind*, 19; Hook, *Out of Step*, 176–7.
29. Kramer, *Twilight of the Intellectuals*, 130–1.
30. Hook, *Out of Step*, 176–7.
31. Cooney, *Rise of New York Intellectuals*, 232.
32. Dorrien, *The Neoconservative Mind*, 28; Hook, *Out of Step*, 260; Stephen J. Whitfield, "The Crusade of a Constructive Conservative," *Academic Questions* 9, no.3 (Summer 1996): 26.
33. Hook, *Out of Step*, 260.
34. Kramer, *Twilight of the Intellectuals*, 136, 309.
35. Hook, *Out of Step*, 432; Dorrien, *The Neoconservative Mind*, 79; Peter Coleman, *The Liberal Conspiracy: The Congress for Cultural Freedom and the Struggle for the Mind of Postwar Europe* (New York: The Free Press, 1989), 11, 15. For biographical sketches of Lasky, following his death, see Richard Bernstein, "Melvin J. Lasky, Cultural Cold Warrior, Is Dead at 84," *New York Times*, May 22, 2004, sec. L; and Daniel Johnston, "A Brusque Little Guy from the Bronx," *Wall Street Journal*, May 26, 2004, sec. 1.
36. The details of Koestler's resignation can be found in Arthur Koestler, *The Invisible Writing* (New York: Macmillan, 1954); *Encyclopedia Judaica*, s.v. "Koestler, Arthur"; Michael Scammell, "Arthur Koestler Resigns," *The New Republic*, May 4, 1998, 30.
37. Coleman, *The Liberal Conspiracy*, xi; Dorrien, *The Neoconservative Mind*, 51; Hook, *Out of Step*, 421.
38. Coleman, *The Liberal Conspiracy*, 67. The first issue of *Encounter* appeared in October 1953. The *Times Literary Supplement* described it as a journal of "negative liberalism" and "hatred and fear of Communism." Who was ever called negative, Kristol retorted, "because of his hatred and fear of fascism?"
39. Hook, *Out of Step*, 334.
40. Arnold A. Offner, *Another Such Victory: Truman and the Cold War, 1945–1953* (Stanford, CA: Stanford University Press, 2000).

41. David McCullough, *Truman* (New York: Simon and Schuster, 1992), 553–4.
42. Melvin Lasky, "Why the Kremlin Exports Confessions," *Commentary*, January 1952, 5.
43. Timothy Garton Ash, "Orwell's List," *New York Review of Books*, September 25, 2003, 10.
44. Coleman, *The Liberal Conspiracy*, 6.
45. Tanenhaus, *Whittaker Chambers*, 342.
46. Richard Gid Powers, "Roy Cohn and Right-Wing Jewish Anticommunism" (author's files, n.d.).
47. Hook, *Out of Step*, 570.
48. Diana Trilling, "How McCarthyism Gave Anti-Communism a Bad Name," *Newsweek*, January 11, 1993, 32.
49. Diana Trilling, *We Must March My Darlings* (New York: Harcourt Brace Jovanovich, 1977), 63; Ronald Radosh, "The Legacy of Anti-Communist Intellectuals," *Partisan Review* 67, no. 4 (Fall 2000): 552–3.
50. Trilling may have been on shaky ground here. Oppenheimer's role in facilitating Soviet espionage "by surrounding himself with people willing and able to turn over information" is still not clear. Ernest Lawrence and Edward Teller doubt that he was a spy. He was, however, a member not only of the party but also of a secret cell at the University of California in the 1930s and 1940s. That particular cell discouraged members from disclosing their membership and helped to set policy and write party literature. Oppenheimer denied such membership, although he conceded that he had joined many front organizations in the 1930s. It is clear that he would have been denied the leadership post had his membership been known. See Harvey Klehr, review of *Sacred Secrets: How Soviet Intelligence Changed American History* by Jerrold and Leona Schechter, *The Weekly Standard*, July 1 and 8, 2002, 39. See also William J. Broad, "Book Contends Chief of A-Bomb Team Was Once a Communist," *New York Times*, September 8, 2002, sec. 1.
51. As quoted in Radosh, "The Legacy," 553.
52. Trilling, "How McCarthyism," 32.
53. Nathan Glazer, "The Method of Senator Joe McCarthy," *Commentary*, March 1953, 266.
54. Elliot Cohen, "The Free American Citizen, 1952," *Commentary*, September 1952, 229.
55. Michael J. Ybarra, "Blacklist Whitewash: The Real Story of the Hollywood Ten," *The New Republic*, January 5 and 12, 1998, 20–3.
56. Haynes and Klehr, *Venona*, 10.
57. Ibid., 3, 7. The literature dealing with Soviet spying activities during this time is now greatly enlarged: see, in addition to other books already noted in the text and endnotes, Allan Weinstein, *The Rosenberg File*, 2nd ed. (New Haven, CT: Yale University Press, 1997); John E. Haynes, *Red Scare or Red Menace? American Communism and Anti-Communism* (Chicago: Ivan R. Dee, 1996); and Allan Weinstein and Alexander Vassiliev, *The Haunted Wood* (New York: Random House, 1998).
58. Dorrien, *The Neoconservative Mind*, 52.
59. Hook, *Out of Step*, 449; Coleman, *The Liberal Conspiracy*, 244.

60. Gerson, *The Neoconservative Vision*, 52; Irving Kristol, "Memoirs of a 'Cold Warrior,'" *New York Times Magazine*, February 11, 1968, 17. See also Hugh Wilford, *The New York Intellectuals: From Vanguard to Institution* (New York: Manchester University Press, 1995). Wilford argues that the intellectuals had a commonality of purpose in their connections with the CIA and never betrayed their radical principles. Also of interest is Arthur M. Schlesinger, Jr., "Symposium: Liberal Communism Revisited," *Commentary*, September 1967, 70. Schlesinger was not troubled by CIA funding. "During the last days of Stalinism... the non-Communist trade-union movements and the non-Communist intellectuals," he wrote, "were under the most severe, unscrupulous, and unrelenting pressure. For the United States government to have stood self righteously aside at this point would have seemed to me far more shameful than to do what, in fact, it did – which was through intermediaries to provide some of these groups subsidies to help them do better what they were doing anyway." As quoted in Coleman, *The Liberal Conspiracy*, 231.
61. Ibid., 47; Gerson, *The Neoconservative Vision*, 51. See also Frances S. Saunders, *The Cultural Cold War: The CIA and the World of Arts and Letters* (New York: The Free Press, 1999).
62. Tom Braden, "Why I'm Glad the CIA Is Immoral," *Saturday Evening Post*, May 20, 1967, 10–14.
63. Coleman, *The Liberal Conspiracy*, 243.
64. Kristol, *Neo-Conservatism*, 14, 18–19.
65. Irving Kristol, "'Civil Liberties': 1952 – A Study in Confusion," *Commentary*, March 1952, 235–6.
66. Ibid., 233–4.
67. Bloom, *Prodigal Sons*, 212; Gerson, *The Neoconservative Vision*, 3.
68. Bloom, *Prodigal Sons*, 420.
69. Radosh, "The Legacy," 563–4.
70. Hook, *Out of Step*, 4.
71. As quoted in John H. Bunzel, "The Intellect as a Weapon for Freedom," *Academic Questions* 9, no. 3 (Summer 1996): 34.
72. Dorrien, *The Neoconservative Mind*, 73, 76–8; Coleman, *The Liberal Conspiracy*, 63; Hook, *Out of Step*, 332.
73. Dorrien, *The Neoconservative Mind*, 79.
74. Irving Kristol, telephone conversation with the author, May 8, 1999; Kristol, *Neo-Conservatism*, 24–5.
75. De Toledano, *Lament*, 145.

Chapter 5

1. Lionel Trilling, *The Liberal Imagination* (Garden City, NY: Doubleday, 1953), 5–6; Lee Siegel, "Cultural Misconceptions," *The New Republic*, August 2, 1992, 2.
2. Lee Edwards, *The Conservative Revolution: The Movement That Remade America* (New York: The Free Press, 1999), 107.

3. As quoted in Arthur Schlesinger, Jr., *Postmasters: Some Essays on American Historians*, ed. Marcus Cunliffe and Robert Winks (New York: Harper Torchbooks, 1969), 310.
4. As quoted in Blumenthal, *Rise of the Counterestablishment*, 41.
5. Nash, *The Conservative Intellectual Movement*, 10.
6. Joseph Keeley, *The China Lobby Man: The Story of Alfred Kohlberg* (New Rochelle, NY: Arlington House, 1969), 205.
7. Diggins, *Up from Communism*, 453; Nash, *The Conservative Intellectual Movement*, 27, 89; Chamberlain, *A Life*, 142; Rusher, *Rise of the Right*, 33–4; Hodgson, *The World Turned*, 71.
8. Chamberlain, *A Life*, 147; David Brooks, ed., *Backward and Upward: The New Conservative Writing* (New York: Vintage Books, 1996), xiv; Tanenhaus, *Whittaker Chambers*, 485–6; Laurence Zuckerman, "How '*Firing Line*' Transformed the Battleground," *New York Times*, December 18, 1999, sec. B.
9. Judis, *William F. Buckley*, 13, 26.
10. Ibid., 84–5.
11. As quoted in Hodgson, *The World Turned*, 77.
12. Schneider, *Cadres for Conservatism*, 14.
13. As quoted in Judis, *William F. Buckley*, 107; as quoted in Powers, *Not without Honor*, 282.
14. Powers, *Not without Honor*, 282.
15. Tanenhaus, *Whittaker Chambers*, 178.
16. Hodgson, *The World Turned*, 70; Tanenhaus, *Whittaker Chambers*, 486–7.
17. Smant, *Principles and Heresies*, 35.
18. Judis, *William F. Buckley*, 108; Smant, *Principles and Heresies*, 36.
19. Edwards, *The Conservative Revolution*, 79.
20. Ibid., 80.
21. Alfred Kazin, *New York Jew* (New York: Knopf, 1978), 60.
22. Nash, *The Conservative Intellectual Movement*, 135, 146, 149, 382; William Rusher, telephone conversation with the author, May 4, 1996; Chamberlain, *A Life*, 146.
23. Kazin, *New York Jew*, 59–62; Chamberlain, *A Life*, 146; Smant, *Principles and Heresies*, 38.
24. Judis, *William F. Buckley*, 155.
25. Chamberlain, *A Life*, 145.
26. Edwards, *The Conservative Revolution*, 15.
27. Chamberlain, *A Life*, 145.
28. Gerson, *The Neoconservative Vision*, 43; Gottfried, *The Conservative Movement*, 34; Nash, "Forgotten Godfathers," 122; Diggins, *Up from Communism*, 37; Powers, *Not without Honor*, 282–4.
29. William F. Buckley, *Nearer My God: An Autobiography of Faith* (New York: Doubleday, 1997), 227.
30. Diggins, *Up from Communism*, 360–1; Judis, *William F. Buckley*, 145
31. As quoted in Tanenhaus, *Whittaker Chambers*, 22.
32. Ibid., 160–1.
33. Powers, *Not without Honor*, 284; Arthur M. Schlesinger, Jr., review of *Whittaker Chambers: A Biography* by Sam Tanenhaus, *New York Times Book Review*,

March 9, 1997, 5; Tanenhaus, *Whittaker Chambers*, 165; Judis, *William F. Buckley*, 161.

34. Judis, *William F. Buckley*, 172; as quoted in Tanenhaus, *Whittaker Chambers*, 505–7.
35. Judis, *William F. Buckley*, 166, 172; Tanenhaus, *Whittaker Chambers*, 505.
36. Tanenhaus, *Whittaker Chambers*, 454; Gerson, *The Neoconservative Vision*, 56.
37. Diggins, *Up from Communism*, 149; Frank Meyer, "The Meaning of McCarthyism," *National Review*, June 14, 1958, 566.
38. Judis, *William F. Buckley*, 173; John P. Judis, "The End of Conservatism," *The New Republic*, August 31, 1992, 29; Gerson, *The Neoconservative Vision*, 44; Smant, *Principles and Heresies*, 161.
39. Smant, *Principles and Heresies*, 159; Hodgson, *The World Turned*, 62.
40. Smant, *Principles and Heresies*, 173; Nash, *The Conservative Intellectual Movement*, 275–6; Judis, *William F. Buckley*, 246; Rusher, *Rise of the Right*, 189.
41. Smant, *Principles and Heresies*, 256; Maurice Isserman and Michael Kazin, *America Divided: The Civil War of the 1960s* (New York: Oxford University Press, 2000), 220.
42. Edwards, *The Conservative Revolution*, 105; see also Diggins, *Up from Communism*, 406; Hodgson, *The World Turned*, 34–5; Tanenhaus, *Whittaker Chambers*, 501.
43. As quoted in Robert L. Bartley, review of *Getting It Right* by William F. Buckley, Jr., *Wall Street Journal*, March 6, 2003, sec. 2.
44. Schneider, *Cadres for Conservatism*, 48–9; Smant, *Principles and Heresies*, 162; Tanenhaus, *Whittaker Chambers*, 409, 487; William F. Buckley, *The Red Hunter* (Boston: Little, Brown, 1999), 392.
45. Willie Schlamm, "Across McCarthy's Grave," *National Review*, May 18, 1957, 471.
46. Nash, *The Conservative Intellectual Movement*, 111; Smant, *Principles and Heresies*, 45.
47. Diggins, *Up from Communism*, 282–8.
48. As quoted in Nash, "Forgotten Godfathers," 138.
49. As quoted in Nash, *The Conservative Intellectual Movement*, 114–15; Toledano, *Lament*, 206.
50. Diggins, *Up from Communism*, 407–8.
51. Smant, *Principles and Heresies*, 42, 207, 299–310.
52. Ibid., 210; Hodgson, *The World Turned*, 81; Judis, *William F. Buckley*, 166.
53. Smant, *Principles and Heresies*, 114–15.
54. Ibid., 30–1, 74.
55. Toledano, *Lament*, 520.
56. Nash, *The Conservative Intellectual Movement*, 27–31; E. Victor Milione, "Ideas in Action: Forty Years of Educating for Liberty," *Intercollegiate Review* 29, no. 1 (Fall 1993): 51–7.
57. E. Victor Milione, telephone conversation with the author, June 10, 1996.
58. Nash, *The Conservative Intellectual Movement*, 290; Milione, "Ideas in Action," 53.
59. Milione, "Ideas in Action," 54.

60. Mary C. Brennan, *Turning Right in the Sixties: The Conservative Capture of the GOP* (Chapel Hill: University of North Carolina Press, 1995), 12; Evans, *Revolt on the Campus* (Chicago: Regnery, 1961), 34–5.
61. Nash, *The Conservative Intellectual Movement*, 31; Gottfried, *The Conservative Movement*, 31, 33, 171; Brennan, *Turning Right*, 12.
62. As quoted in Schneider, *Cadres for Conservatism*, 17.
63. Nash, *The Conservative Intellectual Movement*, 30; Andrews, *The Conservative Revolution*, 31; Schneider, *Cadres for Conservatism*, 32.
64. Liebman, *Coming Out Conservative*, 55–65, 88; Andrews, *The Conservative Revolution*, 64.
65. Andrews, *The Conservative Revolution*, 30, 47, 54, 65.
66. Ibid., 76; Schneider, *Cadres for Conservatism*, 33, 37.
67. Andrews, *The Conservative Revolution*, 57 (see also Appendix A, 221–2); Hodgson, *The World Turned*, 94.
68. Judis, *William F. Buckley*, 184–90; Ribuffo, "The Problem of American Conservatism," 445; Hodgson, *The World Turned*, 95; Milione, telephone conversation with the author; Andrews, *The Conservative Revolution*, 64.
69. Schneider, *Cadres for Conservatism*, 32, 40; Nash, *The Conservative Intellectual Movement*, 305.
70. S. M. Lipset and P. G. Altbach, "Student Politics and Higher Education," in *Student Politics*, ed. S. M. Lipset (New York: Basic Books, 1967), 219–20; Richard G. Braungart, "SDS and YAF: Backgrounds of Student Activists" (Pennsylvania State University, Department of Sociology, University Park, PA, 1966, mimeographed), 9–11; Robert McNamara, *In Retrospect: The Tragedy and Lessons of Vietnam* (New York: Times Books, 1995), 284.
71. Andrews, *The Conservative Revolution*, 1, 21, 57; Daniel Bell, *The End of Ideology: On the Exhaustion of Political Ideas in the Fifties* (Cambridge, MA: Harvard University Press, 1988), 16, 120–1.
72. Brennan, *Turning Right*, 1.
73. Rick Perlstein, "Who Owns the Sixties?," *Lingua Franca*, May/June 1998, 30–7; see also Patricia Cohen, "New Slant on the 60's: The Past Made New; Reassessing a Tumultuous Decade," *New York Times*, June 13, 1998, sec. B.
74. As quoted in Dan Wakefield, *New York in the 50s* (Boston: Houghton Mifflin, 1992), 270.
75. Jack Cassidy (ed.), *Goldwater by Barry Goldwater* (New York: Doubleday, 1988), 106.
76. Moses Rischin, "Jacob Rader Marcus: Historian-Archivist of Jewish Middle America," review of *This I Believe: Documents of American Jewish Life* by Jacob Rader Marcus, *American Jewish History* 85, no. 2 (June 1997): 177.
77. Edwards, *The Conservative Revolution*, 88.
78. Smant, *Principles and Heresies*, 141, 182.
79. Adam Clymer, "Barry Goldwater Is Dead at 89; Conservatives' Standardbearer," *New York Times*, May 30, 1998, sec. A.
80. Hodgson, *The World Turned*, 96; Andrews, *The Conservative Revolution*, 46; Schneider, *Cadres for Conservatism*, 27.
81. Andrews, *The Conservative Revolution*, 50.
82. Ibid., 45.
83. Ibid., 25.

84. As quoted in Evans, *Revolt*, 188–9.
85. Smant, *Principles and Heresies*, 143; Andrews, *The Conservative Revolution*, 45, 78; Frank Meyer, "Principles and Heresies," *National Review*, December 19, 1959, 555.
86. Liebman, *Coming Out Conservative*, 167–8.
87. Hodgson, *The World Turned*, 91; Robert Alan Goldberg, *Barry Goldwater* (New Haven, CT: Yale University Press, 1996), 206.
88. Schneider, *Cadres for Conservatism*, 87.
89. Ibid., 88.
90. Hodgson, *The World Turned*, 108–9.
91. Ibid., 112; Liebman, *Coming Out Conservative*, 178.

Chapter 6

1. Friedman, *What Went Wrong?*, 213.
2. Brent Staples, *Parallel Time* (New York: Pantheon Books, 1994), 148.
3. John P. Judis, "The Spirit of '68," *The New Republic*, August 31, 1998, 24.
4. Murray Friedman, "The Jews," in *Through Different Eyes: Black and White Perspectives on American Race Relations*, ed. Peter Rose, Stanley Rothman, and William J. Wilson (New York: Oxford University Press, 1973), 155.
5. As quoted in Goldberg, *Barry Goldwater*, 137.
6. Joshua Michael Zeitz, "If I Am Not for Myself . . . : The American Establishment in the Aftermath of the Six Day War," *American Jewish History* 88, no. 2 (June 2000): 253–6.
7. As quoted in Brent Staples, "Enter Patty Hearst, and Some Other Ghosts from the 60's," *New York Times*, February 2, 2002, sec. A.
8. Dennis Hale, review of *The Long March: How the Cultural Revolution of the 1960s Changed America* by Roger Kimball, *Society*, March/April 2002, 93.
9. Alex Rosen, Foreword to *Case Study of a Riot: The Philadelphia Story* by Lenora E. Berson (Philadelphia: American Jewish Committee, 1966), 6.
10. As quoted in Fred Siegel, *The Future Once Happened Here: New York, D.C., L.A., and the Fate of America's Big Cities* (San Francisco: Encounter Books, 1997), 61.
11. *Report of the National Advisory Commission on Civil Disorders* (New York: Bantam Books, 1968), vii.
12. As quoted in Smant, *Principles and Heresies*, 216.
13. Tamar Jacoby, *Someone Else's House: America's Unfinished Struggle for Integration* (New York: Basic Books, 1998), 156–8. See also James Q. Wilson, review of *Someone Else's House: America's Unfinished Struggle for Integration* by Tamar Jacoby, *The New Republic*, May 11, 1998, 36.
14. As quoted in Siegel, *The Future Once Happened Here*, 58.
15. Jason De Parle, "What Welfare-to-Work Really Means," *New York Times Magazine*, December 20, 1998, 58.
16. Siegel, *The Future Once Happened Here*, 59–60.
17. De Parle, "What Welfare," 58.
18. Ibid.
19. Siegel, *The Future Once Happened Here*, 56, 70; Douglas J. Besharov, "The Past and Future of Welfare Reform," *The Public Interest*, no. 150 (Winter 2003): 9.

20. Daniel Patrick Moynihan, "The Professors and the Poor," *Commentary*, August 1968, 19–28.
21. Fred Siegel, "Succeeding Giuliani," *Commentary*, January 2002, 40; Siegel, *The Future Once Happened Here*, 64. See also Nathan Glazer, "Neoconservatism and Liberal New York," in *Rethinking the Urban Agenda*, ed. John Mollenkopf and Ken Emerson (New York: Century Foundation Press, 2001), 27.
22. Jacoby, *Someone Else's House*, 158; Kai Bird, *The Color of Truth: McGeorge Bundy and William Bundy: Brothers in Arms* (New York: Simon and Schuster, 1998), 382; Jerold E. Podair, *The Strike That Changed New York: Blacks, Whites and the Ocean Hill Brownsville Crisis* (New Haven, CT: Yale University Press, 2002), 38.
23. Jacoby, *Someone Else's House*, 159; Siegel, *The Future Once Happened Here*, xii; Podair, *The Strike*, 41.
24. Siegel, *The Future Once Happened Here*, xii, 46.
25. Bird, *The Color of Truth*, 384.
26. Podair, *The Strike*, 165.
27. John Tierney, "'Other Half' Is Living a Little Better," *New York Times*, June 29, 2001, sec. B; Siegel, "Succeeding Giuliani," 39–40; Jacoby, *Someone Else's House*, 162. See also Glazer, "Neoconservatism and Liberal New York," 27.
28. Podair, *The Strike*, 6, 12; Siegel, *The Future Once Happened Here*, 49; Friedman, *What Went Wrong?*, 257–63.
29. Anemona Hartocollis, "Growing Outrage Leads Back to Centralized Leadership," *New York Times*, June 7, 2002, sec. B; Joseph Berger, "The Odd Circle of School Control: 'Power to the People' Is Now Seen as 'Amateur Hour,'" *New York Times*, June 16, 2002, sec. 1.
30. Robert Kagan, "When America Blinked," *The New Republic*, December 3, 2001, 29.
31. Powers, *Not without Honor*, 198.
32. Marilyn Berger, "Clark Clifford, a Major Advisor to Four Presidents, Is Dead at 91," *New York Times*, October 11, 1998, sec. 1; R. W. Apple, Jr., "Gone Are the Political Wise Men and the Culture That Bred Them," *New York Times*, October 12, 1998, sec. A.
33. Bird, *The Color of Truth*, 20; Gabriel Schoenfeld, review of *In Retrospect: The Tragedy and Lessons of Vietnam* by Robert S. McNamara with Brian Van DeMark, *Commentary*, June 1995, 34, 52.
34. Apple, "Gone Are the Political Wise Men."
35. Sam Tanenhaus, review of *Secrecy: The American Experience* by Daniel Patrick Moynihan, *New York Times Book Review*, August 17 and 24, 1998, 15.
36. Powers, *Not without Honor*, 322.
37. As quoted in Norman Podhoretz, "Return of the 'Jackal Bins,'" *Commentary*, April 2002, 30.
38. Powers, *Not without Honor*, 320; Tristram Coffin, *Senator Fulbright: Portrait of a Public Philosopher* (New York: Dutton, 1966), 251; Peter Schweizer, *Reagan's War: The Epic Story of His Forty Year Struggle and Final Triumph over Communism* (New York: Doubleday, 2002), 191.
39. As quoted in Powers, *Not without Honor*, 321; Coffin, *Senator Fulbright*, 251–2.
40. Robert Kagan, "How Dean Acheson Won the Cold War," *The Weekly Standard*, September 14, 1998, 31.
41. As quoted in Robert Kagan, "When America Blinked," *The New Republic*, December 3, 2001, 32.

42. William Appleman Williams and Gerald Kolko, "The Cold War Revisited," *Foreign Policy Research Note* 5, no. 6 (September 1998): 1.
43. Bunzel, *Political Passages*, 215.
44. As quoted in David M. Herszenshorn, "Word for Word/Dear Abbie; or, How He Learned to Stop Worrying and Love to Sell Books," *New York Times*, September 3, 2000, sec. 4.
45. As quoted in Kimball, *The Long March*, 81–99.
46. Ibid. See also Joseph Epstein, "Intellectuals – Public and Otherwise," *Commentary*, May 2000, 49; Podhoretz, *My Love Affair*, 88; Edward Renehan, Jr., "Lest We Forget: The Case against Jane Fonda," review of *Aid and Comfort: Jane Fonda in North Vietnam* by Henry Mark Holzer and Erika Holzer, Front Page Magazine.com, September 24, 2002 <http://www.frontpagemag.com/Articles/Printable.asp?ID=3316>; Carol Iannone, "A Dissent on Grace Paley," *Commentary*, August 1985, 55.
47. Irving Howe, *A Margin of Hope* (New York: Harcourt Brace Jovanovich, 1982), 316; Scott Malcomson, review of *Martin Luther King, Jr.* by Marshall Frady, *New York Times Book Review*, January 27, 2002, 10.
48. Stephen J. Whitfield, *The Culture of the Cold War* (Baltimore: Johns Hopkins University Press, 1991), 206.
49. See Mona Charen, *Useful Idiots: How Liberals Got It Wrong in the Cold War and Still Blame America* (Chicago: Henry Regnery, 2003).
50. Gerson, *The Neoconservative Vision*, 115–18.
51. As quoted in Robert Leiter, "Guilty as Hell, Free as a Bird," *Jewish Exponent*, January 24, 2002, 26.
52. Howe, *A Margin of Hope*, 315–16.
53. As quoted in Norman Podhoretz, "My War with Alan Ginsberg," *Commentary*, August 1997, 38.
54. As quoted in Andrew Delbanco, review of *Selected Essays by Lionel Trilling*, ed. Leon Wiesleiter, *New York Review of Books*, January 11, 2001, 40. On Cox's statement, see Trilling's observation in "Culture and the Present Moment: A Round-Table Discussion," *Commentary*, December 1974, 48, 54.
55. Ibid.
56. Whitfield, *The Culture of the Cold War*, 220–1; Arthur M. Schlesinger, Jr., "Symposium: Liberal Anti-Communism Revisited," *Commentary*, September 1967, 69.
57. Arthur M. Schlesinger, Jr., *A Life in the Twentieth Century: Innocent Beginnings, 1917–1950* (Boston: Houghton Mifflin, 2000), 507–9; Kramer, *The Twilight*, 137–42.
58. As quoted in Edward Rothstein, "An Open Mind amid Growing Ideologues," *New York Times*, January 4, 2003, sec. B.
59. David Brooks, "A Moment to Be Seized," *The Weekly Standard*, January 14, 2002, 7–8.

Chapter 7

1. Howe, *A Margin of Hope*, 234.
2. As quoted in Gerson, *The Neoconservative Vision*, 243–4.

3. Irving Kristol, "America's Exceptional Conservatism," *Wall Street Journal*, April 18, 1995, sec. 1. See also Norman Podhoretz, "Neoconservatism," *Commentary*, March 1996, 19.
4. Irving Kristol, "American Conservatism, 1945–1995," *The Public Interest*, no. 121 (Fall 1995): 86; Podhoretz, "Neoconservatism," 28; J. David Hoeveler, *Watch on the Right: Conservative Intellectuals in the Reagan Era* (Madison: University of Wisconsin Press, 1991), 87.
5. Kristol, *Reflections*, x–xi; Hoeveler, *Watch on the Right*, 81–2, 150–1. In her writings, Kristol's wife, Bea, spelled out these ideas more fully. In one essay, she contrasted the British and French forms of the Enlightenment. The former took the form "not of regeneration but of melioration." Secular and religious institutions, civil society and the state, public relief and private charity complemented and cooperated with each other. It did not create "an unbridgeable divide between reason and religion." By contrast, the French Enlightenment, coming on the heels of the French Revolution, was "a social revolution, with a conscious, truly revolutionary social ethic and agenda" that "inevitably culminated in the Terror." The two Enlightenments, the Kristols argued, were not a passing phase in history but have been played out in one form or another throughout history. See Gertrude Himmelfarb, "The Idea of Compassion: The British vs. the French Enlightenment," *The Public Interest*, no. 145 (Fall 2001): 20–3.
6. As quoted in Glazer, "Neoconservatism and Liberal New York," 29.
7. Dorrien, *The Neoconservative Mind*, 88; Irving Kristol and Daniel Bell, "What Is *The Public Interest*?," *The Public Interest*, no. 1 (Fall 1965): 4; Gerson, *The Neoconservative Vision*, 94.
8. Daniel Patrick Moynihan, *Family and Nation* (New York: Harcourt Brace Jovanovich, 1987), 27; Adam Clymer, "Daniel Patrick Moynihan Is Dead; Senator from Academia Was 76," *New York Times*, March 27, 2003, sec. A. The full text of Moynihan's "The Negro Family: The Case for National Action" can be found on the U.S. Department of Labor's website at <http://www.dol.gov/asp/programs/history/webid-moynihan.htm.>.
9. Hodgson, *The World Turned*, 66–8; Michael Barone, "Daniel Patrick Moynihan," *Wall Street Journal*, March 28, 2003, sec. 1.
10. Godfrey Hodgson, *The Gentleman from New York: Daniel Patrick Moynihan, a Biography* (Boston: Houghton Mifflin, 2000), 124.
11. Ibid.
12. Ehrman, "*Commentary, The Public Interest*," 159–81; Gottfried, *The Conservative Movement*, 69.
13. Daniel Bell, *The Cultural Contradictions of Capitalism* (New York: Basic Books, 1976), xi.
14. Kristol, *Neoconservatism*, 31; Gerson, *The Neoconservative Vision*, 349; Hodgson, *The World Turned*, 133; Glazer, as quoted in Bloom, *Prodigal Sons*, 359.
15. James Q. Wilson, "On the Rediscovery of Character," *The Public Interest*, no. 81 (Fall 1985): 4; Glazer, "The New Left and Its Limits," *Commentary*, July 1968, 35.
16. Kristol, "American Conservatism," 85.
17. Dorrien, *The Neoconservative Mind*, 89.
18. Ibid., 88.

19. Kristol, *Reflections*, xii.
20. Gerson, *The Neoconservative Vision*, 97.
21. Kristol, *Reflections*, xiii.
22. Nathan Glazer, "Letter to the Editor: Neoconservatives, Then and Now," *New York Times*, October 26, 2003, sec. 4.
23. Dorrien, *The Neoconservative Mind*, 135; Podhoretz, *Ex-Friends*, 6–7.
24. The editors, "A Short History of Commentary," in *What* Commentary *Hath Wrought: An Anthology of the First Pages of Articles and Stories of Particular Note, with a Short History of the Magazine, in Honor of Norman Podhoretz* (New York: Commentary, 1999), 1–2.
25. Podhoretz, *Ex-Friends*, 78.
26. Ehrman, *The Rise of Neo Conservatism*, 42; Podhoretz, *Breaking Ranks*, 49, 92.
27. Alexander, *Irving Howe*, 111.
28. Richard Gid Powers, "Norman Podhoretz and the Cold War" (New York, March 11, 2003, typescript), 14, 29.
29. Dorrien, *The Neoconservative Mind*, 157; Podhoretz, *Breaking Ranks*, 316; *What* Commentary *Hath Wrought*, 5.
30. Norman Podhoretz, "Following Irving," in *The Neoconservative Imagination: Essays in Honor of Irving Kristol*, ed. Christopher DeMuth and William Kristol (Washington, DC: AEI Press, 1995), 59; Dorrien, *The Neoconservative Mind*, ix.
31. Podhoretz, *Making It*, xi. Podhoretz had personal as well as ideological reasons for his crusade, especially when it came to the *New York Review of Books*. Jason Epstein, an editor at the magazine (along with his then-wife, Barbara) and once Podhoretz's close friend, had advised him not to publish *Making It*, and then had compounded the problem by assigning Edgar Z. Friedenberg to review the book in the pages of *New York Review*. Friedenberg was highly critical of the book.
32. Dorrien, *The Neoconservative Mind*, 161.
33. Ian Buruma, "How to Talk about Israel," *New York Times Magazine*, August 31, 2003, 32.
34. Irving Howe, "The New York Intellectuals: A Chronicle and a Critique," *Commentary*, October 1968, 29–51; Gerson, *The Neoconservative Vision*, 118–22.
35. Gerson, *The Neoconservative Vision*, 118–22.
36. Podhoretz, *My Love Affair*, 172
37. Ibid., 174.
38. Emil Fackenheim, "Jewish Faith and the Holocaust," *Commentary*, August 1968, 31–2.
39. Nathan Glazer, "Jewish Interests and the New Left," *Midstream*, February 1971, 35.
40. Dorrien, *The Neoconservative Mind*, 164.
41. Michael Harrington, *Fragments of the Century* (New York: Saturday Review Press, 1973), 145.
42. As quoted in Podhoretz, *Breaking Ranks*, 355.
43. Podhoretz, *Ex-Friends*, 21; Daniel Bell, "The New Class: A Muddled Concept," *Society*, January/February 1979, 17.
44. Podhoretz, "Following Irving," 58.
45. Gerson, *The Neoconservative Vision*, 86.

46. Podhoretz, *Breaking Ranks*, 218.
47. Stanley Rothman and S. Robert Lichter, *Roots of Radicalism* (New York: Oxford University Press, 1982), 80–145; Michael Lind, *Up from Conservatism: Why the Right is Wrong for America* (New York: The Free Press, 1996), 26–7.
48. Jacob Weisberg, "Profile: The Family Way," *The New Republic*, October 21, 1996, 183; Podhoretz, "Neoconservatism: A Eulogy," *Commentary*, March 1996, 21.
49. Kristol, *Reflections*, xii.
50. Frank S. Meyer, "Principles and Heresies," *National Review*, June 14, 1958, 566.
51. Ehrman, *The Rise of Neoconservatism*, 43, 45.
52. Irving Kristol, "On the Burning Deck," review of *Up from Liberalism* by William F. Buckley, Jr., *Reporter*, November 26, 1959, 48; Gerson, *The Neoconservative Vision*, 45–6.
53. Kristol, telephone conversation with the author, Gerson, *The Neoconservative Vision*, 20; Kristol, "American Conservatism, 1945–1995," 83.
54. Podhoretz, *Ex-Friends*, 70–1.
55. Kristol, "Capitalism, Socialism, and Nihilism," *The Public Interest*, no. 34 (Spring 1973): 12–13.
56. Kristol, *Reflections*, 32; Gerson, *The Neoconservative Vision*, 201.
57. Kristol, *Reflections*, 32.
58. James A. Smith, *The Idea Brokers: Think Tanks and the Rise of the New Policy Elite* (New York: The Free Press, 1991), 177.
59. Kristol, *Neo-Conservatism*, 33.
60. Ibid., 34, 37; Dorrien, *The Neoconservative Mind*, 102; Blumenthal, *The Rise of the Counter-Establishment*, 37, 38.
61. David Grann, "Robespierre of the Right," *The New Republic*, October 27, 1997, 20.
62. Lind, *Up from Conservatism*, 80–1.
63. David Brock, *Blinded by the Right: The Conscience of an Ex-Conservative* (New York: Crown, 2002), 17; Blumenthal, *The Rise of the Counter-Establishment*, 66; Kristol, telephone conversation. On launching the conservative foundation movement, see James Pierson, "You Get What You Pay For," *Wall Street Journal*, July 21, 2004.
64. Gottfried, *The Conservative Movement*, 121, 127; author's interview with Kristol, May 8, 1996.
65. Weisberg, "The Family Way," 184.
66. Blumenthal, *The Rise of the Counter-Establishment*, 148, 159; Jon Weiner, "Dollars for Neo-Con Scholars: The Olin Money Tree," *The Nation*, January 1, 1990, 12–14; Dorrien, *The Neoconservative Mind*, 102. See also People for the American Way, "Buying a Movement: Right-Wing Foundations and American Politics," 1996, <http://www.pfaw.org/pfaw/general/default.aspx?oid=2052>.
67. James H. Jones, "Dr. Yes," *The New Yorker*, August 25 and September 1, 1997, 107.
68. See Dan Himmelfarb, "Conservative Splits," *Commentary*, May 1988, 54–8.
69. As quoted in Maisel, *Jews in American Politics*, 202.
70. Gottfried, *The Conservative Movement*, 121–2.
71. As quoted in Maisel, *Jews in American Politics*, 203.
72. As quoted in Dorrien, *The Conservative Mind*, 12.

73. Maisel, *Jews in American Politics*, 208.
74. Blumenthal, *The Rise of the Counter-Establishment*, 155.
75. Edward S. Shapiro, "Jews and the Conservative Rift," *American Jewish History* 87 (June 1999 and September 1999): 195–215.
76. Clarence Page, "Remembering Daniel P. Moynihan's Mind," *Philadelphia Tribune*, April 4, 2003, sec. 1. Moynihan, who always remained fiercely independent, voted against welfare reform legislation because of time limits it placed on welfare recipients.
77. Weisberg, "The Family Way," 103; Blumenthal, *The Rise of the Counter-Establishment*, 161.
78. Smant, *Principles and Heresies*, 259.
79. As quoted in Dorrien, *The Neoconservative Mind*, 73.
80. Hoeveler, *Watch on the Right*, 57.

Chapter 8

1. Deep distrust of Richard Nixon, however, forced both Nathan Glazer and Daniel Bell to vote for McGovern. Glazer, "Letter to the Editor," October 26, 2003; Ehrman, *The Rise of Neo-Conservatism*, 59; Jay Winik, *On the Brink: The Dramatic Saga of How the Reagan Administration Changed the Course of History and Won the Cold War* (New York: Simon and Schuster, 1996), 109.
2. Winik, *On the Brink*, 80.
3. Tuck, *The Liberal Civil War*, 223; Blumenthal, *The Rise of the Counter-Establishment*, 126–7.
4. Patrick Glynn, *Closing Pandora's Box: Arms Race, Arms Control, and the History of the Cold War* (New York: Basic Books, 1992), 184; Richard Pipes, "Team B: The Reality behind the Myth," *Commentary*, October 1996, 27.
5. Robert Kagan, review of *Years of Renewal* by Henry Kissinger, *The New Republic*, June 21, 1999, 42; Jerry W. Sanders, *Peddlers of Crisis: The Committee on the Present Danger and the Politics of Containment* (Boston: South End Press, 1983), 261, 275.
6. As quoted in Elmo R. Zumwalt, Jr., *On Watch: A Memoir* (New York: Times Books, 1976), 248; Winik, *On the Brink*, 78; Kagan, review of *Years of Renewal*, 44; George Weigel, "Who Won the Cold War? How? So What?," *Ethics and Public Policy Center Newsletter* 6, no. 10 (December 1992): 78.
7. Weigel, "Who Won the Cold War?," 77; Stephen J. Whitfield, *The Culture of the Cold War* (Baltimore: Johns Hopkins University Press, 1991), 9.
8. Schweizer, *Reagan's War*, 55, 58, 293.
9. Ibid., 143.
10. Powers, *Not without Honor*, 8; Thomas Powers, "The Black Arts," *New York Review of Books*, February 4, 1999, 20–4. See also William E. Odom, *The Collapse of the Soviet Military* (New Haven, CT: Yale University Press, 1998).
11. Powers, "The Black Arts," 22.
12. Schweizer, *Reagan's War*, 59–61.
13. Glynn, *Closing Pandora's Box*, 215–21.
14. As quoted in Derek Leebaert, *The Fifty-Year Wound: The True Price of America's Cold War* (Boston: Little, Brown, 2002), 454.
15. Glynn, *Opening Pandora's Box*, 304; Weigel, "Who Won the Cold War?," 78.

16. Pipes, "Team B," 28.
17. Glynn, *Opening Pandora's Box*, 216.
18. Judith Miller, "After the War: Intelligence; Scientist Was the 'Bane of Proliferators,'" *New York Times*, July 21, 2003, sec. A. See also Ken Alibek and Stephen Handelman, *Biohazard: The Chilling True Story of the Largest Covert Biological Weapons Program in the World* (New York: Random House, 1999).
19. As quoted in Glynn, *Opening Pandora's Box*, 268.
20. As quoted in ibid., 271.
21. As quoted in Schweizer, *Reagan's War*, 126–7.
22. Adam Garfinkel, "How to Learn Lessons from History," *Footnotes: The Newsletter of FPRI's Marvin Wachman Fund for International Education* 7, no. 1 (May 2001): 5.
23. Winik, *On the Brink*, 80–1.
24. As quoted in Anne Hessing Cahn, *Killing Détente: The Right Attacks the CIA* (University Park: Pennsylvania State University Press, 1998), 26.
25. Winik, *On the Brink*, 108–9; Cahn, *Killing Détente*, 27.
26. Winik, *On the Brink*, 110; Bill Keller, "The Sunshine Warrior," *New York Times Magazine*, September 22, 2002, 84.
27. Sanders, *Peddlers of Crisis*, 217.
28. Richard Pipes, "Why the Soviet Union Thinks It Could Fight and Win a Nuclear War," *Commentary*, July 1977, 21–34; Michael Sherry, *In the Shadow of War: The United States since the 1930s* (New Haven, CT: Yale University Press, 1995), 353; Winik, *On the Brink*, 110; Powers, *Not without Honor*, 369.
29. Hodgson, *The World Turned Upside Down*, 237.
30. Leebaert, *The Fifty-Year Wound*, 450–1. Richard Pipes, *VIXI: Memoirs of a Non-Belonger* (New Haven, CT: Yale University Press, 2003), 132–42.
31. Cahn, *Killing Détente*, 148.
32. Pipes, "Team B," 33.
33. Keller, "The Sunshine Warrior," 55.
34. Pipes, "Team B," 35. For a dissent on Team B's conclusions with regard to estimates of Soviet strength, which also sees a pattern of neocon overstatement in general, see Fareed Zakaria, "Exaggerating the Threats," *Newsweek International*, June 16, 2003.
35. Pipes, *VIXI*, 139.
36. Leebaert, *The Fifty-Year Wound*, 151. On scholarly opinion, see Richard H. Immerman to the author, July 22, 2003. Cahn takes a sharply critical view of Team B's report in *Killing Détente*. See also Pipes, "Team B," 25–40.
37. Winik, *On the Brink*, 55; Strobe Talbott, *Endgame: The Inside Story of SALT II* (New York: Harper and Row, 1979), 53.
38. Sanders, *Peddlers of Crisis*, 235; Christopher Bright, "The Neoconservatives and the Reagan Adminstration," *World Affairs* 53 (Fall 1990): 48.
39. Ehrman, *The Rise of Neo-Conservatism*, 103; Marilyn Berger, "Cyrus R. Vance, Confidant of Presidents Who Resigned Top Post, Dies at 84," *New York Times*, January 14, 2002, sec. B; Leebaert, *The Fifty-Year Wound*, 452.
40. Gerson, *The Neoconservative Vision*, 188; Sanders, *Peddlers of Crisis*, 236.
41. Leebaert, *The Fifty-Year Wound*, 492; Schweizer, *Reagan's War*, 101–2.
42. Dorrien, *The Neonconservative Mind*, 170; Winik, *On the Brink*, 28–9, 75, 83.
43. Powers, *Not without Honor*, 380–3.

44. Hodgson, *The World Turned Upside Down*, 236; Winik, *On the Brink*, 111, 237; Pipes, "Team B," 40.
45. Powers, *Not without Honor*, 303.
46. Podhoretz, *Ex-Friends*, 100–1.
47. Powers, *Not without Honor*, 340–1.
48. Ruth R. Wisse, "The Maturing of *Commentary* and of the Jewish Intellectual," *Jewish Social Studies* 3, no. 2 (1999): 35–6.
49. Neil Kozoday, telephone conversation with the author, May 22, 2002. Kozoday has a collection of such articles in Polish, issued clandestinely in pamphlet form by Solidarity.
50. Dorrien, *The Neoconservative Mind*, 166; Norman Podhoretz, "My Negro Problem," 101.
51. Howe, *A Margin of Hope*, 6; Ehrman, "The Rise of Neo Conservatism," 39–41, 108–109.
52. Powers, typescript, 16.
53. Zipperstein, "*Commentary* and American Jewish Culture," 19.
54. Bernard Avishai, "Breaking Faith: *Commentary* and the American Jews," *Dissent* 28, no. 2 (Spring 1987): 237.
55. Dorrien, *The Neoconservative Mind*, 184.
56. Hodgson, *The Gentleman from New York*, 218–21, 240–2, 257.
57. As quoted in Dorrien, *The Neoconservative Mind*, 167.
58. Friedman, *What Went Wrong?* 323–4.
59. On Carter shifting ground, see Cahn, p. 187; Powers, typescript, 5. At the instigation of Brzezinski, Carter's national security adviser, a study of Team B's findings was secretly mounted two years after the group had been disbanded. The conclusions, partially released in January–February 1979, held that the Kremlin did not agree with MAD and was putting together forces that would make it possible to engage in a nuclear war. Specifically, it declared that the Soviets would be ready in five years to destroy many United States Minuteman missiles stored in underground silos. Pipes, *VIXI*, 142.
60. Daniel Patrick Moynihan, "A New American Foreign Policy," *The New Republic*, February 9, 1980, 20; Sanders, *Peddlers of Crisis*, 281.
61. As quoted in Sanders, *Peddlers of Crisis*, 282, 312.
62. Ibid., 262.
63. Keith L. Shimko, "The Prince of Darkness and the Evil Empire: Richard Perle, the Soviet Union, and U.S. Arms Control Policy," *International Interactions* 18, no. 4 (1993): 285–308.
64. Robert Kagan, "When America Blinked," *The New Republic*, December 3, 2001, 35.
65. Peter Schweizer, "The Cuban Missle Crisis, Reconsidered," *The Weekly Standard*, October 21, 2002, 29.
66. Schweizer, *Reagan's War*, 123.
67. Peter Rodman, "Uncle Joe's Cabin," *National Review*, December 31, 1997, 51–2; Marc Dollinger, *Jews and Liberalism in Modern America* (Princeton, NJ: Princeton University Press, 2000), 11; Norman Podhoretz, "The Riddle of Ronald Reagan," *The Weekly Standard*, November 9, 1998, 24, 29; Sam Tanenhaus, "The GOP, or Goldwater's Old Party," *The New Republic*, June 11, 2001, 40. For a discussion of the communist attempt to take over Hollywood's labor unions

beginning in 1935 and Reagan's role in frustrating it, see Chapter 1 of Schweizer, *Reagan's War*.

68. Schweizer, *Reagan's War*, 20; Edwards, *The Conservative Revolution*, 85; Tanenhaus, "The GOP," 42.
69. Schweizer, *Reagan's War*, 35–6.
70. Friedman and Friedman, *Two Lucky People*, 390; Sanders, *Peddlers of Crisis*, 282; Jerry Z. Muller, *The Mind and the Market: Capitalism in Western Thought* (New York: Knopf, 2002), 382.
71. Rodman, "Uncle Joe's Cabin," 308; Powers, typescript, 6.
72. Keller, "The Sunshine Warrior," 88; Alessandra Stanley, "A Nation at War: The TV Watch; Ubiquitous Messenger Drives Home U.S. Policy," *New York Times*, April 7, 2003, sec. B.
73. Winik, *On the Brink*, 235; Dorrien, *The Neoconservative Mind*, 10–11.
74. Jeane Kirkpatrick, "Why I Am Not a Republican," *Common Sense*, Fall 1979, 34, quoted in Gerson, *The Neoconservative Vision*, 251–2.
75. See Robert Kagan, "Democracies and Double Standards," *Commentary*, August 1997, 19–26.
76. Christopher Bright, "The Neoconservatives and the Reagan Administration," *World Affairs* 53 (Fall 1990): 55.
77. Winik, *On the Brink*, 117.
78. On the efforts of the Reagan administration to bring about change in the authoritarian governments it supported, see Bright, 66–7.
79. Winik, *On the Brink*, 274; Edwards, *The Conservative Revolution*, 243–4.
80. Cannon, *Ronald Reagan*, 316; Winik, *On the Brink*, 274.
81. Schweizer, *Reagan's War*, 188; Bright, "The Neoconservatives and the Reagan Administration," 71–3.
82. Schweizer, *Reagan's War*, 159; Edwards, *The Conservative Revolution*, 244–6; Leebaert, *The Fifty-Year Wound*, 451. Schweizer refers to the Pipes analysis as NSSD 11–82, but Pipes, in his fuller exposition, describes it as NSDE 75, VIXI, 188–202.
83. Schweizer, *Reagan's War*, 167, 169; Pipes, *VIXI*, 173. A campaign to discontinue the sanctions, Pipes reports, was instigated by U.S. allies abroad and a number of businesses in this country. To his dismay, the situation having been seen as improved by some, the pipeline embargoes were dropped in November 1982. Ibid., 184.
84. George P. Schultz, *Turmoil and Triumph: My Years as Secretary of State* (New York: Scribners, 1993), 512–13.
85. Shimko, "The Prince of Darkness," 290–1; Winik, *On the Brink*, 411.
86. Winik, *On the Brink*, 158, 178; Schweizer, *Reagan's War*, 180–1, 221. Schweizer has a detailed description of the funding of protest groups in the "peace movement" in West Germany – including KFAZ (the Committee for Peace, Disarmament and Cooperation) and the German Peace Union – by the East German intelligence operation Stasi. He quotes Sergei Grigoriev, a former senior official in the International Department of the Communist Party of the Soviet Union, as saying that his department "led an active campaign in Western Europe, funding dozens of peace groups through various public organizations and a number of communist parties."

87. Charles Krauthammer, "The Obsolescence of Deterence," *The Weekly Standard*, December 9, 2002, 23.
88. Schweizer, *Reagan's War*, 223, 227.
89. Winik, *On the Brink*, 166, 178; Talbott, *Endgame*, 61–3; Shimko, "The Prince of Darkness," 300; Rodman, "Uncle Joe's Cabin," 318; Sanders, *Peddlers of Crisis*, 327. On the propaganda purpose of the zero-level option, see "The Surprising Effect of the Nuclear Freeze Movement on the Administration of Ronald Reagan" by Lawrence Wittner, a professor of history at the State University of New York at Albany, taken from an installment of his trilogy, *The Struggle against the Bomb* (Stanford, CA: Stanford University Press, 2003), vol. 3.
90. For a defense of SDI in retrospect, see Robert C. McFarlane, "Missile Defense, Then and Now," *New York Times*, May 4, 2000, sec. A.
91. Winik, *On the Brink*, 316.
92. For a critical history of SDI, see Frances Fitzgerald, *Way Out There in the Blue* (New York: Simon and Schuster, 2000).
93. Rodman, "Uncle Joe's Cabin," 340; Bill Keller, "Missile Defense: The Untold Story," *New York Times*, December 29, 2001, sec. A.
94. Richard Perle, *Hard Line* (New York: Random House, 1992), ix, 19.
95. Caspar W. Weinberger, *Fighting for Peace: Seven Critical Years in the Pentagon* (New York: Warner Books, 1990), 323; Schweizer, *Reagan's War*, 269; Winik, *On the Brink*, 403, 514–15; David Frum, "A Perle Before...," *The National Review*, April 23, 2003, 56.
96. Charles Krauthammer, "Arms Control: The End of an Illusion," *The Weekly Standard*, November 1, 1999, 15.
97. Weinberger, *Fighting for Peace*, 323; Winik, *On the Brink*, 403.
98. Anatoly Dobrynin, *In Confidence: Moscow's Ambassador to Six Cold War Presidents* (Seattle: University of Washington Press, 2001), 499.
99. John Whitehead and Georgy Shaknazarov, "Understanding the End of the Cold War, 1980–1987," paper presented at an Oral History Conference, Brown University, Providence, RI, May 7–10, 1998, 226–8.
100. Late in 2004, an interceptor rocket failed to launch as expected from the Marshall Islands (*New York Times*, December 16, 2004). On Aegis, see *Philadelphia Inquirer*, September 26, 2004. In July 2004, the initial interceptor for a national missile defense system was mounted at Fort Greeley, Alaska. Frances Fitzgerald, "Indefensible," *The New Yorker*, October 2, 2004, 33–4.
101. Strobe Talbott, *Deadly Gambits* (New York: Knopf, 1984), 17. See also Cannon, *Ronald Reagan*, 303.

Chapter 9

1. Schweizer, *Reagan's War*, 103, 299.
2. Michael Radu, interview with the author, Philadelphia, PA, October 13, 2003. See Michael Radu, *Latin American Revolutionaries* (New Brunswick, NJ: Transaction Books, 1988).
3. Theodore Draper, *A Very Thin Line: The Iran-Contra Affairs* (New York: Hill and Wang, 1991), 16.

4. Christopher's comments, delivered in December 1979, appear in a March 1980 Department of State bulletin, quoted in Schweizer, *Reagan's War*, 110.
5. Schweizer, *Reagan's War*, 110.
6. Gioconda Belli, *The Country under My Skin: A Memory of Love and War* (New York: Knopf, 2002), 13; Mary Anastasia O'Grady, "Chavez's Tyranny Emboldens Nicaragua's Ortegar," *Wall Street Journal*, December 24, 2004.
7. Draper, *A Very Thin Line*, 16.
8. As quoted in Jeane Kirkpatrick, "U.S. Security and Latin America," *Commentary*, January 1981, 38.
9. Robert Kagan, *A Twilight Struggle: American Power and Nicaragua, 1977–1990* (New York: Simon and Schuster, 1985), xiv; Schweizer, *Reagan's War*, 207; Winik, *On the Brink*, 423.
10. Kagan, *A Twilight Struggle*, xiv; C. G. Jacobson, "Soviet Attitudes toward Aid to and Contacts with Central American Revolutionaries," unpublished paper, April 10, 1984, 5; Schweizer, *Reagan's War*, 207; Winik, *On the Brink*, 423.
11. Schweizer, *Reagan's War*, 96–7.
12. Ibid., 98
13. For a discussion of both Brzezinski and Linowitz, see Kirkpatrick, "U.S. Security," 30–1.
14. As quoted in Kirkpatrick, "U.S. Security," 38.
15. Kagan, *A Twilight Struggle*, xiv.
16. Elliot Abrams, *Undue Process: A Story of How Political Differences Are Turned into Crimes* (New York: The Free Press, 1993), 5.
17. Schweizer, *Reagan's War*, 109.
18. Kirkpatrick, "U.S. Security," 29.
19. Sanders, *Peddlers of Crisis*, 302–5.
20. Draper, *A Very Thin Line*, 16; Abrams, *Undue Process*, 6.
21. Jacobson, "Soviet Attitudes," 3; Mark Falcoff, "Why We Were in Central America," *Commentary*, May 1999, 45.
22. Kagan, *A Twilight Struggle*, xv.
23. Stephen Schwartz, *A Strange Silence: The Emergence of Democracy in Nicaragua* (San Francisco: Institute for Contemporary Studies, 1992), 10, 21.
24. Falcoff, "Why We Were in Central America," 47.
25. Schwartz, *A Strange Silence*, 23–4.
26. Kagan, *A Twilight Struggle*, 263; Falcoff, "Why We Were in Central America," 47. Senator John Kerry was among the strongest critics of the administration's policies in Nicaragua. In 1985, he visited Sandinista leadership and opposed military aid to the Contras. Mary Anastasia O'Grady, "With Friends Like These? Kerry's Latin Fans," *Wall Street Journal*, July 30, 2004.
27. Draper, *A Very Thin Line*, 18; Christopher Marquis, "Edward P. Boland, 90, Dies, a Longtime Representative," *New York Times*, November 6, 2001, sec. A. The Boland Amendment, however, did permit expenditures for attempting to destabilize nearby governments.
28. Winik, *On the Brink*, 419; Cannon, *Ronald Reagan*, 358–60; Max Singer, "Losing Central America," *Commentary*, July 1986, 11–14.
29. Cannon, *Ronald Reagan*, 360, 365, 367.
30. Ibid., 369. In a broad-ranging essay in *Time* (April 1, 1985), Krauthammer seized on a passage in Reagan's State of the Union address a few months earlier, in which the president had urged this country not to break faith with those

elements around the world, from Afghanistan to Nicaragua, who would "defy Soviet supported aggression and secure rights that have been ours since birth." Krauthammer named the speech "the Reagan Doctrine." Winik, *On the Brink*, 457–8.

31. Cannon, *Ronald Reagan*, 380; Winik, *On the Brink*, 422, 424.
32. Robert Kagan, "Spotlight on Colin Powell," *Philadelphia Inquirer*, February 12, 2002, sec. A.
33. Cannon, *Ronald Reagan*, 378.
34. As quoted in Blumenthal, *Rise of the Counterestablishment*, 162.
35. Ibid.
36. Winik, *On the Brink*, 428.
37. Ibid., 433–5.
38. Kagan, *A Twilight Struggle*, 210. There is a startling parallel between this doctrine and the Bush Doctrine released following the Iraq War, which the younger Bush amplified on November 7, 2003. Addressing Arab allies Saudi Arabia and Egypt, Bush called upon them to embrace democratic traditions and to see in the overthrow of Saddam Hussein the opportunity for a global democratic revolution. It is this kind of response that has led some to believe that Bush's policies have been Reaganesque rather than modeled on those of his father's administration.
39. Ibid., 420; Winik, *On the Brink*, 419, 436.
40. Kagan, *A Twilight Struggle*, 420; Abrams, *Undue Process*, 4–5; Winik, *On the Brink*, 447.
41. Draper, *A Very Thin Line*, 19–22.
42. Ibid., 24.
43. Kagan, *A Twilight Struggle*, 414–15.
44. Winik, *On the Brink*, 473, 475–6; Kagan, *A Twilight Struggle*, 430, 435.
45. Kagan, *A Twilight Struggle*, 453.
46. As quoted in Draper, *A Very Thin Line*, 369.
47. Kagan, *A Twilight Struggle*, 475; Winik, *On the Brink*, 483.
48. Draper, *A Very Thin Line*, 370.
49. Ibid., 184, 354, 363–73, 465.
50. Winik, *On the Brink*, 605; Abrams, *Undue Process*, 116.
51. Winik, *On the Brink*, 483.
52. Hoeveler, *Watch on the Right*, 82.
53. Elliott Abrams, telephone conversation with the author, October 28, 1998.
54. James Risen, "C.I.A. Says It Used Nicaraguan Rebels Accused of Drug Ties," *New York Times*, July 17, 1998, sec. A; Joshua Phillips, "The Case against the Generals," *Washington Post Magazine*, August 17, 2003, 6–11, 19, 25.
55. Schweizer, *Reagan's War*, 113, 208.
56. Jeane Kirkpatrick, "Dictatorships and Double Standards," *Commentary*, November 1979, 102.
57. Winik, *On the Brink*, 136–8, 270–1.
58. Friedman, *What Went Wrong?*, 232, 317; Kaufman, *Broken Alliance*, 9, 206–8.
59. David D. Kirkpatrick, "*New Republic*'s Longtime Owner Sells Control to 2 Big Financiers," *New York Times*, January 28, 2002, sec. C.
60. Winik, *On the Brink*, 454–7.
61. Kagan, *A Twilight Struggle*, xv; Schwartz, *A Strange Silence*, 132; Mary Anastasia O'Grady, "Sandinistas Still Hold Nicaragua in Thrall," *Wall Street Journal*, October 3, 2003, sec. 1.

62. Schweizer, *Reagan's War*, 4; Steven F. Hayward, "Reagan's Triumph," *Claremont Review of Books* 3, no. 1 (Winter 2002): 4. A more recent view of Reagan's role, developed by Stefan Halper and Jonathan Clarke in *America Alone – The Neo Conservatives and the Global Order*, is that Reagan was primarily a negotiator rather than a Cold Warrior and would not have pursued the policy of George W. Bush in Iraq. The authors cite an article by Norman Podhoretz of May 2, 1982 – "The Neo Conservative Anguish over Reagan's Foreign Policy" – which faulted Reagan for not pursuing a harder line with the Soviet Union. Following the appearance of the article, Reagan called Podhoretz and in effect said "trust me." Reagan told him in the half-hour conversation that the Soviets were in deep trouble economically and that the administration was going "to put the squeeze on them." Commenting on this conversation in 2004, Podhoretz said that he had a more charitable view of Reagan now. Podhoretz also felt that President Bush was essentially following the Reagan approach in Iraq. Halper and Clarke, *America Alone*, 165. See also John Tierney interview with Podhoretz, "What Would He Have Done in Iraq?," *New York Times*, June 13, 2004.
63. Schweizer, *Reagan's War*, 210, 219.
64. Ibid., 279.

Chapter 10

1. Robert L. Pollock, "Capitalism for Consenting Adults," *Wall Street Journal*, January 28, 2002, sec. 1. For a fuller discussion of the controversies surrounding the capitalist idea, see Jerry Z. Muller, *The Mind and the Market: Capitalism in Modern European Thought* (New York: Knopf, 2002).
2. Irving Kristol, "Class and Sociology: 'The Shadow of Marxism,'" *Commentary*, October 1957, 193.
3. Irving Kristol, "An Odd Lot," *Encounter*, December 1960, 62–3.
4. Irving Kristol, "The Credibility of Corporations," *Wall Street Journal*, January 17, 1974, sec. 1.
5. Kristol, *Reflections*, 172; Gerson, *The Neoconservative Vision*, 213.
6. Irving Kristol, "Capitalism, Socialism, and Democracy," *Commentary*, April 1978, 29.
7. Gerson, *The Neoconservative Vision*, 199.
8. As quoted in Gerson, *The Neoconservative Vision*, 228.
9. Ibid., 215.
10. Gerson, *The Neoconservative Vision*, 200.
11. The quotations are from Pollock, "Capitalism for Consenting Adults."
12. Sanford Lakoff, *Max Lerner: Pilgrim in the Promised Land* (Chicago: University of Chicago Press, 1998), 255.
13. Kristol, "Capitalism, Socialism," 53–4.
14. Gertrude Himmelfarb, "Victorian Values/Jewish Values," *Commentary*, February 1989, 31.
15. Dorrien, *The Neoconservative Mind*, 97.
16. Irving Kristol, *Two Cheers*, 166.
17. Hoeveler, *Watch on the Right*, 95.
18. Bell, *The Cultural Contradictions*, 21.

19. Hoeveler, *Watch on the Right*, 96.
20. As quoted in Gerson, *The Neoconservative Vision*, 183.
21. Kristol, *Reflections*, ix, x; Dorrien, *The Neoconservative Mind*, 104.
22. Robert L. Bartley, *Seven Fat Years* (New York: The Free Press, 1992), 63.
23. Kristol, *Neo-Conservatism*, 35.
24. Jude Wanniski, telephone conversation with the author, May 30, 2000.
25. Kristol, *Neo-Conservatism*, 35; Wanniski, telephone conversation.
26. Jonathan Chait, "Prophet Motive," *The New Republic*, March 21, 1997, 21–4.
27. David Stockman, *The Triumph of Politics: Why the Reagan Administration Failed* (New York: Harper and Row, 1986), 39; Wanniski, telephone conversation.
28. As quoted in Dorrien, *The Neoconservative Mind*, 102.
29. Irving Kristol, "The Economics of Growth," *Wall Street Journal*, November 16, 1978, sec. 1.
30. Nash, typescript, 14. See also Samuel McCracken, "A Theology of Capitalism," *Commentary*, July 1982, 74, 76–7.
31. As quoted in Chait, "Prophet Motive," 24.
32. As quoted in Weisberg, "The Family Way," 186.
33. B. J. Phillips, "A Recycling of Reaganomics," *Philadelphia Inquirer*, August 7, 1996, sec. 1; Gary Wills, "It's His Party," *New York Times Magazine*, August 11, 1996, 28–59.
34. Cannon, *Ronald Reagan*, 255, 260–1.
35. Bartley, *Seven Fat Years*, 107, 168.
36. Ibid., 174.
37. Kristol, *Neo-Conservatism*, 36–7; Hoeveler, *Watch on the Right*, 101–2; Kristol, "Ideology and Supply Side Economics," *Commentary*, April 1981, 48, 50.
38. Larry Eichel, "On Tax Cuts, Bush Is Reviving Reagan Era Strategy," *Philadelphia Inquirer*, February 24, 2002, sec. 1. See also Daniel Altman, "The End of Taxes as We Know Them," *New York Times*, March 30, 2003, sec. 4. In the 1996 election, the accounting and consulting firm Coopers & Lybrand completed a technical analysis of the plan using a computer model to track the likely fiscal and economic consequences. "The plan pretty much works the way Dole-Kemp says," John Wilkins, who formerly worked for the Treasury and headed the firm's tax policy economics group, declared, if not as entirely effectively as the Dole camp had concluded; see Peter Passell, "Good News for Dole in a New Study of His Tax Plan," *New York Times*, October 24, 1996, sec. D. For more on the Dole-Kemp tax plan, see John B. Taylor, "Supply Side: The Whole Story," *New York Times*, September 1, 2002, sec. 4.
39. As quoted in Steven Greenhouse, "Update on Capitalism: What Do You Mean 'Us', Boss?," *New York Times*, September 1, 2002, sec. 4. On May 29, 2003, President Bush signed into law the Jobs and Growth Tax Reconciliation Act, perhaps the largest supply-side changes to tax law in American history. Conservatives argued that beginning in June, the unemployment rate peaked at 6.3 percent and began dropping in July, a drop that has held steady at 5.6 percent, lower than the typical unemployment rate in the 1970s, 1980s, and 1990s. Critics, however, charged that the major beneficiaries were the rich, who got most of the tax breaks. See a debate between Bill Beach, Rea Hederman, and Tim Kane, "Tax Returned," and Mark Weisbrot, "Redistribution – but It Is in the Wrong Direction," *Philadelphia Inquirer*, September 19, 2004.

Chapter 11

1. Kristol, *Neoconservatism*, 486.
2. Mark Lilla, "A Tale of Two Reactions," *New York Review of Books*, May 14, 1998, 6.
3. Irving Kristol, contribution to a *Commentary* symposium, "Capitalism, Socialism, Democracy," *Commentary*, April 1978, 1.
4. Bell, *The Cultural Contradictions*, xxiii; Gerson, *Neoconservative Vision*, 231.
5. Podhoretz, *Breaking Ranks*, 28, 47, 188, 200–1.
6. Staughton Lynd, "An Exchange with Irving Howe," *New York Review of Books*, December 23, 1965, 28.
7. Podhoretz, *Breaking Ranks*, 38.
8. David Gelernter, "How the Intellectuals Took Over (And What to Do about It)," *Commentary*, March 1997, 34.
9. Podhoretz, *Breaking Ranks*, 306.
10. Ibid.
11. Jeffrey O'Connell and Richard F. Bland, "Moynihan's Legacy," *The Public Interest*, no. 142 (Winter 2001): 104.
12. As quoted in Gerson, *Neoconservative Vision*, 234, 236.
13. Gelernter, "How the Intellectuals Took Over," 34.
14. Hodgson, *The World Turned*, 37.
15. As quoted in Daniel Bell, "The New Class: A Muddled Concept," in *The New Class*, ed. B. Bruce Biggs (New Brunswick, NJ: Transaction Books, 1979).
16. Kimball, *The Long March*, 27.
17. Irving Kristol, telephone conversation with the author.
18. James Q. Wilson, *The Moral Sense* (New York: The Free Press, 1993), 240–4.
19. James Q. Wilson, "Cultural Meltdown," *The Public Interest*, no. 137 (Fall 1999): 99–101.
20. As quoted in Weisberg, "Profile," 182; Easton, *Gang of Five*, 31–3.
21. As quoted in Weisberg, "Profile," 183.
22. Gertrude Himmelfarb, *The Demoralization of Society: From Victorian Virtues to Modern Values* (New York: Knopf, 1995), 36.
23. Ibid., 31, 77.
24. Ibid., 171, 176.
25. Gertrude Himmelfarb, *The New History and the Old* (Cambridge, MA: Harvard University Press, 1987), 17–18, 25–6, 56; Weisberg, "Profile," 183.
26. As quoted in Gerson, *The Neoconservative Vision*, 249.
27. David S. Bernstein, "Closed Book," *National Review*, May 18, 1998, 25–7.
28. Brock, *Blinded by the Right*, 105.
29. Edwin McDowell, "For George F. Will, a Herring That Turned Out to Be Anything but Red," *New York Times*, June 27, 1990, sec. C.
30. Brock, *Blinded by the Right*, 106.
31. Alan Bloom, *The Closing of the American Mind* (New York: Simon and Schuster, 1987), 27, 29–30, 33, 36–9, 202.
32. *New York Times*, August 21, 1996.
33. Ibid.; Wolfe, "The Revolution," 34.
34. Keller, "The Sunshine Warrior," 54; Paul Wolfowitz, interview with Tanenhaus, news transcript, Department of Defense, May 14, 2003.

35. Saul Bellow, *Ravelstein* (New York: Viking, 2000), 11–12, 19.
36. Keller, "The Sunshine Warrior," 88; Wolfowitz, interview with Tanenhaus.
37. "The Cult of Leo Strauss," *Newsweek*, August 3, 1987, 61.
38. Brinkley, "The Problem of Conservatism," 422.
39. James Atlas, *Bellow: A Biography* (New York: Random House, 2000), 387.
40. Saul Bellow, *Mr. Sammler's Planet* (New York: Viking, 1970), 33.
41. Atlas, *Bellow*, 388.
42. "Polemical Prize," *New York Times*, October 2, 1999.
43. Norman Podhoretz, "The Adventures of Philip Roth," *Commentary*, October 1998, 31.
44. Ruth R. Wisse, *The Modern Jewish Canon* (New York: The Free Press, 2000), 320; Podhoretz, "The Adventures of Philip Roth," 39. Another novelist who ran counter to the grain at this time was Herman Wouk, the Pulitzer Prize–winning novelist. His best-seller *The Winds of War* was a celebration of the military at a time of national crisis.
45. Edwards, *The Conservative Revolution*, 194.
46. Dorman, *Arguing the World.*
47. Nathan Glazer, "On Being Deradicalized," *Commentary*, October 1970, 74–80.
48. Podhoretz, *Ex-Friends*, 87.
49. Diane Ravitch, *The Language Police: How Pressure Groups Restrict What Students Learn* (New York: Knopf, 2003).
50. Ellen Messer-Davidow, "Manufacturing the Attack on Liberal Higher Education," in *After Political Correctness*, ed. Christopher Newfield and Ronald Strickland (Boulder, CO: Westview Press, 1995), 60.
51. William H. Honan, "Core Curriculum Vanishing in Top Colleges, Study Says," *New York Times*, March 20, 1996, sec. B; Messer-Davidow, "Manufacturing the Attack," 60–1; John Elson, "Academics in Opposition," *Time*, April 1, 1991, 54; Denise K. Magner, "Ten Years of Defending the Classics and Fighting Political Correctness," *The Chronicle of Higher Education*, December 12, 1997, 13–14.
52. As quoted on the FIRE website at <http://www.fire.org>.
53. As quoted in Magner, "Ten Years," 13.
54. Stephen Balch, telephone conversations with the author, November 27, 2000, and September 25, 2003.
55. Ward Connerly, *Creating Equal: My Fight against Race Prejudices* (San Francisco: Encounter Books, 2000); Balch, telephone conversations.
56. Jennifer Jacobson, "Conservatives in a Liberal Landscape," *The Chronicle*, September 24, 2004, A8–A11.
57. Hoeveler, *Watch on the Right*, 122.
58. Ibid., 130.
59. Hilton Kramer, *The Revenge of the Philistines: Art and Culture, 1972–1984* (New York: The Free Press, 1985), 340.
60. See Martin Peretz's tribute to the publication in *The New Republic*, May 19, 1997, 43; Blumenthal, xiv, 133, Hoeveler, 141; Michael J. Lewis, "Bearing Witness," review of *The Twilight of the Intellectuals* by Hilton Kramer, *Commentary*, June 1999, 66.
61. Gerson, *The Neoconservative Vision*, 332–3.
62. Kurtz, "Beyond Gay Marriage," *The Weekly Standard*, August 11, 2003, 26–33. See also Sam Schulman, "Gay Marriage and Marriage," *Commentary*, November

2003, 35–40; Adam Wolfson, "Conservatives and Neo Conservatives," *The Public Interest*, Winter 2004, 44

63. As quoted in a profile of Bloom in the *New York Times*, October 16, 1998.
64. Laurence W. Levine, *The Opening of the American Mind: Canons, Culture, and History* (Boston: Beacon Press, 1996), 17.
65. Murray Friedman, "Economic Growth and Civil Rights," *Journal of Contemporary Studies*, Winter 1981, 51–7.
66. Nancy Haggard-Gilson, "Against the Grain, Black Conservatives and Jewish Neo Conservatives," in *African-Americans and Jews in the Twentieth Century*, eds. V. P. Franklin, Nancy L. Grant, Harold M. Kletnick, and Genna Rae McNeil (Columbia: University of Missouri Press, 1998), 165–90.
67. *New York Times*, May 27, 2002.
68. John McWorter, "My Master's House," *Wall Street Journal*, September 9, 2003.
69. As quoted in Haggard-Gilson, "Against the Grain," 167.
70. See Glen Loury, *The Anatomy of Racial Inequality* (Cambridge, MA: Harvard University Press, 2002).
71. Shelby Steele, "A Victory for White Guilt," *Wall Street Journal*, June 26, 2003, A16.
72. Podhoretz, "Going Too Far for the Trillings," *Ex-Friends*, 91.
73. Podhoretz, *Ex-Friends*, 101.
74. See her excerpt, "The Beginning of the Journey," in her book *Lionel Trilling and His Critics*, 372–3. Also Carol Iannone, "Lionel Trilling and the Barbarians at the Gate," *Academic Questions*, Winter 2001–02, 13.

Chapter 12

1. Iran N. Forman, "The Politics of Minority Consciousness," in Maisel and Forman, *Jews in American Politics*, 153.
2. Jay P. Lefkowitz, "Jewish Votes and the Democrats," *Commentary*, April 1993, 38–41.
3. Alan Brinkley, "The Problem of American Conservatism," *American Historical Review* 98, no. 2 (April 1993): 38–41.
4. See Joel Carpenter, *The Reawakening of American Fundamentalism* (New York: Oxford University Press, 1997).
5. Edwards, *The Conservative Revolution*, 187, 197–8.
6. As quoted in A. James Reichley, *Religion in American Public Life* (Washington, DC: Brookings Institution, 1985), 320.
7. Judis, "The End of Conservatism," 28–31; David Horowitz, *The Politics of Bad Faith: The Radical Assault on America's Future* (New York: Simon and Schuster, 1998), 198.
8. As quoted in Edwards, *The Conservative Revolution*, 198. See also Jeremy Rabkin, "The Supreme Court in the Culture Wars, *The Public Interest*, no. 125 (Fall 1996): 12.
9. The terms "Christian Right" and "religious right" are used here essentially as a matter of convenience. In a strict sense, there is no one religious right. There are Pentecostalists and non-Pentecostalists, moderates and nonmoderates, those who seek to work with other elements in society and those who do not. There are significant theological differences among these groups and in their attitudes

about using government to deal with social welfare issues. See Marc D. Stern, "Talking with the Religious Right," *Congress Monthly*, March/April 1995, 10–11.

10. John C. Green, "The Christian Right at the Millennium," pamphlet published by the American Jewish Committee, September 2000, 15.
11. Reichley, *Religion in American Public Life*, 321.
12. Robert D. Woodberry and Christian S. Smith, "Fundamentalism et al.: Conservative Protestants in America," *Annual Review of Sociology* 24 (1998): 44–5; Ralph Reed, *Active Faith: How Christians Are Changing the Soul of American Politics* (New York: The Free Press, 1996), 104–5; Dinesh D'Souza, *Falwell before the Millennium: A Critical Biography* (Chicago: Regnery Gateway, 1984), 111–90; Rabkin, "The Supreme Court," 12. In 2002, John C. Green reports in his essay "The Undetected Tide," high-church-attending white evangelicals constituted 41 percent of the Republican vote in the South, more than all other white Protestants combined and nearly twice the percentage for high-church-attending evangelcials in the rest of the country. *Religion in the News* 6, no. 1 (Spring 2003): 6.
13. Naomi W. Cohen, "Natural Adversaries or Possible Allies: American Jews and the New Christian Right," pamphlet published by the American Jewish Committee, May 1993, 20.
14. Seymour Martin Lipset and Earl Raab, "The Election and the Evangelicals," *Commentary*, March 1981, 28. The anti-Christ remark is from *Religious News Service Digest*, January 19, 1999.
15. Lipset and Raab, "The Election and the Evangelicals," 28.
16. As quoted in Cohen, "Natural Adversaries," 7.
17. Barry Kosmin, telephone conversation with the author, August 1, 2003.
18. As quoted in Brinkley, "The Problem of American Conservatism," 428.
19. Kristol, "American Conservatism," 88–90.
20. Lipset and Raab, "The Election and the Evangelicals," 26.
21. Anti-Defamation League, January 8, 1989.
22. Jewish Telegraphic Agency, e-mail news report, October 14, 2002.
23. Cohen, "Natural Adversaries," 28.
24. Lucy Dawidowicz, "Politics, the Jews, and the '84 Election," *Commentary*, February 1984, 28.
25. Irving Kristol, "Irving Kristol Writes," *Commentary*, October 1984, 17, in connection with letters about "The Political Dilemma of American Jewry."
26. Cohen, "Natural Adversaries," 31–2. Graham's role as a bridge between evangelicals and Jews was momentarily tarnished early in 2002 when it became known that during a 1972 conversation with President Nixon (captured on tape) he made derogatory remarks about Jews, including an observation that they wielded too much power in the United States. The elderly and sickly Graham later appologized.
27. Ralph Reed, *Active Faith*, 207.
28. Daniel Kurtzman, Jewish Telegraphic Agency, e-mail news report, December 15, 1995; *Washington Jewish Week*, December 7, 1995.
29. *Forward*, February 2, 2001.
30. Yechiel Eckstein, "Christians Aren't the Enemy," *Wall Street Journal*, August 18, 2002, sec. 1.
31. Yechiel Eckstein, *Forward*, July 12, 2002.

32. Stephen M. Cohen, *Religion and the Public Square: Attitudes of American Jews in Comparative Perspective* (survey, Center for Jewish Community Studies, Baltimore, June 2000), 31.
33. Cohen, "Natural Adversaries," 14.
34. Ibid., 25.
35. Marc Tannenbaum in conversation with Murray Friedman. This was an informal conversation that I recall from memory and not an interview.
36. Rabkin, "The Supreme Court," 12; Daniel J. Balz and Ronald Brownstein, *Storming the Gates: Protest Politics and the Republican Revival* (Boston: Little, Brown, 1996), 310; Cohen, "Natural Adversaries," 20.
37. Reed, *Active Faith*, 111.
38. John C. Green, "Understanding the Christian Right," pamphlet published by the American Jewish Committee, May 1996, 17. See especially Green's note 21, which contains a very full listing of recent scholarly works on the Christian Right.
39. William C. Brennan, *America's Right Turn: From Nixon to Bush* (Baltimore: Johns Hopkins University Press, 1994), 62; Eugene D. Genovese, *The Southern Front and Politics in the Cultural War* (Columbia: University of Missouri Press, 1995), 249.
40. Reed, *Active Faith*, 12–14.
41. Robert W. Fogel, *The American Enterprise*, November/December 1995, 879–80.
42. Ralph Reed, telephone conversation with the author, March 11, 1999.
43. Easton, *Gang of Five*, 135–8; Jack Abramoff, telephone conversation with the author, July 19, 1996.
44. Reed, *Active Faith*, 22–3; Easton, *Gang of Five*, 203.
45. Richard John Neuhaus, "Ralph Reed's Real Agenda," *First Things*, October 1996, 43.
46. Reed, *Active Faith*, 28, 262.
47. Adam Wolfson, "God and Country," review of *Active Faith* by Ralph Reed, *Commentary*, July 1996, 71.
48. Easton, *Gang of Five*, 344.
49. Ibid., 324.
50. Ibid., 326; Jason DeParle, "The Christian Right Confesses Sins of Racism," *New York Times*, August 4, 1996, sec. 4.
51. Brinkley, "The Problem of Conservatism," 426.
52. Woodberry and Smith, "Fundamentalism et al.," 26–7; see also Stephen L. Carter, *God's Name in Vain: The Wrongs and Rights of Religion in Politics* (New York: Basic Books, 2000).
53. Nicholas D. Kristof, "God, Satan, and the Media," *New York Times*, March 4, 2003, sec. A.
54. Mark I. Rozell and Clyde Wilcox, *Second Coming: The New Christian Right in Virginia Politics* (Baltimore: Johns Hopkins University Press, 1996), 215–16; see also Easton, *Gang of Five*, 325.
55. Easton, *Gang of Five*, 347. See also *Philadelphia Inquirer*, February 23, 1996; Kenneth Stern, American Jewish Committee backgrounder on Pat Buchanan; Green, *The Christian Right*, 19.
56. Jewish Telegraphic Agency news report in the *Jewish Exponent* (Philadelphia), August 19, 1994; David Levitas, "ADL and the Christian Right," *The Nation*, June 19, 1995, 882–5.

57. Michael Lind, "Rev. Robertson's Grand International Conspiracy Theory," *New York Review of Books*, February 2, 1995, 22–5.
58. Reed, *Active Faith*, 208.
59. Ibid., 208–10; Gustav Niebuhr, "Pat Robertson Says He Intended No Anti-Semitism in Book He Wrote Four Years Ago," *New York Times*, March 4, 1995, sec. 1.
60. Pat Robertson, *Wall Street Journal*, April 4, 1995, sec. 1; Nash, typescript, 22.
61. Midge Decter, telephone conversation with the author, December 22, 1998; David Klinghoffer, *Why American Jews Should Learn to Stop Worrying and Love Conservative Christians: Modern Problems, Ancient Solutions* (Mercer Island, WA: Toward Tradition, n.d.), 11.
62. Jewish Telegraphic Agency, e-mail news report, July 15, 1994.
63. The Boshwitz statement is in the *Jewish Exponent* (Philadelphia), November 11, 1994. The resignations of two ADL leaders were reported in the *Washington Times*, August 25, 1994.
64. Norman Podhoretz, "In the Matter of Pat Robertson," *Commentary*, August 1995, 27–32. A clearer picture of Robertson's ambiguity toward Jews can be seen in the minutes of an almost two-hour, off-the-record meeting Robertson held with American Jewish Committee leaders on April 19, 1995, at his Virginia Beach headquarters, the minutes of which were given to me by Rabbi James Rudin, who recorded them. Robertson told the group he recognized the rift that existed between him and the Jewish commuity. He blamed it on "anti-evangelical Christian" feelings among Jews and "left-wing" critics. He gave as examples of those not "benign to him" Robert Abrams, a former New York State Attorney General; *New York Times* columnists Frank Rich and Anthony Lewis; Richard Cohen, a *Washington Post* editorial writer; as well as singer Barbara Streisand and Norman Lear, the television producer and leader of People for the American Way. Asked why he described these people as "Jews" rather than as individual critics, he responded heatedly, according to the minutes, "Because they are!" Robertson went on to describe the many positive ways he had responded to Jewish needs and interests. The minutes make no mention of the reaction of Reed, who was also present, but whom I suspect was uncomfortable with Robertson's responses.
65. As quoted in Hoeveler, *Watch on the Right*, 113.
66. As quoted in Weisberg, "Profile," 189.
67. Irving Kristol, "The Coming 'Conservative Century,'" *Wall Street Journal*, February 1, 1993, sec. 1, quoted in Gerson, *The Neoconservative Vision*, 269.
68. Bell, *The Cultural Contradictions*, xxix.
69. As quoted in Gerson, *The Neoconservative Vision*, 284.
70. Irving Kristol, "The Future of American Jews," *Commentary*, August 1991, 24.
71. Irving Kristol, "Why Religion Is Good for the Jews," *Commentary*, August 1994, 21.
72. Irving Kristol, "The Future of American Jews," 24–5.
73. Reed, *Active Faith*, 211.
74. As quoted in Goldberg, *Jewish Power*, 110.
75. Ibid.
76. Frank Rich, "Bait and Switch," *New York Times*, April 6, 1995, sec. A.
77. As quoted in Reed, *Active Faith*, 212.
78. Christopher Hitchens, *The Nation*, October 9, 1995, 18.

79. Katherine Q. Seeyle, "Christian Coalition's Ralph Reed Quits for New Political Role," *New York Times*, April 24, 1997, sec. B; Reed, *Active Faith*, 190; Rabkin, "The Supreme Court," 20.
80. Easton, *Gang of Five*, 389.
81. Reed, *Active Faith*, 154.
82. David Brooks, "Social Issues Strike Back," *The Weekly Standard*, February 16, 1996, 13.
83. Easton, *Gang of Five*, 366.
84. Woodberry and Smith, "Fundamentalism, et al.," 47–8.
85. Easton, *Gang of Five*, 366.
86. Green, "The Christian Right," 1.
87. Jewish Telegraphic Agency, e-mail to the author, June 11, 2003.
88. David Firestone, "Evangelical Christians and Jews United for Israel," *New York Times*, June 9, 2002, sec. 1.
89. David Firestone, "DeLay Is to Carry Dissenting Message on a Mideast Tour," *New York Times*, July 25, 2003, sec. A.
90. See the JCPA resolution on evangelical–Jewish relations adopted by the 2003 Plenum of the JCPA. On this and criticism of this move toward rapprochement, see Leonard Fein, "An Unholy Alliance," *Forward*, April 25, 2003. On liberal Protestant church groups moving toward divestment, see *Forward*, October 1, 2004.

Chapter 13

1. Norman Podhoretz, "Neoconservatism: A Eulogy," 19–29. In his 1995 book *Neoconservatism: The Autobiography of an Idea*, Irving Kristol asked, "Where stands Neoconservatism today?" and answered his question, "It is clear that what can fairly be described as the neoconservative impulse ... was a generational phenomenon, and has now been pretty much absorbed into a larger, more comprehensive conservatism." Quoted in Adam Wolfson, "Conservative and Neoconservatives," *The Public Interest*, no. 155 (Winter 2004): 33.
2. Mary Ann Glendon, "The Women of Roe v. Wade," *First Things*, June/July 2003, 21. On teenagers and abortion, see E. J. Graff, "Apocalypse Not," *The New Republic*, May 31, 2004, 14.
3. Nina Bernstein, "Behind Fall in Pregnancy, a New Teenage Culture of Restraint," *New York Times*, March 7, 2004, sec. 1. Leslie Kaufman, "It's a Trend: Births out of Wedlock Are Falling Statewide," *New York Times*, October 2, 2004.
4. Wolfe, "The Revolution," 42.
5. Dorrien, *The Neoconservative Mind*, 369.
6. Nash, "The Transformation of American Conservatism," 6.
7. Podhoretz, "Neoconservatism: A Eulogy," 24.
8. Kristol, *Wall Street Journal*, April 18, 1995, sec. 1.
9. For a discusson of this struggle, see Edward Shapiro, "Right Turn? Jews and the Conservative Movement," in Maisel and Forman, eds., *Jews in American Politics*, 196–211.
10. Samuel Lipman, "Can We Save Culture?," *National Review*, August 26, 1991, 36. See also Lipman as quoted in Gerson, *The Neoconservative Vision*, 273–4.

11. William F. Buckley, Jr., "Toast to Tomorrow," *National Review*, December 22, 1997, 46–9. See also Kristol, *Neoconservatism*, 37.
12. Jonah Goldberg, "Bush Pioneering a New Vein of Conservatism," *Philadelphia Inquirer*, July 23, 2003, sec. A.
13. Walzer as quoted in *Forward*, January 31, 2003, 14.
14. Edward Rothstein, "Left Has Hard Time in Era of Terrorism," *New York Times*, December 21, 2002, sec. B.
15. As quoted in Sam Tanenhaus, *New York Times*, September 9, 2002, sec. 1.
16. Dan Balz and Ronald Brownstein, *Storming the Gates: Protest Politics and the Republican Revival* (Boston: Little, Brown, 1996), 40–2.
17. David Frum, *The Right Man: The Surprise Presidency of George W. Bush* (New York: Random House, 2003), 238.
18. A number of essays of these younger neocons, as well as those of other conservatives, have been reprinted in David Brooks, *The New Conservative Writing* (New York: Vintage Books, 1996).
19. Rifka Rosenwein, "Backward March," *Brill's Content*, June 2000, 105–7.
20. "After the Acquittal," *Forward*, February 19, 1999.
21. Hanna Rosin, "Memo Master," *The New Republic*, November 7, 1994, 22–8; Weisberg, "The Family Way," 186.
22. Easton, *Gang of Five*, 46.
23. Weisberg, "The Family Way," 188.
24. Sam Tanenhaus, "Bush's Brain Trust," *Vanity Fair*, July 2003, 168.
25. Easton, *Gang of Five*, 271.
26. Ibid., 271–5.
27. Weisberg, "The Family Way," 188.
28. Ehrman, "*Commentary, The Public Interest*," in Friedman, ed., *American Jewish Conservatism*, 178.
29. David Brooks, telephone conversation with the author, January 15, 1996.
30. Kristol, *Neoconservatism*, 4.
31. Dorrien, *The Neoconservative Mind*, 138.
32. Ibid., 19; Kristol, telephone conversation with the author. See also Kristol, "Why Religion Is Good for the Jews," 19–21.
33. David Brooks, *Atlantic Monthly*, March 2003, 26.
34. Abrams, *Faith or Fear*, 19, 181.
35. Wendy Shalit, *A Return to Virtue: Discovering the Lost Virtue* (New York: The Free Press, 1999), 49.
36. Kay S. Hymowitz, "Bringing Up Parents," *Commentary*, June 2003, 51.
37. Gerson, *The Neoconservative Vision*, 287.
38. Irving Kristol, "The Future of American Judaism," *Commentary*, August 1991, 26.
39. Kristol, telephone interview.
40. Evan Gahr, "The Religious Right: Not for Christians Only," *Insight*, August 2, 1993, 26.
41. As quoted in Gerson, *The Neoconservative Vision*, 291.
42. Sarna and Dalin, *Religion and State*, xi.
43. As quoted in David G. Dalin, *American Jews and the Separationist Faith* (Washington, DC: Ethics and Public Policy Center, 1993), 15.
44. Sarna and Dalin, *Religion and State*, 125–6.

45. Ibid., 126.
46. Abrams, *Faith or Fear*, 90.
47. Jeffrey Rosen, "Is Nothing Secular?," *New York Times Magazine*, January 30, 2000, 40–4; Murray Friedman, "Voucher Decision Ushers in a New Era," *Philadelphia Inquirer*, June 30, 2002, sec. A.
48. Irwin M. Stelzer, "Big Business's Bad Behavior," *The Weekly Standard*, July 22, 2002, 22–6. See also Stelzer, "The Corporate Scandals and American Capitalism," *The Public Interest*, no. 155 (Winter 2004): 19–31.
49. David Cay Johnston, "Very Richest's Share of Income Grew Even Bigger, Data Show," *New York Times*, June 26, 2003, sec. A; Sarah Luek, "Facing a Crunch, States Drop Thousands from Medicaid Rolls," *Wall Street Journal*, June 26, 2003, sec. 1; Joshua B. Bolten, "We Can Cut the Deficit in Half," *Wall Street Journal*, December 10, 2003, sec. 1.
50. Nathan Glazer, telephone conversation with the author, June 7, 2003.
51. Nicholas Lehmann, "Postscript: Daniel Patrick Moynihan," *The New Yorker*, April 7, 2003, 98.
52. James Q. Wilson, "Gentleman, Politician, Scholar," *The Public Interest*, no. 154 (Summer 2003): 117.
53. Glazer, telephone conversation. See also Nathan Glazer, "The Hard Questions," *The New Republic*, January 27, 1997, 25.
54. See, for example, Charles Krauthammer, "Leave Affirmative Action to Voters," *Philadelphia Inquirer*, June 27, 2003, sec. A; and Thomas Sowell, "Surrendering to the Multiculturalists," *Forbes*, June 16, 1997, 72–3.
55. Murray Friedman, "Are Jews Moving to the Right?," *Commentary*, April 2000, 50; Ralph J. Sonenshein, *Politics in Black and White: Race and Power in Los Angeles* (Princeton, NJ: Princeton University Press, 1993), 290. See also Stephen M. Cohen, "Survey Sees Historic Shift to Right," *Forward*, January 17, 2003, sec. 1; Thomas B. Edsall, "GOP Makes Gains with Jewish Voters," *Washington Post*, June 25, 2002, sec. A; Murray Friedman, "Are Jews Moving to the Right?," *Moment*, October 1997, 50; Murray Friedman, "Capturing the Jewish Vote," *B'nai Brith IJM*, Summer 2003, 19, 21, 59.
56. See Laurie Goodstein, "A National Challenge: Civil Liberties; Jewish Groups Endorse Tough Security Laws," *New York Times*, January 3, 2002, sec. A.
57. Alan M. Fisher, "Where the Jewish Vote Is Going," *Moment*, March 1989, 41.
58. Murray Friedman, "Democrats, Maybe, but Fewer Liberals," *Forward*, June 7, 2002, sec. 1.
59. Nash, "*Commentary* and American Conservatism," 28.
60. Dorrien, *The Neoconservative Mind*, 375.
61. Sam Tanenhaus, "The Hard-Liner," *Boston Globe*, November 2, 2003.
62. Dorrien, *The Neoconservative Mind*, 376.
63. Ibid., 375–6. The Kristol quote is from Stefan Halper and Jonathan Clarke, *America Alone: The Neo Conservatives Are the Global Order* (Cambridge: Cambridge University Press, 2004), 100.
64. Muravchick, "The Bush Manifesto," 23–30.
65. Todd S. Purdum, "The Brains behind Bush's War Policy," *New York Times*, February 1, 2003, sec. B.
66. James Mann, *The Rise of the Vulcans: The History of Bush's War Cabinet* (New York: Viking, 2004), 21–9.

67. Ibid., 28.
68. The Wolfowitz Khalilzad article is discussed in ibid., 209–15.
69. Dick Polman, "Neoconservatives," *Philadelphia Inquirer*, May 4, 2003, sec. C.
70. *New York Times*, November 7, 2003, sec. A. See also *Wall Street Journal*, March 21, 2003, sec. 1; and Polman, "Neoconservatives," *Philadelphia Inquirer*, May 4, 2003.
71. Steven R. Weisman, "Pre-emption Evolves from an Idea of Official Action," *New York Times*, March 23, 2003, sec. A; Robert S. Greenberger and Karby Legett, "President's Dream: Changing Not Just Regime but a Region," *Wall Street Journal*, March 21, 2003, sec 1.
72. David E. Sanger, "Bush Asks Lands in the Middle East to Try Democratic Ways," *New York Times*, November 7, 2003, sec. A.
73. As quoted in Polman, "Neoconservatives."
74. See also David Frum, "He That Stands It Now," *National Review*, March 22, 2004, 35–8.
75. Mark Helprin, "No Way to Run a War," *Wall Street Journal*, May 17, 2004, sec. 1.
76. As quoted in Leslie H. Gelb, "What Comes Next?," *Wall Street Journal*, May 20, 2004, sec. 1.
77. See Tom Donnelly, "Swift Invasion, Slow Victory," *The Weekly Standard*, May 17, 2004, 12–14; Stephen F. Hayes, *The Connection* (New York: HarperCollins, 2004). See also Hayes, "The 9–11 Commission and the Connection," *The Weekly Standard*, July 26, 2004, 9. The connection is a crucial issue that the *New York Times* and other media have missed. The *Times* treated the 9/11 Commission report as a "smoking gun," confirming, according to the *Times* in June 2004, "No Al Qaeda Tie." This contradicted assertions by Vice President Cheney and the Democratic co-chair of the 9/11 Commission, Lee Hamilton. The latter asserted that he did not know what the fuss was all about. "We don't disagree with that [Cheney's and his own remarks]." No one, including the Bush administration, claimed that Saddam Hussein was involved in the 9/11 attacks. What was argued was that the intimacy of that connection was a potential threat, a judgment that the Senate Intelligence Committee report published on July 19, 2004, corroborated. "Any indication of a relationship between these two hostile elements could carry great danger to the United States."
78. David Brooks, "In Iraq, America's Shakeout Moment," *New York Times*, May 18, 2004, sec. A.
79. Peter Beinart, "An Argument for a New Liberalism: A Fishting Faith," *The New Republic*, December 13, 2004, 19.
80. Daniel Henniger, "Blue Democrats Lost Red America Back in 1965," *Wall Street Journal*, November 5, 2004.
81. Jewish Telegraphic Agency, November 4, 2004.
82. See Irving Kristol, "The Neoconservative Persuasion," *The Weekly Standard*, August 25, 2003, 17.
83. A. J. Bacevich, "*Commentary* Gets Religion," *The Weekly Standard*, December 4, 1995, 34.
84. David Gelernter, "Judaism beyond Words: Conclusion," *Commentary*, July–August 2003, 46.
85. Irving Kristol, "American Conservatism," 87.

Index